faith
TRIUMPHANT

ROBERT H. PIERSON

"It occurred to me that it would be well to recheck all these accounts from first to last and after thorough investigation to pass this summary on to you, to reassure you of the truth of all you were taught" (Luke 1:3, 4, T.L.B.).

REVIEW AND HERALD PUBLISHING ASSOCIATION
WASHINGTON, D.C.

Editor: Raymond H. Woolsey
Cover Design: Harry Knox

DEDICATION

To the nearly 3 million members of the Advent family—
men and women and youth—who gather week by week in our
Sabbath schools and churches in nearly two hundred countries
of earth, these personal devotional messages are dedicated.

One member of this family must be singled out for special
mention in this dedication—the one who has spent many hours
in helping me prepare this book, and who for more than forty
years I have been proud to call my wife—Dollis Mae Pierson.

RECIPE FOR A HAPPY NEW YEAR

Hitherto have ye asked nothing in my name: ask, and ye shall receive, that your joy may be full. John 16:24.

Years ago from a brochure long since discarded I copied this "Recipe for a Happy New Year":

"Take twelve fine full months—see that they are thoroughly free from all old memories of bitterness, rancor, hate, and jealousy. Cleanse them completely from every clinging spite; pick off all specks of pettiness and littleness; in short, see that these months are freed from all the past, and have them as fresh and clean as when they first came from the great storehouse of Time.

"Divide each of these months into thirty or thirty-one equal parts—each one except the second; divide that into twenty-eight equal parts. Do not try to make up the year's batch all at one time (many spoil the broth in that way), but prepare one day at a time, as follows:

"Into each day put twelve parts of faith, eleven of patience, ten of courage, nine of work (some omit this ingredient and so spoil the flavor of the rest), eight of hope, seven of loyalty, six of liberality, five of kindness, four of rest (leaving this out is like leaving the oil out of the salad—don't do it), three of prayer, two of meditation, and one well-selected resolution. To this add a dash of fun, a sprinkle of play, and a heaping cupful of good humor.

"Pour into the whole mixture love ad libitum, and mix with a vim. Cook thoroughly with fervent heart, garnish with smiles and a sprig of joy, then serve with quietness, unselfishness, and cheerfulness, and *A Happy New Year* is certainty."

Humanly speaking, this is an appropriate recipe. We can learn much from it. There is one thing—*One Person*—missing. You can't have a truly Happy New Year without *Him*—Jesus.

One cannot speak of true faith, courage, hope, loyalty, liberality, or kindness without Him. He is the very essence of them all! If we desire that our "joy may be full" during the coming year we must open the door of our heart and invite Him in. "As long as you look to Christ, you are safe."—*Testimonies,* vol. 4, p. 522.

FROM THE BEGINNING TO THE END

And he said unto me, It is done. I am Alpha and Omega, the beginning and the end. I will give unto him that is athirst of the fountain of the water of life freely. Rev. 21:6.

When Jesus declared Himself to be the Alpha and Omega (He would say, the A and the Z, to those of us who speak the English language), He stated a great truth that should never be forgotten—a truth peculiarly relevant to you and to me as we enter this new year.

Jesus said, "I am *the beginning.*" When things began the Son of God was there to begin them. Centuries before His birth in Bethlehem's manger, Christ was the Creator. We are introduced to Him in the first five words of inspired Scripture: "In the beginning God created" (Gen. 1:1).

The apostle John tells the story of "the beginning": "Before the world was created, the Word already existed; he was with God, and he was the same as God. From the very beginning, the Word was with God. Through him God made all things; not one thing in all creation was made without him" (John 1:1-3, T.E.V.).

"The Word became a human being and lived among us. We saw his glory, full of grace and truth. This was the glory which he received as the Father's only Son" (verse 14, T.E.V.).

The Creator of the universe became our Redeemer. The One who is our "Beginning" promises: "I will give unto him that is athirst of the fountain of the water of life freely" (Rev. 21:6). He became the Author of our faith (see Heb. 5:9). The hand that created the sun, the moon, the countless stars, that flung the unnumbered worlds into space, centuries later was nailed to a cross of shame. But it became a cross of victory.

He who was "the beginning" is also "the end." He is our glorious consummation. When the drama of good and evil is finished Christ Himself will ring down the curtain. At His second advent He will usher in a breathtaking, sinless eternity. "The kingdoms of this world are become the kingdoms of our Lord, and of his Christ; and he shall reign for ever and ever" (Rev. 11:15).

"I am Alpha and Omega, the beginning and the end," He declares. "I want to become everything to *you today!*"

8

POLAROID OR TINTYPE?

For the wages of sin is death; but the gift of God is eternal life through Jesus Christ our Lord. Rom. 6:23.

The prophet Jeremiah declares: "The heart is deceitful above all things, and desperately wicked: who can know it?" (Jer. 17:9). Unfortunately we cannot limit the prophet's words to the past tense. We cannot say that the heart *was* deceitful or *used to be* desperately wicked. The words of inspiration are as terribly true today as they were when Jeremiah penned them centuries ago. Man's heart is still deceitful and desperately wicked.

The apostle Paul recorded an important truth: "All have sinned, and come short of the glory of God" (Rom. 3:23). His words were true in A.D. 60. They are also true in 1975. A criminal plans a bank robbery in a jet plane traveling five hundred miles an hour just as his forebear may have planned one on horseback at five or eight miles an hour decades before. A wife can hate her husband in a modern kitchen surrounded with all the gadgetry of the 1970's, just as a woman did in a sod house a century ago. The motive has not changed, only the times and the locale.

Greater knowledge, higher, more specialized education, sophisticated living have not changed the human heart. The world is still full of present-day Pharisees, Sadducees, publicans, harlots, Mary Magdalenes, Judas Iscariots—sinners of every ilk. A picture is not altered because it is a Polaroid instead of a tintype.

Man's expanded intellect has not altered his naturally wicked heart. The passage of time has changed technology but it has not changed the technologist's heart or nature. By nature man is still a sinner. His need of salvation is just as desperate today in the midst of an opulent society as it was two thousand years ago in a humbler, simpler setting.

And "the wages of sin is [still] death." We dare never forget it. This is one wage rate that has not changed with the fluctuating fortunes of the laborer.

But, thank God, neither has the way of escape been altered: "The gift of God is [still] eternal life through Jesus Christ our Lord." In a changing world He is still our changeless Saviour!

THE NAME THAT CONQUERS

And she shall bring forth a son, and thou shalt call his name Jesus: for he shall save his people from their sins. Matt. 1:21.

In many parts of the world considerable significance is attached to names given both to persons and places. In the Tamil country of South India, for example, a rather common Christian name is Yesuratnam. *Yesu* is the Tamil for "Jesus." *Ratnam* means "jewel." So Yesuratnam means "jewel of Jesus."

The greatest name in the Orient, or in any part of the world, is Jesus Christ. The Scriptures refer to Him by many names, each one giving a little insight into His life, His character, or His ministry.

The name "Jesus" comes from the Hebrew *Jehoshua,* Joshua, meaning, "Yahweh is salvation." Yahweh, or Jehovah, is the omniscient, omnipresent, omnipotent God of heaven, who was Israel's provider and protector. Hoshea is another form of the same name. Hoshea was the original name of Joshua, son of Nun. One writer suggests Joshua received his name in anticipation of the deliverance God would enable him to effect on behalf of His chosen people.

Some fifteen hundred years after the death of Joshua another Jehoshua, or Jesus, was born into the land of His enemies. He came not only to take back a good report to His Father but to wrest that land outright from the hands of the great deceiver. This deliverance assured that one day our planet in rebellion would be subdued and restored to its originally intended place in the universe—a perfect, sin-free habitation of redeemed saints.

In this all-prevailing name Jesus sent forth His early disciples to become world conquerors. "Christ's name was to be their watchword, their badge of distinction, their bond of union, the authority for their course of action, and the source of their success. Nothing was to be recognized in His kingdom that did not bear His name and superscription."—*The Acts of the Apostles,* p. 28.

He is *your* Jesus, *your* Redeemer, *your* Lord. He is able to save *you* from *your* sins!

IT'S BEAUTIFUL!

Hitherto have ye asked nothing in my name: ask, and ye shall receive, that your joy may be full. John 16:24.

A young man in Kansas was listening to the Voice of Prophecy broadcasts. Through the Christ-filled messages he found Jesus as his personal Saviour and Friend.

"I found God in my bedroom all by myself as I listened to your broadcasts," he wrote. "Jesus came into my heart like the sun rising in the morning. He raised me out of my bed and put me on my knees. I couldn't believe it was happening to me, but I am so thankful. I am going to praise His name always.

"During my lifetime I have tried many times to change my living patterns but to no avail. I have always failed. I find now all you have to do is ask God, and He will help you.

"Now God has shown me the right way to live. I've been a Christian only a short time, but I feel my life finally has meaning. I praise the Lord for giving me a chance to live the life God meant me to live. I feel He wants me to tell the whole world about my new-found life. It is beautiful."

Recently a spiritual awakening came onto the campus of one of our colleges. Many students found Jesus for the first time. Their testimony? Listen:

"I am so happy," a young woman exclaimed. "I never thought it could happen to me. I've sold books. I've been an Adventist all my life, but now I have given my heart to Jesus for the first time. I'm so happy!"

"The wall between me and Jesus is gone," one boy declared. "Now we really communicate."

"My boy friend and I know we haven't been as good or as serious about religion as we should be," a young woman confessed. "We decided to go to the retreat, and it happened. I'm so happy. It was beautiful there. They told us it would seem different. We won't let it die; we're going to have a revival!"

Another youth describes his new experience: "I gave my heart to Jesus. Now it's real. We shouldn't be surprised. It's happening. It's great. I'm drained emotionally but I'm not down. God is here. I know He's with me. It's beautiful."

It *is* beautiful! *Your* joy also will be full. It is for you!

IS SAYING ENOUGH?

He that saith, I know him, and keepeth not his commandments, is a liar, and the truth is not in him. 1 John 2:4.

"I am a Christian; I belong to Christ. I am on my way to heaven." Fine! This would be a wonderful world in which to live if every one would make this declaration—and truly mean it. But this is only the first step. Being a Christian is much more than merely saying so.

You see, there is a difference between *saying* and *doing.* Saying is good but there must also be some doing. I have seen people—and no doubt you have seen them too—who said, "I have accepted Christ. I am a Christian. I'm on my way to heaven." Perhaps a brief prayer commitment was thrown in for good measure, and that was all there was to it. For them this was all there is to the Christian life.

The apostle John makes it clear that there is more to being a Christian than just saying and praying! Listen to these words: "Someone may say, 'I am a Christian; I am on my way to heaven; I belong to Christ.' But if he doesn't do what Christ tells him to, he is a liar" (1 John 2:4, T.L.B.).

"Many are continually saying, 'All that we have to do is to believe in Christ.' They claim that faith is all we need. In its fullest sense, this is true; but they do not take it in its fullest sense. To believe in Jesus is to take Him as our redeemer and our pattern. If we abide in Him and He abides in us, we are partakers of His divine nature, and are doers of His word. The love of Jesus in the heart will lead to obedience to all His commandments. But the love that goes no farther than the lips, is a delusion; it will not save any soul. Many reject the truths of the Bible, while they profess great love for Jesus; but the apostle John declares, 'He that saith, I know Him, and keepeth not His commandments, is a liar, and the truth is not in him.' "—*Historical Sketches of SDA Missions,* pp. 188, 189, orig. ed.

Accepting Christ is more than verbal affirmation; it includes the confession of sin, forgiveness for sin, obedience to the commandments of God, victorious living through the imparted strength of the indwelling Christ.

FOOLISHNESS CONFOUNDS THE GREAT

But God hath chosen the foolish things of the world to confound the wise; and God hath chosen the weak things of the world to confound the things which are mighty. 1 Cor. 1:27.

Abraham Lincoln once said, "The Lord prefers common-looking people. That is the reason He makes so many of them." Perhaps He also desired the world to see what transformations of His grace might be wrought among those not so blessed with the bounties of life. The apostle Paul writes:

"Notice among yourselves, dear brothers, that few of you who follow Christ have big names or power or wealth. Instead, God has deliberately chosen to use ideas the world considers foolish and of little worth in order to shame those people considered by the world as wise and great. He has chosen a plan despised by the world, counted as nothing at all, and used it to bring down to nothing those the world considers great, so that no one anywhere can ever brag in the presence of God" (1 Cor. 1:26-29, T.L.B.).

Dr. Godfrey Anderson graphically depicts the truth of Paul's words as he describes the power of the gospel at work on the hearts and lives of members in the church in its early days of struggle:

"When the Pagan detractors of the early Christian church claimed scornfully that its members were the ragtag of society —slaves, plebeians, artisans—the church answered proudly that herein lay its power. It could take the lowest members of society and, by the power of the cross, make them noble persons. Thieves and tax gatherers became honest; prostitutes left their sordid lives behind; slaves gained new dignity as members of the household of faith. Although it had a particular appeal for the lowly, who found in the gospel a new and worth-while identity, it also attracted the intellectuals and the high-born who gave early Christianity the dignity and prestige of their support."—GODFREY T. ANDERSON, "The Power of the Cross," in the *Review and Herald,* April 4, 1968.

We dare not despise the day of small things nor the contributions of common people.

13

HE TELLS IT LIKE IT IS!

In hope of eternal life which God, who never lies, promised ages ago.
Titus 1:2, R.S.V.

The Bible tells it like it is! Jesus Christ is the only perfect hero in the Holy Scriptures. The weaknesses as well as the strengths of Bible characters stand out for all to see. There is no covering up or touching up—no adjusting of halos to improve the image of some halting saint.

Take David for an example. This leader in Israel comes down to us as perhaps the greatest sinner and the greatest saint in the Word. He is a man after God's own heart. He is also a man whom God pointedly rebuked. His ways were at once laudable and lamentable. No chapter of David's life is tucked away in a closet to spare him in generations to come.

We laud him as a man of mercy when he spares Saul's life in the cave. We grieve as we read the sad story of his experience with Bathsheba so faithfully and fully recorded. In horror we hear his order to Joab that sent Uriah to his death and left David not only an adulterer but a murderer. Old Testament writers indeed tell it as it is.

Those who penned the New Testament followed their example. "Holy men of God spake as they were moved by the Holy Ghost" (2 Peter 1:21). God cannot lie (see Titus 1:2). He guides men's pens to chronicle events just as they occurred, to describe men just as they were.

We usually think of the disciple John as the apostle of love. And he was. He was numbered among the inner circle of the Saviour's followers. Inspiration also reveals a John who was proud and ambitious. He coveted one of the highest places in Christ's kingdom (see Mark 10:35-37). He was a son of thunder on occasions—a testy, turbulent fellow (see chap. 3:17). He was self-confident (see chap. 10:38, 39). He was vindictive and quick tempered (see Luke 9:54). Inspiration tells it as it is! You can count on it. You can trust the Bible!

You may be assured Paul spoke the truth when he said, "For the wages of sin is death, but the free gift of God is eternal life in Christ Jesus our Lord" (Rom. 6:23, R.S.V.).

Good or bad, God's Word tells it as it is!

HE TELLS IT LIKE IT OUGHT TO BE

"If my people who are called by my name humble themselves, and pray and seek my face, and turn from their wicked ways, then I will hear from heaven, and will forgive their sin and heal their land." 2 Chron. 7:14, R.S.V.

The writers of sacred writ not only reveal the weak and the strong points in Bible characters, they put their fingers on men and women today and tell it like it is. Sometimes it hurts. But this hurt may be good for us. It may well lead us to something better.

When you and I look into the Bible mirror, what we see doesn't give us anything of which to boast. God's brush paints it as it is: "All have sinned, and come short of the glory of God," Paul reminds us (Rom. 3:23). Earlier, as he wrote to the believers in Rome, he brought the picture more into focus by describing just what kind of reprobates men without Christ are: "Their lives became full of every kind of wickedness and sin, of greed and hate, envy, murder, fighting, lying, bitterness, and gossip. They were backbiters, haters of God, insolent, proud braggarts, always thinking of new ways of sinning and continually being disobedient to their parents. They tried to misunderstand, broke their promises, and were heartless—without pity" (Rom. 1:29-31, T.L.B.).

This is as it is. Here is what it ought to be: God calls for a humbling of heart, for confession of sin, for earnest prayer. "If my people, which are called by my name, shall humble themselves, and pray, and seek my face, and turn from their wicked ways; then will I hear from heaven, and will forgive their sin, and will heal their land" (2 Chron. 7:14).

"For stricken Israel [to whom these words were spoken] there was but one remedy—a turning away from the sins that had brought upon them the chastening hand of the Almighty, and a turning to the Lord with full purpose of heart."—*Prophets and Kings,* p. 128. Inspiration tells it as it ought to be. God's appeal to His people in Elijah's day comes to us today. The need of the sinner now is no different than it was in the prophet's day. There must be a turning from sin to holiness and it must be a 180-degree turn with God's help. This is as it ought to be!

HE TELLS IT LIKE IT CAN BE

If we are living in the light of God's presence, just as Christ does, then we have wonderful fellowship and joy with each other, and the blood of Jesus his Son cleanses us from every sin. 1 John 1:7, T.L.B.

The Bible is not only a book in which inspired writers tell it as it is and as it ought to be, it faithfully describes it *as it can be.* The Scriptures reveal not only sinners lost. They acclaim saints saved. Holy men of God not only lament the weakness of man, they proclaim the power of God. The sacred pages speak not only of a hell to shun, they glow with the inspired account of a heaven to gain. There is not only a church militant, there is a church triumphant. You and I want to be part of that victorious multitude that no man can number, who will stand at the last day before the throne of God. *It can be—* God's Word declares it!

The Bible is the only book that reveals man's Saviour. The Koran, the Bhagavad Gita, the writings of Buddha, Confucius, and Zoroaster, all contain some commendable moral ethics. But they offer no Saviour. They leave man in his hopeless, lost state.

Man needs help. He needs it urgently. He is not a naughty child who needs reproving. He is not a sick patient who needs healing. He is a lost sinner who needs saving. The Bible is the only book with a plan to do for man what must be done if he is to be rescued from his lost condition.

I have watched Hindus offer their sacrifices in India. The slaying of goats and buffaloes speaks of an inner longing for something better—but these sacrifices do not point backward gratefully or forward hopefully to a Saviour.

How different the experience of a born-again Christian! "God commendeth his love toward us, in that, while we were yet sinners, Christ died for us" (Rom. 5:8). "The blood of Jesus Christ his Son cleanseth us from all sin" (1 John 1:7). The sinner can be forgiven, cleansed, restored. God's Word declares it. The way into the kingdom then lies straight before the justified one. By God's grace and by His strength, eternal life becomes the prize of every redeemed one! God says so and God tells it as it can be!

DO WE REALLY NEED GOD TODAY?

They have belied the Lord, and said, It is not he; neither shall evil come upon us. Jer. 5:12.

Can a person truly believe in God in these enlightened days? Centuries ago in times when men widely believed in demons and witches, when disease and fear were rampant, men felt a Higher Power was indispensable. But what about our day? With all our scientific inventions and wonder drugs, does man really need a power outside himself?

In many areas where man once felt his need of God, the scientist now fulfills the requirements with the apparent miracles of his laboratory. Man no longer fears many of the terrors from which, in the past, he believed only a Higher Power could deliver him. Today he is protected by sanitation, germ control, immunization, antibiotics. He can now dispense with Newton's God, for he has Newton's laws of motion. He feels quite self-sufficient! Is there a place in the twentieth-century milieu for the God of the Bible? What can this Supreme Being do for us that the modern scientist cannot?

No one would deny that science has performed amazing feats in recent decades. There are, however, still some questions the scientist has not answered, some problems technology has not solved, some human needs laboratories cannot supply.

Science has given no conclusive proofs for the beginning of man and his planet Earth. Men of science have promulgated many hypotheses, yet they have not produced a more likely explanation for the beginning than by a divine fiat Creation. Man of himself is able to go back into the misty past just so far; then he encounters difficulties. Even that first tiny spark of life he reckons as the beginning must have come from some living force outside the power of man.

Science has found no remedy for the blight of sin that has marred this earth and its inhabitants. Machines do not provide the way for man to "live soberly, righteously, and godly, in this present world" (Titus 2:12). Neither do test tubes create formulas for life eternal. Sinful man still needs God.

WHY DO YOU BELIEVE?

Without faith it is impossible to please him: for he that cometh to God must believe that he is, and that he is a rewarder of them that diligently seek him. **Heb. 11:6.**

Why do you believe in God? Strange question, you say, but just pause a moment and analyze your prayers. Do you spend most of your time with God *asking* Him for something—help in trouble, protection in time of danger, health in illness, temporal assistance in the hour of adversity? Our prayer petitions offer a fair index to our concept of the God in whom we believe and just why we believe in Him.

Think about it. If you believe in God and go to Him only because He is able to provide for you, protect you, and give you what you need, just what *is* your basis for faith?

If you believe chiefly because God can make your life secure, then when life flows serenely along, why not dispense with Him? According to this philosophy, you really don't need Him when everything is moving along satisfactorily. Someone has said, "There are no atheists in foxholes." Perhaps there are plenty on the beaches and in the night clubs.

Truly now, why do you believe in God?

The God of the Bible is no cosmic magician at hand merely to supply our every need, real or imagined. He asks for recognition and love before we are aware of advantages or benefits. He wants us to believe in Him and love Him for what He *is*—not because of what He can do for us temporally and physically.

Our heavenly Father is more than a filler of gaps, One who makes up for our inability to do things. Rather He is the center of our life, the One in whom "we live, and move, and have our being" (Acts 17:28). We believe in God because He is, because He created us, and because He has recreated us. We have felt His energizing power, His transforming grace at work in our lives. We have experienced the warmth of His love in a world filled with hate.

The advantages and the benefits? Of course they will follow, just as He has promised. But remember, we believe and love because He *is,* not because of what we expect to receive from Him.

THE MAN WHO LOVED THIS PRESENT WORLD

For Demas hath forsaken me, having loved this present world. **2 Tim. 4:10.**

What an epitaph to be placed upon any erstwhile Christian's memorial stone. How many other names might here replace that of Demas. "[He] hath forsaken me, having loved this present world." The *New English Bible's* version of Paul's words has, "because his heart was set on this world."

We may well think of Demas with sadness and sympathy rather than in condemnation, for there are so many of his spiritual kinsmen among us even in 1975. For too many it is much more inviting to choose the fun-filled way of life—the way of the bright lights and raucous laughter. Too many love comfort and hilarity more than they love Christ and heaven. The promise-packed way of the world with its present potential bids strongly for every human heart. Demas yielded. He chose the immediate, easy way.

"Demas' love of worldly gain and honor is in sharp contrast with the love of genuine Christians for the 'appearing' of Christ. The desire for worldly honor may make it impossible for a Christian to fight successfully 'a good fight' and finish his 'course.' "—*The SDA Bible Commentary,* on 2 Tim. 4:5.

Dr. Taylor makes the apostle James's words current and relevant as he warns potential present-day Demases: "Don't you realize that making friends with God's enemies—the evil pleasures of this world—makes you an enemy of God? I say it again, that if your aim is to enjoy the evil pleasure of the unsaved world, you cannot also be a friend of God" (James 4:4, T.L.B.).

"The evil pleasure of the unsaved world" may become Satan's Trojan horse in the heart of the halting saint. At first the heart is shared with Christ, then little by little, often imperceptibly, the Saviour is crowded out. The world takes over. Like Demas the self-seeking Christian becomes a deserter. It is a subtle, evil process. It may at first eat painlessly, like a cancer, but its end is desertion and death. Christ cannot long reign in a divided heart.

"Set your affection on things above," Paul pleads, "not on things on the earth" (Col. 3:2).

WHAT THE WORD WILL DO!

And a certain Jew named Apollos, born at Alexandria, an eloquent man, and mighty in the scriptures, came to Ephesus. Acts 18:24.

What a glorious honor to be numbered among God's great men in the Holy Scriptures as one who was "mighty in the scriptures." This was Apollos. He was a man of native ability and natural power, but when Priscilla and Aquila studied the Scriptures further with him at Ephesus he grew even more as a man of the Word.

The Word of God does something for any man or woman who feeds on it. It did something for Apollos, the converted Jew from Alexandria. It played an important part in making him eloquent for God. Adequate preparation always begets confidence in any endeavor, and Apollos was prepared. He filled his mind with the precious truths of the Word. Knowledge of the Scriptures made him confident. The Spirit of God rested upon him and he spoke with freedom and power of Christ's love and ministry.

When a man is "instructed in the way of the Lord," as was Apollos, it makes a new person of him, fills him with a holy zeal, and sends him out to burn for God. It makes him "fervent in the spirit" and he will do "diligently the things of the Lord."

A thorough knowledge of Scripture removes fear from timid souls. Apollos "began to speak boldly" (verse 26) of his new-found Saviour. His zeal led him into the very den of opposition—the synagogue. When a worker for God possesses both a knowledge and a zeal, something happens. Results under the blessing of the Spirit are assured. Inspiration records of Apollos, "For he mightily convinced the Jews, and that publickly, shewing by the scriptures that Jesus was Christ" (verse 28).

The Holy Spirit through the Scriptures made Apollos eloquent, He made him zealous for God, He took away any natural fear he may have experienced, and He made him a successful soul winner!

Given similar opportunity He will do the same in 1975 through us!

IT MUST BE IN YOU!

Being confident of this very thing, that he which hath begun a good work in you will finish it until the day of Jesus Christ. Phil. 1:6, margin.

Elder A. G. Daniells, a former president of the General Conference, was in Europe. His heart was heavily burdened to see the work of God finished and to see Jesus come. He had with him a copy of *Christ's Object Lessons.* It is reported that in his hotel room as he pondered and prayed, the man of God cried out to the Lord, "O God, if there is any message in this book that will help me lead Thy people into an experience that will prepare them to meet Thee soon, please show it to me!"

Elder Daniells took *Christ's Object Lessons* and opened it. His eyes fell upon these words: "As you receive the Spirit of Christ—the Spirit of unselfish love and labor for others—you will grow and bring forth fruit."—Page 68.

"Bring forth fruit"—these words conjured up in the leader's mind a great evangelistic thrust that would challenge the church to a program of soul winning, calculated to quickly take God's message to every kindred, tongue, and people.

But he read on—

"The graces of the Spirit will ripen in your character. Your faith will increase, your convictions deepen, your love be made perfect. More and more you will reflect the likeness of Christ in all that is pure, noble, and lovely."—*Ibid.*

From these words Elder Daniells knew the Lord's servant was not speaking of a great public evangelistic thrust. She was writing of consistent character development. "More and more you will reflect the likeness of Christ"—"He which hath begun a good work *in you* will finish it." The apostle declares this work must be done in the individual life—in *you* (and in *me*)—in the life of every professing Seventh-day Adventist Christian.

A finished work in your life and mine is the development of a Christlike character in which the fruits of the Spirit will be evident to all:

" 'The fruit of the Spirit is love, joy, peace, longsuffering, gentleness, goodness, faith, meekness, temperance' (Gal. 5: 22, 23). This fruit can never perish, but will produce after its kind a harvest unto eternal life."—*Ibid.,* pp. 68, 69.

"WHEN THE FRUIT IS BROUGHT FORTH"

When the fruit is brought forth, immediately he putteth in the sickle, because the harvest is come. Mark 4:29.

There is a very close relationship between the spiritual condition of the church, a finished work, and the return of our Lord. Ellen White makes this clear in *Christ's Object Lessons:* "When the character of Christ shall be perfectly reproduced in His people, then He will come to claim them as His own." —Page 69.

This is what Jesus was talking about in His parable of the blade, the ear, and the full corn. The fruit spoken of in the parable refers to the fruits of the Spirit. As we read yesterday, " 'The fruit of the Spirit is love, joy, peace, longsuffering, gentleness, goodness, faith, meekness, temperance' (Gal. 5:22, 23). This fruit can never perish, but will produce after its kind a harvest unto eternal life."—*Ibid.*, pp. 68, 69.

"The harvest is the end of the world" (Matt. 13:39). In our text for today Jesus is saying, "When the fruits of the Spirit are brought forth in the lives of My people, immediately I will put in the sickle at My second coming because the harvest [end of the world] is come." To simplify it even more: "When My people reflect My character I will come to claim them as My own."

Frequently we say it is not time, but a task that separates us from our eternal inheritance. While this is in a degree true, there is something more—not only is there a message to be preached, there are characters to be perfected—your character and mine! The Advent message must not only enter Tibet and Arabia, it must find a permanent home in our own lives. It must not only change the people in primitive, underdeveloped spots of earth, it must produce the fruits of the Spirit in Robert H. Pierson—and every other candidate for the kingdom.

The third angel's message must not only make Sabbathkeepers in Africa and Asia, it must reproduce the character of the Lord of the Sabbath in church members everywhere.

When the fruit is brought forth in the lives of God's people, our Saviour will immediately put in the sickle, because the harvest will then be fully ready! No more waiting.

I BELIEVE IN PROTEST!

Cry aloud, spare not, lift up thy voice like a trumpet. Isa. 58:1.

Of course I believe in protest. I am a *"Protestant."* Although not all forms of protest are right, Seventh-day Adventist Christians have not only a right but a duty to protest. Let's make ample use of well-sought publicity provided by every possible news medium. I am for protest—provided it does not violate the principles and methods of Christ.

What shall we protest? We might well begin with a protest against the inroads of worldly preoccupation and materialism within the ranks of our own church. "If any man love the world, the love of the Father is not in him" (1 John 2:15).

While we are protesting, why not mount a crusade against the decline of the family altar and the deadly effects of spiritual neglect in Adventist homes? "Shew piety at home . . . ," Paul says, "for that is good and acceptable before God" (1 Tim. 5:4). How many family altars are in disrepair! Too many Adventist Bibles are dusty with disuse. Secular interests have taken over. What a challenge for holy protest!

As we consider protest priorities, the blight of Laodiceanism that holds us in its stupefying grip should stand high on our list. " 'I know you well. . . . You say, "I am rich, with everything I want; I don't need a thing!" And you don't realize that spiritually you are wretched and miserable and poor and blind and naked' " (Rev. 3:15-17, T.L.B.). With the banner of Christ our Righteousness over us, we should make an effective attack on this anesthetizing condition that strangles our church into near impotency!

In the world about us we can protest the spiritual vacuum and moral decline of society. "Human beings have confederated with satanic agencies to make void the law of God. The inhabitants of the world are fast becoming as the inhabitants of the world in Noah's day. . . . The powers of Satan are at work to keep minds diverted from eternal realities."—*Testimonies,* vol. 9, p. 43.

Publicly in preaching missions, personally in one-to-one witness, we need to protest the effective subtleties of Satan.

GOD'S SPIRIT WITHDRAWN

My spirit shall not always strive with man. Gen. 6:3.

"The condition of things in the world shows that troublous times are right upon us. The daily papers are full of indications of a terrible conflict in the near future. Bold robberies are of frequent occurrence. Strikes are common. Thefts and murders are committed on every hand. Men possessed of demons are taking the lives of men, women, and little children. Men have become infatuated with vice, and every species of evil prevails."—*Testimonies,* vol. 9, p. 11.

Have we not seen such grisly crimes committed in our day? When has this world beheld the multimurders that have been committed in our day, in our land? Snipers pick off innocent victims from vantage points as they walk the streets below. Young men in Texas killed during sadistic parties. Twenty-six laborers slain in California.

What do these heinous crimes mean? The Lord's messenger has the answer: They mean "the restraining Spirit of God is even now being withdrawn from the world" *(ibid.,* vol. 6, p. 408). "The Spirit of God is gradually but surely being withdrawn from the earth."—*Ibid.,* vol. 9, p. 11.

Ellen White also speaks of another evidence of the Spirit's withdrawal. "Men have become infatuated with vice."

In an article describing erotic art shows and entertainers dancing nude in New York City, is the following remarkable quote: "We're living in a Babylonian society perhaps more Babylonian than Babylon itself. . . . The emphasis in our society today is on the senses and the release of the sensual. All old codes have been broken down."—MAX LERNER, quoted in *Newsweek,* Nov. 13, 1967.

"My spirit shall not always strive with man," God reminds us. Today His restraining Spirit holds back the powers of evil that, when they burst unchecked upon our world, will bring carnage and woe on a scale never before imagined. Then the time of trouble *will* be upon us.

Trouble ahead? Yes! Even now it is brewing, but in Christ we have an assured and an assuring place of refuge! There we may be safe *now*—and then!

BEAUTIFUL SEPULCHERS

Even so ye also outwardly appear righteous unto men, but within ye are full of hypocrisy and iniquity. Matt. 23:28.

Father and mother are sitting comfortably in the family room. The TV is blaring. On the screen an old movie holds their attention. Academy-age Junior bursts upon the scene.

"Mom, the kids are going to a show and they want me to go with them!"

"No, Junior, you know Seventh-day Adventists don't go to the theater," mother responds, one eye riveted to the TV screen.

"But, Mom . . . ," Junior protests.

"It's settled. You are *not* going!"

You may well imagine the sequel to this little drama as Junior withdraws sullenly, muttering something about "hypocrites" and "the church" under his breath.

The scene changes—

I want to share with you a cartoon I saw in the paper recently.

A scruffy Mod and Moll are shuffling out from their pad for another routine day of prattle and protest.

"I'll run over and pick up my unemployment check," the male is saying, "then I'll go over to the U and see what's holding up my Federal Education Grant, and then pick up our food stamps.

"Meanwhile you go to the free VD Clinic and check up on your tests, then pick up my new glasses at the Health Center, then go to the Welfare Department and try to increase our eligibility limit again. Later we'll meet at the Federal Building for the mass demonstration against the stinking, rotten establishment."

Hypocrisy is both timeless and ageless. It is not some strange malady that strikes a person when he reaches a certain age in life. It is a spiritual illness that God condemns at any age. "God hates hypocrisy."—*The Acts of the Apostles*, p. 72. "Hypocrisy always met the severest rebuke from Jesus."—*Testimonies*, vol. 4, p. 326.

"IS THERE ANY WORD FROM THE LORD?"

Then Zedekiah the king sent, and took him out: and the king asked him secretly in his house, and said, Is there any word from the Lord? Jer. 37:17.

During a period of national apostasy in Judah, King Zedekiah found the Babylonians battering at the gates of his capital. With the kingdom slipping from his grasp, with captivity or death just ahead, the backslidden Zedekiah managed a few thoughts for God. He remembered Jeremiah the prophet whom he had placed in a pit. In the hour of dire extremity the king sent for the harassed prophet. His first question when the man of God appeared was, "Is there any word from the Lord?"

This is the question that should be uppermost in the mind of every Seventh-day Adventist today. The world is full of pressures, frustrations, and problems. Some of these problems affect the church, our schools, our medical institutions.

The one question we must press with perseverance today—*"Is there any word from the Lord?"*

The world shouts loudly its proposed solutions. We know what the accrediting bodies say, what the labor unions demand, what the community wants, what the government requires. The strident tones of worldly forces about us come through loud and clear. We have no problem hearing and understanding their insistent clamor. But the question still persists, *"Is there any word from the Lord?"*

Today the evil one works in a more subtle manner. What he cannot destroy by overt attack he seeks to subvert through the erosion of faith. The church today is much more in danger of *seduction* than of *persecution*.

The word of the Lord comes to us through different channels. God speaks through His Holy Bible. He speaks by His Holy Spirit. He speaks through nature rightly interpreted. He speaks to God's remnant through His appointed messenger—Ellen White.

When we face problems in our churches or institutions, in our board and committee meetings today, the first area of solution we seek must be God's will. "Is there any word from the Lord?" must take precedence over all other proposals.

DOES DOCTRINE MATTER?

If any man will do his will, he shall know of the doctrine, whether it be of God, or whether I speak of myself. John 7:17.

"Don't talk to us about doctrine," the young college junior said to me, "just speak to us about Jesus. This is all we need. We have heard so much about the Sabbath, about last-day events, and the Second Advent. Just tell us about Jesus. He is all we need!"

Agreed! Jesus *is* all we need—and how much we do need Him! But how can we know Jesus unless we first know who He is, where He came from, what He believed and taught, what works He did, and what happened to Him? In addition to all of this we must experience Him!

How can we learn these things about the greatest Person who ever lived? The place to learn about Jesus is in His Book, the Word of God. Doctrine (teaching) reveals these things to us.

For instance, take the "doctrine" of the seventh-day Sabbath —what can we learn about Jesus from this cardinal point of faith we hold? We can learn a great deal. The seventh-day Sabbath is the memorial of Creation. This fact introduces to us the Lord of the Sabbath as the Creator who "made heaven, and earth, and the sea, and the fountains of waters" (Rev. 14:7). Christ as Creator with the Father is revealed as the omnipotent Lord of all. If He has power to bring forth a universe out of nothing, this reveals a great deal about Him. He is all-powerful. Surely we can trust our all to His keeping. The doctrine of the Sabbath reveals this great truth about God the Son.

The "doctrines" of the law, the cross, the resurrection, the priestly ministry of Jesus and His second advent, even Christ's teaching about tithing, all give us insights into the kind of divine-human Person He was and is. They give us an understanding of what He believed and taught, from whence He came, where He went, and what we may expect from Him now and in the future. Doctrine and inspired history reveal Christ to us—make Him a real Person to us. We cannot truly know Him and experience Him without doctrine!

It is important that we both do His will and know of the doctrine!

"PROVE ALL THINGS"

Despise not prophesyings. Prove all things; hold fast that which is good.
1 Thess. 5:20, 21.

In these words to the believers Paul was speaking specifically about the manifestation of the Spirit mentioned in verses nineteen and twenty. There have been true prophets. There are also self-proclaimed prophets and prophetesses in the world today. I have met some of these professed seers in mission lands. There are those in our own land who declare they possess the gift of prophecy.

Four basic proofs should be applied to professing prophets. First, do they confess Christ by example as well as by precept? If a person's lips say one thing and his life says another, the apostle John warns you had better be careful. A man's deeds must square with his words (see 1 John 4:1-4). If they do not, God has not sent him.

A true prophet takes his stand unequivocally on the divinity of the Lord Jesus Christ. Anyone who is uncertain on this basic precept of the gospel is an impostor, the Word declares. "Who is the liar? Who but he that denies that Jesus is the Christ? He is Antichrist, for he denies both the Father and the Son: to deny the Son is to be without the Father; to acknowledge the Son is to have the Father too" (1 John 2:22, 23, N.E.B.). This requirement will sort out many others professing the gift of prophecy.

If a person is moved by the Spirit of God, his teachings will accord with the precepts of Scripture. The Holy Spirit is not divided against Himself. He does not say one thing to a person directly that is contradictory to what He has said in the Word of God. "If any man preach any other gospel unto you than that ye have received, let him be accursed" (Gal. 1:9). The ranks of professed prophets will be thinned out materially by this test!

The fourth test is the fruitage of a prophet's teaching. Is it good or bad? (Read Matt. 7:18-20.) This is important!

Thank God that Ellen White, the one whom the Lord placed in the remnant church with the gift of prophecy, stands all these and other tests. So, as Paul says, "Hold fast that which is good."

MODERN SCIENCE NOW AGREES

When a prophet speaks in the name of the Lord, if the word does not come to pass or come true, that is a word which the Lord has not spoken; the prophet has spoken it presumptuously, you need not be afraid of him. Deut. 18:22, R.S.V.

"For approximately fifty years Ellen G. White wrote extensively in the field of health and nutrition," wrote U. D. Register, Ph.D., chairman, Department of Nutrition, Loma Linda University School of Public Health, in the booklet, *Medical Science and the Spirit of Prophecy.* "She advocated many principles of health for which there was no available scientific evidence. Although written at a time when health fallacies were prevalent, the principles have been verified by science in a remarkable way."—Page 1.

This booklet comes packed full of scientific confirmations of statements from the pen of the messenger of the Lord. Its pages reveal how her inspired predictions have come true.

In the year 1884 Ellen White wrote that "nine tenths of the wickedness among the children of today is caused by intemperance in eating and drinking" *(Temperance,* p. 150). "Doubtless the imbibing of alcoholic drinks, tea, and coffee would be included in these indictments of 'intemperance.' "—*Medical Science and the Spirit of Prophecy,* p. 11. "In 1890 Mrs. White declared that 'the diet materially affects the mind and disposition.' "—*Ibid.* Following these statements are excerpts from a number of sources giving scientific evidence of our day "that better-fed teen-agers get the best grades in school," thus confirming Ellen White's writings.

"In the *Testimonies . . .* bearing date of 1868, Ellen White warned certain overweight individuals of their being 'liable to acute attacks of disease, and to sudden death' if they continued a dietary program in which animal fats figured largely."—*Ibid.,* p. 14. "The American Heart Association in 1960 cautiously advised the reduction or control of fat consumption, particularly the use of saturated fats, because of the risk of heart attacks and strokes."—*Ibid.*

How thankful we should be for the special light God has given this people through the gift of prophecy!

THE DIVINE IMPERATIVE

I have no right to boast just because I preach the gospel. After all, I am under orders to do so. And how terrible it would be for me if I did not preach the gospel! 1 Cor. 9:16, T.E.V.

I first met Urbano Castillo when I visited the Philippines in 1967. He didn't look at all as I had pictured him. From reports in the *Review and Herald* I pictured Urbano as a tall, muscular man with a physique that could stand the rigors of opposition—a man who traveled and preached constantly. Brother Castillo is a short man, but a man who stands tall with God and his fellow countrymen.

During World War II when most foreign missionaries in his country had either been interned or sent home, Urbano Castillo sensed a need for lay workers to step into the breach and help national preachers proclaim the Advent message. So this slight, bespectacled, dental technician secured a tent from the mission and went to work in public evangelism.

"I manufacture dentures for a living," Brother Castillo told me, "but my main business is winning souls to Christ."

Eking out a meager existence in his trade, this little man of God is rich in the Word and he preaches with power. The last report I had of Urbano's work, he had raised up nearly thirty churches, with approximately 1,500 persons baptized.

"When the Lord helps me raise up a new church, the first thing I want to do is to see that they have their own church home, so we build a church building right away," he explained.

Fifteen hundred baptisms, thirty new churches—what a monument to the commitment of one little man with a big vision, a large faith, and a will to serve his Lord. Urbano Castillo experienced the divine imperative resting upon him. Nothing could stop him. This demonstrates how God can use just one person who is fully dedicated to Him. "There is no limit to the usefulness of one who, by putting self aside, makes room for the working of the Holy Spirit upon his heart, and lives a life wholly consecrated to God."—*The Desire of Ages,* pp. 250, 251.

What would happen if even one tenth of the Seventh-day Adventist Church membership possessed the commitment and the zeal of Urbano Castillo?

"SHE PLEASETH ME WELL"

And Samson said unto his father, Get her for me; for she pleaseth me well. Judges 14:3.

"Samson went down to Timnath, and there he saw a woman, one of the Philistines. When he came back, he told his father and mother that he had seen a Philistine woman in Timnath and asked them to get her for him as his wife. His father and mother said to him, 'Is there no woman among your cousins or in all our own people? Must you go and marry one of the uncircumcised Philistines?' But Samson said to his father, 'Get her for me, because she pleases me' " (Judges 14: 1-4, N.E.B.).

"Get her for me; for *she pleaseth me well.*" These words of history's best-known strong man are familiar to most of us. Samson knew what God had said about alliances with daughters of the Philistines.

It so happened in this situation that what God said did not agree with what Samson wanted—what pleased him. He was insistent. In essence he demanded, "Regardless of what God says, get her for me; for she pleases me well."

Deciding what to do in a given situation on the basis of what a person wants, what pleases him, rather than by what God declares to be right or wrong did not cease with the death of Israel's strong man. Today many decisions are made the Samson way—on what one wants. What friends to make, what literature to read, what pictures to watch, what clothes to wear, what food to eat, where to go, or what to do are decided purely upon what pleases the individual.

"Everything that belongs to the world—what the sinful self desires, what people see and want . . ." John says, "none of this comes from the Father; it all comes from the world" (1 John 2:16, T.E.V.).

God does not bring fire down upon us when we walk in the ways of our own inclination, but He reminds us: "Rejoice, O young men, in thy youth; and let thy heart cheer thee in the days of thy youth, and walk in the ways of thine heart, and in the sight of thine eyes: but know thou, that for all these things God will bring thee into judgment" (Eccl. 11:9).

How are *you* making *your* decisions these days?

PRAY OR SAY YOUR PRAYERS?

Seek the Lord and his strength, seek his face continually. 1 Chron. 16:11.

Some Christians pray; others, parrotlike, merely "say their prayers." There is a difference. The Word of God makes this plain. On the occasion of the return to Jerusalem of the ark of God, David describes true communication with his heavenly Father. "Seek the Lord and his strength," the sweet singer admonishes, "seek his face continually."

True prayer involves true seeking. True prayer is a continuing experience.

I once heard of a young woman whose prayer relationship was so limited that in an hour of extreme peril the only prayer she could call to mind was the grace she had learned to say at mealtime. Of course, it is good to use all the prayer power at one's command on such an occasion, but it is far more reassuring to be on better speaking terms with the Almighty than relying upon just a perfunctory recitation.

It requires faith—often a tenacious expectation that one will realize the fruition of his prayers—to truly communicate with God. It pays to linger long in the presence of the Most High—to continue until the blessing is assured.

Years ago the Hindu headman of a small South Indian community invited Seventh-day Adventists to come to his village and open work. When we responded he met us with an earnest appeal. "Your Bible says a person who wants something should ask and seek and knock," he declared. "For many months I have been asking, I have been seeking, I have been knocking. At last you have come." His continuing prayers were rewarded. We established work in his village. Aruldas was baptized. This headman served many years as a church elder before he died.

"If you will seek the Lord and be converted every day; . . . if with gladsome consent of heart to His gracious call, you come wearing the yoke of Christ, . . . all your difficulties will be removed, all the perplexing problems that now confront you will be solved."—*Thoughts From the Mount of Blessing,* p. 101.

This promise is for the one who truly seeks the Lord continually!

EARNEST PRAYER CAN WORK MIRACLES

And the people murmured against Moses, saying, What shall we drink? And he cried unto the Lord. Ex. 15:24.

I like this text. In the hour of need Moses "cried unto the Lord." The story continues to a blessed conclusion: "the waters were made sweet." When Moses "cried unto" Him, the Lord did something about it. A miracle was performed. The people needed pure drinking water. Only a miracle could provide such water. Moses cried. God heard. The bitter "waters were made sweet." Earnest prayer works miracles.

Many years later a godly woman was distressed. She had no child. Reproach was upon her. "I am a woman of a sorrowful spirit," Hannah declared to Eli, "but have poured out my soul before the Lord" (1 Sam. 1:15).

When Hannah poured out her soul to God in earnest petitions God heard. Again He performed a miracle. "The Lord hath given me my petition which I asked of him," she declared joyfully (verse 27). Samuel was born. Hannah's reproach was removed. Earnest prayers can work miracles.

Some years later Samuel himself "cried unto the Lord." The inspired record declares that "the Lord heard him." "The Lord thundered with a great thunder on that day upon the Philistines, and discomfited them; and they were smitten before Israel" (chap. 7:9, 10). The children of Israel had strayed far from God. The prophet had frankly set forth the conditions for a return of the Lord's blessing among them. "If ye do return unto the Lord with all your hearts, then put away the strange gods and Ashtaroth from among you, and prepare your hearts unto the Lord, and serve him only: and he will deliver you out of the hand of the Philistines" (verse 3).

The day of God's miracle-working power is not past. Too many of us, though, have not learned the science and the power of persevering prayer. Too few of us know what "crying to the Lord" truly is.

The conditions of answered prayer—of restored blessing—to the wandering saint is made clear in Samuel's experience. One must *repent, return, reform,* and *cry unto the Lord.* Then miracles can happen. They happened in Samuel's day. They can happen in your day and mine.

EVERYTHING QUESTIONED

Pilate saith unto him, What is truth? John 18:38.

In the world today there are those who question everything. Nothing must be settled finally. Everything must be probed, pulled apart, and challenged.

There were people of this ilk in Jesus' day. Some of them were the theologians of their time. They questioned everything. They questioned Jesus' birth. They questioned His life, His character. They challenged His authority, His doctrine. They denied His divinity!

By the time His ministry closed, the fruit of their skepticism was apparent. They had reached some firm conclusions. Christ, the Revelation of God, was an impostor. The spotless Lamb of God, Righteousness Incarnate, was a bad man! "If he were not a malefactor, we would not have delivered him up unto thee" (John 18:30).

Their probing, questioning, challenging, criticizing, had warped their thinking. Their pedantic display of human logic ended in spiritual bankruptcy. In the end their carping criticism led to a cross where they crucified the Lord of glory.

To Pilate Jesus declared His kingship. He did more. He affirmed His divinity, "My kingdom is not of this world." He revealed His high destiny, "To this end was I born." He declared His divine mission, "For this cause came I into the world." Then He added, "That I should bear witness unto the truth. Every one that is of the truth heareth my voice" (verses 36, 37).

Immediately Jesus was challenged. His clear, positive declaration was questioned. "What is truth?" Pilate demanded. "I am not sure I understand what you are talking about. I, too, believe in truth, but I am not one of your followers. Define your terms. Tell me what truth really is!"

"What is truth?"—the words and the spirit of unsatisfied challenge sounds strangely familiar to our ears in the nineteen seventies.

May God grant that our questioning today may not end with a vanishing faith nor in spiritual bankruptcy, but rather to a confirmed faith, to a greater confidence in God, in His Book, and in His last-day message.

THE FAITH FACTOR

Without faith it is impossible to please him: for he that cometh to God must believe that he is, and that he is a rewarder of them that diligently seek him. Heb. 11:6.

We must face it frankly—there are problems posed by our expanding technology. Certain data presented by some geologists, for example, cannot be fully gainsaid by a surface reaction or simplistic explanation.

It is quite probable that this side of eternity there will always be a faith factor—we will, as believers in the Word of God, accept some aspects of Bible truth in simple faith. We may well say, "Some things I cannot explain, but I believe God's Word. Someday He will make plain those things I may not fully understand today."

We accept the Bible account of Creation by faith. The evolutionist also accepts his hypothesis of beginnings by faith! Only God was present during those first six days when He made the world and all that is in it. "Through faith we understand that the worlds were framed by the word of God, so that things which are seen were not made of things which do appear" (Heb. 11:3).

The unbelieving scientist has not produced an incontestable hypothesis of his explanation of the origin of man and of this world. He postulates, but he has not proved it!

In this controversy *the Bible and the Spirit of Prophecy are not on trial!* "The Bible is not to be tested by men's ideas of science, but science is to be brought to the test of this unerring standard."—ELLEN G. WHITE, in *The Signs of the Times,* March 13, 1884.

Someday those points not fully revealed to us now will be made plain. "We may rejoice that all which has perplexed us in the providences of God will then be made plain, things hard to be understood will then find an explanation; and where our finite minds discovered only confusion and broken purposes, we shall see the most perfect and beautiful harmony."—*Steps to Christ,* p. 113. This may well apply to some of the blind spots in science as well as to the vicissitudes of life.

A faith factor may always be required, but we may with certainty *trust* Him where we cannot always trace Him!

SOME THINGS ARE SETTLED

For ever, O Lord, thy word is settled in heaven. **Ps. 119:89.**

The word "settled" in our text for today comes from a Hebrew root meaning "to establish," "to make stand." A dictionary definition of this word is "to secure permanently," "to resolve conclusively," "to become established."

I am glad to belong to a people who believe in the Bible as the inspired and authoritative Word of the living God. We settled that point decades ago. It is established in our hearts and lives. To our satisfaction we have resolved conclusively some of the problems that continue to perplex many people in the world today. With Seventh-day Adventists the Bible has been secured permanently—it not only contains the Word of God, it indeed *is* the Word of God.

"God's word is settled for all time and is unchangeable. It is high above the accidents of chance and stands fast both in heaven and in earth. Man's teachings concerning the word may change, but the word stands immovable."—*The SDA Bible Commentary,* on Ps. 119:89.

It does not necessarily follow that all the problems are *solved,* but they are *settled.* When God speaks that settles the matter with a committed follower of His. There will be problems until our Lord returns. There will be some things in the field of science we may not understand this side of the kingdom.

There may even be issues raised by man's theology—or because too frequently God is left out of today's theology. Such questions may concern us but they will not unsettle us. They will not disturb our faith in God and in His last-day message. We settled these matters in our hearts when we turned our lives over to Him.

God declares we have some starting points. Some bases of faith have already been established and settled. These starting points for Seventh-day Adventists are to be found in revelation —the Bible and the writings of the Spirit of Prophecy.

"Eternal is thy word, O Lord, planted firm in heaven" (Ps. 119:89, N.E.B.).

Thank God for this assurance in a confused, unsettled world. This confidence will see us through to the kingdom.

SOMEONE TO TIE TO

He also said: "You, Lord, in the beginning created the earth, and with your own hands you made the heavens. They will all disappear, but you will remain. They will all grow old like clothes; you will fold them up like a coat, and they will be changed like clothes. But you are the same, and you will never grow old." Heb. 1:10-12, T.E.V.

There have been more amazing changes in the world during the past two or three decades than in centuries before. Think of the political changes. The appearance of scores of new nations have redrawn our maps, old ideologies have given place to new and perhaps untried philosophies. In the world of technology fantastic trips into outer space no longer belong to the comic strips. They have burst upon a startled world with breath-taking reality. I hesitate to predict what technologists have in future store, lest by the time this book appears in print the predictions will be outdated.

In the spiritual world there have been astonishing changes —not all of them in favor of faith. Denominational walls have been crumbling. Likewise, many of the old landmarks of truth long accepted as foundation pillars of the gospel have been washed away. As one hymnwriter wrote, "Change and decay in all around I see."

Despite the apparently unending chain reaction of change, the great facts of human existence remain unaltered. The political, religious, technological, and physical changes with which we are beset are surface changes. Man's basic needs have not changed.

Despite exciting breakthroughs in technology our world is still filled with the sick and the dying. In spite of advances on the psychiatric front and the development of potent drugs, institutions for the mentally ill are filled to overflowing. Prisons and houses of correction are still overcrowded. Man, embroiled in a crucible of change, still needs help, help from outside himself—a changeless Helper.

That changeless Helper is Christ. Speaking of Jesus, Paul declares, "Thou remainest . . . thou art the same." What blessed assurance! We have something, Someone, to whom we may tie with confidence in this changing, need-filled world—Jesus Christ!

JESUS SPEAKS ABOUT HYPOCRISY

For ye are like unto whited sepulchres, which indeed appear beautiful outward, but are within full of dead men's bones, and of all uncleanness. Matt. 23:27.

Driving with his wife along a northern California highway one fall day, Mr. Blank saw two young men standing by the road looking for a ride. As they were well-dressed, clean-cut youths, he applied his brakes.

Back into the cruising speed of the highway, Mr. Blank, his wife, and the two boys, Bill and Earl, proceeded to get acquainted. They visited cordially for some time.

"Mind if I smoke?" one of the young men called from the back seat.

"All right with me," the driver replied agreeably.

The conversation turned to the trouble on school campuses across the country.

"We don't have any trouble like that on our campus," Earl volunteered as he pulled on his cigarette.

"No?" Mr. Blank responded with interest. "What college do you attend?"

"We go to a small private school called Blank Union College," explained Bill.

"Blank Union College? Isn't that a Seventh-day Adventist school?" the driver queried.

"Yes," was the reply.

"Seventh-day Adventists?" the man at the wheel mused. "I know Seventh-day Adventists well. In fact, you probably know Elder Leader in the General Conference. He's my brother-in-law!"

Bill and Earl gulped and looked at each other sheepishly.

"Say, mister," Bill began, "here's where we get down. Thanks a lot for the lift."

"Here?" the driver asked with surprise. "I thought you were going a hundred miles with me?"

"No, we'll get down here," the two chorused.

Jesus had a word for such persons, whether they are young or old. He called them hypocrites.

JUST HOW PECULIAR ARE YOU, ANYWAY?

But ye are a chosen generation, a royal priesthood, an holy nation, a peculiar people; that ye should shew forth the praises of him who hath called you out of darkness into his marvellous light. 1 Peter 2:9.

I knew a man once who called himself a Seventh-day Adventist lay preacher. Most of us would question this brother's method of drawing crowds. When I saw him first he was lying in the middle of a busy street, tying up traffic in order to attract attention. The police had to carry him away bodily to get the honking motorists moving again.

Brother Brown was peculiar, without doubt. Is this what the apostle Peter meant when he wrote that we are to be God's "peculiar" people? Does it mean involving ourselves in all sorts of strange antics to attract attention?

The old English usage of *peculiar* is in a sense of possession —we belong to God. But another definition of *peculiar* holds meaning for us, that of being "different from the usual or the normal." God's people are not to be eccentric or queer. They are to be "different from the usual" run of people in the community where they live or work.

Usually this difference is manifest in a thousand little ways that seldom make newspaper headlines. Yet every one is noted by our heavenly Father. To make it practical think of it this way.

When you are patient at the traffic light in the midst of bumper to bumper traffic and you are eager to get home, you are being different from the usual. When your waitress adds up your lunch bill incorrectly and you could save thirty-five cents by keeping quiet, but you don't—that's being peculiar today.

When you worship your Lord on His Sabbath instead of honoring the world's rest day, you are peculiar. When you confess a fault to your brother, when you make restitution for money or property you have unlawfully taken, when you decline an invitation to the theater, when you dress like a child of God, you are peculiar in today's world.

Being peculiar in God's vocabulary is not being eccentric or odd, it is merely being Christlike, demonstrating that we are His cherished possession.

"ALL YE ARE BRETHREN"

But be not ye called Rabbi: for one is your Master, even Christ; and all ye are brethren. Matt. 23:8.

"All ye are brethren," or, as *Today's English Version* records it, "you are all brothers of one another." In these words Jesus describes the true relationships and the fraternal love that must exist among God's people.

The Seventh-day Adventist Church is an international church. God intended that it should be. We are a worldwide movement. Prophecy decreed it. Believers were to be gathered out from every land on earth. Read Revelation 10:1, 2 and chapter 14:6. God's last-day movement must be broadly based. It should embrace the world.

Bringing together men and women, young and old, from "every nation, and kindred, and tongue, and people" creates a situation inherent with problems. Living in a part of the world where all people speak the same language and are of the same racial background still has its hazards. But with a church membership gathered from nearly two hundred lands, with different cultural heritages, divergent social, political, and religious backgrounds, welding them together into Christian unity could be difficult.

Imagine Israelis and Arabs, Pakistanis and Indians, Russians and Americans, North Koreans and South Koreans, Frenchmen and Germans, Watusi and Bahutu, Laos and Kikuyus, Moslems and Hindus, all in the same caldron. Talk about potential explosions, you have them here.

Yet out of all this diversity must come a unity, a oneness, that is a foretaste of the togetherness we will experience in the earth made new. These loved ones, gathered out from all nations, tribes, and races of earth are to be brought together in a Christian brotherhood that will be a marvel to the universe.

In a world filled with hatred, injustices, inequities, suspicion, mistrust, and violence, how can we ever hope to effect this unity?

The answer is simple—*Christ our Elder Brother does it for us.* His last-day message molds us together. All the ideological differences, all the suspicions, all the tribal and national hatreds, disappear at the cross. Here we become one.

WORKERS TOGETHER FOR GOD

For we are labourers together with God: ye are God's husbandry, ye are God's building. 1 Cor. 3:9.

When the apostle Paul found the believers in Corinth forming cliques, some supporting Peter, some uplifting Christ, and still others who were his own staunch supporters, he was distressed. He proceeded to explain that men of varied talent may work together in love and unity. One man's methods may appeal to certain seekers for truth. Others will be led to Christ and His message through quite a different approach used by another committed worker.

One worker for God may be used of the Holy Spirit to sow seeds of truth in human hearts that will not bring forth fruit for months or years. Another agent for God comes along and waters the seed sown. Still another may reap the harvest. Paul explains this sharing of gospel cooperation: "I have planted, Apollos watered; but God gave the increase. So then neither is he that planteth any thing, neither he that watereth; but God that giveth the increase. Now he that planteth and he that watereth are one: and every man shall receive his own reward according to his own labour. For we are labourers together with God" (1 Cor. 3:6-9).

Close cooperation in the church today is still the secret of success in God's work as it was in Paul's day. One could even use Isaiah's words out of context: "So the carpenter encouraged the goldsmith, and he that smootheth with the hammer him that smote the anvil, saying, It is ready for the sodering: and he fastened it with nails, that it should not be moved" (Isa. 41:7). "They helped every one his neighbour; and every one said to his brother, Be of good courage" (verse 6).

God has given His people varied talents. Some, like Apollos, are eloquent public speakers, others like Priscilla and Aquila are strong personal workers. God has placed some in the church who are gifted musicians. Others excel in the work of the Sabbath school, or the young people's work. Some have received the gift of "helps." Some plant, others water, and still others reap the precious grain at the time of the harvest.

Whatever our role, our reward is certain, "for we are labourers together with God."

PENTECOST OR FAILURE

And behold, I send the promise of my Father upon you; but stay in the city, until you are clothed with power from on high. **Luke 24:49, R.S.V.**

The awesome scenes of Calvary were in the past. Days of heartbreak and disappointment now gave way to moments of hope and joy. The Master once again stood in the midst of His disciples. But the hour of His departure was at hand. Once more they clung to His every word and crowded near, loath to have Him leave them alone again.

Now He was leaving His farewell message, "Behold, I send the promise of my Father upon you: but tarry ye in the city of Jerusalem, until ye be endued with power from on high" (Luke 24:49).

"Tarry ye in . . . Jerusalem." Why did Jesus not tell them to go to Nazareth, to Bethlehem, to Capernaum, and get to work preaching His gospel, to be about the work of taking His message to "all the world for a witness unto all nations" (Matt. 24:14)?

Instead Jesus instructed His followers to go to Jerusalem and remain until a certain experience came to them. They were not to go anywhere, preach any sermons, witness for Him in any way, until they were prepared—*until the Holy Spirit came upon them.* "Before one book of the New Testament was written, before one gospel sermon had been preached after Christ's ascension, the Holy Spirit came upon the praying apostles."—*The Desire of Ages,* p. 672.

In these words Jesus wishes to impress upon His followers a great truth that is still basic in 1975. They could not succeed in the worldwide challenge He had entrusted to them in their own strength. To proclaim His message then or now requires a power above and beyond man. The power that alone will enable us to preach the gospel to all the world in this generation is the power the disciples received at Pentecost—a massive outpouring of the Holy Spirit.

The disciples were to go to Jerusalem and wait—*it was either Pentecost or failure.* With the people who are proclaiming God's message in the final fleeting moments of this world's history likewise, *it is either Pentecost or failure!*

WHY DID THIS HAPPEN TO ME?

His answer was, "My grace is all you need; for my power is strongest when you are weak." 2 Cor. 12:9, T.E.V.

"I don't know why this had to happen to me!" There was a tinge of bitterness in my young friend's voice as he described the most recent misfortune that had befallen him. "It seems like all the trouble, all the sickness, all the bad luck, come my way!"

He paused, looked me defiantly in the eye and demanded: "For years I have been a Christian. I know I'm not perfect, but I have tried to live a decent life and set a good example to those around me. *Why* then do all these misfortunes have to happen to *me?*"

Of course Ronnie was not the first Christian to ask this question. Possibly you and I both have felt in the same mood ourselves sometimes. We have felt that good Christians should not be plagued with reverses, insults, accidents, sickness, and death. It is so easy then to ask: "Why did God permit this to happen to me?"

God does not promise that His child shall escape all tribulation in this present life. If He made such promises many people would become Christians just to assure for themselves safety on the highways, to escape arthritis, or to avoid lung cancer.

God did not spare His only begotten Son insults, suffering, and death. But He sustained and strengthened Jesus during His testing time. *He promises to do the same for us today*—His grace is all we need. He does not withhold the cup of trial, but He supplies grace when we are called upon to drink it. He assures us of His love and presence when we pass through the fires of affliction.

The next time you feel sorry for yourself remember, "You should overcome the idea that you are a martyr, and lay claim to the promise of Christ, who says, 'My grace is sufficient for thee.' "—*Messages to Young People*, p. 92.

"God lives and reigns; and He will give us all the help we need. It is our privilege at all times to draw strength and encouragement from His blessed promise, 'My grace is sufficient for you.' "—*Evangelism*, p. 98.

COSTING US SOMETHING

And the king said unto Araunah, Nay; but I will surely buy it of thee at a price: neither will I offer burnt offerings unto the Lord my God of that which doth cost me nothing. 2 Sam. 24:24.

In numbering Israel David disobeyed God. Because he repented the Lord permitted him to choose the punishment that would befall Israel—seven years of famine, three months at the hands of Israel's enemies, or three days' pestilence from God.

"Let us fall now into the hand of the Lord;" David responded, "for his mercies are great: and let me not fall into the hand of man" (2 Sam. 24:14).

The retribution suffered by Israel was awesome. When seventy thousand of his countrymen fell victim to God's pestilence David cried out for mercy and the cessation of slaughter.

The Lord instructed David to erect an altar and offer a sacrifice on the threshingfloor of Araunah, the Jebusite. When the king made known his desire to purchase the plot from Araunah, he replied, "Oh, king, take the land. It is yours for nothing. I will gladly give you not only land but the oxen and the wood for the sacrifice. It is yours freely."

Then comes our text for the day. "And the king said unto Araunah, Nay; but I will surely buy it of thee at a price: neither will I offer burnt offerings unto the Lord my God of that which doth cost me nothing."

King David's words should ring in our ears today—*a faith worth having is one that costs us something.* Being a Christian, a Seventh-day Adventist Christian, has cost some followers of the Master their friends, families, jobs—for some, even their lives.

Sometimes we are a bit perturbed when we are slightly inconvenienced for Him. May God have pity on us if we are not willing that our faith should cost us something, if we have never missed a meal, never gone without a night's sleep, never lost a friend, for our Lord!

"I cry to God, Raise up and send forth messengers . . . who are determined not to bring to God a maimed sacrifice, which costs them neither effort nor prayer."—*Gospel Workers,* p. 114.

What have *you* given up for *your* Master?

GUNMEN IN CHURCH

They display the effect of the law inscribed on their hearts. Their conscience is called as witness, and their own thoughts argue the case on either side, against them or even for them. Rom. 2:15, N.E.B.

"Everybody stand up and be quiet!" The masked man with a gun in his hand meant business. "Now, in single file come past me here in the back of the church and put your wallets and your money at my feet."

Another masked and armed accomplice took a strategic position in the church and motioned his pistol menacingly.

In a matter of minutes the members of the small congregation had deposited some four hundred dollars in the stipulated spot and the two gunmen disappeared with their loot.

Nearly a year later some of the sisters in the Adelphi church organized a weekly prayer band. They prayed for relatives and friends, for the progress of the work, and the outpouring of the Holy Spirit.

"Why don't we pray for those men who held up our church some months ago?" one of the members suggested before their weekly prayer session. So they began praying for the men who had taken their money.

About three weeks later a plain envelope addressed to the pastor was delivered. Inside was some money and a letter. "We are the ones who robbed your church some months ago," the letter read. "We are very sorry we did this. Please forgive us. We are returning all of the money to you. If you can, kindly pray for us." There was, of course, no name or address on the note.

I do not know whether the conscience of these gunmen ever brought a full surrender to Christ. If He has not already done so, I hope the workings of the Holy Spirit will lead them to this experience of conversion.

"Paul points to the exercise of conscience among the Gentiles as further evidence that they still possessed some awareness of the will of God, despite their ignorance of the written law."—*The SDA Bible Commentary,* on Rom. 2:15.

Whether we be halting saint or overt sinner, God bids us open our ears to the voice of conscience. It may be His voice speaking to us!

THOUGH THE HEAVENS FALL

And they said one to another, We are verily guilty concerning our brother, in that we saw the anguish of his soul, when he besought us, and we would not hear; therefore is this distress come upon us. **Gen. 42:21.**

With the guilt of 4 million murders resting upon him Auschwitz Concentration Camp commandant Rudolf Hoess was asked at his trial before the International Military Tribunal in Nuremburg, "How could you have gone through with this action?"

Hoess's reply, as recorded in the record of his trial, was, "Whenever assailed by doubts, I had one deciding argument to support me, namely, the strict orders and their motives, as transmitted to me by Reichsführer SS, Himmler."

The slight stabs of conscience this brutal murderer experienced were quickly smothered. The blame for his bestial crimes was imputed to others. Conscience silenced, Hoess continued to deal out suffering and death to thousands who had the misfortune of coming under his "care." Later he himself perished in the same camp where he had slain his thousands. I once stood in front of the gallows where he paid for his disregard of conscience.

A guilty conscience is difficult to live with. "It is dangerous for you to trifle with the sacred demands of conscience, dangerous for you to set an example that leads others in a wrong direction."—*Testimonies,* vol. 8, p. 195.

"Conscience is the voice of God, heard amid the conflict of human passions; when it is resisted, the Spirit of God is grieved."—*Ibid.,* vol. 5, p. 120.

We cannot lightly explain our misbehavior or pass on the blame to others. Each of us bears responsibility for the choices we make, the paths we pursue. God calls us to full obedience to the dictates of Christ-controlled conscience.

"The greatest want of the world is the want of men—men who will not be bought or sold, men who in their inmost souls are true and honest, men who do not fear to call sin by its right name, men whose conscience is as true to duty as the needle to the pole, men who will stand for the right though the heavens fall."—*Education,* p. 57.

AN ISLAND IS BORN!

In the beginning God created the heavens and the earth. Gen. 1:1, R.S.V.

The *Isleifur II* was plowing slowly through the frigid waters off the southern coast of Iceland. Through the morning twilight, the cook glimpsed a strange object in the distance.

As the day dawned, the cook, looking through his binoculars, beheld smoke and eruption columns rising out of the sea. A new volcano was being born before his eyes! November 14, 1963, was Surtsey's birthday and ever since that date this square mile of lava and ash has been under careful and continuous scientific observation.

The Scriptures declare, "In the beginning God created the heavens and the earth." "In the beginning" was a long, long time ago by anyone's reckoning. For centuries Bible scholars and scientists estimated the age of the earth at about six thousand years. Now atheistic evolutionists declare the earth to be hundreds of millions of years old. These scientists point to the strata of the rocks, the geological column, the fossils that are found in these layers of earth. They interpret the past on the basis of the present. The brief history of Surtsey reveals some chinks in this armor.

"If the history of Surtsey were not known," writes Dr. Harold Coffin of the Geoscience Institute in Berrien Springs, Michigan, "it would be difficult to arrive at a correct knowledge of its age from the study of the rocks alone. The rate of erosion of the cliffs and the rounding of the blocks by the force of the waves was unexpectedly rapid. Even the rate of cooling seemed faster than expected. . . . Surtsey should cause scientists to be cautious about jumping to conclusions concerning the rates of geologic processes."—*The Youth's Instructor,* Jan. 7, 1969, p. 30.

Dr. Coffin further explains that careful study of these cataclysmic forces of nature on a small scale reveal "that developments which geologists have been taught take thousands of years are accomplished here in a few days or weeks. . . . Surtsey teaches us that the concept of uniformity is unrealistic and that catastrophism, which the Bible clearly supports, is a much better basis for interpreting the earth."

WE HEAR WHAT WE WANT TO HEAR

Which say to the seers, See not; and to the prophets, Prophesy not unto us right things, speak unto us smooth things, prophesy deceits. Isa. 30:10.

Communication—getting through to people—has its complications. If you don't believe that people have communication filters, read "Letters to the Editor" in the *Review and Herald* or *Time* magazine. Many times individuals are reacting differently to what they read, or thought they read, in the same article. One person reads an article and calls it great. Another person reading the same article is wholly incensed.

We differ in our background, our environment, in our nationality, culture, education. We usually hear what we want to hear. Our "filter" shuts off what we don't want to hear. It is little wonder we sometimes have communication problems and misunderstandings with people around us.

You know, sometimes God has communication problems with church members, too. When He speaks to them through His Word or through Ellen White, His appointed messenger, He has a difficult time getting through. Too frequently we hear what we want to hear instead of what *He* wants us to hear. Both old and young have problems in this area.

The apostle Paul admonishes "that no man put a stumbling-block or an occasion to fall in his brother's way" (Rom. 14:13). Some youth read this as a rebuke to "over thirties" because they mention the externals so frequently. Many among the youth culture are weary of hearing quotations from the Word and from Ellen White on dress, proper grooming, and kindred topics. Some of the same youth overlook the fact that these very things can be stumblingblocks to the older saints as well.

Many youth are disturbed, rightly perhaps, by what they feel is hypocrisy in their elders. Parents who ban the movies in the theater watch the late show on TV. They condemn marijuana while swallowing an endless amount of drugs in pills. The parent reads the Spirit of Prophecy statements one way; the child another. Too many in both groups cry out in their hearts, "Speak unto us smooth things."

Today God needs urgently to get through to all of us regardless of our age, and we need to learn that He says what He means and means what He says.

WHEN JESUS SAYS NO

So he got back into the boat. The man who had been possessed by the demons begged Jesus to let him go along. But Jesus said no. Mark 5:18, 19, T.L.B.

It was only natural that the man from Gadara whom the Saviour had delivered from the demons wished to stay with Him. With Christ were help, hope, security against possible attacks of the future. To remain with Jesus offered solutions to all of the man's problems. Naturally he desired to remain close to his Deliverer.

"But Jesus said no." The Master had other plans for the freed man. He was to be the first missionary to the people of Gadara. Though this was not the man's plan for himself, it was God's plan for him—so "Jesus said no."

Years ago when the Pierson family was looking forward to service in the cause of God, we had some definite ideas of our own about just where we wanted to work—and where we didn't want to work. If the Lord had plans for us to work in the homeland, for some strange reason unfathomable to us now we were not keen on working in Georgia. For some equally unfathomable reason we did not want to go to India. Africa, South America—these were our choices.

You guessed it. "Jesus said no." He sent us first to Georgia and then to India—and how we loved them both! Where could anyone find more lovable people or a more challenging task than in Georgia or India? How thankful we are now that the Lord said No to our plans and gave us the privilege of serving first in these two places. Later He took us to both Africa and South America.

When Jesus says No we should trust Him.

"Our plans are not always God's plans. He may see that it is best for us and for His cause to refuse our very best intentions, as He did in the case of David. But of one thing we may be assured, He will bless and use in the advancement of His cause those who sincerely devote themselves and all they have to His glory. If He sees it best not to grant their desires He will counterbalance the refusal by giving them tokens of His love and entrusting to them another service."—*The Ministry of Healing,* p. 473.

HOLINESS IN BUSY-NESS

And thou shalt make a plate of pure gold, and grave upon it, like the engravings of a signet, Holiness to the Lord. **Ex. 28:36.**

The Lord instructed that a plate of gold should be placed upon the miter that the priest wore upon his head. On this golden plate were to appear the words "Holiness to the Lord."

Seventh-day Adventists, members and denominationally employed workers alike, are a busy people. There is something dynamic about the Advent message that kindles a fire in the bones of those who accept it. There is work inside and outside ever pressing to be done. The church inreach requires committed church officers—men and women willing to sacrifice their own time in order to do God's work. The church outreach challenges selfless men and women to go to the homes of friends and neighbors, both near and far, with the precious truths they themselves have found bring peace and joy.

Yes, Seventh-day Adventists are a busy people. Busy working for the Lord.

Perhaps Moses has a word of caution for busy people in his words about the golden plate on the priest's miter—ever think about it that way?

The priest, of course, was busy about the work of the sanctuary. It was a demanding routine—ever pressing for attention. There were not many spare moments from his round of service for God. *In the midst of his busy-ness God wanted His anointed ones never to forget that there must also be holiness!* In fact, busy-ness without holiness produces a sterile activity that God cannot bless and prosper.

> Our numbers grow, our cares increase,
> From plans and push we never cease.
> Like Martha we are on the go—
> We seem to rush and worry so.
>
> Lord, slow us down; Lord, stand us still,
> Make clear to us Thy holy will,
> And help us see we've lost the day
> When we're too rushed to watch and pray.

"YOU ARE HIS PERSONAL CONCERN"

Humble yourselves under God's strong hand, and in his own good time he will lift you up. You can throw the whole weight of your anxieties upon him, for you are his personal concern. **1 Peter 5:7, Phillips.**

What a precious promise for every child of God. *"You are his personal concern."* If the head of some great nation should undertake a personal interest in you and assure you the full weight of his power and financial assistance, you would be grateful indeed. Our promise today is an even more blessed assurance. Earthly rulers rise and fall; their ability to help may wane and disappear quickly or suddenly. The One who declares you and me to be His personal concern is the Omnipotent God, the Ruler of the universe. His ability to help is limitless. His love for us surpasses all conception.

"Throw the whole weight of your anxieties upon him," we are invited. How full of cares and anxieties this world of ours is. Perhaps your life is weighted down with some heavy anxiety, some unspoken fear. This promise then is *for you!*

Anxiety is defined by Webster as "painful uneasiness of mind respecting an impending or anticipated ill." "Anxiety" is a synonym for "care," which in turn is defined as "mental suffering; grief. A burdensome sense of responsibility; anxiety."

Are *you* experiencing mental suffering? Has grief but recently rested a heavy burden upon your life? Is the responsibility of your home, your work, your educational program, more than you are able to bear alone? Then the promise in God's text is for *you* today. *"Throw the whole weight of your anxieties upon him, for you are his personal concern."*

The Lord's messenger adds these precious words of encouragement: "When we really believe that God loves us, and means to do us good, we shall cease to worry about the future. We shall trust God as a child trusts a loving parent. Then our troubles and torments will disappear; for our will is swallowed up in the will of God."—*Thoughts From the Mount of Blessing,* p. 101.

Then we are reminded to live one day at a time. Tomorrow's cares and perplexity will care for themselves when we are safely in God's overshadowing care.

YOU HAVE A PART TO PLAY!

Take ye away the stone. John 11:39.

There was a stir on the mission compound. A Chinese servant of the missionary family was overcome by fumes from a charcoal heater. Several anxious members of the family gained entrance to his tiny room by knocking the door down. Inside they found the servant on the bed unconscious.

"Let us pray for him," one devout searcher exclaimed.

"Let us open the windows first," someone else, just as devout, suggested.

The windows were opened. Prayer was offered. The stricken man revived. The question is, Was opening the windows a manifestation of a lack of faith? Could God not have healed the man with the windows closed as easily as with air flowing in through open windows?

Of course He could! But God also expects us to do our part in answering prayer! Jesus Himself demonstrated this concept of answered prayer.

Lazarus was sick. His sisters Mary and Martha sent for Jesus to come quickly and heal their brother. But Lazarus died and was buried before the Saviour arrived.

A short time later Christ stood before the closed tomb where Lazarus lay.

"It was a cave, and a stone lay upon it. Jesus said, Take ye away the stone" (John 11:38, 39).

The drama unfolds rapidly. "Then they took away the stone. . . . Jesus lifted up his eyes, [and prayed]. . . . And when he thus had spoken, he cried with a loud voice, Lazarus, come forth. And he that was dead came forth" (verses 41-44). Christ's prayer was answered.

Was rolling away the stone a manifestation of faithlessness? Could not Jesus have raised Lazarus with the stone in front of the door of the tomb? Of course He could! But Jesus wished to teach His people of all ages that they are to cooperate—to do their part in answering their prayer petitions. Sometimes it is opening the windows. Sometimes it is rolling away a stone, but we must do what we can. Then God takes over!

GOD *WILL* ANSWER!

He shall call upon me, and I will answer him: I will be with him in trouble; I will deliver him, and honour him. Ps. 91:15.

God's word and His honor are at stake. He declares, "He shall call upon me, and I will answer him." Every sincere prayer of longing saint or repentant sinner will be answered!

God's word declares it!

Twice the gospel prophet assures us, "Then shalt thou call, and the Lord shall answer; thou shalt cry, and he shall say, Here I am" (Isa. 58:9). Then again this precious promise, "And it shall come to pass, that before they call, I will answer; and while they are yet speaking, I will hear" (chap. 65:24). Although this last promise is for those who inhabit the new earth, many of God's faithful ones can testify to its fulfillment in this life.

The prophet Zechariah repeats the Lord's promise, "I will bring the third part through the fire, and will refine them as silver is refined, and will try them as gold is tried: they shall call on my name, and I will hear them: I will say, It is my people: and they shall say, The Lord is my God" (Zech. 13:9).

"They shall call . . . I will hear." The promise is sure. There may be a refining process—trials and suffering, as Zechariah indicates to God's people in his day, but when we can truly say, "The Lord is my God," and He can say of us, "It is my people," then *they shall call . . . I will hear.*"

Jesus Himself adds His weight of testimony: "Ask, and it shall be given you; seek, and ye shall find; knock, and it shall be opened unto you" (Luke 11:9).

This is the Saviour's way of saying, "You call, I will hear!"

The assurance is timeless. It was for the psalmist's day many centuries ago. It was for Isaiah's day nearly seven centuries before Christ. It was for Jesus' day two thousand years ago. It is for your day and mine. "He shall call upon me, and I will answer him." And, blessed thought, the prophet Isaiah projects the truth of a prayer-hearing and prayer-answering God on into the earth made new. We can never exhaust His willingness or His ability to provide for every need of His people.

"THE PLACE OWES ME A COAT—
IT IS ALL RIGHT!"

He that saith, I know him, and keepeth not his commandments, is a liar, and the truth is not in him. 1 John 2:4.

A few years ago a woman wrote to a popular columnist who advises correspondents on family problems. Fred had taken the young woman to a first-class restaurant for dinner. On entering the restaurant he hung his coat on a hook near the door. When they were ready to leave, the coat was gone. Fred made fervent but futile representations to the manager. The restaurant was not responsible.

A week or so later the couple returned to the same eating place, had dinner, and on the way out Fred helped himself to a beautiful coat that just fit him. The young woman remonstrated vigorously.

"I'm not stealing," Fred insisted, "the place owes me a coat, and under the circumstances it is all right for me to take this one."

The shocked young woman wrote to the columnist asking, "Is this true? Was Fred not stealing? Are there some times when a person is justified in taking what does not belong to him?"

The reply was refreshing, coming as it did in this permissive age: "When a person takes something that does not belong to him, it's stealing no matter what the rationalization. Fred is as big a thief as the person who stole his coat, and you can tell him I said so."

The so-called new morality condones sin and leaves the sinner uncondemned. Sin is not sin anymore according to the reckoning of some theologians of our age.

The contentions of apostles of the new morality notwithstanding, *sin is still sin!* When we break one of the Ten Commandments we sin. We may rationalize. We may contend the situation justifies our action. We may explain our misdeeds to our own satisfaction, but God says plainly, "sin is the transgression of the law."

GOD'S WAYS AND OUR WAYS

For my thoughts are not your thoughts, neither are your ways my ways, saith the Lord. Isa. 55:8.

In 1955 the Southern Union School of Bible Prophecy sent Elder O. B. Gerhart, their Kentucky-Tennessee representative, the address of a woman in Lexington reportedly much interested in the message. With O. R. Henderson, pastor of our Lexington, Kentucky, church, Brother Gerhart found 315 Spring Street in the city and knocked at the door.

The Bible school report stated that the interested woman was already keeping the Sabbath, so early in the conversation Elder Gerhart mentioned this fact. He was surprised at her reply.

"No," she said, "I am not keeping the Sabbath, and I have never taken the Bible course you have mentioned, but I have often thought I should keep the seventh-day Sabbath."

"Years ago as a child," the lady of the house explained, "I read in the Bible that the seventh day of the week is the Sabbath. I found nothing that even remotely suggested the first day of the week was a day of rest. I spoke with my family and friends about the Sabbath, but they either ignored or ridiculed me."

The woman paused, then continued: "The reaction of those around me led me to feel that probably I was wrong. But try as I did, I could not dismiss the impression that we were observing the wrong day as the Sabbath."

"You will be interested to know that there is an entire Christian denomination with more than a million members who also keep the seventh-day Sabbath," the brethren explained.

A recheck of the Bible interest cards revealed that by mistake some Lexington, Tennessee, cards had been sent with the Lexington, Kentucky, interests, and Elder Gerhart should have been visiting a woman at 315 Spring Street, Lexington, Tennessee, instead of Kentucky!

Both Elder Gerhart and Sister Belden were convinced that the mix-up was not coincidental, but providential, for she took the studies, was baptized, and became a member of the Lexington, Kentucky, Adventist church.

WAKE UP!

Awake to righteousness, and sin not. 1 Cor. 15:34.

"There must cease to be practice of all known sin, and no longer neglect of known duty."—A. G. DANIELLS, *Christ Our Righteousness*, p. 109. This is God's goal for His people. Righteousness (right doing) and victory over sin are synonymous. Only when victory is ours is the robe of Christ's righteousness ours!

"But while God can be just, and yet justify the sinner through the merits of Christ, no man can cover his soul with the garments of Christ's righteousness while practicing known sins or neglecting known duties," Ellen White explains. "God requires the entire surrender of the heart, before justification can take place; and in order for man to retain justification, there must be continual obedience, through active, living faith that works by love and purifies the soul."—*Ibid.*, pp. 109, 110.

"Wake up!" Paul cries. Evidently someone is asleep. The faltering saint's conscience has been deadened by evil influence. Such a person is in peril. He must wake up, for "the voice of duty is the voice of God" *(Sons and Daughters of God,* p. 175). "Christ is ever sending messages to those who listen for His voice."—*Testimonies,* vol. 4, p. 542.

The bandit must stop holding up banks. The murderer must stop killing. The adulterer must cease his impurity. Surely such persons can have no inheritance with the saints. All would agree.

Ever make the application more personal? We may not hold up banks but do we ever rob God of tithes or offerings? Are we dishonest in our business relationships? We might recoil in horror if someone suggested we take the life of a fellow human being, but do we shrink from character assassination? Do we harbor hatred in our hearts? We may never overtly break the seventh commandment, but is your heart the resting place for evil thinking? In God's sight, which is more reprehensible?

Dishonesty, bitterness, hatred, impurity, evil-speaking, jealousy, covetousness, Sabbathbreaking, profanity, loosespeaking, destructive criticism, temper—all must go if we are to be covered with the robe of Christ's righteousness!

THE VALLEY OF DRY BONES

And ye shall know that I am the Lord, when I have opened your graves, O my people, and brought you up out of your graves. And shall put my spirit in you, and ye shall live, and I shall place you in your own land: then shall ye know that I the Lord have spoken it, and performed it, saith the Lord. Eze. 37:13, 14.

"The valley of dry bones" doesn't sound like a very challenging title for a devotional reading—a rather dry subject, one might say. But the thirty-seventh chapter of Ezekiel contains a thrilling message. Let us notice some of the high points.

In verse one the Lord in vision takes the prophet and sets him down "in the midst of the valley which was full of bones." As Ezekiel walked among the bones the Lord spoke to him. "Ezekiel," He said, "do you think these bones can ever live again?"

The prospect was not hopeful. "I don't know," the prophet replied, "You would be the only One who could answer such a question."

"You speak to the bones," the Lord instructed His servant. "Tell them God will cause breath to enter them once more and they shall indeed live."

Ezekiel, acting upon faith, followed the instruction of the Lord. He spoke. In vision he saw a miracle take place before His eyes. The bones responded. They "came together." Flesh and sinews clothed them once again and skin covered them. The prophet spoke again—"breath came into them, and they lived, and stood up upon their feet" (Eze. 37:10). What is more, they became "an exceeding great army."

This prophecy, of course, can apply to the resurrection of the dead—hope for Israel—an assurance of God's love and His power to deliver His people. Perhaps it has a 1975 application as well. It can be and should be a challenge to revival and reformation at this late hour. It may also be a *promise!* "[I] . . . shall put my spirit in you, and ye shall live, and I shall place you in your own land: then shall ye know that I the Lord have spoken it, and performed it, saith the Lord" (verse 14).

Revival will come! The Lord has promised it! We dare not say, "Our hope is lost: we are cut off" (verse 11). He has power to breathe life into His church and make us live.

WHAT ABOUT THE POOR AMONG US?

Jesus said unto him, If thou wilt be perfect, go and sell that thou hast, and give to the poor, and thou shalt have treasure in heaven: and come and follow me. Matt. 19:21.

In a large country I visited recently I found unbelievable poverty. Unemployment was at its peak during my visit. Multitudes in the villages were without work and without food. Once daily for five days a week the leader of the Adventist church supervised the distribution of food provided through Adventist channels to several hundred people. This meager ration was all the nourishment most of these hapless human beings received during the day. I was glad to see members of God's remnant church about the Master's business in helping to meet the needs of the poor. This was as it should be.

Through the centuries God has had much to say about the attention His people should pay to the unfortunate in their midst:

"If there be among you a poor man of one of thy brethren within any of thy gates in thy land which the Lord thy God giveth thee, thou shalt not harden thine heart, nor shut thine hand from thy poor brother" (Deut. 15:7).

During His earthly ministry, the Saviour Himself instructed one seeking the way of eternal life: "Sell that thou hast, and give to the poor" (Matt. 19:21).

The Lord's present day messenger reminds us: "We cannot come in touch with divinity without coming in touch with humanity; for in Him who sits upon the throne of the universe, divinity and humanity are combined. Connected with Christ, we are connected with our fellow men by the golden links of the chain of love. Then the pity and compassion of Christ will be manifest in our life. We shall not wait to have the needy and unfortunate brought to us. We shall not need to be entreated to feel for the woes of others. It will be as natural for us to minister to the needy and suffering as it was for Christ to go about doing good."—*Christ's Object Lessons,* pp. 384, 385.

"Blessed is he that considereth the poor: the Lord will deliver him in time of trouble" (Ps. 41:1).

Are we doing all we should for the less fortunate among us?

POVERTY IS NOT YOUR DESTINY

They are the seed of the blessed of the Lord. Isa. 65:23.

The following paragraphs describe poverty in affluent United States: "Welfare for 6.2 million persons in 1950 cost 2.5 billion dollars. Now, 14.4 million are on relief, and the expenditures in February, 1971, were running at an annual rate of about 18 billion dollars.

"During that time, governments at all levels have also been spending other billions to help to end poverty through education, counseling, job training, and community improvements.

"Today, beckoning still is the elusive dream: that poverty in America can be totally eliminated, once and for all." (From a copyrighted article in *U.S. News and World Report,* July 12, 1971, p. 52.)

Poverty is not a problem confined to the United States. In some Oriental countries, streets and public buildings are crowded with unfortunate people who have no homes. Some were born on the streets, they live on the streets, and many will die on the streets. They have never enjoyed a sustained diet of healthful food, never known the luxury of a clean bed or a place they can call home.

Through the years governments in many lands have sought to eradicate poverty. In some countries considerable success has attended these efforts. The standard of living has been raised. Men and women have been provided with a modicum of the good things of life.

In the United States we have had New Deals, Fair Deals, promises of the Great Society and the fulfillment of the great American Dream—all have assured the voters that Utopia for all was just around the corner. No doubt some of these programs have provided many benefits for the people. But poverty is still with us.

Hope and help for the faithful poor are just ahead! Political pundits will not provide it. Human ingenuity will not devise the total solution to poverty. But if you are faithful, poverty is not your destiny. God has prepared something better for you! In God's plan there will be no crop failures, no mortgage foreclosures, no evictions from home. God's social security provides food, clothing, and shelter for all.

THE APOSTLE OF ENCOURAGEMENT

May the Lord bless Onesiphorus and all his family, because he visited me and encouraged me often. His visits revived me like a breath of fresh air. 2 Tim. 1:16, T.L.B.

The story of Onesiphorus is told in the King James Version by Paul in sixty-seven words. What a brief biography, yet what a blessed one. How much we learn of the old apostle's friend in four of those words—"he oft refreshed me." Dr. Taylor brings Onesiphorus to life for our day with this paraphrase of Paul's words: "He visited me and encouraged me often. His visits revived me like a breath of fresh air."

Onesiphorus was an apostle of encouragement. The world was a brighter, better place in which to live because he was there. His contacts were like breaths of fresh air.

His was a legacy of encouragement to future generations. What a wonderful thing to be remembered by posterity as a person who brought courage to all those with whom he came in contact who needed help—one who revived persons like a breath of fresh air.

Some men and women are like that. Wherever they go new life and new hope burst into hearts like flowers after a spring shower. Life is worth living, the skies are bluer, the sun is brighter, because they came your way. They, too, are apostles of encouragement—of the twentieth century.

The old apostle felt that an unusual reward was due such a purveyor of hope and courage as Onesiphorus. "May the Lord give him a special blessing at the day of Christ's return," he wrote (2 Tim. 1:18, T.L.B.). Men and women like this deserve something extra—both in this life and in the life to come.

It is a great thing to be an Onesiphorus—to be an apostle of encouragement, to cheer the downcast, to inspire the dispirited, to revive hope, to bring the sunshine back into skies too long darkened with problems and discouragement.

The prophet Isaiah describes well how this experience comes about: "They helped every one his neighbour; and every one said to his brother, Be of good courage" (Isa. 41:6).

SO YOU ARE A GRANDMOTHER?

When I call to remembrance the unfeigned faith that is in thee, which dwelt first in thy grandmother Lois, and thy mother Eunice; and I am persuaded that in thee also. 2 Tim. 1:5.

So you are a grandmother—or a grandfather, perhaps—and you think your influence doesn't count for much, that you are on the shelf and that you are unimportant? Listen, grandparents, I have news for you. You may be living the most important years of your life.

Tucked away in Paul's Second Epistle to Timothy is a cheering message for grandparents: "When I call to remembrance the unfeigned faith that is in thee, which dwelt first in thy grandmother Lois, and thy mother Eunice; and I am persuaded that in thee also."

Someone has said that in order to become a success in life a man should be able to choose his grandparents. The influence and the genes they pass on to their grandchildren surely play an important role in the success of any man or woman.

Grandmother Lois and Timothy's mother Eunice were united in their efforts to rear the young man of God. "The faith of his mother and his grandmother in the sacred oracles was to him a constant reminder of the blessing in doing God's will."—*The Acts of the Apostles,* p. 203. Their efforts bore fruit. "Those who had taught Timothy in his childhood were rewarded by seeing the son of their care linked in close fellowship with the great apostle."—*The SDA Bible Commentary,* Ellen G. White Comments, on 2 Tim. 3:14, 15, p. 918.

I knew a grandmother who experienced the heartache of seeing her daughter and her daughter's husband leave the church and go into a life of faithless worldliness. The grandmother, however, was able to keep her grandson in church school and to have him with her as much as possible. Today that grandson is a successful missionary in a distant land because of the influence of his grandmother. What a star there will be in her crown someday.

God bless the faith-filled grandmother Loises in the world today!

WHY? WHY? WHY?

But not as the offence, so also is the free gift. For if through the offence of one many be dead, much more the grace of God, and the gift by grace, which is by one man, Jesus Christ, hath abounded unto many. Rom. 5:15.

With his sister clinging to his arm, Duncan stood by the open grave of his brother-in-law. Two little boys and a tiny girl stared sad-eyed into the gaping hole where daddy lay.

"Why, why, *why*, O God, did You have to let *him* be taken? Here is a wife with three little children to be reared without a father!" the words burned mercilessly in Duncan's mind.

Duncan is not the first child of God who, in a moment of unspent grief, sobbed out those pathetic words: "Why, *why, why*, O God, does it have to be? How can a God of love let a small act of disobedience six thousand years ago in a perfect garden open the floodgates of woe, and in its relentless rush bring sorrow and death to me centuries later?"

Our text for today helps answer this trauma-filled question.

If death and the grave seem unjust to us, what greater injustice Jesus suffered in taking man's guilt upon Himself and yielding His life upon the cross to pay a debt He did not owe. "For he hath made him to be sin for us who knew no sin" (2 Cor. 5:21). The perfect, sinless Christ not only bore our sins, He was made sin for us!

Through this single matchless act of grace Christ opened the doors of salvation to all who would by faith accept His substitutionary death upon the cross. All men deserved to die. God, through His "gift by grace" provided a way of escape for all who would accept it! Though Adam's one sin brought death and grief, "one man"—Christ by His death—brings hope and eternal life.

"On the mount of crucifixion a fountain opened deep and
   wide,
      Through the floodgates of God's mercy flowed a vast
      and gracious tide.
Grace and love, like mighty rivers, poured incessant
   from above,
      Heaven's peace and perfect justice kissed a guilty world
      in love."

—*The Pulpit Commentary*, Vol. VI, p. 279.

IS IT ALL RIGHT "SOMETIMES"?

How then can I do this great wickedness, and sin against God? Gen. 39:9.

Joseph was no marble statue. He was young. He was "handsome and good looking" (Gen. 39:7, N.E.B.). As a slave, how could he refuse the favors of his master's wife? No human being would ever know if he responded to her sensuous invitation. If he refused—then what? Perhaps Potiphar didn't "understand" his wife—it might even be "the loving thing" for Joseph to do in this situation. The young Hebrew had much to gain and apparently nothing to lose—nothing, that is, except his self-respect, God, and heaven!

Joseph in this hour of burning temptation realized that God was aware of every situation that leads to sin. Joseph was no situation ethicist. He was convinced that God has some constants—that breaking the seventh commandment is sin under any circumstance and in any situation.

Joseph could say "No" with a bang! No parleying with the evil one. No seeking reason to excuse himself. No blaming the situation. Sin was sin—then—any time—in his master's home under the cloak of secrecy—any place. That was that!

Many modern theologians are not as definite and as positive in their attitude toward violations of the Ten Commandments as was Joseph. We are told today the seventh commandment should now read: "Thou shalt not commit adultery—ordinarily." Given the right situation it is "the loving thing" to gratify the baser passions. Sometimes "unmarried love is better than married unlove." There are circumstances and conditions under which it is perfectly permissible to commit adultery, even some men of the cloth tell us.

A prominent exponent of situation ethics is ready to argue that Christian obligation sometimes calls for lies, adultery, fornication, theft, promise-breaking, and killing, depending on the situation.

Joseph, the son of Jacob, did not believe this philosophy. He knew that sin involved not only Potiphar's wife and himself but also God—and sin against God! He believed God meant what He said when He declared, "Thou shalt not commit adultery" (Ex. 20:14).

IN PROSPERITY AND IN ADVERSITY

Hear me, Asa, and all Judah and Benjamin: The Lord is with you, while you are with him. If you seek him, he will be found by you, but if you forsake him, he will forsake you. 2 Chron. 15:2, R.S.V.

Israel was in apostasy. Since Jeroboam's death there had been a steady spiritual decline. Nadab, Baasha, Elah, Zimri, and Omri ruled with a rod of evil over a period of some forty years.

In the south, in Judah, the situation was different. Here good King Asa reigned. "And Asa did what was good and right in the eyes of the Lord his God" (2 Chron. 14:2, R.S.V.). Asa destroyed the high places and the altars of the strange gods. He demolished the idols. He cut down the groves. The images to the sun were broken down.

"And the kingdom had rest under him," the Inspired Word declares (verse 5, R.S.V.).

Then disaster threatened Judah. Zerah, the Ethiopian, with a great army invaded Asa's kingdom. It was an hour of crisis. In this time of peril good King Asa did not rely upon his visible resources alone. He had done all he could to prepare for such an eventuality. He had fortified his cities. He had trained a strong army. But in this hour of decision Asa turned to the Lord.

The king's first concern was the spiritual condition of his people. Was the living God first in their lives? Had every known sin been confessed and forgiven? Humanly speaking the odds heavily favored the invading force. Asa, however, had learned how to serve and trust his God during times of peace. Now when destruction threatened, he trusted in the One whom he served. In prosperity and in adversity King Asa was a leader who could trust God to care for him.

It was then that Asa poured out his heart to God. "O Lord," the man of God pleaded, "there is none like thee to help, between the mighty and the weak. Help us, O Lord our God, for we rely on thee, and in thy name we have come against this multitude. O Lord, thou art our God; let not man prevail against thee" (verse 11, R.S.V.). The Lord heard His faithful servant. "The Lord defeated the Ethiopians before Asa and before Judah, and the Ethiopians fled" (verse 12, R.S.V.).

If we stay with the Lord in prosperity, He will stay with us in the hour of adversity.

"IF YOU ONLY KNEW WHAT I KNOW!"

For all the ancient scriptures were written for our own instruction, in order that through the encouragement they give us we may maintain our hope with fortitude. Rom. 15:4, N.E.B.

Teen-age Al was a real Western novel addict. His favorite character was Dynamic Dan, a law-enforcement agent who always came out on top in every brush with breakers of the law.

One night the light in Al's room was on much later than usual, and his father went to investigate. As he neared Al's door he heard his son explode with gusto, "If you only knew what I know! If you only knew what I know!"

"It's late, Al. How about those exams tomorrow? What are you doing?"

"I'm reading, Dad," Al replied. "I got so interested I couldn't put my book down."

"That's one of the reasons novels are bad for you, Al. But I heard you say something, 'If you only knew what I know,'" his father continued. "What were you talking about?"

"Well, you see, Dad," Al explained, "in all of his other books Dynamic Dan always outwitted the criminals. No matter how well laid their plot was, he was one step ahead of them. But this book is different. I've read half of it, and Dan is having a rough time. He has been thwarted at every turn. The criminals are ahead. So I turned over to the last chapter and read it. Everything comes out all right. Dan takes care of the mobsters and they all end up in jail. Guess you heard me talking to one of the gangsters that was 'on top'—if he only knew what I know about what's ahead for him!"

"If you only knew what I know!" These words started me thinking. We live in a world filled with sin, heartache, illness, and tragedy. How much discouragement and despair there is around us. Thousands end it all by taking their own lives.

"If such individuals only knew what we know"—if they only knew God's glorious ending to man's tragic sin story! If they would but turn to God's Word and read His last chapter. The coming of Jesus, the end of the great controversy, the beautiful home of the saved in that breath-taking, sinless, painless, sorrowless, deathless world—if they only knew!

It is your business and mine to let them know!

BUILDING UP THE REDEEMER'S KINGDOM

By this shall all men know that ye are my disciples, if ye have love one to another. John 13:35.

You and I are both eager to see God's kingdom built up, the work finished, and Jesus come. The Lord's messenger sets forth one of the simplest and most effective contributions that you and I can make to this end:

" 'By this shall all men know that ye are my disciples, if ye have love one to another.' The more closely we resemble our Saviour in character, the greater will be our love toward those for whom He died. Christians who manifest a spirit of unselfish love for one another are bearing a testimony for Christ which unbelievers can neither gainsay nor resist. It is impossible to estimate the power of such an example. Nothing will so successfully defeat the devices of Satan and his emissaries, nothing will so build up the Redeemer's kingdom, as will the love of Christ manifested by the members of the church."—*Testimonies,* vol. 5, pp. 167, 168.

Strangely enough, Ellen White does not say that we need more money, more equipment, more facilities, or even more workers. She says what the church needs to build up the Lord's kingdom today is more *love*—"Nothing will so build up the Redeemer's kingdom, as will the love of Christ manifested by the members of the church."

Whom are we to love? We are to love our neighbor (see Matt. 19:19). We are to love *all* of the saints (see Col. 1:4), we are also to love those who do not love us, those who do not treat us kindly (see Matt. 5:44). This is not easy, but it is Christlike!

Jesus also makes it clear that we are to love as He loved (see John 13:34). This is a wholehearted sacrificial love that loves without discrimination.

How does this kind of love build up God's kingdom and help finish the work? "When those who profess the name of Christ shall practice the principles of the golden rule, the same power will attend the gospel as in apostolic times."—*Thoughts From the Mount of Blessing,* p. 137.

The love of Pentecost will bring the spirit of Pentecost and the power of Pentecost. This is what God says we need to build up His kingdom and to see the work finished.

RETURN AND SHOW

Return to thine own house, and shew how great things God hath done unto thee. And he went his way, and published throughout the whole city how great things Jesus had done unto him. **Luke 8:39.**

Arriving "at the country of the Gadarenes" the Master went ashore. "When he went forth to land, there met him out of the city a certain man, which had devils long time, and ware no clothes, neither abode in any house, but in the tombs. When he saw Jesus, he cried out, and fell down before him, and with a loud voice said, What have I to do with thee, Jesus, thou Son of God most high? I beseech thee, torment me not. (For he had commanded the unclean spirit to come out of the man)" (Luke 8:27-29).

What a glorious release for this tormented creature. Little wonder his heart went out in love to his great Benefactor. Small wonder, either, he should want to go with Jesus—to stay with Him always!

But Christ had other plans for the man of Gadara!

"Jesus sent him away, saying, return to thine own house, and shew how great things God hath done unto thee" (verses 38, 39).

Recently I was speaking with a group of college-age young people.

"Elder," they queried anxiously, "what can we do—what shall we say in witnessing for Christ? We love Him. We want to help others know and love Him but we don't know where to begin. What can we say?"

These are good questions. Jesus has the answers. We begin witnessing with our own experience. We are to go and "shew how great things God hath done" for *us personally.* We are to be living witnesses of the power of God at work in our lives. The stories of our own deliverance, of our own transformation, of our own daily and hourly help from above, are the greatest testimony we can bear for Christ!

In many of the pages to follow I want to share with you what Christ has done for us!

NOT WHERE BUT HOW

The churches of Asia salute you. Aquila and Priscilla salute you much in the Lord, with the church that is in their house. 1 Cor. 16:19.

In the early Christian church believers in "the way" had no sanctuaries of their own in which to worship God. No vaulted roofs reverberated to the singing of those men and women who followed their new-found Lord. Not even humble chapels gave a listening ear to their earnest petitions. Those first disciples of a risen Lord worshiped in the homes of fellow believers. In our text today, Paul, in sending greetings to the Corinthian Christians, speaks of a church that met in the home of Priscilla and Aquila.

What a wonderful experience—to go down in sacred history as members who provided sanctuary for the children of God to meet Sabbath by Sabbath. It is not where God's people worship, but the spirit in which they worship, that counts with God.

In the earlier days of the Advent Movement intrepid pioneers met frequently in the homes of those who professed like precious faith. In these homes the Holy Spirit was poured out in mighty power upon the earnest seekers of truth. The humbleness of the meeting place did not impede the blessing God had in store for His people. It is not where God's people worship, but the spirit in which they worship that matters with Him.

As a preteen-age boy, my earliest memories of worship center on two homes—my grandmother's and my own home in the little town of Brooklyn, Iowa. We were the only Seventh-day Adventists in the community. As isolated members we rarely were blessed with a visit from a conference worker. But the Sabbath school at home brought blessing to us all and laid a solid foundation of Adventism in our lives.

By mentioning the churches that met in the homes of early believers, writers of Scripture perhaps wished to impress upon the saints of all generations a truth we must never forget: *It is not where we worship, but how we worship that matters in God's sight!*

The place of worship is what God and the worshiper make it!

"MY SON, GIVE ME THINE HEART"

My son, give me thine heart, and let thine eyes observe my ways.
Prov. 23:26.

"Mother critically ill, come quickly." Through misty eyes I read the telegram several times. Mother had been in poor health for several years. Reports from Florida in recent months indicated she was failing rapidly. My worst fears were confirmed. If I wanted to see her alive I would need to drive the fifteen hundred miles from Iowa to Florida with few stops.

My mother was a Seventh-day Adventist. My grandmother was a Seventh-day Adventist. My great-grandmother was a Seventh-day Adventist. I was a fourth-generation Seventh-day Adventist. But we were isolated members, and in those days cars were not so dependable and roads were not as serviceable as they are today. Our church attendance was irregular. Occasionally pastors would visit us. My youthful heart was not too seriously inclined toward the church.

Public high school in Florida with its athletics and social functions took their spiritual toll. Admittedly, I was more interested in sports than I was in church. After graduation I returned to Iowa to work in a cooperative creamery and to pursue my first love—athletics—as time and occasion afforded. God and the church were crowded almost out of my reckoning.

Then the telegram came. It was a severe blow that shocked me to my senses. Within hours I was on my way to Florida and mother. I arrived too late. She had lapsed into a coma some hours before my arrival. For several days I kept vigil by her bedside. Then came the day when she breathed her last. My heart was broken.

"Dear Lord," I sobbed soon after I had seen her take those last halting breaths, "I surrender. I have wasted years. What do You want me to do?"

Then came the voice of God to me: "My son, give me thine heart, and let thine eyes observe my ways." My heart was what the Saviour wanted, for when He has our hearts He has our all.

"Before I was afflicted I went astray: but now have I kept thy word" (Ps. 119:67).

WHAT WE SAY OR WHAT WE DO?

Not every one that saith unto me, Lord, Lord, shall enter into the kingdom of heaven; but he that doeth the will of my Father which is in heaven. Matt. 7:21.

"They will go to church, yes, but they won't really believe anything they hear" (2 Tim. 3:5, T.L.B.), or as the King James Version states succinctly, they have "a form of godliness" but deny "the power thereof."

As a young man this was my experience. I was a nominal church member. There was no Adventist church in my hometown. I was baptized. I believed at least theoretically in the Second Advent. I kept the Sabbath. I paid tithe on the few dollars I earned during those depression years. I attended church and Missionary Volunteer meetings when it was convenient. I didn't smoke or drink. I was a good moral youth.

I attended a public high school in Florida and was deeply involved in almost every activity—football, basketball, baseball, track, the school paper, social activities, and all. I was the only Seventh-day Adventist in the school. During the four years of high school very few, if any, athletic contests or major social events were held on Friday night or Saturday. My regard for the Sabbath would have precluded my participation during the hours of God's holy day. Out of deference to the conscience of a student with religious convictions, all of these events were scheduled "so Bob Pierson can participate."

During those years I was nominally a Seventh-day Adventist Christian with high standards so far as morals and ethics were concerned, but I knew very little of the power of Christ in my heart and life. To me Jesus was a character of history who beautifully lived and heroically died two thousand years ago in old Palestine—or perhaps He still lived somewhere in heaven. It was a comfortable feeling to go to Him for help in times of emergency. In my heart was no overwhelming sense of need. There was no abiding Friend or Companion, whom to love and serve is the great obsession of a Christian.

All of that came a few years later when I met Jesus and was truly converted.

The outward forms are not enough. Knowing Christ, doing His will—is the only way!

"THE INCREMENT IS YOURS!"

But seek ye first the kingdom of God, and his righteousness; and all these things shall be added unto you. Matt. 6:33.

As a teen-ager Bob was working in a cooperative creamery in the Midwest. His work was to receive the cream from customers, help run butterfat tests, assist in pasteurizing the cream, making the butter, and being generally involved in the work of the plant.

Then one day the chairman of the cooperative board came to the young worker.

"Bob," he said, "we need you in the plant on Saturdays. As you know, this is the biggest day of the week. We need you. We are also looking for an assistant buttermaker. This job will pay more money than you are receiving. If you will work on Saturdays the job and pay increase are yours. But if you can't work on Saturday . . ."

Bob knew what he was going to say and started to interrupt.

"Think it over," the board chairman continued before the young man could speak, "and let me know how you feel in a week's time. We hope you will stay with us."

"Mr. de Meuleanere," Bob replied thoughtfully, "I do not need a week to think over your proposition. I can give you my answer right now. I like the work here. I've enjoyed working with you men. I appreciate the confidence you have manifested in offering me something even better; but if it means working on the Sabbath, you will have to find someone else."

The week passed. The board met. Bob waited anxiously for their decision. A smiling board chairman met him.

"Well, Bob," he beamed, "we have decided to keep you on. The buttermaking job is yours. The increment is yours, too! The board decided they could do with a few more young fellows who place their conscience first and their jobs second."

Bob learned what every child of God knows—our heavenly Father never fails. He has not promised ice cream and cake or the luxuries of life. But the necessities of life will be ours. "He will give them to you if you give him first place in your life" (Matt. 6:33, T.L.B.).

I know this story is true and that God fulfills His promises, for I am Bob.

HOW DOLLIS FOUND CHRIST

I will put my spirit within you, and cause you to walk in my statutes.
Eze. 36:27.

Dollis, a teen-age teacher in a Florida elementary school, found herself for the first time at a Seventh-day Adventist camp meeting. Her only previous contacts with Seventh-day Adventists had been through a high school friend and his family. Mostly, Adventism had meant that Bob did not participate in athletic events on Saturday. Well, that was his business!

The first early-morning meeting made a tremendous impact upon her. Never before had she seen members of her peer group stand and express their love for Christ.

A few hours later Dollis was sitting in the rear of the large tent listening to Elder J. A. Stevens, of the General Conference, present a stirring Sabbath morning message. At the speaker's invitation all sat with bowed heads as the appeal was made. For some months a new and strange power had been at work in Dollis' heart. The healing of Bob's sister, Ruth, from cancer had made a deep impression upon her.

"Won't those who wish to accept Christ this morning stand?" Elder Stevens invited.

Unhesitatingly, Dollis responded.

"Won't those of you who wish to go all the way with Christ this morning come down front for special prayer?"

"All the way"—suddenly the realization of just what this meant startled the youthful teacher. A conflict arose in her heart. "No, I can't . . . I won't," she said to herself, and sat down.

The preacher paused a moment. Then continuing, he directed his appeal to the one who had just been seated. "That young lady in the very back who was standing a moment ago, won't you come? Come now!"

Dollis gripped her chair tightly for several seconds as the battle in her heart ebbed and flowed. Suddenly the struggle ceased. Fear vanished. The victory was won. Slowly but resolutely she arose and made her way to the front of the tent in a full surrender to Jesus and His last-day message.

For more than forty years now Dollis and Bob have been preaching the Advent message in many lands.

"DON'T BE ANXIOUS ABOUT TOMORROW"

So don't be anxious about tomorrow. God will take care of your tomorrow too. Live one day at a time. **Matt. 6:34, T.L.B.**

I was a child of the great depression in the late twenties and early thirties. I know what it is to get along with the bare necessities of life. I was born into a home of affluence. My father was the president of the Poweshiek County Savings Bank in a small Midwestern town. My earliest recollections were of having almost everything I needed or wanted.

The closing of the banks and the onset of the depression wiped out all of that in a few months' time. Fortunately my father had taught all of his children to work, even though we really didn't need to. This stood us in good stead when we had to—and I had to in my early teens. I knew what it was to work hard before and after school and on Sundays and holidays. It was good for me!

Dollis and I were married just three days before we entered Southern Junior College in Collegedale, Tennessee. Years later, on the occasion of a baccalaureate sermon, I described to the graduating class our apartment, "with three bedrooms, a study, a living room, a dining room, and kitchen"—all in one room! I told the class of our "private bath"—private for all nineteen of us who lived on the second floor of the old normal building.

But God was good. We never lacked the necessities of life. We didn't have much cake and ice cream, but our bread and water (and other good, wholesome food in abundance) was always ours. In those days we worked for twenty-five cents an hour and—blessed thought—we could draw 10 per cent of that amount in cash! The balance paid school bills and bought food at the college store.

Why do we tell these personal experiences? As a testimony to God's goodness during hard times—to assure any struggling reader who may be experiencing adversities that God can and does provide for those who are in need temporally. We know from experience. We know also He added a lot of love and happiness to those depression days.

God fulfills His promises. We have tested Him!

"FOR HIM"

Peter therefore was kept in prison: but prayer was made without ceasing of the church unto God for him. **Acts 12:5.**

A great prayer meeting is described in the twelfth chapter of Acts. You doubtless know the story well.

"About that time King Herod moved against some of the believers, and killed the apostle James (John's brother). When Herod saw how much this pleased the Jewish leaders, he arrested Peter during the Passover celebration and imprisoned him, placing him under the guard of sixteen soldiers. Herod's intention was to deliver Peter to the Jews for execution after the Passover. But earnest prayer was going up to God from the church for his safety all the time he was in prison" (Acts 12:1-5, T.L.B.).

I like the words of the King James Version, "for him." The church was praying for someone definite—someone in need. "Prayer was made without ceasing . . . unto God *for him*"— doubtless by name!

I believe in praying for individuals by name. I believe in prayer lists.

One day soon after I entered the ministry I was looking through the drawers of an ancient family roll-top desk I had inherited. In one of the pigeon holes I found an old envelope marked, "Ocala MV Society Prayer List."

I opened the envelope and glanced down a list of some fifteen or twenty names. Imagine my surprise when I found *my* name among the others. During a period in my young life when I needed spiritual help, when I was not praying for myself as frequently or as earnestly as I should, someone was praying *for me by name!*

"Prayer . . . for him"—talking to the Lord on behalf of individuals personally who are in need—is effective prayer. It is good to pray for the missionaries, the colporteurs, and other groups in general—God surely hears these intercessory petitions—but somehow I feel that in regard to the "for him" prayers—when we single out individuals and plead with the Lord in their behalf personally—the results will be even more amazing!

Why not try it more often?

74

ONLY ONE NAME

Neither is there salvation in any other; for there is none other name under heaven given among men, whereby we must be saved. Acts 4:12.

Every day as I drove into the city of Bombay from our home in the suburbs I would see him sitting there, a Hindu holy man who wore only a grimy loincloth. His body was covered with cow-dung ashes. He sat complacently upon a bed of spikes, smoking a pipe. The spikes were sharp, too, I learned upon investigation one day.

When I asked him why he had been sitting thus for eleven long years his answer did not surprise me. Through self-inflicted punishment he was seeking to somehow "atone" for his misdeeds, to balance accounts with his god and thus earn salvation.

In non-Christian lands millions of burdened souls seek deliverance through "side doors." I have seen men travel for days by lying down in the busy road, measuring their body length, arising, and repeating the procedure until they reach some distant, presumably holy, place. I have seen them packed into railway carriages by the thousands, traveling on pilgrimages to some sacred shrine or "holy" river. They cut and maim themselves in quest of deliverance. They are searching, searching.

It is not alone in so-called heathen lands that questing souls seek to earn salvation. Millions in so-called Christian lands follow the same course, perhaps not consciously, but surely just as futilely. Perhaps some of us as Seventh-day Adventists have a tendency to want to "work" our way into the kingdom by our good deeds or by depending upon moral codes for salvation.

The Lord's messenger has a word for us when we begin to depend upon our works or upon our own moral finery: "Education, culture, the exercise of the will, human effort, all have their proper sphere, but here they are powerless. They may produce an outward correctness of behavior, but they cannot change the heart; they cannot purify the springs of life. There must be a power working from within, a new life from above, before men can be changed from sin to holiness. That power is Christ. His grace alone can quicken the lifeless faculties of the soul, and attract it to God, to holiness."—*Steps to Christ*, p. 18.

Jesus is our only hope!

MORE THAN WE HAD DREAMED OF!

And all that dwell upon the earth shall worship him, whose names are not written in the book of life of the Lamb slain from the foundation of the world. Rev. 13:8.

I have watched Hindu worshipers offer their sacrifices to the goddess Kali in Calcutta, India. It is a sight one never forgets. The head of a terrified little animal is placed in a specially constructed instrument. Some water from the sacred Ganges is sprinkled upon its neck. With one stroke of a large knife the head is severed from the body. The blood is spilled. Some sort of propitiation (the worshiper is not just certain how it happens) is made.

In the council of eternity—before the creation of the world—the plan of redemption was laid. This involved the creation of man as a free moral agent. If this new creature should choose to do wrong, the penalty for sin—death—would rest upon him. At this juncture Jesus offered to be man's substitute if he fell. He would become man's sacrifice!

In a sense Jesus entered the shadow of the cross from that time onward. With His divine foreknowledge, Calvary was a certainty from that very moment. Millennia before the scenes of Calvary, Christ indeed became "the Lamb slain from the foundation of the world."

When Adam and Eve sinned in the Garden of Eden, the shadows of the cross deepened. In the death of each animal sacrifice from that day forward Christ was reminded that He Himself must shed His blood to end all sacrifices. For centuries Christ continued to walk in the shadow of the cross.

Which is the greater suffering for a man condemned to death—the few seconds it takes for the trap to be sprung and his body to hurtle into space and for death actually to take place, or the mental anguish during weeks and perhaps months that he spends in the death cell waiting, dreading the day of execution? You know the answer.

Perhaps this crude illustration will help us better understand what John meant when he wrote that Jesus was "the Lamb slain from the foundation of the world"! What a sacrifice! What love!

HOW EARLY?

They brought children for him to lay his hands on them with prayer. The disciples rebuked them, but Jesus said to them, "Let the children come to me; do not try to stop them; for the kingdom of Heaven belongs to such as these." And he laid his hands on the children, and went his way. Matt. 19:13, 14, N.E.B.

Many years ago I was invited to conduct a Week of Prayer in one of our colleges. Just before the first meeting a father came to me in deep concern.

"Please do all you can for my daughter this week," he appealed. "She has never been baptized although she is 18 years old."

The father paused, then continued, "When Linda was nine years old she wanted to be baptized but her mother and I thought she was too young. We were not as patient and understanding in explaining this to her as we should have been, and we quenched the tiny flame of love for Jesus that had been kindled in her heart. Through the years she has never again expressed the desire to be baptized and to join the church. Please speak to her and try to help her make the decision she should."

Tears were in this anguished father's voice as he appealed on behalf of his daughter. He longed to see his daughter open her heart to Christ and to follow Him in complete obedience.

The Lord was good during that special week of devotion. Linda responded to the appeals of the Holy Spirit and she surrendered her life to Christ. She was baptized and for many years has been a worker in the cause of God herself. But all stories do not have such happy endings!

When should a child be encouraged to give his heart to Jesus and prepare for baptism? Ellen White reminds us: "God wants every child of tender age to be His child, to be adopted into His family.

"An eminent divine was once asked how old a child must be before there was reasonable hope of his being a Christian. 'Age has nothing to do with it,' was the answer. 'Love to Jesus, trust, repose, confidence, are all qualities that agree with the child's nature. As soon as a child can love and trust his mother, then can he love and trust Jesus as the Friend of his mother. Jesus will be his Friend, loved and honored.' "—*Child Guidance*, p. 486.

ABOUT ETERNITY AND CERTAINTY

That I might make thee know the certainty of the words of truth; that thou mightest answer the words of truth to them that send unto thee? **Prov. 22:21.**

In the summer of 1942 the Pierson family boarded a large troopship in Bombay, India, returning to America after seven years in the mission field. The vessel was crowded with missionaries, crews from sunken merchant ships, servicemen, and an assortment of other passengers. Women and children were assigned certain areas of the ship. Men and older boys occupied other quarters. Male passengers signed statements to the effect that they knew there were not sufficient lifeboats for use if the ship should be sunk.

It was the beginning of a strange, uncertain, and eventful voyage. We sailed under sealed orders, we were told, and that is about all that we were told during the forty-two day journey. When we steamed out of Bombay harbor no one knew for sure where we were going or what route we were taking to get there. Speculation was rife. Would we go east or west? Would we go via the Red Sea or the Cape of Good Hope? Was our destination a port on the West or the East Coast of the United States? Or would we dock in Jacksonville, New Orleans, or some other Southern port? New rumors laden with unfounded speculations were the order of the day. New "information" based upon "they say" spread through the ship almost hourly. The only certainty was uncertainty.

Uncertainty grips too many Christian churches today. Too many professed Christians do not know where they are going or how they are going to get there. Across the Western world religious unrest is becoming more and more evident. Traditional positions on church doctrine are under bold assault. Denominational walls are crumbling. The only certainty in many Christian quarters is uncertainty.

In such an hour when the foundations are being severely shaken, when doubt and discredit are the order of the day, you and I, young and old alike, must turn to our Bibles. Prayerfully and perseveringly we must peruse the sacred pages. Our eternity must be built upon certainty. We need not fear to test the Advent message by the Word of God. For more than a century it has stood the closest scrutiny. But we must *search* and *know!*

LAL SINGH, AND YOU!

Ever learning, and never able to come to the knowledge of the truth. 2 Tim. 3:7.

Years ago I was conducting an evangelistic crusade in Poona, India. One young man—we will call him Lal Singh—attended the meetings regularly and came to my office several times a week for personal Bible studies. He knew the message well. I felt certain he would be among the first to take his stand for the truth. So one day I pressed him.

"Lal Singh," I said, "we have been studying the Holy Bible together for some months now. What do you think of this Holy Book?"

"I believe it is God's Word," he replied unhesitatingly.

"That is good," I said hopefully. "And what do you think of Jesus Christ?"

"I believe He is the Son of God," he replied without hesitation.

"Fine," I replied. "And what about the Ten Commandments?"

"I intend to keep them," was his prompt answer.

I felt sure everything was developing as hoped for. "Then you plan to be a Seventh-day Adventist Christian, don't you?" I pressed prayerfully.

Lal Singh looked at me amazed—Become a Christian? He really hadn't thought of that. He believed he could include Jesus with his other gods, and keep the commandments and still remain a Hindu!

Lal Singh was not the first, nor will he be the last, to be "ever learning, and never able to come to the knowledge of the truth." Many both outside and inside the church are afflicted by this syndrome.

There are even some church members who attend services regularly and who study the Word faithfully but who refuse to let the Spirit of God make new creatures of them! They, too, are ever learning but never able to come to the true, practical knowledge of the truth!

Which is to be condemned the most—Lal Singh or the halting church member?

NO SMOKING ON SABBATH!

All these evil things come from within, and defile the man. Mark 7:23.

Years ago I was pastoring our church in Bombay, India. One morning a man in distress came to the mission bungalow looking for help. Often drifters would stop by to get a free meal or a loan of a few rupees, so I questioned the man carefully.

He was a Seventh-day Adventist, "Brother Professor" assured me. He had been baptized by Pastor Hamilton. To prove his *bona fides* he reeled off the names of workers and lay members in the Calcutta church whom he knew well.

"If you will just lend me enough money to purchase my ticket home," he appealed, "I will return the money as soon as I reach Calcutta."

Here was a brother in distress. His story sounded plausible. He needed help. My heart was touched. I was at the point of handing over the necessary rupees to buy his ticket when my telephone rang. Excusing myself, I went inside, completed the call, and returned to the front veranda to perform my good deed for the day.

Imagine my surprise when I found Brother Professor complacently smoking a cigarette!

"I thought you told me you were a Seventh-day Adventist!"

"I am," he replied, without batting an eyelid.

"Do you mean that Elder Hamilton baptized you?" I pressed.

"Yes, he did," the man with the cigarette replied.

"Why then are you smoking a cigarette?" I demanded. "Don't you know Seventh-day Adventists do not smoke?"

"But it isn't Sabbath!" Brother Professor replied calmly.

"It isn't Sabbath?" I gasped incredulously. "What do you mean?"

"Well," my caller explained simply, "Pastor Hamilton told me not to smoke on the Sabbath!"

We smile, but when you come to think of it, don't many of us have rather strange attitudes and concepts about the message and living it out in our lives that might sound just as strange in the Lord's ears as not "smoking on the Sabbath"?

THEY WASHED THEIR CLOTHES

And the Lord said unto Moses, Go unto the people, and sanctify them to day and to morrow, and let them wash their clothes, and be ready against the third day: for the third day the Lord will come down in the sight of all the people upon mount Sinai. Ex. 19:10, 11.

She was very young and, I am sure, very sincere. For the new year the pastor had delivered a Spirit-filled sermon on service. In response to his earnest appeal for a new commitment, hundreds in the large, crowded church surged forward for the consecration prayer.

Before the prayer the pastor asked whether anyone had anything he wished to say. Without hesitation our dark-haired young lady, wearing a modest white sweater and blue skirt, hurried to the rostrum.

She spoke for several minutes with deep emotion of what Christ had come to mean to her. After bearing her own testimony she rebuked the members of the large church for their indifference toward the unwashed and poorly clothed in the community around them.

"They are so busy working for Christ," she declared with feeling, "they do not have time to work for money to buy good clothes and to groom themselves well. *You don't want them in your church!*"

While she bore her testimony of what Christ had done for her, my heart was warmed. I was right with her. When she declared the church did not want some of her unkempt peer group to come to church, I felt she had deviated from the truth. I have visited hundreds of Seventh-day Adventist churches around the world. There may be some who would object to the presence of individuals with unwashed bodies, uncut hair, and offensive clothing, but I doubt there are very many.

There are two sides to this coin also. The true religion of Christ cleans people up outside as well as inside. I have seen this times without end in mission lands. Before the people went up to the mount to meet God they were admonished to wash their clothes and clean up for the occasion. Cleanliness is still closely akin to godliness. We honor God with clean bodies and clothing in His house of worship.

NEEDING HELP?

His name shall be called . . . Counsellor, The mighty God, The everlasting Father, The Prince of Peace. Isa. 9:6.

Eight years in an emerging, exploding Africa taught me many valuable lessons. There was trouble in almost every land during the explosive sixties. Political furore, states of emergency, martial law or open warfare at one time or another, upset all eight of our unions. Many times we simply did not know which way to turn or what to do!

Thank God, we did not face those trials and perils alone, unaided. The precious assurance "Lo, I am with you alway, even unto the end of the world" (Matt. 28:20) sustained us during days of violent upheaval.

Do you sometimes come to the place where you don't know what to do, where to turn? The promises are for *you* as well. Jesus the mighty God, the everlasting Father, desires to become your Counselor!

"If . . . any of you does not know how to meet any particular problem he has only to ask God—who gives generously to all men without making them feel foolish or guilty—and he may be quite sure that the necessary wisdom will be given him" (James 1:5, Phillips).

When we face difficulties and problems it is so human to seek counsel and guidance from a trusted friend or acquaintance. There is nothing wrong in this. "In the multitude of counsellors there is safety" (Prov. 11:14). But many of us toss and turn on sleepless beds before help comes. Why do we subject ourselves to such punishment? Why not take our problem to the One who "gives generously to all men"?

Note these inspired words of counsel:

"We are not to let the future, with its hard problems, its unsatisfying prospects, make our hearts faint, our knees tremble, our hands hang down. . . . Those who surrender their lives to His guidance and to His service will never be placed in a position for which He has not made provision. . . . If we are doers of His word, . . . whatever our perplexity, we have a sure Counselor; whatever our sorrow, bereavement, or loneliness, we have a sympathizing Friend."—*The Ministry of Healing*, pp. 248, 249.

IS YOURS A SECONDHAND EXPERIENCE?

For I know whom I have believed, and am persuaded that he is able to keep that which I have committed unto him against that day. 2 Tim. 1:12.

Knowing Christ must be a personal experience. The apostle Paul declared, "I know whom I have believed." Some Samaritans, deeply impressed by the testimony of the woman at the well, "believed on him for the saying of the woman," but "many more believed because of his own word. . . . Now we believe, not because of thy saying: for we have heard him ourselves, and know that this is indeed the Christ, the Saviour of the world" (John 4:39-42).

A secondhand experience with Jesus is not sufficient. What the Master has done for someone else may encourage me, but it will never save me. *I* must know Him personally myself. *I* must know the joy of sins confessed and forgiven. *My* prayers must reach through to the throne of grace. He must do something for *me*.

Jesus is the Saviour of the world—there is no question about this. But you and I could fail to appropriate the salvation He extends to all. We must choose Him as our Saviour. He must be *ours*.

Christ cleansed countless lepers during His earthly ministry, but unless we turn to Him personally for help today, we may perish from the leprosy of sin in 1975. We must seek his cleansing power personally.

The Master delivered men and women from demon possession two thousand years ago. We need deliverance from evil habits today. His power of deliverance has not diminished one whit through the centuries, but we must experience this great power in *our* lives.

What Jesus did for the human race two thousand years ago is of great importance. We dare not minimize it. But what we let Him do for us today is of even greater import to *our* eternal welfare.

Not what He did for Mary Magdalene, not what He did for the widow of Nain, or for Lazarus, or the devil-possessed man of Gadara, or the thief on the cross, but what we permit Him to do for us personally—this will determine our eternal destiny!

IT SHALL NOT RETURN VOID

So shall the word which comes from my mouth prevail; it shall not return to me fruitless without accomplishing my purpose or succeeding in the task I gave it. Isa. 55:11, N.E.B.

A truck driver in one of our large Tennessee cities discovered a damaged carton of religious books lying in a dark corner of an old warehouse. The container was broken and the books had fallen onto the floor. Nobody seemed interested in doing anything about the situation. So the books had been there for some time.

The truck driver picked up one of the books and glanced through it. Since the title *Bible Readings for the Home* reminded him of his wife's recently aroused interest in the study of the Bible, he decided to take the book home for her. The wife had been in the hospital for surgery and had there met a congenial Seventh-day Adventist woman who visited her daughter, who was in the same room. Our sister's Christian conduct made a deep impression on the patient.

As the truck driver's wife studied the book her husband brought, she began to connect its contents with Seventh-day Adventists. One day she reached for her telephone and called the Seventh-day Adventist church, requesting someone to visit her. A representative called, and Bible studies were arranged. The pastor gave the studies. The husband soon asked for Sabbath off from his work and stopped smoking. Together this couple found their way into the remnant church because of a damaged carton of *Bible Readings* and the faithful witnessing of a Christian visitor in a large city hospital.

Perhaps you have worked and prayed for a friend, a neighbor, or a member of your own family without visible results. Or it may be you are a literature evangelist knocking on doors, placing literature in offices and homes—you don't see the results of your efforts immediately. The promise in our text today is yours!

Do not become discouraged. Keep on sowing. God *will* bring the increase.

GARY'S DEATH WAS NOT IN VAIN

Ye have said, It is vain to serve God: and what profit is it that we have kept his ordinance? Mal. 3:14.

Gary Abrahamson graduated from Oak Park Academy in Iowa, and a few months later was inducted into the service of his country. On July 1, 1970, he left for Vietnam. On the night of September 20, Gary laid down his life for his country while on patrol as a medic.

Gary's body was flown home to a hero's reception and burial. A military honor group served as pallbearers. A color guard from the local American Legion paid him honor. Flags flew at half-mast in his hometown the day of the funeral.

According to Elder F. J. Kinsey, who had charge of the funeral service, Gary did not die in vain. Later a classmate wrote these words to Elder Kinsey: "I very much appreciated your sermon at Gary Abrahamson's funeral. It meant a lot to me and said a lot to me.

"You probably remember that you baptized me. . . . Since that time I have strayed from what I should have been doing, but your message and Gary's funeral brought me back. I think your speculation about the possible reason for his death was true—both reasons, especially the second reason—that was for me, of that I am sure. I wish I could have done something but I can't.

"I know I will have a hard time on the road I have chosen, but God is on my side, for that I am glad. Please pray for me and send me a copy of the sermon as soon as you can."

The death of any person, especially of a young man or woman in the flower of youth, is a traumatic experience. Hearts of loved ones are bowed down in deep grief. Yet even from such a heartbreaking experience come blessings. Evidently Gary had lived an exemplary life. That life was not lived in vain. He died a hero's death. His death was not in vain. Through it all one young man's heart was touched and he returned to God.

We little know the results upon others of our lives or our words. Sometimes God uses a hero's death and a pastor's words to bring eternal life to one who is without it. Gary's death was not in vain.

YOU CAN'T GO IT ALONE!

I am the vine, ye are the branches: He that abideth in me, and I in him, the same bringeth forth much fruit: for without me ye can do nothing. John 15:5.

Years ago in the West Indies I knew a layman burning with zeal to preach the Advent message. Every time he heard a sermon on soul winning he could scarcely contain himself. He *must* preach. But Brother Brown had a great handicap. He could not read. He could not distinguish one word from another, or even one letter from another. The Bible, the books, the papers he needed for source material seemed as inaccessible to him as diamonds on the moon. He did not know the alphabet.

Brother Brown, however, determined by God's grace to change that situation—and he did. He learned the alphabet and learned to read. The twenty-six letters unlocked a whole new world for him when they became his tools.

The alphabet is absolutely indispensable to one who wishes to possess the treasures of any library. The inviting vistas of travel, history, poetry, and religion are barred and bolted against the one who is without the key—the alphabet. Without this vehicle the searcher is helpless. It is a necessity!

What the alphabet is to literature, Jesus is to true life, for He is the key to life. Without Him we cannot know from whence we came, why we are here, or where we are going. Without Him we find the choicest treasures of this life totally inaccessible. "Without me ye can do nothing," He reminds us.

Jesus reveals God the Father to us. "He that hath seen me hath seen the Father; and how sayest thou then, Shew us the Father?" (John 14:9). From Christ we learn to love God and to serve Him. We discover the peace that comes with bringing our lives into harmony with His will. We experience the great joy of helping others. Our present life takes on new meaning. Christ teaches us there is also life beyond—sinless, sorrowless, deathless—for those who accept and follow Him! Only through Jesus are revealed the radiant raptures of the Christian life here and now and the glorious life in the earth made new.

EASIER TO EVALUATE THAN TO PARTICIPATE

Let us not therefore judge one another any more: but judge this rather, that no man put a stumblingblock or an occasion to fall in his brother's way. **Rom. 14:13.**

I met a man at camp meeting one time who promptly informed me he would never hold a church office despite the fact that he had been a member for some twenty years. Before I could ask for an explanation he volunteered one: "Too many hypocrites!" he scoffed. "I've seen too many of them in my time. They make a big show up front, but when it comes to living what they preach, mighty few of them do it!"

I had what I considered a good suggestion for my disillusioned brother.

"Why don't you accept the first office the church offers you?" I urged, "and show them what kind of a life a genuine church officer should live. You have a wonderful opportunity to be an example to the believers."

My "good suggestion" apparently fell on stony ground. "Not me," he muttered, and shuffled off to visit with someone else.

Later I saw him again. His countenance had changed.

"Elder," he said thoughtfully, "I think you are right. Instead of criticizing others, I believe it would be better if I got into the harness and set a good example."

It is much easier to evaluate than to participate. In fact, it is easier to falsify than to testify. It doesn't require much intelligence to sit back and criticize, to question, or impugn the motives of the leader who is up front probably doing his best to do the job he was asked to do. Being a church elder, a deacon, a deaconess, a Sabbath school superintendent, or most any other officer exposes one to criticism or evaluation. Sometimes the remarks are so unkind it causes the officer to "step down."

"He that covereth a transgression seeketh love; but he that repeateth a matter separateth very friends" (Prov. 17:9).

Dr. Taylor sums up the apostle Paul's counsel nicely when he writes: "So don't criticize each other any more. Try instead to live in such a way that you will never make your brother stumble by letting him see you doing something he thinks is wrong" (Rom. 14:13, T.L.B.).

SMOKE IN MY NOSE

Which say, Stand by thyself, come not near to me; for I am holier than thou. These are a smoke in my nose, a fire that burneth all the day. Isa. 65:5.

There it was, a painting high in the outside front gable of the cathedral. I looked at the figures with considerable interest, and, I must admit, with just a little amusement. There I saw South American Indians of 400 years ago decked in the gay regalia of their day. Colonial settlers were dressed in the costumes of the same period. A priest in his vestments, and (and this is the incredible part of it) there in the midst of these people of yesterday were two modern businessmen dressed in twentieth-century attire, complete with pocket handkerchiefs! How incongruous they looked fellowshiping with men of the sixteenth century! Then I learned the story behind the painting.

A few years before, the local bishop decided the front gable of his cathedral should be enhanced with a commemorative painting of the first mass said on the South American continent. Of course, such a painting, done by a reputable artist, would cost a fair amount of money. Where would this money come from?

The bishop approached two of his wealthy parishioners urging them to provide the needed cash. They agreed—with one provision—they should both appear in the painting!

"Impossible!" the bishop exploded. "How could two modern businessmen be included in a scene that took place four hundred years ago? Impossible!"

"All right," the men replied, "then perhaps you can find your money from some other source!"

"Let us think it over," the bishop continued evasively. "We'll give you our final word in a day or two." The "final word" is on the cathedral today—two twentieth-century men standing with a group of sixteenth-century nationals and colonials at a mass celebrated four centuries ago!

Interesting? Amusing? Ridiculous? Yes, of course, but after all, pride in the heart of almost any man or woman may produce some very ridiculous if not disastrous results!

God says the conceited or proud person is smoke in His nose.

NO BLACK, NO WHITE!

There is neither Jew nor Greek, there is neither bond nor free, there is neither male nor female: for ye are all one in Christ Jesus. Gal. 3:28.

Mrs. Pierson and I were leaving Jamaica after two thrilling weeks spent with workers and members we had learned to love during five years of service on the island years before. At the Montego Bay airport more than four thousand Adventists and friends, old and young, packed every square foot of the airport building to sing and wave good-by.

Arriving by the same plane on which we were scheduled to depart was a sizable part of black leaders of various political organizations from the United States. When they disembarked and saw the airport packed with singing, waving people, their reaction was immediate!

"What is this big crowd here for?" one of them asked Elder H. S. Walters, president of the West Indies Union Conference.

"We have come to say good-by to one of our church leaders and his wife," Brother Walters replied.

"One of your leaders?" the questioners asked. "Is he black?"

"No," replied our Jamaican president with a broad grin, "he is white. You see, in the Seventh-day Adventist Church we don't make any difference in black and white—we are all brothers and sisters in Christ!"

"No black and white—all brothers and sisters in Christ!" I wish this were always true. Certainly this is our Master's desire for the people of His remnant church—full brotherhood in Him. In Christ there cannot be the slightest trace of superiority on the part of any race. There can be no demeaning attitudes or actions when Christ reigns supreme in these hearts of ours. It is not a matter of the color of our skin; it is a question of the condition of our heart that counts with God.

"Christ tears away the wall of partition [the self-love], the dividing prejudice of nationality [or race], and teaches a love for all the human family. He lifts men from the narrow circle which their selfishness prescribes; He abolishes all territorial [and ethnic] lines and artificial distinctions of society."—*The Desire of Ages*, p. 823.

JESUS PREACHED—SUICIDE SAVED

Then Philip opened his mouth, . . . and preached unto him Jesus.
Acts 8:35.

The dedication of the new Colonial Pantitlan Chapel in Mexico City was held on, of all days of the week, Thursday, the only time that could be worked into my heavy program. The service opened with the usual animated song service. The little building was crowded to capacity.

While God's people and their friends were singing happily inside the chapel and enjoying the festive occasion, less than 250 yards from the sanctuary a woman was making the fearful decision to take her own life. There had been problems in the home—problems with sons and their wives, problems with her own self. She was unhappy and confused. Hope for anything better had disappeared. There seemed no way out but to end it all.

As she made her way to a fateful rendezvous with death she drew near the beautiful little Adventist chapel. She heard beautiful singing from inside. Strange, she thought, that people would be in church for a service on Thursday.

Something drew Maria irresistibly to the door of the chapel. A faithful deacon, spotting the stranger, hurried to her side and drew her inside the building. "Come inside, señora!" he urged. "You are very welcome here today."

Maria was too timid to permit herself to be taken into the crowded sanctuary and soon she found herself sitting in the pastor's study listening to the first words of the dedicatory sermon. Something in the message that day reached this poor soul's heart. According to a report published later by Angel Ramirez, "By the time the meeting was over Maria had found peace in her soul and things seemed a little brighter. With tears in her eyes she confessed to God and the brethren her dreadful thoughts and determination."

God's instructions are: "There should not a sermon be given unless a portion of that discourse is to especially make plain the way that sinners may come to Christ and be saved."—*Evangelism*, p. 188.

How thankful I am that the Lord helped me that day to "make plain the way."

TWO PRAYERS ANSWERED IN TWO HOURS

Pray without ceasing. 1 Thess. 5:17.

In ten minutes I was scheduled to leave the hotel in Zurich, Switzerland, to catch my Swiss Air plane to London. Confidently I collected my baggage and reached into my pocket for my plane ticket and passport. They were not there.

Carefully I went through the contents of my brief case. I could not find my travel documents. Taking out my Bible, sermon notebook, *Working Policy* book, papers, letters, and other contents, I searched carefully for the wallet. Still I did not locate it.

Turning to my carefully packed suitcase, I unlocked it and hurriedly felt around the edges and under the clothes. The familiar object did not meet my touch. Not very hopefully I unpacked my suitcase, feeling each article in vain anticipation.

Sensing a feeling of despair I began ransacking the room. I simply must have my ticket and passport to get out of Switzerland into England—appointments in England made that imperative.

"Dear Lord," I prayed, "You know I have to have those travel documents. You know I've looked every place I can in this room. Please help me!"

Just as I finished praying the telephone rang. It was the division office in Berne. "We have bad news for you," the voice on the other end of the line said. "Elder Powers has just found your passport and plane ticket in his brief case. What shall we do with them?"

I glanced at my watch—it was about an hour and a half until my plane was scheduled to leave the airport. Could the documents be brought by car to Zurich airport in time? They would try.

At the airport the airline representatives were not hopeful. It takes two hours to drive from Berne to Zurich, they assured me grimly. I requested them to hold my reservation. This time I prayed for a speedy and safe trip for the ones bringing the wallet.

Fifteen minutes before the plane was scheduled to depart Dr. and Mrs. Zurcher drove up with all my documents.

Two answers to prayer in less than two hours!

TOO BAD—NO SPECIAL DISPENSATION

I have chosen the way of truth; thy judgments have I laid before me.
Ps. 119:30.

Several years ago a retired Air Force colonel called to see me in Washington. He represented a national tennis association. I wondered what anyone in the tennis world wanted to see me about. I soon learned.

"You see, Mr. Pierson," the genial colonel across the desk explained, "there are two outstanding tennis players here in the States who are Seventh-day Adventists. They enter a tournament early in the week, win their matches, then when the finals fall on Saturday they cannot participate because they will not play on your Sabbath."

"Yes," I encouraged, "and what can I do to help you?"

"Well, you understand that this is very disrupting to our tournament program and these men could, no doubt, win some of the final matches. We all admire the faithfulness to conscience of your members, but we would like to see them win some of the laurels."

I waited to hear his solution to the problem.

"You see, sir, in another church where there are conflicts like this, the matter is easily resolved. The person in difficulty is able to secure a special dispensation that temporarily frees him from the requirements of his church, and there is no problem. Now I have come to request such a special dispensation for these two friends of mine, so they can play tennis on Saturday when necessary."

The colonel paused, watching hopefully for my response. He was disappointed, but I don't think he was surprised when I replied, "These men wouldn't play on the Sabbath even if the church could grant them permission. You see, this is not a matter between the individual and his church only; it is a matter between him and God." Then I explained the true meaning of the Sabbath.

"I understand now," the colonel smiled when I had finished speaking. "And I honor you for your stand."

With God, right is right. There are no special dispensations that can be granted by human agencies permitting a person to deviate for a season from the path of rectitude.

IS SINCERITY ALWAYS ENOUGH?

Now therefore fear the Lord, and serve him in sincerity and in truth.
Joshua 24:14.

I should have looked at my plane ticket carefully, but I didn't. My secretary always attached a pink slip to my ticket so the information regarding the airport from which I was leaving was gleaned at a glance. Unfortunately, my secretary was on vacation. Unfortunately, also, there are three airports that serve Greater Washington—National, Dulles, and Baltimore-Washington International.

With very few minutes to spare we rolled up in front of the American Airlines departure building at National Airport. I jumped out, took my bags, and hurried to check in at the ticket counter. I handed the man behind the counter my ticket and placed one piece of baggage on the scales, eager to be on my way to Gate No. 11.

"Which flight are you going on this morning, sir?" the attendant asked.

"Flight 263 to Dallas, leaving at 11:15," I replied with assurance.

"I am sorry, sir, but flight 263 leaves from Baltimore. You are in the wrong airport!" he explained kindly.

I have heard people say, "I am sincere in observing the first day of the week instead of the seventh day." Or, "I am perfectly sincere in doing this or that." This was their defense for actually doing what they wanted to do despite the fact that their course of action was not in harmony with the teachings of God's Word.

Sincerity is a must, but alone it is not always enough. I was perfectly sincere in going to National Airport to catch my plane for Dallas. There was no question whatsoever in my mind as I handed my ticket to the airline representative. But I was mistaken in my sincerity.

I had to add truth to my sincerity by following what the airline schedule said. I went to Dallas only when I followed its information—on another flight than the one I had planned.

In serving God, sometimes sincerity is not enough; we must be sure that we are also following the truth of His Word!

IF THERE BE ANY SICK AMONG YOU

Is there any one of you who is sick? He should call the church elders, who will pray for him and pour oil on him in the name of the Lord. James 5:14, T.E.V.

The letter was dated July 8, 1970. It was written by Mrs. C. W. Pine, whose husband was pastor of our Staunton, Virginia, church at the time. It brought back memories of an experience that had taken place in 1958:

"You will not remember this date as I do, but it was twelve years ago today that you were in Ardmore, Oklahoma, getting your physical in preparation for service in Africa. My husband had had surgery a few days before for cancer of the kidney and was very ill. Dr. Joers told me that day that the chances for recovery for very long were very slim, medically speaking. You kindly consented to join with seven other ministers from the Oklahoma Conference in anointing my husband. I believe the text, 'the effectual, fervent prayer of a righteous man availeth much.' Your prayers and those of our friends were answered that day. He never had to have a hypo from then onward, though there were times when he was in great pain. It did take him some months to regain his health.

"He is in excellent physical condition. He has baptized many people since his recovery, has raised up and built five churches, and has, I believe, carried on a good, well-rounded program.

"My three daughters and I thank the Lord each day for sparing his life and sending the sincere workers there that day to pray with us."

My heart is always encouraged when I receive letters such as this. My confidence in the prayer-hearing and prayer-answering God whom I serve is strengthened. The Jesus who healed the sick two thousand years ago is more real to me, for I know He still lives in 1975 and He is still the Great Physician.

In an age of eroding faith, you and I need to treasure well these personal contacts with a living Saviour. He is not only our Saviour, He is our Great Physician.

HE IS RISEN!

He is not here, but is risen: remember how he spake unto you when he was yet in Galilee. Luke 24:6.

I looked at the return address on the envelope with an Indian stamp on it: P. K. Barse, Poona, India. Neither the name nor the address "rang a bell" at first, but when I read the letter dated January 1, 1959, the whole story flooded my memory again.

In 1952, assisted by the Southern Asia Division office staff, I conducted an evangelistic crusade in the downtown section of the old city of Poona. For three months, five nights a week, we preached the message in an area where we had no Adventist church.

A young Marathi journalist, P. K. Barse, was one of the regular attendants at the meetings, but when the hour of decision came he, like many other non-Christian interested persons, faltered. He did not decide for Christ and His last-day message. Two years later we returned to America, served four years in our homeland, and then in 1959 we were back in the mission field—this time in the South African Division.

Then came the letter. I read it eagerly. "You probably will not remember me," Mr. Barse wrote. Then after identifying himself as the young journalist who had attended our meetings seven years before, he continued. "I shall never forget the night you spoke on the resurrection of Christ. Several times you used the words, 'He is not here, He is risen!' Those words burned their way into my mind. Through the past seven years I could never forget them. They made a tremendous appeal. I just want you to know that recently, after a great struggle, I have accepted the risen Lord as my Saviour and I have been baptized. It all began with your words, 'He is not here, He is risen!' "

Those words, of course, were not mine. I had taken them from Dr. Luke's Gospel as recorded in our verse for the day.

There is still power in the resurrection. The power that raised Jesus from the dead nearly twenty centuries ago today still raises men and women from many lands to spiritual life and a new experience in Christ Jesus!

ARE YOU A CHRISTIAN OR JUST
A CHURCH MEMBER?

Having a form of godliness, but denying the power thereof. 2 Tim. 3:5.

I was attending a meeting of literature evangelists in Auburn, Washington. It was inspiring to listen to the miracles of God's grace working in and through these men and women of the Bookman's Army in the Washington Conference. My heart warmed and glowed as they recounted the miracles of God's grace in their behalf.

A young businessman had recently sold his real-estate agency in favor of more intimate involvement in the Lord's work. Within a few days he and his wife would be knocking on doors for God.

Brother New-worker was telling his experience.

"I have been a Seventh-day Adventist all of my life," he explained. "I was baptized about fifteen years ago. I have been a Christian four months." I was not certain I had heard him correctly—a Seventh-day Adventist all his life, baptized fifteen years ago, a Christian only four months? How could this be? Are not all baptized Seventh-day Adventist church members Christians?

Theoretically a church member is a Christian. Actually, a Christian is one who has experienced a meaningful encounter with Christ. This confrontation has done something to such a person's life. His living patterns have changed. He is a new man in Christ Jesus. He trusts fully in the crucified Saviour for salvation. The fruits of the Spirit and Christian works appear in his life as the result of this new Christ-relationship.

"A Seventh-day Adventist all my life . . . baptized fifteen years ago . . . a Christian four months."

Then I realized what Brother New-worker meant. He had believed the doctrines. He had belonged to the church. Outwardly he had adhered to the requirements of church membership. He had gone through the motions, but something—Someone—was missing—Jesus!

"A Seventh-day Adventist all my life . . . baptized fifteen years ago . . . a Christian four months."

Do these words cast any warning light on your pathway?

WHY ARE WE HERE?

And I saw another mighty angel come down from heaven, clothed with a cloud: and a rainbow was upon his head, and his face was as it were the sun, and his feet as pillars of fire: and he had in his hand a little book open: and he set his right foot upon the sea, and his left foot on the earth. Rev. 10:1, 2.

Two thoughts in our text for today I would like you to especially notice. The angel had in his hand a little book open. Then notice that one of the angel's feet was "upon the sea," and the other was "on the earth." John's vision had something very definite to do with Seventh-day Adventists today. It has a message of confidence for you and me.

The little book in the angel's hand was open when John saw it. It had not always been open. Another prophet centuries before had been instructed to close this same book. You can read this in the book of Daniel, chapter 12, verse 4: "But thou, O Daniel, shut up the words, and seal the book, even to the time of the end."

The visions, dreams, and instruction God gave to the prophet Daniel, according to these words, were not for his day. They were to be "shut" and "sealed" until a time in earth's history known as "the time of the end"—a short period in this world's history just before the second coming of Jesus. We must conclude, then, that the little book with its special messages for such an awesome hour would be opened.

It is interesting to note that some of the basics of what we call the Advent message are found in "the little book" of Daniel. The rise and fall of nations, the second coming of Christ, and the setting up of His kingdom, are in the little book. So are the great judgment scene and certain aspects of the ministry and Messiahship of Christ.

For centuries the little book remained closed.

Then, when the time of the end arrived toward the end of the eighteenth century, the little book was opened, just as our text today foretold. In many parts of the world—"upon the sea, and . . . on the earth"—adults and children, ministers and laymen, began to explain the message that was used of God to call the Seventh-day Adventist Movement into existence.

A BITTER EXPERIENCE

And I went unto the angel, and said unto him, Give me the little book. And he said unto me, Take it, and eat it up; and it shall make thy belly bitter, but it shall be in thy mouth sweet as honey. Rev. 10:9.

"How can the Seventh-day Adventist Church be God's true church when your founders predicted that Jesus would return in 1844, and they suffered such a great disappointment when He did not appear?"

This is a fair question. Almost every Adventist sometime in his experience is confronted with this challenge. It would be an embarrassing question were it not for several facts.

In the first place, *the Seventh-day Adventist Church has never set a date for the return of Christ*—in 1844 or any other date. The Seventh-day Adventist Church was not organized until 1863, nineteen years after the 1844 disappointment, so it could not have made such a prediction. It is true, however, that some people who later became Seventh-day Adventists were part of the Millerite movement at the time of the great disappointment in 1844.

The belief that their Saviour would soon appear was a precious hope. Large numbers believed with all their hearts. Some sold their property, confessed their sins, made wrongs right with their fellow men in preparation for the Master's return. When October 22, 1844, passed without Jesus' appearing, it was a bitter experience.

But does the fact that there was a great disappointment mean that the Lord was not in the movement? Consider another bitter disappointment that came to the forerunners of the apostolic church in Christ's day. During His earthly ministry the disciples of Christ were convinced that Jesus was going to set up an earthly kingdom and that some of them would occupy favored positions in that kingdom. They were bitterly disappointed when Christ's ministry ended, not on a throne but on a cross! Did this mean that God was not in that early Christian movement because great disappointment was experienced? Of course not.

In both the disappointment in Christ's day and in 1844 God was testing those who professed to be His followers, but He did not forsake them!

FROM DISAPPOINTMENT TO APPOINTMENT

And he said unto me, Thou must prophesy again before many peoples, and nations, and tongues, and kings. **Rev. 10:11.**

After the bitter disappointment of 1844 word came to the early believers in the Advent, "Thou must prophesy again before many peoples, and nations, and tongues, and kings."

The Lord then directed His faithful ones to two more great truths that have helped to make us the Advent people. Some of the disappointed ones continued to search the Scriptures and pray earnestly for light. Their attention was directed to the words of John in Revelation 11:1, 2 and to Revelation, chapter 14. Here they discovered the sanctuary truth. Shortly afterward, the message of the seventh-day Sabbath was brought to them by a Seventh Day Baptist.

It became clear to those early Adventists that the seventh-day Sabbath is a memorial to God's creative power. Therefore, it was important. The messages of Revelation 14 came into focus, for here God was calling for men and women everywhere to "worship him that made heaven, and earth, and the sea, and the fountains of waters" (Rev. 14:7). They were likewise enjoined "to keep the commandments of God" (verse 12). The seventh-day Sabbath of the fourth commandment was indeed in the heart of God's holy law. He expected them to bring their lives into harmony with this precept and also to teach others this blessed truth.

Sabbathkeeping Adventists now began to understand God's plan for them. The Lord in His goodness had sent a special message to them—not only a message of salvation through Christ and the Saviour's soon return but they were also to tell the world that men and women should bring their lives into harmony with God's holy law, including the fourth commandment. Without this, people would not be prepared for the judgment and the advent of Jesus. Those early believers now better understood what God wanted them to do.

No other church was preaching these messages. God had entrusted this unique mission to them! From this small beginning the Advent message of which you and I are a part has, under God's blessing, reached out into almost every country on earth. This is indeed God's doing.

YOU MAY SAY IT WITH CONVICTION

And I say also unto thee, That thou art Peter, and upon this rock I will build my church; and the gates of hell shall not prevail against it. Matt. 16:18.

A Seventh-day Adventist chaplain in the U.S. Army was discussing religion with a fellow army officer.

"I am going to join the Roman Catholic Church," the officer declared.

"Yes?" our chaplain responded. "And what has led you to this decision?"

There followed an hour or so of straightforward discussion, during which the officer explained at length the reason for his decision. As the conversation neared its close, Colonel Blank looked squarely into the eyes of our chaplain and burst out, "Christ did found a church during His earthly ministry and He declared that the gates of hell would never prevail against it." He paused a moment, then continued. "That church must still be in existence today, and if it isn't the Roman Catholic Church, which is God's true church?"

There was no hesitancy in our chaplain's reply. "Colonel," he said, "the Seventh-day Adventist Church is God's true church."

I do not know how this conversation ended, but I applaud men and women who are members of God's remnant church who are courageous and will speak their convictions.

We are not in existence today merely as one among many of a great Protestant brotherhood of churches, keeping Saturday instead of Sunday, adhering to a few dietary laws, and doing a little welfare work. We are definitely not here as just another church. We are here as the result of fulfilled prophecy. We are here with a message that God, through holy men, declared must be proclaimed to prepare a people for the second advent of Christ. The rise of this movement is foretold in prophecy—in Revelation 10 and 11. The message is found in Revelation 14. No other church is preaching this message.

This does not mean that there are not many children of God in other churches. Neither does it mean that only those who are Seventh-day Adventists today will be saved. During the next few days we will study what it does mean. And what we learn will confirm our faith.

HOW WE MAY BE CERTAIN

And now I have told you before it come to pass, that, when it is come to pass, ye might believe. **John 14:29.**

Holy men of God through whom He spoke during the days of the Old Testament were given various insights into the birth, life, ministry, death, burial, and resurrection of the Messiah to come. Micah foretold the place of the expected One's birth, Bethlehem. Isaiah delineated many events associated with the miraculous birth, the extreme sufferings, and the death of the Messiah. The psalmist sang of His glorious resurrection. Other inspired writers contributed to the Messianic mosaic that serves as convincing evidence that Jesus Christ was indeed the promised Saviour of the world. He, and He alone, fulfilled the prophetic utterances that must be reckoned with.

"Now I have told you before it come to pass," Jesus declared concerning events in His life and the sending of the Holy Spirit, "that, when it is come to pass, ye might believe."

As it was with Jesus Christ's life and ministry, so it is with the rise and progress of His last-day church. There is close agreement between promise and fulfillment. Concerning this important facet of faith Jesus might well repeat His words: "I have told you before it come to pass, that, when it is come to pass, ye might believe."

The Advent Movement *arose on time* in the early 1830's—soon after the 1260-year period of papal persecution had ended.

Our spiritual progenitors *came with the right message*—the basic Adventist doctrines of the little book of Daniel. It was the judgment-hour message found in Revelation 14 as well as in Daniel. This message was Bible based and Christ centered.

The message would go with great speed. It would "fly in the midst of heaven" to "preach unto them that dwell on the earth, and to every nation, and kindred, and tongue, and people" (Rev. 14:6). In one century the Advent message as preached by the Seventh-day Adventist Church has gone from one language and one country to almost all the major languages and to almost all countries of the earth. It was promised. The promise has been fulfilled. This is God's church!

IT APPEARED ON TIME

And the woman fled into the wilderness, where she hath a place prepared of God, that they should feed her there a thousand two hundred and threescore days. Rev. 12:6.

"Do you believe that the Seventh-day Adventist Church constitutes the remnant church, and do you desire to be accepted into its membership?" the pastor was asking a group in the front of the sanctuary.

In unison the baptismal candidates replied, "Yes."

This question from the *Church Manual* is one that confronts every person who applies for membership in the Seventh-day Adventist Church. Its answer should be more than just a "yes" in a chorus of candidates. The affirmative reply should come from a clear understanding that this is indeed God's true church of the remnant.

One of the reasons we may be certain that this is God's true church is that it was called into being at the time the prophetic writers foretold.

In Revelation 12:6 the revelator declares that the woman (the church) would emerge from a 1260-year exile in the wilderness. This prophetic time period covering the era of papal persecution ended in 1798 as almost every Adventist understands. Hence we should look for the emergence of God's remnant soon after that date.

A careful study of the events comprising the sounding of the seventh trumpet of the Apocalypse indicates that these happenings were to occur between 1844 and the second advent of Christ. See chapters 7, 8, and 9 of Daniel, and 11 and 16 of Revelation.

Likewise, some Bible students have held that August 11, 1840, marked the close of the sixth seal of Revelation 9.

These years—1798, 1840, and 1844—comprise a period in prophetic history that must be reckoned with. At least twice Scripture declares that sometime during this period God's last-day church would burst upon the scene.

The rise of the Advent Movement with its messages emphasizing the imminent return of Christ fits precisely into this period of history beginning about 1831.

God's remnant appeared on time!

IT ALL ADDS UP!

Hold fast the form of sound words, which thou hast heard of me, in faith and love which is in Christ Jesus. **2 Tim. 1:13.**

If your life depended upon correctly adding a long column of figures, you would add them once, and then you would go back over the figures and check and recheck them to be absolutely certain you had the correct answer. You must be absolutely certain.

Your eternal life depends upon your understanding and acceptance of the truths of God's Word. Make no mistake about it—you must know God's will and way, and this knowledge must be translated into a life of faith and obedience.

I once heard a man say, "The trouble with you Seventh-day Adventists is that you are right and you know you are right." He meant these words as a slurring rebuke. God's people should never be proud or boastful, but if there is one thing we must make certain, it is that we are following God's Holy Word to the very best of our understanding. We must be right and we must know that we are right. There must be no question about it. Eternal life is too precious for us to gamble on any "hope so's." With Paul we must be able to say with assurance, "I know whom I have believed, and am persuaded that he is able to keep that which I have committed unto him against that day" (2 Tim. 1:12).

Of God's last-day message you may be certain. The prophetic portion adds up like an arithmetic problem. You can check and recheck it to be absolutely certain.

We are living in the very last days. The time of the end is upon us. Jesus is coming soon, very soon.

The message of Daniel and Revelation must be preached to prepare men and women for this climactic event.

Those who claim to be God's remnant will be preaching this message. They will not only profess Christ as their Saviour and Lord, they will keep His Ten Commandments, including the fourth.

They will also have in their midst "the testimony of Jesus" which is "the spirit of prophecy" (Rev. 12:17; 19:10).

This movement must be a worldwide movement.

"YOU HAVE TO BELONG TO THE FAMILY"

For this cause I bow my knees unto the Father of our Lord Jesus Christ, of whom the whole family in heaven and earth is named. **Eph. 3:14, 15.**

Bonnie and Billy were riding with their parents through an affluent part of their city. Passing a large home with huge iron gates barring the driveway, Bonnie spotted two shiny red bicycles and other toys just inside the gates.

"Oh, Mamma," Bonnie squealed with delight. "Let's stop and go in and play with the lovely toys!"

Billy eyed his little sister with big-brother disdain. "Silly girl," he said. "You can't go in there and ride those bicycles and play with those toys. Don't you know you have to belong to the family to play with those things!"

"You have to belong to the family to play with those things!" The words carry a challenge far beyond the world of primary-age youngsters longing for toys. Belonging to the family—God's family—is the most blessed prospect any of us could desire.

The apostle Paul speaks of the family in heaven and the family on earth. Today God is making up His family on earth in preparation for the time so soon to come when the family of God on earth will become the family of God in heaven.

We become members of the family by birth or by adoption. Jesus Himself declared, "Ye must be born again" (John 3:7). The natural birth does not prepare us for the family of God. There must be a change—a transformation of life that begets the attributes, the characteristics, of our heavenly Father's family. With this change comes the adoption process. Paul refers to this as "the adoption of sons" (Gal. 4:5). What a privilege! "God can bestow no higher honor upon mortals than to adopt them into His family, giving them the privilege of calling Him Father."—*Fundamentals of Christian Education,* p. 481.

When we belong to the family we then have access not only to the joys or the toys of this life that soon are gone but "to an inheritance . . . that fadeth not away" (1 Peter 1:4).

What joy when we truly belong to the family.

COWARDS AND WEAKLINGS

As for us, we have this large crowd of witnesses around us. Let us rid ourselves, then, of everything that gets in the way, and the sin which holds on to us so tightly, and let us run with determination the race that lies before us. Heb. 12:1, T.E.V.

On the wall of the Iowa State Capitol building in Des Moines is a challenging mural. The work of art portrays the spirit of the pioneers who conquered the West during the past century. The scene depicts a young husband and wife moving across hostile plains in a covered wagon. The wife holds a babe in one arm and drives a team with the other. The man, his face tense, holds a gun prepared for any eventuality.

Beneath the mural are these words: "The cowards never started and the weaklings dropped out along the way."

Stop and consider these words a moment. They are worth a second thought. "The cowards never started and the weaklings dropped out along the way."

It requires true courage for many a person to take his stand for God's last-day message. For some it means giving up a good position demanding Sabbath attendance. Some have had their own family or friends turn against them when they allied themselves "with those strange people." On some rare occasions men and women have had to decide between the truth and life itself. *The cowards never start.*

To be a loyal Seventh-day Adventist one must not only make a brave beginning, he must persevere—sometimes under discouraging circumstances. For like the Iowa pioneers, *the weaklings drop out along the way.*

It is easier to rationalize than to stabilize, to postulate than to practice. It is less difficult to yield than to stand—to be a Demas than to be a Daniel. Pluralism is more popular than hewing steadfastly to unique truth. It is easier to quit than to conquer—to give up than to give all. Being a true Seventh-day Adventist in our permissive age requires a holy tenacity, for the weaklings drop out along the way.

But there is help. "Lo, I am with you alway, even unto the end of the world," Jesus assures us (Matt. 28:20). So let us "run with determination the race that lies before us."

105

THE RIVER HE COULD NOT CROSS

Afterward he measured a thousand; and it was a river that I could not pass over: for the waters were risen, waters to swim in, a river that could not be passed over. Eze. 47:5.

In May, 1971, I walked across the Mississippi River in five steps! This, of course, was not in New Orleans, Louisiana, or in Memphis, Tennessee. It was in central Minnesota where this legendary river rises. I stood on the shores of lovely Lake Itasca and watched the crystal-clear waters overflow and begin their long journey to the sea. You can take your choice in crossing the river at this point. Large smooth stones provide a slippery pathway for the more daring. A well-placed sign warns venturesome tourists that the stones are slippery. I chose the heavy plank that spans Ole Miss a few feet downstream. I made it in five easy steps.

On a nearby rustic sign we read these words: "Here 1,475 feet above the ocean the mighty Mississippi begins to flow on its winding way 2,552 miles to the Gulf of Mexico."

As I stood with Elder and Mrs. J. L. Dittberner gazing into the cool clear waters I marveled at the thought that this twisting, turning, growing, widening stream would make its way through and around all sorts of obstacles until it reached its destination hundreds of miles south. It reminded me of the words of the prophet Ezekiel: "When the man that had the line in his hand went forth eastward, he measured a thousand cubits, and he brought me through the waters; the waters were to the ankles. Again he measured a thousand, and brought me through the waters; the waters were to the knees. Again he measured a thousand, and brought me through; the waters were to the loins. Afterward he measured a thousand; and it was a river that I could not pass over: for the waters were risen, waters to swim in, a river that could not be passed over" (Eze. 47:3-5).

This in turn reminds me of the onward progress of God's message. Beginning as a tiny rill a century ago, it is now reaching flood stage. In the lifetime of Seventh-day Adventists now living, this truth has grown from one language in one country to more than 523 languages in 193 countries. And yet God's mighty river flows on!

BE READY ALWAYS

If anybody asks [you] why you believe as you do, be ready to tell him, and do it in a gentle and respectful way. 1 Peter 3:15, T.L.B.

I was a guest on a nationwide TV hookup in a country far from the United States. The master of ceremonies on the interview program was the owner of the station, and one who knew Seventh-day Adventists favorably. Among those on our program panel was the defense minister of the country, a senator who at one time had served as vice-president of the federal government, a Moslem governor, a former cabinet member, and two or three others.

Turning to me, the M.C. asked, "And just what does that name *Seventh-day Adventist* mean?" This is always the question I am pleased to be asked under such circumstances, for it affords fine opportunity "to give . . . a reason of the hope that is in" me. I took time carefully to explain our hope in a soon-coming Saviour and that as Christians we follow Christ in the observance of the seventh-day Sabbath.

Turning to the minister of defense and the senator, the M.C. asked, "I presume you two gentlemen are Christians; which day of the week do you observe as your day of rest?"

"We observe Sunday," both replied.

"Why?" was the next question that followed quickly.

The two surprised officials looked at each other rather helplessly and stammered, "We don't know just why!"

Turning to the Moslem governor, the M.C. continued, "You are a Moslem, I believe. Sir, which day of the week do the Moslems observe as their day of rest?"

"Moslems observe Friday as their holy day," came back the quick reply.

"And why do you observe Friday?" came the next pointed question.

The Moslem gentleman smiled nervously. "I'm sorry, I am not very much up on these religious matters. I am afraid I can't explain just why we observe Friday."

I am glad the great truths of the Advent message are Bible based and Christ centered. They are defensible We need not fear embarrassment or defeat when we explain in a gentle and respectful way why we believe as we do.

SQUEEZED INTO THE WORLD'S MOLD

Note this first: in the last days there will come men who scoff at religion and live self-indulgent lives. **2 Peter 3:3, N.E.B.**

Many people today appear to believe that anything is moral if you enjoy doing it. If the majority of the people around you are doing it, it's all right. If there isn't any visible "harm" in your actions—go ahead—there isn't anything wrong about it! If it seems "the loving thing" to do, an aura of respectability is cast about the questionable action.

"These sociological views have influenced jurisprudence considerably. Thus the Supreme Court of the United States, starting with a moral and ethical relativity first articulated by Justice Oliver Wendell Holmes, has come to accept as normative the codes and conduct common to the community. In effect this means that if the community finds nudity, pornography, and homosexuality acceptable, these things are juridically legitimate. There are no absolute standards that are controlling at all times and under all circumstances. What the community accepts today is the rule of life. If it changes to something else tomorrow, this new thing becomes normative even if it is the exact opposite of what was in force yesterday." —HAROLD LINDSELL, in *Christianity Today,* Sept. 11, 1970, p. 4. Copyright 1970 by *Christianity Today.* Reprinted by permission.

The apostle Peter viewed the free-wheeling, indulgent days in which we live. He recognized them as "the last days." "There will come men who scoff at religion and live self-indulgent lives."

To yield to the permissiveness of our times is not the course the true child of God will choose. Seventh-day Adventists are to be a called-out people. A morality gap should set us apart from those who present merely "a form of godliness" (2 Tim. 3:5).

Our privilege, our high destiny, is to be different. As followers of Christ everything is not open-ended, not situational —wrong today, right tomorrow. Just because the majority around us are doing it does not make it right. Morality is not judged by the majority. The majority have often been wrong.

We do not scoff—we obey!

A 400,000 TRILLION, TRILLION, TRILLION, TRILLION TO ONE CHANCE!

By faith we understand that the world was created by the word of God, so that what is seen was made out of things which do not appear. **Heb. 11:3, R.S.V.**

"What I believe about the supernatural is derived from what I was taught by my parents, and what they taught me was derived from what they were taught, and so on," wrote Edmund R. Leach in the last published issue of the *Saturday Evening Post*. "But such beliefs are justified by faith alone, never by reason, and the true believer is expected to go on reaffirming his faith in the same verbal formula."

For more than a century atheistic evolutionists have belittled Creation and the Creator by such sweeping statements, disparaging faith. Such detractors of God and God's Word would seek to create the illusion that in the hypothesis of evolution there is no need of faith—all is a proved fact. This is not true!

When it comes to the question of ultimate origin, that first cause still has not been proved. Life, we are told, had its origin when living protoplasm suddenly appeared in a sea of mud multiplied millions of years ago. Where did the *original* molecule, the first neutron, electron, proton, come from?

There has to be a first cause. Life had to begin sometime, somewhere. A rose, a cat, a horse, a tree, a child, a heaven full of stars—they are all here. We see them. We know they exist. But life had to have some point of beginning. The believer finds this beginning in God as Creator.

"The odds were against the right combination of circumstances occurring to evolve intelligent life on earth—about 400,000 trillion trillion trillion trillion to one," Sir John Eccles, Nobel laureate in neurophysiology, is quoted in the June, 1970, issue of *These Times.* Though Sir John indicated his belief in such a hypothesis he admitted it was "fantastically improbable."

To me it is much more logical to accept the inspired words of Paul and believe in an omniscient Creator, than in a vast and complex universe originating from nothing by a multiplied-trillions-to-one chance!

PUNCTUALITY HELPS!

So teach us to number our days, that we may apply our hearts unto wisdom. Ps. 90:12.

A friend of mine was reared in a Lutheran home in Denmark years ago. Emmanuel's parents were sticklers for punctuality. When appointments were made they were met promptly.

One evening the Lutheran parents were invited to hear a prominent minister of another Protestant faith. The meeting was scheduled to begin at eight o'clock. At ten minutes after eight the speaker strode onto the platform. Rightly or wrongly, Emmanuel's parents paid scant heed to what he had to say "because he did not keep his appointments" and "if his faith permitted laxness here, perhaps there were other weaknesses." The good Lutheran parents never went again to hear this speaker.

Then a Seventh-day Adventist evangelist came to town. Friends heard Pastor Raft speak. They were favorably impressed with the truths from God's Word. They invited Emmanuel's parents to attend. The invitation was accepted.

Exactly at eight o'clock, the time scheduled for the meeting to begin, Pastor Raft strode, Bible in hand, onto the platform. The Lutheran parents were impressed. He was on time. They were even more impressed with the message of truth to which they listened. Night after night they returned. Each night the meeting opened promptly as the clock pointed the hour. Each sermon was packed full of good things from the Word.

In this instance truth and punctuality, hand in hand, brought a family into God's remnant church.

The Lord may not bless you with a soul if you are always punctual, but many people with whom you associate will rise up and call you blessed if you don't waste their time by causing them to have to wait for you to meet an appointment. In addition, if you watch your minutes, the hours will take care of themselves and you will have improved your own status in life.

We need to learn to hoard our minutes as well as to number our days!

UNCONDITIONAL SURRENDER DOES IT!

Presumptuous are they, selfwilled. 2 Peter 2:10.

Reformation that follows true revival requires that the individual place his will on God's side. The struggle against sin at best is traumatic. Arrayed on one side of the controversy is God the Father, Jesus the Son, the Holy Spirit, and the angels. Opposing these powers of righteousness are Satan and all the sinister influence of fallen angels. The battleground is the human heart. The tempted one, with eternity at stake, has a very important role to play. He must *choose* to do what is right—*he must place his will on God's side if he expects to win the battle!*

The apostle Peter describes those who are lost as "presumptuous, selfwilled." The redeemed, those who wear the robe of Christ's righteousness, have fully surrendered their wills to God. The Lord did not force them. They *willed* to do right.

"The Lord does not design that human power should be paralyzed; but by cooperating with God, the power of man may be efficient for good. God does not design that our will should be destroyed; for it is through this very attribute that we are to accomplish the work He would have us to do."—*Selected Messages,* book 1, pp. 375, 376.

There can be no question about God's desire to cleanse and keep us from sin. His will is clear. He hears, forgives, cleanses, strengthens. Our part is clear. We "come unto the knowledge of the truth" (1 Tim. 2:4). We confess our sins and give ourselves wholly to God. We *will* to serve Him. Just as surely as we do this, God fulfills His word to us.

Just as Christ submitted His will to the Father's—"Not my will, but thine, be done" (Luke 22:42)—so you and I will find victory when we surrender our will to the Saviour and say simply, "Thy will be done." With our will and His will bound together in complete oneness there can be no failure. We can safely say, "Lord, You just take complete charge. Lead and direct every step of the way. My yesterdays, todays, and tomorrows are all in Your hands."

Faith-filled and fully surrendered, we need have no fear. Victory is ours.

IS HE IN THE PROTEST MOVEMENT?

Jesus said: "My kingdom does not belong to this world; if my kingdom belonged to this world, my followers would fight to keep me from being handed over to the Jews. No, my kingdom does not belong here!" John 18:36, T.E.V.

A tiny tot, caught up in the spirit of her times, approached her teacher. "Miss Jennings, I want to protest," she lisped earnestly, then paused thoughtfully, "but I don't know what to protest about." Contention and opposition to anything and everything are in the very air we breathe.

As I write, for many months the campuses of American colleges and universities have been aboil with violent protest demonstrations. The streets of American cities have been bathed in blood and littered with debris by protesters of every ilk. Countless persons have been injured. Many have lost their lives in this violent vortex of protest.

I have learned sadly that all who write and march and demonstrate are not moved by the Spirit of Christ. I do not find Christ in the stoning, the brutal battling, the occupying, the violent protesting too prevalent in many parts of the world today. There are some words from the Lord that apply to this means of seeking redress.

"Put up again thy sword" (Matt. 26:52), Jesus commanded when Peter resorted to violence. Would He not say the same today?

"The government under which Jesus lived was corrupt and oppressive; on every hand were crying abuses,—extortion, intolerance, and grinding cruelty. Yet the Saviour attempted no civil reforms. He attacked no national abuses, nor condemned the national enemies. He did not interfere with the authority or administration of those in power. He who was our example kept aloof from earthly governments. Not because He was indifferent to the woes of men, but because the remedy did not lie in merely human and external measures. To be efficient, the cure must reach men individually, and must regenerate the heart."—*The Desire of Ages*, p. 509.

"I am meek and lowly in heart," Jesus declares (chap. 11:29). The way of Christ is the way of peace, the way of love, the way of reason.

WHAT IT IS ALL ABOUT

They that shall be of thee shall build the old waste places: thou shalt raise up the foundations of many generations; and thou shalt be called, The repairer of the breach, The restorer of paths to dwell in. Isa. 58:12.

Repairers—restorers—how much this world of ours needs such people today!

The word *restorer* is derived from a Hebrew root meaning "to return (back)," "to bring back home," "to cause to recover," "to cause to rescue," "to cause to return." It is the same original from which the verb in Psalm 23:2 comes: "He restoreth my soul."

The gospel of the kingdom is a message of restoration—restoration of obscured, forgotten, or ignored Bible truth. This message calls men and women back to "the old paths." "Thus saith the Lord, Stand ye in the ways, and see, and ask for the old paths, where is the good way, and walk therein, and ye shall find rest for your souls" (Jer. 6:16).

Seventh-day Adventists are more "restorers" as was Elijah than we are initiators as was Moses. "Jesus answered and said unto them, Elias truly shall first come, and restore all things" (Matt. 17:11). The work of the Elijah message, in a sense, is a message that calls men and women to restore truths that have long been neglected, ignored, or forgotten.

The Rotherham translation of our text for the day declares that we are to be restorers "of paths leading home." In reviving the proclamation of vital truths long obscured by the darkness of tradition, Seventh-day Adventists are in reality preparing the way for the last stretch homeward bound. This is a challenging assignment, indeed.

Man's mortal nature, the imminent visible return of Christ, the millennium, and other truths of the Word, had become distorted or forgotten through the centuries. These must be restored to their rightful place in God's temple of truth. Repairers of the breach were called into being from many lands, and the great work of restoration has now been under way for well over a century.

This is what the Christ-centered Advent Movement is all about.

WHAT ABOUT SOCIAL ACTION?

These ought ye to have done, and not to leave the other undone. Matt. 23:23.

There are myriads of problems in the world today, and men and women, young and old, are seeking valiantly to solve them in many different ways. Change by social service plays an important role in many of these solutions. Community uplift is a noble undertaking. Many sincere government agencies and socially oriented youth seek to extinguish the fires of unrest and need by a host of poverty programs, social reforms, improved living, and industrial conditions.

But social action alone is not enough. Such programs alone provide only a scab on the wound. The causes of the inequities, the seething ferment, remain. Prejudice, frustration, hate, still smolder. A permanent change must search deeper. The source of the problem, not the result, must be dealt with. The Good News must accompany the good works.

Jesus not only "went about doing good," He declared that the "remission of sins should be preached in his name" (Acts 10:38; Luke 24:47). He instructed the men from whom He had cast out devils, "Go home to thy friends, and tell them how great things the Lord hath done for thee" (Mark 5:19). We are to do good. We are to go tell.

"Man is not only hungry and needs to be fed, He is not only ignorant and needs to be educated, He is not only naked and needs to be clothed. He is spiritually lost and needs to be redeemed. . . . The basic problem of man is the fundamental derangement and disharmony at the very center of human nature, his estrangement from God."—J. T. SEAMANDS, *The Supreme Task of the Church* (Grand Rapids: Eerdman's, 1964), p. 18.

To substitute anthropology for theology is not enough. To replace faith in God with faith in man is no permanent solution to the problems of the poor and needy in our time. Christ's saving grace and Christ's example must be in the picture as well as Christ's works. Were He on earth today He would doubtless say, "These ought ye to have done, and not to leave the other undone." Here is the Master's blueprint of service for young and old in our day.

A DAY IN CAPERNAUM

The Son of man came not to be ministered unto, but to minister. Matt. 20:28.

It was Sabbath in Capernaum. As men gathered within the halls of their large stone synagogue they heard the melodious voice of a young Galilean speaking. It was Jesus of Nazareth teaching the people: "They were astounded at his teaching, for what he said had the note of authority" (Luke 4:31, 32, N.E.B.).

Suddenly a loud shriek rang out, drawing their attention from the Saviour's words, as a madman pushed his way to the front. Somehow in his demon-possessed mind he must have realized he was in the presence of One who could set him free. The agony of his soul, expressed through the crying out of demons within, reached the ear of One who could and would help. At Christ's command the demons came out and the cleansed man fell prostrate at His feet, whole.

That same day, in a fisherman's cottage, another miracle followed. Peter's mother-in-law lay suffering with a high fever. Standing over her, Jesus rebuked the fever. Immediately she arose and served her family and guests. It would seem from the record that Jesus now might have had food and a little rest—but not for long.

As soon as the sun set all in Capernaum evidently knew where to find Jesus, for "from the homes, the shops, the market places, the inhabitants of the city pressed toward the humble dwelling that sheltered Jesus. The sick were brought upon couches, they came leaning upon staffs, or, supported by friends, they tottered feebly into the Saviour's presence."—*The Desire of Ages,* p. 259.

"Hour after hour they came. . . . Never before had Capernaum witnessed a day like this."—*Ibid.*

Jesus healed them all. He did not stop His work of healing until far into the night—not until the last sufferer was made whole and had gone to his home. Then Jesus lay down on His bed to rest, tired but happy. "He rejoiced in His power to restore them to health and happiness."—*Ibid.*

What a wonderful day in the life of our Saviour! He would have His followers emulate and strive to follow His example.

DO WHAT I DO!

*And he said unto them, Look on me, and do likewise: and, behold, when
I come to the outside of the camp, it shall be that, as I do, so shall ye do.
Judges 7:17.*

When Gideon spoke these words to his followers he had no
thought of theology. He was speaking to the camp of Israelites explaining his strategy for attacking the Midianites. Success
in their undertaking lay in their close attention to his example, and following explicitly what he would do.

" 'Watch me,' " he instructed his men: " 'when I come to the
edge of the camp, do exactly as I do. When I and my men blow
our trumpets, you too all around the camp will blow your
trumpets, and shout, "For the Lord and for Gideon" ' " (Judges
7:17, 18, N.E.B.).

Actually, this bit of military strategy and instruction pro-
pounded by Gideon before he went into battle fourteen centuries before Christ contains some vital counsel for those of us
engaged in the Christian warfare today.

Look on me, and do likewise. These words bear no expression of humility. Where is Christ our example in such a command? "It shall be that, as I do, so shall ye do" are not words
bolstering a Christ-centered philosophy. Should not Christ
and not ourselves be the pattern for Christian conduct?

This is true. Christ should and must be our example. But
think of it this way—you and I should be following our great
Exemplar so closely that our lives will reflect His. We will probably never lead a victorious army as did Gideon but in the
Christian warfare we must reflect the attributes of Jesus so
that we will be able to say, "Look on me, and do likewise."

Centuries later the apostle Paul had this same thought in
mind when he wrote to the believers in Philippi. "Those
things, which ye have both learned, and received, and heard,
and seen in me, do: and the God of peace shall be with you"
(Phil. 4:9).

What people hear of and from us and what they see in us
influences them. Paul realized this and by God's grace he was
determined to so live that no one would be caused to stumble
because of his wrong example.

"I WANT TO BE LIKE YOU!"

From the very beginning God decided that those who came to him—and all along he knew who would—should become like his Son. **Rom. 8:29, T.L.B.**

A group of Seventh-day Adventist youth from one of our colleges were at work in a nearby inner city. One child from the streets sat daily in the classes. Henry's clothes were ragged, his feet were bare. It was evident he had very little of this world's goods.

Then one day Henry appeared in class well dressed, well groomed. He was a different child. His youthful tutor, who, despite counsel from those who supervised his work, came perhaps too well groomed each day, was surprised.

"Well, Henry, you are all dressed up today," his teacher exclaimed. "Is this some special day for you?"

The lad looked up into the face of his friend. A broad grin creased his face. "I want to be like you!" Henry exclaimed enthusiastically.

"I want to be like you"—what a testimony! What a tribute! What a challenge!

"From the very beginning," from the days of eternity when the Father and the Son counseled together about the creation of man, it has been God's desire and intention that the creatures of His hands would "become like his Son."

In this life man's physical likeness to his Creator has been sadly marred by sin. Six thousand years of transgression have so degraded him that today man's physical resemblance to his Maker must be faint indeed.

Yet we are to "become like his Son" in character. Through justification and sanctification—the imputed and imparted righteousness of Christ—the child of God may become more and more like his divine Example. It is the good news of the gospel that such a marvelous transformation is possible.

"The change is effected by the union of the human with the divine. As the Son of God took upon Himself our human nature, so Christians may become the temples of the Holy Spirit (1 Cor. 6:19), and Christ will dwell in them (John 14: 23). Thus the believer becomes a partaker of the divine nature (2 Peter 1:4)."—*The SDA Bible Commentary*, on Rom. 8:29.

"YOU ARE THE WORLD'S SEASONING"

You are the world's seasoning, to make it tolerable. If you lose your flavor, what will happen to the world? And you yourselves will be thrown out and trampled underfoot as worthless. Matt. 5:13, T.L.B.

As Adventists, we frequently encounter interesting people on the buses, trains, ships, and planes. Take the experience of Mrs. Ruth Hagen Wade on a flight from New Orleans to Omaha. Mrs. Wade found herself sitting by a Catholic priest. Soon they were discussing world conditions.

"What do you think about the second coming of Christ?" Ruth asked.

"Well," the cleric replied, "you know there are many different theories on the subject." The man of the cloth paused thoughtfully, then continued, "Now you take the Seventh-day Adventists, for instance. They have a clear-cut doctrine on the Second Advent."

Mrs. Wade's interest heightened. "Yes?" she queried, attempting to conceal her rising interest.

"Yes," the priest continued, "the Adventists have it down pat. They explain it all from the Bible. I am not an Adventist," he hastened to add, "but I confess their teaching on the subject is quite clear."

There was a pause. The priest did not yet know to which church Ruth belonged. Then, "You know, those Adventists are interesting people and they have quite a program going around the world. I've seen their work in the Far East and down in South America, and it is something to be admired. The lives of the people they serve are surely changed. The morals and the way of life of a community are different after the Adventists arrive. My church could learn much from the way these people work in different parts of the world."

"He kept on extolling the virtues of Seventh-day Adventist medical and educational work for fifteen or twenty minutes," Ruth said later, telling the experience to her father.

We are most grateful for this change of attitude on the part of so many. It does, however, place a tremendous responsibility upon us. If we are to be the world's seasoning, we must live up to the expectations of both God and our fellow men! By God's grace we dare not fail either!

WRITING OUR OWN TICKETS

The just man walketh in his integrity: his children are blessed after him.
Prov. 20:7.

The honesty and integrity of the normal practicing Adventist does not go unnoticed among those not of our faith. Reporting on good credit risks, one issue of *Burroughs Clearing House* stated, "Seventh-day Adventists, who take their religion seriously, can virtually write their own tickets."

A dictionary definition declares integrity is an "unimpaired condition—adherence to a code of moral, artistic, or other values." The Word of God declares that integrity is one of the first fruits of Christian ethics. In a time when the new morality scorns the constant rule of right and wrong, the child of God still adheres to a code of morals—that which the Word of God sets forth.

"Better be poor and above reproach," the wise man says, "than rich and crooked in speech" (Prov. 19:1, N.E.B.). Integrity, even though on rare occasions it may lead to poverty, is to be chosen above devious speech and action and great riches. In other words there are still Christian business ethics to which the follower of the Nazarene adheres.

It is encouraging to know that "Seventh-day Adventists, who take their religion seriously, can virtually write their own tickets." The serious Adventist is conscientious about meeting his financial obligations on time.

Nearly a century ago an editor of the Healdsburg, California, paper wrote of the Adventists of his day and of his community:

"They are a class of people who seem to strive to practice what they profess; they are industrious and abstemious to the last degree. They seem to have a good way of minding their own business, paying their debts, saying but little brag of themselves and no ill of their neighbors. They are a class that will never do Healdsburg any harm but are a valuable acquisition. We are pleased at their strength."—HAROLD OLIVER McCUMBER, *Pioneering the Message in the Golden West*, p. 160.

Not a bad set of principles for Seventh-day Adventists of 1975, is it? May the Lord help us to continue to be able to "write our own tickets."

MIGHTY TO SAVE

Who is this that cometh from Edom, with dyed garments from Bozrah? this that is glorious in his apparel, travelling in the greatness of his strength? I that speak in righteousness, mighty to save. Isa. 63:1.

Seven centuries before His incarnation, the Son of God foretold His mission of might. "Travelling in the greatness of his strength," the man of Galilee would "speak in righteousness," confirming His words with deeds of Omnipotence. Daily He revealed Himself "mighty to save" through the miracles of grace that He performed.

The words in righteousness spoken by the world's Redeemer transformed a raving, restless demoniac among the wilds of Gadara into a quiet, obedient disciple. The apostle Mark describes this devil-possessed person before he came into contact with Jesus: "This man lived among the gravestones, and had such strength that whenever he was put into handcuffs and shackles—as often he was—he snapped the handcuffs from his wrists and smashed the shackles and walked away. No one was strong enough to control him. All day long and through the night he would wander among the tombs and in the wild hills, screaming and cutting himself with sharp pieces of stone" (Mark 5:3-5, T.L.B.).

Then Jesus came. The scene quickly changed. The raving ceased. The savage became sober. The taunts became entreaties. The demoniac became a suppliant. The destroyer became a disciple. The wilderness soon became a babble of humanity. Never had the onlookers witnessed such a spectacle.

The great Deliverer still walks the hills and dales of this earth's needs. Jesus is "mighty to save" from the more common devil possession of our sophisticated society. The devils of alcohol, tobacco, or drug addiction, of impure thoughts and practices, of unruly tongues, the imps of dishonesty and untruthfulness, are just as deadly as the possession experienced by the man of Gadara.

Thank God He is still mighty to save from these as well!

BABYLON IS BACK!

Thou art wearied in the multitude of thy counsels. Let now the astrologers, the stargazers, the monthly prognosticators, stand up, and save thee from these things that shall come upon thee. Isa. 47:13.

I turned on the radio. For a few minutes I listened to a warm feminine voice advising, "You who were born under the sign of Capricorn have a surprise coming today." I could almost see thousands of young Capricorn children lean forward to catch every word. They were interested in surprises.

"You will receive some money from an unexpected source," the radio voice continued. I had heard that one many times in the Orient from unsophisticated street-walking fortunetellers in Bombay.

The occult explosion with all of its subtitles—astrology, magic, tarot, Satan worship, séances—and its ten thousand professional astrologers and forty million Americans, has helped turn the zodiac into a colossal business.

People gather in Minneapolis for a ten-week course in witchcraft. Hundreds of others come for classes in astrology, yoga, and palmistry. Small church groups have developed courses that acquaint their members with the world of mystery. It is a new day for the occult.

But what's new in this renaissance of black magic, séances, and metaphysical madness? Nothing much! It was the "in thing" in Daniel's day 600 years before Christ. It was a "well-developed and important science in ancient Babylon. The heavens were carefully studied for portents of coming events." —*The SDA Bible Commentary,* on Isa. 47:13, p. 273.

What good did it do in Daniel's day? Not much! "The labors of Babylonian stargazers were to no purpose. Isaiah challenges the Babylonian wise men to continue with their practice of the occult arts and find out for themselves what advantage it might bring them at the hour of doom the Lord had foretold."—*Ibid.,* on Isa. 47:13.

The Lord of heaven would no doubt issue the same challenge today to those who choose the occult to the living God. The astrologers and the stargazers can no more save sinners from the wrath to come in our day than they could in Daniel's or Isaiah's!

THE WHOLE CHURCH NEEDS REVIVAL

Wilt thou not revive us again: that thy people may rejoice in thee? **Ps. 85:6.**

The revival and reformation experience into which God is calling His people reaches into every area of the remnant church. The call is to churches, to schools, to medical institutions, and to publishing houses.

To workers in our hospitals and clinics the servant of the Lord says: "A work of reformation is to be carried on in our institutions. Physicians. workers, nurses, are to realize that they are on probation."—*Testimonies,* vol. 6, p. 253. Those who serve the Great Physician are to become like the Great Physician. Such an experience calls for revival and reformation.

Inspiration faithfully depicts the need for revival in our schools: "Should Christ enter our institutions for the education of the youth, He would cleanse them as He cleansed the temple, banishing many things that have a defiling influence."— *Counsels to Parents and Teachers,* p. 25. Only a Heaven-sent revival can cleanse some of the educational institutions of worldliness and traces of modernism.

If our medical and educational institutions are to become all that God would have them be, our churches must be revival-based bastions of righteousness. A great need for revival exists within our churches. "We need a thorough reformation in all our churches," says the Lord's messenger. "The converting power of God must come into the church."—*Testimonies to Ministers,* p. 443.

Our institutions are to a certain extent what our churches make them. The leaders in our hospitals, schools, and publishing houses are first Seventh-day Adventist church members— the product of the spirituality or the lack of spirituality of the church.

"Satan is very artful, busy, and active. His special power is brought to bear upon those who are now engaged in the work of preaching or publishing the present truth."—*Testimonies,* vol. 1, p. 586.

Churches are made up of individuals—just like you, like me, and like thousands more. We all need revival and reformation. O Lord, "wilt thou not revive us again?"

WHEN TROUBLE COMES

I am with thee, saith the Lord. Jer. 1:19.

The prophet Jeremiah had his troubles. Everyone, it seemed, joined to make his life miserable.

When King Jehoiakim heard the words of the prophet read by Jeremiah's friend, Baruch, he ordered the rolls destroyed. "When Jehudi had read three or four columns of the scroll, the king cut them off with a penknife and threw them into the fire in the brazier. He went on doing so until the whole scroll had been thrown on the fire" (Jer. 36:23, N.E.B.).

The chief governor of the house of the Lord joined those who persecuted the prophet. "Then Pashur smote Jeremiah the prophet, and put him in the stocks that were in the high gate of Benjamin, which was by the house of the Lord" (chap. 20:2).

His neighbors plotted against Jeremiah. "I had been like a sheep led obedient to the slaughter; I did not know that they were hatching plots against me and saying, 'Let us cut down the tree while the sap is in it; let us destroy him out of the living, so that his very name shall be forgotten'" (chap. 11:19, N.E.B.).

Even the friends of the man of God sought opportunity to wreak revenge upon the hapless prophet. "For I heard many whispering, 'Denounce him! we will denounce him.' All my friends were on the watch for a false step, saying 'Perhaps he may be tricked, then we can catch him and take our revenge'" (chap. 20:10, N.E.B.).

To make his cup even more bitter Jeremiah's own family turned against him. In fact, everyone—"all the people"— denounced the prophet of doom and demanded his death. "So the priests and the prophets and all the people heard Jeremiah speaking these words in the house of the Lord. Now it came to pass, when Jeremiah had made an end of speaking all that the Lord had commanded him to speak unto all the people, that the priests and the prophets and all the people took him, saying, Thou shalt surely die" (chap. 26:7, 8).

Yet through it all the Lord stood by Jeremiah. "I am with thee, saith the Lord" (chap. 1:19).

When God is on our side we are in the majority. We need not fear though troubles come.

WOMEN PLAY A PART

She stretched out her hand to the poor; yea, she reached forth her hands to the needy. **Prov. 31:20.**

Throughout Scripture one finds women playing an important role in the world and in the church. Miriam was both a prophetess and a musician. She also wielded much power in the days of Moses and Aaron. Some decades later "Deborah, a prophetess, the wife of Lapidoth, she judged Israel at that time" (Judges 4:4).

Abigail, wife of Nabal, displayed unusual talents in diplomacy in David's day. Anna was a prophetess. Mary, the mother of Jesus, was a deep student of Scripture. Dorcas displayed outstanding talent as a welfare worker. Paul called Priscilla one of his "helpers in Christ Jesus" (Rom. 16:3).

"Many women . . . followed Jesus . . . ministering unto him" (Matt. 27:55). Other women were close to the Saviour, distinguishing themselves during His life and at His death and after His resurrection. A woman anointed the Saviour's head at the home of Simon the leper and wiped His feet with her hair (see Mark 14:3 and Luke 7:37). A woman was the last one at the cross when the Saviour died (see Mark 15:47). One was first at the tomb following His resurrection (see John 20:1). A feminine voice was the first to proclaim the resurrection (see Matt. 28:8).

In our day women are playing an increasingly important role in public life. Around the world they are making their contribution to the welfare of the people.

In Alliance, Ohio, Mrs. Cleatus Young, teacher's aide and mother of two college students, organized a Faith-in-Action program through which hundreds of unemployed found jobs. In White River, Arizona, Mrs. Minnie Guenther, after rearing nine youngsters of her own, acted as "mother" to thousands of Apache Indian children. In New York City, Mrs. Mae Hendrickson, an 86-year-old volunteer, received the United Hospital Fund's highest award for 25,000 hours of service. In Chagrin Falls, Ohio, Mrs. Gini Laurie ran an international information service for the handicapped.

This is as it should be and it is only a beginning in the long saga of feminine accomplishments.

IT'S FOR REAL!

We rejoice in God through our Lord Jesus Christ, who has now made us God's friends. **Rom. 5:11, T.E.V.**

A hard-bitten young army nurse was driving along an Eastern highway "looking for a pole to crash into," she later confessed bitterly.

"I wanted so much to die," she wrote. "I can still remember what kind of day it was. The sun was just coming up, throwing a red haze over the snow-covered mountains. It was oh, so beautiful, but I was so full of hate! For me there was no such thing as love in the whole wide world. I had no love in me then. I had no friends. I was alone."

In her bitterness, Linda (let's call her that) pressed hard on the accelerator, half hoping the speed on the icy mountain roads would send her hurtling into oblivion. Her radio was blaring. Then it happened. The Voice of Prophecy program came on. Something new and different crept into her heart.

"I can still remember the words as though they were spoken yesterday," Linda testified. "I needed a friend. I needed love and someone to love. I heard Pastor Richards say something about the love of Jesus for everyone. I couldn't believe what I was hearing."

Linda pulled her car over to the side of the road and stopped to listen.

"I heard the speaker tell about a real and everlasting Friend *I* could have. And yet I didn't know whether 'it was for real.' Praise God, today I know He *is* real!"

Linda went on to describe an illness that overtook her soon after her conversion. There were weeks in bed—weeks of pain. The doctors gave her up. Despair threatened. Then Linda's new-found Saviour became her Great Physician. She was restored to health. Again Christ proved He is for real in sickness and in health.

"I am so thankful to God," Linda now declares. "I can never put my feeling into words. I feel so close to Him. He is part of me. He is all of me. He is mine and I am His."

Just now, would you like to say with Linda, "Now I belong to Jesus, and Jesus belongs to me, Not for the years of time alone, but for eternity"?

OUR MINISTRY OF RESTORATION

Brethren, if a man be overtaken in a fault, ye which are spiritual, restore such an one in the spirit of meekness; considering thyself, lest thou also be tempted. Gal. 6:1.

I can still see a pair of appealing eyes looking into mine. They are the eyes of my first baptismal candidate that I personally had laid beneath the waters many years ago. His experience had been up and down—sometimes spiritually abounding and in the church, sometimes discouraged and out on the fringes. He was a brilliant man of talent but highly emotional. Here he was, sitting beside me—thirty years since I had last seen him.

"Elder," he said sadly, "the church members want to give me Bible studies." He faltered, then continued. "I know those doctrines well. It is not teaching of doctrine that I need; it is love and understanding."

"Love and understanding"—here are two important tools of restorers.

Usually when a person drifts away from the church it is not because he or she has changed his mind about doctrine. Many times a person leaves because he is lonely, discouraged, or just plain bored. He needs a friendly visit. He needs encouragement. He needs a Calvary more than he needs a Sinai.

I was attending a large church meeting not long ago. As I made my way through that great mass of people following the service I was conscious of a hand on my arm. Turning, I saw a familiar face. It was the face of a friend I had had part in saving many years before. The man had made a mistake. We could have dismissed him, given him up, but we gave him another chance.

"Elder," he said, his face lightened with joy, "I drove 150 miles to this meeting today to tell you I have not let you down. I have made good."

We are to save people, not to crush them. Wherever we can do so, as church leaders and as laymen, we should *save* men— restore them—and let them make good.

"If a man should do something wrong, . . . you who are endowed with the Spirit must set him right again *very gently*" (Gal. 6:1, N.E.B.).

CERTAINTY OF THE PROPHETIC WORD

All this only confirms for us the message of the prophets, to which you will do well to attend, because it is like a lamp shining in a murky place, until the day breaks and the morning star rises to illuminate your minds.
2 Peter 1:19, N.E.B.

Peter spoke from experience. He and his companions personally witnessed the fulfilling of many prophetic predictions of the Old Testament. The coming of the Messiah, the circumstances surrounding His birth, His ministry, His rejection, and finally His death, burial, resurrection, and ascension all had been foretold by "holy men of God . . . as they were moved by the Holy Ghost" (2 Peter 1:21). The disciples had witnessed these moving events. They spoke from a position of firsthand experience. They knew they could put confidence in the prophetic word. It was certain.

Dr. Luke also knew "the certainty" of these things in which the church of his day had been instructed (Luke 1:4). Doubtless these and other prophetic utterances were included in this ongoing instruction.

Notice this inspired statement from Ellen White:

"The history which the great I AM has marked out in His word, uniting link after link in the prophetic chain, from eternity in the past to eternity in the future, tells us where we are today in the procession of the ages, and what may be expected in the time to come. All that prophecy has foretold as coming to pass, until the present time, has been traced on the pages of history, and we may be assured that all which is yet to come will be fulfilled in its order."—*Education*, p. 178.

The rise and fall of nations—Babylon, Medo-Persia, Greece, and Rome—the breaking up of the Roman Empire; all have been fulfilled in harmony with divine prediction. The great papal power appeared and remains on the stage of action. The great earthquake of 1755, the Dark Day, the falling of the stars, took place on time as the prophets predicted. The rise of the Advent Movement, religious revival and apostasy have appeared on time.

"We have not been telling you fairy tales," Peter declares (2 Peter 1:16, T.L.B.). We may be assured that all which is yet to come will be fulfilled in its order.

WHAT IS JUST AHEAD?

Therefore rejoice, ye heavens, and ye that dwell in them. Woe to the inhabiters of the earth and of the sea! for the devil is come down unto you, having great wrath, because he knoweth that he hath but a short time. **Rev. 12:12.**

Did you ever notice that most Seventh-day Adventist prayers, public and personal, include an earnest appeal for God to finish His work in the earth and to send His Son Jesus to gather the redeemed at His second advent? This is right. We should pray for our Saviour's early return. We are weary of this sin-cursed existence and long for the day of deliverance already too long delayed.

But did you ever stop to think of it this way—the answer to that prayer for the early Advent inevitably must include the most awesome, perhaps most terrifying, period in this world's history!

The Lord's messenger, after quoting our text for today, says, "Fearful are the scenes which call forth this exclamation from the heavenly voice. The wrath of Satan increases as his time grows short, and his work of deceit and destruction will reach its culmination in the time of trouble."—*The Great Controversy*, p. 623.

In awful crescendo the evil one vents his wrath upon those whom he has already made captives. The righteous likewise will be subjected to his vicious attacks—but only as God permits.

Just ahead is the most fantastic era of this planet's existence! Events great and challenging, as well as horrifying and destructive, are before us. The outpouring of the latter rain, the sealing work, the loud cry, the shaking, the closing of the third angel's message, Christ's work in the heavenly sanctuary completed, the time of trouble, Sunday law legislation, the exodus from the cities, the death decree, and final glorious deliverance—these may come, yes, must come, in our day. In our study during this month of May we will consider these thrilling, challenging events!

Come what may, if you and I maintain a close relationship with our Saviour the days ahead will be days of glorious victory and final deliverance!

THIS IS THE END!

The hour has come, the hour is striking, and striking at you, the hour and the end! **Eze. 7:5, 6, Moffatt.**

The end is near. Bible prophets declare it. Social and political events about us affirm it.

Our harassed world is coming apart at the seams. Worse than this, it is literally exploding as the result of social, economic, and political pressures that have been building up a fearful head of disaster for decades. When the explosion will come only God knows—but come it will!

"Our world is on fire," declares Evangelist Billy Graham, "and man without God will never be able to control the flames. The demons of hell have been let loose. The fires of passion, greed, hate, and lust are sweeping the world. We seem to be plunging madly toward Armageddon."—Excerpt from *World Aflame* by Billy Graham. Copyright © 1965 by Billy Graham. Reprinted by permission of Doubleday & Company, Inc.

As Ezekiel said, the hour and the end are striking!

The world of technology confirms the prophet's words. During the past half century, planet Earth has rocketed through more scientific, social, and economic change than in all the previous centuries of mankind's total history combined. Yet ever new and breath-taking inventions pour forth from Pandora's box of technology. Still more bewildering creations of man's expanded intellect are on the drawing board. Apparently now man has it within human capability to blot civilization out of existence. We are being rapidly propelled to the end time when God will write "finished" as His final footnote to human history as we know it today.

Events crowding in upon us from every side are alarming. Facts with which we are confronted demand that an alarm be sounded. As the late Arthur Maxwell once said, "Something *is* coming to an end. Call it the 'present order' if you will. Call it 'the age' or 'the world.' The name matters little. What is important is that all signs point to the approaching terminus of history as we know it."—"This Is the End," in the *Signs of the Times,* January, 1968.

We are nearing the end—the sure word of prophecy declares it. It is a thought that should thrill every Advent heart!

HE *WILL* COME

For yet a little while, and he that shall come will come, and will not tarry.
Heb. 10:37.

Environmental technologists are fighting to save Earth from man. Our air is befouled with carbon monoxide, hydrocarbons, lead compounds, sulfur dioxide, and countless other noxious substances. Ecologists estimate that 150 million tons of air pollutants are spewed into the atmosphere every year in the United States alone. Car-clogged streets, sewage-filled rivers, contaminated lakes, polluted air, combine to tell us the hour is late. Our earth waxes old like a garment.

Charles Y. Clock and Rodney Stark, research sociologists, state: "Perhaps at no time since the conversion of Paul has the future of Christianity seemed so uncertain. Clearly, a profound revolution in religious thought is sweeping the churches. Where will it lead? . . . We have reached two main conclusions: (1) that the religious beliefs that have been the bedrocks of Christian faith for nearly two millennia are on their way out; and (2) that this may well be the dawn of a post-Christian era! [There is] . . . a near majority rejection of such traditional articles of faith as Christ's miracles, life after death, the promise of the second coming, and the virgin birth. . . . It seems clear to us that a return to orthodoxy is no longer possible."— CHAS. Y. CLOCK and RODNEY STARK, "Will Ethics Be the Death of Christianity?" *Trans-Action Magazine,* June, 1968.

Jesus will come soon. Conditions within the church confirm the truth of the prophetic word.

"When the professed people of God are uniting with the world, living as they live, and joining with them in forbidden pleasures; when the luxury of the world becomes the luxury of the church; when the marriage bells are chiming, and all are looking forward to many years of worldly prosperity—then, suddenly as the lightning flashes from the heavens, will come the end of their bright visions and delusive hopes."—*The Great Controversy,* pp. 338, 339.

Inspired prophets declare we are nearing the end—there can be no question about it, for we can have confidence in the holy men God has used to pinpoint the times in which we live. Ours is the sure word of prophecy!

A MESSAGE FROM JESUS

I Jesus have sent mine angel to testify unto you these things in the churches. I am the root and the offspring of David, and the bright and morning star. Rev. 22:16.

The words of our text today are from Jesus Himself. The last book in the Bible is "the Revelation of Jesus Christ" (Rev. 1:1). It contains messages from Him, borne by His angels to His churches. If Jesus has a message for *my* church I want to know what it is, for if the message is from Him it is important to me.

The messages of Revelation are especially for our day—for God's people who are standing upon the threshold of eternity. "Revelation must be studied," the Lord's messenger reminds us. "Especially should Daniel and the Revelation have attention as never before in the history of our work."—*Testimonies to Ministers*, p. 112.

Satan will do all within his power to divert the attention of the Laodicean church from this important book. "Satan has blinded the minds of many so that they have been glad of any excuse for not making the Revelation their study."—*Ibid.,* p. 116.

The evil one seeks to divert God's people from the study of this last book in the Bible for good reason. He knows, "If our people were half awake, if they realized the nearness of the events portrayed in the Revelation, a reformation would be wrought in our churches."—*Ibid.,* p. 118.

The fourteenth chapter of Revelation has a special message for the world and for God's people. Here is found "the three angels' messages" that have made us a distinctive people—a people with God's message for God's hour that will prepare all who will accept it for the soon return of God's Son. We are not here just as another church with a few distinctive doctrines that distinguish us from churches of other faiths. We are God's movement brought into existence in these last hours to proclaim His special message.

Speaking of these three messages, Ellen White says, "Let none ignore this work or treat it as of little importance. The truth is to be proclaimed to the world, that men and women may see the light."—*Testimonies*, vol. 8, pp. 158, 159.

THE FIRST ANGEL'S MESSAGE

Then I saw an angel flying in mid-heaven, with an eternal gospel to pro-claim to those on earth, to every nation and tribe, language and people. He cried in a loud voice, "Fear God and pay him homage; for the hour of his judgement has come! Worship him who made heaven and earth, the sea and the water-springs!" Rev. 14:6, 7, N.E.B.

Seven facts appear prominently in the message of the first angel.

1. *It announces the hour of God's judgment.* The judgment of the whole human family is a solemn work indeed. Not one of us will escape arraignment.

2. *It calls on men to worship God as the Creator.* This message is particularly relevant for our day when too many of earth's inhabitants have fallen for atheistic evolution that substitutes man's theories for divine truth.

3. *It calls attention to the true Sabbath.* Today some men observe Friday as their day of rest. A large percentage of the Christian world "keeps" Sunday either in commemoration of the resurrection or merely as a weekly holiday. Inspiration reminds us that the true Bible Sabbath—the memorial of Creation—is the seventh day of the week.

4. *It will be preached worldwide.* God's last-day message is to go "to every nation and tribe, language and people." To date it is being proclaimed in nearly two hundred countries.

5. *It will go with great speed.* The angel was *"flying* in mid-heaven." Flight is a symbol of speed. During the lifetime of Seventh-day Adventists now living, the message of the first angel has gone from one language to approximately one thousand different tongues.

6. *It was "designed to separate the professed people of God from the corrupting influences of the world* and to arouse them to see their true condition of worldliness and backsliding" *(The Great Controversy,* p. 379). (Italics supplied.)

7. *It arose at the right time.* God raised up men and women and even little children to proclaim the first angel's message at the appointed time—early in the nineteenth century, at the beginning of the time of the end.

There can be no question about it—*prophetic and historic certainty assure this is God's message.*

THE SECOND ANGEL'S MESSAGE

Then another angel followed him through the skies, saying, "Babylon is fallen, is fallen—that great city—because she seduced the nations of the world and made them share the wine of her intense impurity and sin." Rev. 14:8, T.L.B.

"Babylon was founded by Nimrod. . . . From the very beginning the city was emblematic of disbelief in the true God and defiance of His will . . . , and its tower a monument to apostasy, a citadel of rebellion against Him. . . . The founders of Babylon aspired to set up a government entirely independent of God, and had He not intervened, they would eventually have succeeded in banishing righteousness from the earth."—*The SDA Bible Commentary,* on Rev. 14:8.

In later years Babylon became a symbol of spiritual apostasy. Those Christian churches that have accepted men's tradition in place of God's Word—who have drifted away from the truth as it is in Jesus—are described as Babylon.

The second angel's message proclaimed to the world since the middle of the nineteenth century declares that "Babylon is fallen, is fallen." Repetition lends emphasis to the prophet's words. It vividly describes those religious bodies that are in spiritual confusion today.

"Many interpreters realize that theology is now in a state of confusion, even anarchy," Carl F. H. Henry declares. "Some characterize our era as a theological shamble."

This spiritual confusion portrays God as "everything from a celestial gas to a kind of invisible honorary president 'out there' in space" *(Time,* April 8, 1966). Many of Babylon's preachers are apparently more interested in social action than they are in the gospel of Christ. Their topics deal with "guaranteed annual income, how to avoid the draft, civil disobedience, and the like . . . (seeking) . . . to reform society by law, coercion, and government regulation" *(Together,* June, 1968).

God today is calling *His people* out from the spiritual confusion of the fallen Babylon around us. Thank God, in practically every country on earth men and women are responding to this call and are once again placing their feet upon the eternal rock of God's truth.

133

THE THIRD ANGEL'S MESSAGE

Yet a third angel followed, crying out loud, "Whoever worships the beast and its image and receives its mark on his forehead or hand, he shall drink the wine of God's wrath, poured undiluted into the cup of his vengeance. He shall be tormented in sulphurous flames before the holy angels and before the Lamb. The smoke of their torment will rise for ever and ever, and there will be no respite day or night for those who worship the beast and its image or receive the mark of its name." Rev. 14:9-11, N.E.B.

Seventh-day Adventists have a terminology all their own. We love to speak of "accepting the truth" and "finishing the work." Our words are mixed with emotion when we refer to "the close of probation" and "the time of trouble." These phrases, filled with meaning to us, are not always meaningful to those not acquainted with Seventh-day Adventists.

Perhaps the words of greatest importance to the heart of every committed Adventist are "the third angel's message." When we use this phrase we usually include the messages of all three angels described in Revelation 14. In taking this liberty we are supported by God's messenger (see *Evangelism*, p. 196).

The beast to which the revelator refers is the leopardlike beast described in chapter 13. This, we believe, depicts the papal power. Its professed "mark" of authority (Sunday observance) will, in God's time, become a national issue. During this period loyalty to the Creator and His seventh-day Sabbath will be tested by demands that men observe the first day of the week, an admitted papal institution. Failure in this test then results in the disobedient receiving the mark of the beast.

Actually *the choice is between following the commandments of God and the commandments of men.* It is a matter of masters, not merely of twenty-four-hour days.

When one reads the dire punishment to be visited upon those who choose man's tradition in place of God's Word, it is easy to understand the importance God attaches to this message. In a sense every soul will stand before Pilate to make his choice between Christ or the usurper Barabbas. "This is where the fortitude of God's people has its place—in keeping God's commands and remaining loyal to Jesus" (Rev. 14:12, N.E.B.).

How we stand during the days of supreme test *then* may depend upon how we relate to the three angels' messages *now.*

SHOWERS AHEAD!

Ask ye of the Lord rain in the time of the latter rain; so the Lord shall make bright clouds, and give them showers of rain, to every one grass in the field. Zech. 10:1.

Solusi College in Rhodesia is well known for its chronic water problems. Here we have 12,000 acres of parched earth choking for water, *water, water.* One year we experienced an especially severe drought. The hard red earth cracked. The dust was a constant reminder of our pitiable plight. For weeks teachers and students had been praying earnestly for relief.

Then the rains came—with a blessed vengeance. Mrs. Pierson and I drove onto the campus in the midst of the delightful deluge. The fresh, cool rain poured down in silver sheets. The dusty road into the mission suddenly became a river. Our little Vauxhall could scarcely breast the torrent. Cisterns were filled. Dams overflowed, sharing their liquid blessings with anxious farmers downstream.

What a change! What a transformation! From the refreshing deluge Solusi campus came forth robed in live, lush green. Lawns suddenly appeared in living color. The trees and bushes exchanged their drab dresses for fresh new garments. Crops drank deeply and pushed upward with renewed courage and vigor.

For decades the Advent message has been proclaimed. Multiplied thousands in many lands have responded. But the work is not finished. Human effort is not sufficient. More divine help must be ours. This help is promised.

"Near the close of earth's harvest, a special bestowal of spiritual grace is promised to prepare the church for the coming of the Son of man. This outpouring of the Spirit is likened to the falling of the latter rain; and it is for this added power that Christians are to send their petitions to the Lord of the harvest 'in the time of the latter rain.' In response, 'the Lord shall make bright clouds, and give them showers of rain.' 'He will cause to come down . . . the rain, the former rain, and the latter rain' (Zech. 10:1, Joel 2:23)."—*The Acts of the Apostles,* p. 55.

Thank God, showers of power are upon us! *The work will be finished!*

THE SCENES OF PENTECOST WILL BE REPEATED

Be glad, O sons of Zion, and rejoice in the Lord, your God; for he has given the early rain for your vindication, he has poured down for you abundant rain, the early and the latter rain, as before. The threshing floors shall be full of grain, the vats shall overflow with wine and oil. I will restore to you the years which the swarming locust has eaten, the hopper, the destroyer, and the cutter, my great army, which I sent among you. Joel 2:23, 24, R.S.V.

The outpouring of the Holy Spirit in latter-rain power is a baptism for which the Advent people have yearned and prayed for many years. We need this reviving, energizing power both within and outside the church to assure a finished work.

"It is the latter rain which revives and strengthens them [God's people] to pass through the time of trouble."—*The SDA Bible Commentary*, Ellen G. White Comments, on Rev. 18:1, p. 984. "The work will be similar to that of the Day of Pentecost. . . . The 'latter rain' will be given at its [the gospel's] close for the ripening of the harvest."—*The Great Controversy*, p. 611.

The outpouring of the early rain at Pentecost roused the early church and stirred the world. "After the descent of the Holy Spirit the disciples went forth to proclaim a risen Saviour, their one desire the salvation of souls. They rejoiced in the sweetness of the communion with saints. They were tender, thoughtful, self-denying, willing to make any sacrifice for the truth's sake. In their daily association with one another they revealed the love that Christ had commanded them to reveal. By unselfish words and deeds they strove to kindle this love in other hearts."—*Testimonies*, vol. 8, p. 241.

"The disciples were so filled with love for Him and for those for whom He died, that hearts were melted by the words they spoke and the prayers they offered. They spoke in the power of the Spirit; and under the influence of that power, thousands were converted."—*The Acts of the Apostles*, p. 22.

The propecy of Joel "met a partial fulfillment in the days of the apostles," and now "we are living in a time when it is to be even more evidently manifest to the people of God" (*The SDA Bible Commentary*, Ellen G. White Comments, on Joel 2, p. 1175).

Thank God the scenes of Pentecost will be repeated in our day when the latter rain falls upon us!

CONDITIONS OF POWER

I will pour out my spirit upon all flesh. Joel 2:28.

The gift of the Holy Spirit will be realized by God's church when as individual members, by His grace, we make ourselves ready. God has promised this precious gift "but like every other promise, *it is given on conditions*" (*The Desire of Ages,* p. 672). (Italics supplied.)

We do well to study prayerfully and frequently what these conditions are. The messenger of the Lord has set them forth much more clearly than could I. Let us note them well.

"The heart must be emptied of every defilement, and cleansed for the indwelling of the Spirit. It was by the confession and forsaking of sin, by earnest prayer and consecration of themselves to God, that the early disciples prepared for the outpouring of the Holy Spirit on the Day of Pentecost. The same work, only in greater degree, must be done now."—*Testimonies to Ministers,* p. 507.

"Those who come up to every point, and stand every test, and overcome, be the price what it may, have heeded the counsel of the True Witness, and they will receive the latter rain, and thus be fitted for translation."—*Testimonies,* vol. 1, p. 187.

"When one is fully emptied of self, when every false god is cast out of the soul, the vacuum is filled by the inflowing of the Spirit of Christ."—*Gospel Workers,* p. 287.

"Whenever minor matters occupy the attention, the divine power which is necessary for the growth and prosperity of the church, and which would bring all other blessings in its train, is lacking, though offered in infinite plenitude."—*The Acts of the Apostles,* p. 50.

"The great outpouring of the Spirit of God, which lightens the whole earth with His glory, will not come until we have an enlightened people, that know by experience what it means to be laborers together with God. When we have entire, whole-hearted consecration to the service of Christ, God will recognize the fact by an outpouring of His Spirit without measure; but this will not be while the largest portion of the church are not laborers together with God."—*Christian Service,* p. 253.

When you and I meet the conditions the Holy Spirit is ours!

FINAL THRUST TO VICTORY

And after these things I saw another angel come down from heaven, having great power; and the earth was lightened with his glory. And he cried mightily with a strong voice, saying, Babylon the great is fallen, is fallen, and is become the habitation of devils, and the hold of every foul spirit, and a cage of every unclean and hateful bird. Rev. 18:1, 2.

In Adventist terminology this divine extravaganza is known as "the loud cry."

The pen of inspiration has much to say about this final dramatic thrust to victory. "The work will be similar to that of the Day of Pentecost." Ellen White describes the worldwide extent of the glorious 1840-1844 manifestation when "the first angel's message was carried to every missionary station in the world."—*The Great Controversy*, p. 611. Then she declares that the work of the mighty movement of the loud cry will exceed anything that has come before it.

Leading statesmen will respond to the message (see *The Great Controversy*, pp. 610, 611). "The Lord will work in this last work in a manner very much out of the common order of things, and in a way that will be contrary to any human planning . . . God will use ways and means by which it will be seen that He is taking the reins in His own hands. The workers will be surprised by the simple means that He will use to bring about and perfect His work of righteousness."—*Testimonies to Ministers*, p. 300.

"Servants of God, with their faces lighted up and shining with holy consecration, will hasten from place to place to proclaim the message from heaven. By thousands of voices, all over the earth, the warning will be given. Miracles will be wrought, the sick will be healed, and signs and wonders will follow the believers."—*The Great Controversy*, p. 612.

"By these solemn warnings the people will be stirred. Thousands upon thousands will listen who have never heard words like these."—*Ibid.*, p. 606.

What a message! What power! What response! What results! And to think God not only *wants* you and me to have part in this glorious final thrust to victory, He is counting on us! We dare not disappoint Him!

IF YOU AND I HAVE PART

My soul thirsteth for God, for the living God. Ps. 42:2.

God has a role for each one of His people to play in the outpouring of His Holy Spirit in latter-rain power. However, He cannot entrust this potent weapon to members of the human family unconditionally.

God's people must be prepared to receive the Spirit's power. A message is now being proclaimed to accomplish this preparatory work. "It [the Laodicean message] is designed to arouse the people of God, to discover to them their backslidings, and to lead to zealous repentance, that they may be favored with the presence of Jesus, and be fitted for the loud cry of the third angel."—*Testimonies,* vol. 1, p. 186. First comes a sense of our need, followed by a zealous repentance.

Loud-cry power will be entrusted only to "converted people," men and women to whom God's last message "means everything," who "have a true, abiding faith."

"The Lord will work through humble instruments." All the glory for what is accomplished must be God's. He will work with yielded vessels to assure this. "The laborers will be qualified rather by the unction of His Spirit than by the training of literary institutions."—*The Great Controversy,* p. 606.

God will not permit man to step in and lay his plans or place his own mold upon His great work. "There will be those among us who will always want to control the work of God, to dictate even what movements shall be made when the work goes forward under the direction of the angel who joins the third angel in the message to be given to the world."—*Testimonies to Ministers,* p. 300. There will be a turn of events attesting that God "is taking the reins in His own hands" *(ibid.).*

Racial prejudice will disqualify us to receive loud-cry power (see *Testimonies,* vol. 9, p. 209). Recipients of God's special favor will be men and women bound together in close ties of love and unity. "The love of Christ, the love of our brethren, will testify to the world that we have been with Jesus and learned of Him. Then will the message of the third angel swell to a loud cry, and the whole earth will be lightened with the glory of the Lord."—*Testimonies,* vol. 6, p. 401.

You and I must "thirst for God, for the living God."

BUT WHEN?

But you shall receive power when the Holy Spirit has come upon you.
Acts 1:8, R.S.V.

The letter on my desk was from a layman in South Africa. The question the writer posed was a challenging one. "I read in the book of Acts," he wrote, "that one preacher won three thousand souls in one day when the Spirit of God was poured out upon His people. When is the church today going to receive that same power?"

"When is the church today going to receive that same power?" This is not only a good question, it is one of the most vital challenges before God's people today! The Advent message will penetrate closed doors of countries where millions of people live, but it will be as the result of more than mere plans or programs. God's saving truth will witness in more than man's feeble power "to those who dwell on earth, to every nation and tribe and tongue and people" (Rev. 14:6, R.S.V.). Help must come from above—and soon.

Thank God the promise of the Saviour is ours today: "You shall receive power when the Holy Spirit has come upon you" (Acts 1:8, R.S.V.). "We are to feel the power of the Spirit of God in this movement."—*Testimonies*, vol. 9, p. 154.

The promise *will* be fulfilled. There is no question about it. God has given us His guarantee. "He . . . has given us the living guarantee of the Spirit in our hearts" (2 Cor. 1:22, Phillips). God's guarantee, unlike some we receive from earthly sources, will not fail us! The Spirit *will* be ours. The needed power *will* come! He wants the work finished. The awesome thing about it is that God wants to give us the power of His Holy Spirit *now*. He wants His Son Jesus to come and take us home. The power is available at this very moment if we will but meet the conditions and receive it! "At this very hour His Spirit and His grace are for all who need them and will take Him at His word."—*Ibid.*, vol. 8, p. 20.

"You shall receive power when the Holy Spirit has come upon you."

"When is the church going to receive that power?" This is a challenging question. Only you and I can answer it! How much longer are we going to keep God waiting?

NO WAR—WHY?

After this I saw four angels stationed at the four corners of the earth, holding back the four winds so that no wind should blow on the sea or land or any tree. Rev. 7:1, N.E.B.

World events that today rate only page-two attention in the newspapers would have meant *war* a few decades ago! Then America, Britain, and other great powers moved in with force when their nationals were unduly molested or their flag desecrated. Such acts of insult were perpetrated only at the risk of war.

That was yesterday. What of today?

In recent times there have been international border violations, planes shot down, ships fired on, diplomatic ultimatums, flags burned; but these have not frequently resulted in war. The undeclared or limited wars are fought, it is suspected sometime, with "gentleman's agreement" with the enemy or his allies.

Some unseen hand appears to be holding on a leash those forces normally capable of loosing war and strife of Armageddon magnitude. Why do not such terrible wars develop from these explosive situations? "Fear of atomic destruction," one may reply. "Nations are more mature," another suggests. These answers may have their bearing upon the problem, but to most Adventist students of the Word it is apparent there *is* an unseen hand holding in check the forces of war. God has a reason for prolonging peace a little longer.

This is all a part of the Advent message!

"We are standing on the threshold of great and solemn events. Prophecies are fulfilling. Strange and eventful history is being recorded in the books of heaven—events which it was declared should shortly precede the great day of God. Everything in the world is in an unsettled state. The nations are angry, and great preparations for war are being made. Nation is plotting against nation, and kingdom against kingdom. The great day of God is hasting greatly. But although the nations are mustering their forces for war and bloodshed, that command to the angels is still in force, that they hold the four winds until the servants of God are sealed in their foreheads."
—*Selected Messages,* book 1, pp. 221, 222.

THE SEALING WORK

Then I saw another angel rising out of the east, carrying the seal of the living God; and he called aloud to the four angels who had been given the power to ravage land and sea: "Do no damage to sea or land or trees until we have set the seal of our God upon the foreheads of his servants." **Rev. 7:2, 3, N.E.B.**

In our text for today a great sealing work is described. Meanwhile angels hold the winds of strife on earth.

In the Word of God the words *seal, sign,* and *mark* are used interchangeably. Inspiration reveals that the seventh-day Sabbath is God's seal or sign (Ex. 31:13, 17).

The seventh-day Sabbath, made by Christ (John 1:1-3, 14), was set aside as a memorial to the Son of God's creative power in speaking our world into existence. It thus became our planet's birthday. Throughout succeeding generations it was God's plan that it should continue to serve as a sign or mark distinguishing His true followers from those who worshiped false gods. "It was to be a token of their separation from idolatry, and their connection with the true God."—*The Desire of Ages,* p. 283.

Today Christ's seventh-day Sabbathkeeping immediately stamps one as a believer in the Genesis (chapters one and two) Creation account. There can be no evolutionists, modernists, or destructive higher critics within the ranks of God's true Sabbathkeepers.

When a man forgot the true Sabbath he soon turned his back upon the Lord of the Sabbath—the God who "made heaven and earth, the sea, and all that in them is" (Ex. 20:8-11). As a result, we have various non-Christian religions in many parts of the world. They observe Friday or other days as holy days or feast days. In the Nilgiri Hills of South India where we lived for several years one mountain tribe kept Tuesday for their feast day. A large portion of the so-called Christian world observes the first day of the week.

When the world is in such spiritual condition just before the return of our Lord a message goes forth—a message exalting Christ and His Sabbath seal, calling men and women back to worship Him as the Creator. As a Seventh-day Adventist you are a part of that great message and movement!

ARE YOU READY FOR GOD'S SEAL?

And the Lord said unto him, Go through the midst of the city, through the midst of Jerusalem, and set a mark upon the foreheads of the men that sigh and that cry for all the abominations that be done in the midst thereof. Eze. 9:4.

"I am thankful I understand that God's seal is the observance of the seventh-day Sabbath and that I am keeping it," a church member once told me.

Later I pondered my friend's statement. Is knowledge of the true Sabbath and the perfunctory observance of God's holy day sufficient to assure being "sealed" during the sealing work going on around the world today? The Lord has news for us!

"Not all who profess to keep the Sabbath will be sealed. There are many even among those who teach the truth to others who will not receive the seal of God in their foreheads." —*Testimonies,* vol. 5, pp. 213, 214.

These are solemn words. They declare that some who "profess to keep the Sabbath" and some "who teach the truth to others" may not themselves receive the seal of God's approval. This could be church members and church officers. It could include workers in the cause of God. It could include me.

"The seal of God will never be placed upon the forehead of an impure man or woman. It will never be placed upon the forehead of the ambitious, world-loving man or woman. It will never be placed upon the forehead of men or women of false tongues or deceitful hearts. All who receive the seal must be without spot before God—candidates for heaven."—*Ibid.,* p. 216.

It is evident from these words that the work of sealing includes much more than careless "Saturday keeping" or lightly accepted church membership. The Lord makes it clear that those who receive His mark or seal are those who carry a deep concern for the spiritual condition of the church.

The standard is high but there is help and hope.

"No one need say that his case is hopeless, that he cannot live the life of a Christian. Ample provision is made by the death of Christ for every soul. Jesus is our ever-present help in time of need. Only call upon Him in faith, and He has promised to hear and answer your petitions."—*Ibid.,* p. 215.

A GREAT SHAKING

I will give my orders, I will shake Israel to and fro through all the nations as a sieve is shaken to and fro and not one pebble falls to the ground. Amos 9:9, N.E.B.

In India and Pakistan many times I have watched farmers winnowing their grain. In those days there were no sophisticated threshing machines. The member of the family doing the work placed a few handfuls of grain in the sieve, then holding it high in the air he would shake it back and forth. The husks and foreign particles, shaken through the wire mesh, were blown away by the wind.

The Word of God speaks of another shaking—not of grain but of everything without solid foundations. Before Jesus returns the church and every church member personally will face trials of faith spoken of by inspired writers as "the shaking." The prophet Amos described it: "I will give my orders, I will shake Israel to and fro through all the nations as a sieve is shaken to and fro and not one pebble falls to the ground." The apostle Peter experienced the conflict. Jesus spoke of it. " 'Simon, Simon, Satan has asked to have you, to sift you like wheat, but I have pleaded in prayer for you that your faith should not completely fail. So when you have repented and turned to me again, strengthen and build up the faith of your brothers' " (Luke 22:31, 32, T.L.B.). Satan will overtly and subtly endeavor to add as many as possible of God's people to the ranks of apostasy.

"Satan has come down with great power to work with all deceivableness of unrighteousness in them that perish; and everything that can be shaken will be shaken, and those things that cannot be shaken will remain."—*Testimonies,* vol. 9, p. 62.

This work of shaking is now in progress. "The mighty shaking has commenced and will go on, and all will be shaken out who are not willing to take a bold and unyielding stand for the truth and to sacrifice for God and His cause."—*Early Writings,* p. 50.

Thank God for the promise of One who "is able to keep . . . [us] from falling, and to present . . . [us] faultless before the presence of his glory with exceeding joy" (Jude 24).

HOW IS IT WITH YOU?

"Next time," he says, "I will not only shake the earth, but the heavens too." By this he means that he will sift out everything without solid foundations, so that only unshakable things will be left. **Heb. 12:26, 27, T.L.B.**

Yesterday we read of a great shaking time when many halting saints will be sifted out of fellowship with God's people. What causes this shaking?

Love of the world caused one follower of Christ to fall by the wayside. "For Demas hath forsaken me, having loved this present world" (2 Tim. 4:10). Many modern Demases are falling by the wayside now. The attraction of the bright lights and the pleasure marts is too great. Love of the world eclipses love of Christ.

Carelessness and indifference will shake some from fellowship with God's people. Ellen White saw the company of professed followers journeying heavenward growing smaller. "Some had been shaken out and left by the way. The careless and indifferent, who did not join with those who prized victory and salvation enough to perseveringly plead and agonize for it, did not obtain it, and they were left behind in darkness."—*Early Writings*, p. 271.

Some will not be able to stand *the straight testimony of the True Witness.* "I asked the meaning of the shaking I had seen and was shown that it would be caused by the straight testimony called forth by the counsel of the True Witness to the Laodiceans. . . . Some will not bear this straight testimony. They will rise up against it, and this is what will cause a shaking among God's people."—*Ibid.,* p. 270.

"God will arouse His people; if other means fail, *heresies will come in* among them [God's people], which will sift them, separating the chaff from the wheat."—*Testimonies*, vol. 5, p. 707.

"Errors will be presented in a pleasing and flattering manner. False theories, clothed with garments of light, will be presented to God's people. Thus Satan will try to deceive, if possible, the very elect."—*Ibid.,* vol. 8, p. 293.

In such a time of testing our God assures those who will accept His help, "My grace is sufficient for thee" (2 Cor. 12:9). Cling tightly to this precious promise.

FOOLED BY AN ANGEL!

Satan can change himself into an angel of light, so it is no wonder his servants can do it too, and seem like godly ministers. 2 Cor. 11:14, 15, T.L.B.

Remaining faithful to the truth of God in the last days will not be easy. Satan will see to that! "The Devil has come down to you in great anger, knowing that he has little time" (Rev. 12:20, T.L.B.).

But Satan will be well disguised in his anger. He will appear as an angel of light. As such he will "work miracles of all kinds, to deceive, if possible, the very elect" *(Testimonies,* vol. 9, p. 16). He will use counterfeit plans and programs to carry out his work of deception.

He will come with counterfeit doctrines. Already he has counterfeits for many of God's original tenets of truth. Evolution has supplanted Creation in most of the Christian world. A first-day sabbath replaces God's seventh day of rest. The evil one has sought to substitute sprinkling and pouring for God's baptism by immersion. Bazaars and raffles replace tithes and offerings in many religious centers. Don't be surprised.

He will come in counterfeit revivals. Before the Saviour returns God has promised a revival of primitive godliness among His people. Satan knows this. He will seek to imitate this period of refreshing by a false revival of his own. "Before the loud cry of the third angel is given, he raises an excitement in these religious bodies, that those who have rejected the truth may think that God is with them. He hopes to deceive the honest and lead them to think that God is still working for the churches."—*Early Writings,* p. 261.

He will come with counterfeit healing. "Wonderful scenes, with which Satan will be closely connected, will soon take place. God's Word declares that Satan will work miracles. He will make people sick, and then will suddenly remove from them his satanic power. They will then be regarded as healed." Consider what you hear over the radio and watch on your television today, then note the inspired warning, "These works of apparent healing will bring Seventh-day Adventists to the test." —*Selected Messages,* book 2, p. 53.

We will need God's help "to stand against the wiles of the devil" (Eph. 6:11) in that day—and we may have it!

HANDS ACROSS THE GULF

We are not fighting against people made of flesh and blood, but against . . . huge numbers of wicked spirits in the spirit world. Eph. 6:12, T.L.B.

In 1957, an eighteen-year-old South African girl, Joy Aiken, who lived near Pinetown, was murdered by her lover. In an effort to hide his crime, the murderer placed the body in a culvert under a road some seventy miles from her home.

For days police searched in vain for trace of the missing girl. In desperation, Joy's brother approached Nelson Palmer, a retired schoolteacher and spiritualist medium living in the community, asking for his help. When Nelson Palmer came out of a trance a short time later, he led the police and the family straight to the place where the body was hidden.

Spiritualism is not some recent phenomenon. It flourished in Bible times. Modern spiritualism had its birth in the home of the Fox sisters in Hydesville, New York, when mysterious rappings were heard in 1848. The first spiritist church was organized in Sturgis, Michigan, ten years later. By 1910 it was estimated there were some 60 million spiritualists in the world, and today there are two thirds of this number who claim some extrasensory perception in the United States alone.

One Protestant spiritist minister in appealing to fellow clergymen to open their minds to the psychic phenomena, declared such a course would restore the gift of tongues and unite the church in an experience rivaling Pentecost. "Our goal," he declares, "is to win the ministry to our cause."

"When Protestantism shall stretch her hand across the gulf to grasp the hand of the Roman power, when she shall reach over the abyss to clasp hands with spiritualism, when, under the influence of this threefold union, our country shall repudiate every principle of its Constitution as a Protestant and republican government, and shall make provision for the propagation of papal falsehoods and delusions, then we may know that the time has come for the marvelous working of Satan and that the end is near."—*Testimonies,* vol. 5, p. 451.

What is happening in the spirit world and in the churches today reminds us it is later than we think! Prophetic certainties declare it!

FOREVER SETTLED

Let the evildoer still do evil, and the filthy still be filthy, and the righteous still do right, and the holy still be holy. **Rev. 22:11, R.S.V.**

For years Eddie Hart and Reynaud Robinson had looked forward to this hour. They were actually in Munich, Germany, to represent the United States in the 1972 Olympics. For months they had trained rigorously. They had met and defeated some of the best sprinters in America. Now the greatest day of victory was within their grasp. The big moment was here. But when they reached the stadium Hart and Robinson discovered they were too late. The races had been run a few minutes before. Their moment of opportunity had passed.

Noah and his family, the animals, the birds, insects, and reptiles were all safe inside the ark. The great door was swung shut by God's own hand. When the door closed, no one from outside could enter. The day of opportunity had ended. Those who too long had trifled with God's mercy perished outside the ark when the Flood came.

When Jesus completes His work of intercession in the heavenly sanctuary, Heaven's "work for sinners will be done. . . . The probation of all closes when the pleading for sinners is ended. . . . The case of every soul will have been decided, and there will be no atoning blood to cleanse from sin."—*The Faith I Live By,* p. 215.

At this fateful hour the eternal destiny of every human being will have been settled. The decree goes forth, "Let the wicked man continue his wickedness and the filthy man his filthiness; let the good man continue his good deeds and the holy man continue in holiness" (Rev. 22:11, Phillips).

The last sermon is preached. The last song is sung. The last prayer is offered. "The restraining Spirit of God is withdrawn from the earth."—*Ibid.*

With awful speed the last events of earth's history take place. "Satan will then plunge the inhabitants of earth into one great, final trouble."—*Ibid.* The famine for the Word of God, the falling of the seven last plagues, the time of trouble, will be upon mankind in swift retribution. Thank God, through it all the righteous will be kept safely in the secret place of the Most High.

FAMINE AHEAD!

The time is coming, says the Lord God, when I will send famine on the land, not hunger for bread or thirst for water, but for hearing the word of the Lord. Men shall stagger from north to south, they shall range from east to west, seeking the word of the Lord, but they shall not find it. Amos 8:11, 12, N.E.B.

"A world famine striking 'hundreds of millions or even billions of human beings' is near," a scientist-economist warned in an Associated Press report appearing in the Salisbury, Rhodesia, *Herald* (Sept. 2, 1964).

"It will be the most colossal catastrophe in history," declared Dr. R. Ewell, vice-president for research, State University of New York, Buffalo.

"Such a famine in Asia, Africa, and South America by the 1970's and later seems almost inevitable as expanding population outstrips food production, he told the American Chemical Society."

That another famine is coming—and soon—is foretold in the words of our text for today. This famine will be "for hearing the word of the Lord." Now the Bible is readily available. In most parts of the Western world it can be freely preached. Men and women may hear and may decide for or against its claims. This order of things will change just before the return of Jesus.

Speaking of this time, Ellen White writes:

"The last tear for sinners had been shed, the last agonizing prayer offered, the last burden borne, the last warning given. The sweet voice of mercy was no more to invite them. When the saints, and all heaven, were interested for their salvation, they had no interest for themselves. Life and death had been set before them. Many desired life, but made no effort to obtain it.

"Those who had not prized God's Word were hurrying to and fro, wandering from sea to sea, and from the north to the east, to seek the Word of the Lord. Said the angel, 'They shall not find it. There is a famine in the land; not a famine of bread, nor a thirst for water, but for hearing the words of the Lord.' "—*Early Writings*, p. 281.

This is not idle speculation. *The time is surely coming.*

149

THE TIME OF JACOB'S TROUBLE

Alas! for that day is great, so that none is like it: it is even the time of Jacob's trouble; but he shall be saved out of it. Jer. 30:7.

Jacob was headed home. But it was not the usual homecoming that one who had been far away for years might expect. There was no glad welcome, no celebration anticipated. In fact, Jacob was fearful. He had cheated Esau his brother and had been forced to flee from home years before. Now he was returning. How would Esau receive him?

The news was not reassuring. On the borders of his homeland word reached Jacob's camp that Esau was approaching with warriors bent on revenge.

Sending his family away, Jacob finds himself alone with his God. In great distress he intercedes with his Creator. He pours out his heart and confesses his sin. "With deep humiliation he pleads the covenant made with his fathers, and the promises to himself in the night vision at Bethel and in the land of his exile. The crisis in his life has come; everything is at stake. In the darkness and solitude he continues praying and humbling himself before God."—*The Great Controversy,* p. 617.

In the midst of the struggle the hand of God was placed upon Jacob's shoulder, and he was given the assurance of God's love and deliverance.

There is a time of Jacob's trouble ahead for God's chosen ones! "As Satan influenced Esau to march against Jacob, so he will stir up the wicked to destroy God's people in the time of trouble. And as he accused Jacob, he will urge his accusations against the people of God."—*Ibid.,* p. 618.

In the midst of trouble such as the world has never seen before, on the borders of the eternal world, God's people— you and I—will face the greatest struggle of all time.

God's people will pass through a period of mental anguish too awesome to describe. "As they review the past, their hopes sink; for in their whole lives they can see little good. They are fully conscious of their weakness and unworthiness. Satan endeavors to terrify them with the thought that their cases are hopeless."—*Ibid.,* pp. 618, 619.

It will be an agonizing experience, but the faithful "shall be saved out of it." Precious promise!

WILL YOU MAKE IT?

All that will live godly in Christ Jesus shall suffer persecution. 2 Tim. 3:12.

For many hours I sat in the living room of a mission bunga-low listening to tales of torture and deprivation. There had been trouble—bad trouble—in the country, and thousands of our Seventh-day Adventist church members had suffered. Large numbers fled the country in fear of their lives. Hundreds were in prison or detained in concentration camps. I visited them there. I saw the wounds on the back of a church leader after he had been beaten when he refused to work on the Sabbath. I saw the stripes on a dear old pastor's body received when he refused to submit to his tormentors. Homes were ransacked. Houses were burned. Many failed to escape with their lives.

That which I witnessed on this sad occasion was but a re-minder of what the inspired Word tells us is ahead for God's people during the last terrifying days of the great controversy.

"Satan will excite indignation against the humble minority who conscientiously refuse to accept popular customs and tradi-tions. Men of position and reputation will join with the lawless and the vile to take counsel against the people of God. Wealth, genius, education, will combine to cover them with contempt. Persecuting rulers, ministers, and church members will conspire against them. With voice and pen, by boasts, threats, and ridi-cule, they will seek to overthrow their faith. By false representa-tions and angry appeals they will stir up the passions of the peo-ple. Not having a 'Thus saith the Scriptures' to bring against the advocates of the Bible Sabbath, they will resort to oppressive enactments to supply the lack. To secure popularity and patron-age, legislators will yield to the demand for a Sunday law. Those who fear God cannot accept an institution that violates a pre-cept of the Decalogue. On this battlefield comes the last great conflict of the controversy between truth and error. And we are not left in doubt as to the issue. Now, as in the days of Mordecai, the Lord will vindicate His truth and His people."—*Ibid.*, pp. 450, 451.

Only those who love the Lord Jesus and His last-day message more than they love life itself will remain faithful under this intense persecution. It is a sobering thought. Will *you* make it? With God's help you can!

GOD'S STRANGE ACT

Then from the sanctuary I heard a loud voice, and it said to the seven angels, "Go and pour out the seven bowls of God's wrath on the earth." Rev. 16: 1, N.E.B.

Many of us have suffered the piercing pain of an angry boil or a raw carbuncle. Many of us also have found ourselves in a burning desert without water for many hours and experienced the parching discomfort of unquenched thirst. But in due course we have found relief from the nagging sores and slaked our thirst with cool water.

Imagine, if you are able, a man covered with offensive carbuncles in a scorching desert heat, going to a water fountain only to find stenching blood gushing forth. God's Word declares that such an experience is most surely ahead for millions of human beings perhaps living on earth today.

This grievous experience is described in Revelation, chapter 16. It is well for us to read these solemn words again. "Foul malignant sores appeared on those men that wore the mark of the beast and worshipped its image. . . . The sea . . . turned to blood like the blood from a corpse. . . . The rivers and springs . . . turned to blood. . . . The sun . . . was allowed to burn men with its flames. . . . And its kingdom [of the beast] was plunged into darkness. Men gnawed their tongues in agony" (Rev. 16: 2-11, N.E.B.).

Under the sixth plague the nations of earth are gathered for the last great battle of Armageddon (see Rev. 16:12-16). The seventh plague winds down the curtain on the last act of human history with "flashes of lightning and peals of thunder, and a violent earthquake. . . . Huge hailstones, weighing perhaps a hundredweight, fell on men" (verses 17-21, N.E.B.). God intervenes in the last great battle when Jesus comes.

Terrifying? Yes, but this experience need not be yours or mine. In that day God's people will be shielded from His "strange act" (Isa. 28:21). "Neither shall any plague come nigh thy dwelling" (Ps. 91:10). "While the wicked are dying from hunger and pestilence, angels will shield the righteous and supply their wants."—*The Great Controversy*, p. 629. "I the Lord will hear them, I the God of Israel will not forsake them" (Isa. 41:17).

THE TEMPEST IS COMING!

And at that time shall Michael stand up, the great prince which standeth for the children of thy people: and there shall be a time of trouble, such as never was since there was a nation even to that same time: and at that time thy people shall be delivered, every one that shall be found written in the book. Dan. 12:1.

You have seen those signs, "DANGER—BLASTING AHEAD," or "DANGER—ROAD UNDER REPAIR." Some of us have seen signs, "DANGER—FIGHTING IN THIS AREA," "WARNING—YOUR GOVERNMENT CANNOT BE RESPONSIBLE FOR YOUR SAFETY IF YOU PROCEED BEYOND THIS POINT!"

The Lord has erected many signs to warn His people there is trouble ahead! "The tempest is coming!"—*Messages to Young People,* p. 89. "A storm is coming, relentless in its fury."—*Testimonies,* vol. 8, p. 315. "A great crisis awaits the people of God. A crisis awaits the world. The most momentous struggle of all the ages is just before us."—*Ibid.,* vol. 5, p. 711. The prophet Daniel, in our text today, sums it all up as "a time of trouble, such as never was since there was a nation even to that same time."

"Those who honor the law of God have been accused of bringing judgments upon the world, and they will be regarded as the cause of the fearful convulsions of nature and the strife and bloodshed among men that are filling the earth with woe. The power attending the last warning has enraged the wicked; their anger is kindled against all who have received the message, and Satan will excite to still greater intensity the spirit of hatred and persecution."—*The Great Controversy,* pp. 614, 615.

"It is often the case that trouble is greater in anticipation than in reality; but this is not true of the crisis before us. The most vivid presentation cannot reach the magnitude of the ordeal."—*Ibid.,* p. 622.

Some lull themselves to sleep thinking, It will not come in my day. Many may be tragically surprised. *It may well come in our day!* If through the grace of Christ we are prepared, we need not fear. Has not our God said, "At that time thy people shall be delivered, every one that shall be found written in the book" (Dan. 12:1)?

SAFE FROM THE STORM

For in the time of trouble he shall hide me in his pavilion: in the secret of his tabernacle shall he hide me; he shall set me up upon a rock. **Ps. 27:5.**

Travelers making their way across the vast Sahara found themselves suddenly engulfed by a fierce sandstorm. The wind swirled the blinding particles around them in fiendish glee. When all seemed lost they stumbled upon a crude stone building some kind benefactors had erected for the protection of desert travelers. Inside they found refuge and safety until the storm had passed.

"There are troublous times before us; the judgments of God are coming upon our world. The nations of earth are to tremble. There will be trials and perplexities on every hand; men's hearts will fail them for fear. And what shall we do in that day? Though the earth shall reel to and fro like a drunkard, and be removed like a cottage, if we have made God our trust, He will deliver us. 'He that dwelleth in the secret place of the Most High shall abide under the shadow of the Almighty.' 'Because thou hast made the Lord, which is my refuge, even the Most High, thy habitation; there shall no evil befall thee. . . . For he shall give his angels charge over thee, to keep thee in all thy ways' (Ps. 91)."—*Sons and Daughters of God,* p. 354.

After passing through the harrowing experience in Elisabethville, Congo, when we were caught for days between two armies, I wrote to my sister in North Carolina, "If God can take His people safely through the experience that has been ours this past week, I am certain He can and will take us through any trials and troubles He may permit to befall us between here and the kingdom." This I firmly believe.

When the death decree goes forth that those who keep God's commandments should be slain, God's people will not stand alone. In the face of destruction the Lord will invite us to a place of refuge: "Come, my people, enter thou into thy chambers, and shut thy doors about thee: hide thyself as it were for a little moment, until the indignation be overpast" (Isa. 26:20).

In the hour when the outlook is darkest the uplook will be the brightest.

DELIVERANCE AT MIDNIGHT

In a moment shall they die, and the people shall be troubled at midnight, and pass away: and the mighty shall be taken away without hand. Job 34:20.

In the last traumatic struggle of the great controversy God's people will be tried and tested beyond anything human beings have ever experienced. Satan will attack the remnant in all of his fiendish fury.

"Those who honor the Bible Sabbath will be denounced as enemies of law and order, as breaking down the moral restraints of society, causing anarchy and corruption, and calling down the judgments of God upon the earth. Their conscientious scruples will be pronounced obstinacy, stubbornness, and contempt of authority. They will be accused of disaffection toward the government. Ministers who deny the obligation of the divine law will present from the pulpit the duty of yielding obedience to the civil authorities as ordained of God. In legislative halls and courts of justice, commandment keepers will be misrepresented and condemned."—*The Great Controversy*, p. 592.

What a scene—sword, famine, pestilence, bloodshed, physical upheaval and confusion fill the land. The plagues cause unrepentant men and women to suffer and to seek vengeance upon the little band of commandment-keeping Christians whom they charge with being responsible for the holocaust of horror abroad in the land.

"The decree will go forth that they must disregard the Sabbath of the fourth commandment, and honor the first day, or lose their lives."—*Testimonies*, vol. 1, pp. 353, 354.

The servant of the Lord enlarges upon the dreadful drama: "When the protection of human laws shall be withdrawn from those who honor the law of God, there will be in different lands, a simultaneous movement for their destruction. As the time appointed in the decree draws near, the people will conspire to root out the hated sect. It will be determined to strike in one night a decisive blow, which shall utterly silence the voice of dissent and reproof."—*The Great Controversy*, p. 635.

At last in that dark night of agony deliverance comes. God answers the prayers of His people. "He shall call upon me, . . . I will deliver him" (Ps. 91:15).

GATES CLOSED AND LOCKED

So Christ was once offered to bear the sins of many; and unto them that look for him shall he appear the second time without sin unto salvation. Heb. 9:28.

I was on a missionary safari in South West Africa with leaders from the South African Union. We were prospecting in unentered territory for suitable places to open new work. We traveled up through the Etosha Game Reserve en route to Ovamboland on the southern border of Angola. Our base for the last stage of the journey was an old German fort at Namutoni, now a ranger station within the reserve.

Each evening at sundown the gates of the stockade are closed and locked. Returning from Ondangua, tiny capital of the Ovambos, we found ourselves in danger of being locked out. The sun was setting rapidly. We had no illusions about the safety of spending a night out in the open with lions, elephants, and other predatory beasts on the prowl. With less than five minutes to spare we came in sight of our destination.

What a breath-taking scene lay just ahead! Unfolding before us, bathed in the gorgeous hues of a tropical sunset, stood snow-white Namutoni, etched against a crimson sky. Minutes later we drove into the stockade as the watchman was preparing to close and lock the gate. We had made it just in time. The sun had set but we were safe inside.

Today the sun is about to set for the last time on this sin-riven planet. Pilgrims traveling toward eternal safety in the City of God are within sight of home. The shades of night are falling fast around us. Events point unmistakably to the end of all things. Soon the gates of probation will forever close.

"Is there a Christian whose pulse does not beat with quickened action as he anticipates the great events opening before us? The Lord is coming. We hear the footsteps of an approaching God."—*Our High Calling,* p. 346.

> "The sunset burns across the sky;
> Upon the air its warning cry
> The curfew tolls, from tower to tower.
> O children, 'tis the last, last hour!"
> —CLARA THWAITES

GUIDANCE IN A CRISIS

The eyes of the Lord run to and fro throughout the whole earth, to shew himself strong in the behalf of them whose heart is perfect toward him. **2 Chron. 16:9.**

In 1905 subtle, insidious teachings that could rob workers and members of their faith in the gift of prophecy were being taught.

"On Monday night, December 25, a private meeting was held with the leading men in a room at the [Battle Creek] college," Elder A. G. Daniells wrote in a letter. "This meeting was of such a nature that a number of people have told me that if they had not been well grounded, they would have turned away entirely from the *Testimonies*. One said that he would have been driven into infidelity. . . . Two men told me that they slept but little that night."

The preceding Thursday morning, December 21, 1905, Ellen White, far away in California, was awakened early. A deep impression rested upon her. She must copy an entry from her diary that she had written two years previously, January 1, 1904. This message must be sent immediately to Battle Creek.

"Early the next morning after this [private] meeting was held," Elder Daniells wrote, "the message was in our hands and in twenty-four hours after these misleading, bewildering, confusing representations were made to a few men privately, they were openly exposed to nearly two thousand people. . . . When the general meeting closed, three men who had been in the meeting the night before from five to eleven o'clock, came forward and told me that the meeting held the previous night had been clearly described by the testimony I had read."

The counsel needed to meet this crisis had been written two years before and reached Battle Creek at the very hour it was needed. The eyes of faithful members were opened to error and to recognize God's leading through the Spirit of Prophecy.

God's eye still runs to and fro in the earth. His loving counsel is still for us through the writings of His messenger.

What a blessing!

IT IS A MUST

Marvel not that I said unto thee, Ye must be born again. John 3:7.

The Mount of Olives was bathed in the purple haze of a beautiful Palestinian moonlight. With an Arab guide by our side, a friend and I looked out over the jeweled lights of modern Jerusalem. We stood on the Mount of Olives where Jesus once had His memorable interview with a ruler of the Jews.

To the eager heart of Nicodemus, hungry for truth, the Saviour unfolded the gospel plan. The Master did not hedge in meeting the queries of His distinguished guest. He said, "Verily, verily, I say unto thee, Except a man be born again, he cannot see the kingdom of God" (John 3:3).

This new birth of which the Saviour speaks is a joyful new experience. A new heart, a new way of life, a new hope for the future is ours.

Notice the Saviour declared, "Ye *must* be born again."

Here is a message we must not fail to understand. Jesus did not say, "Unless you are born again, you *may* not reach the kingdom of heaven." He did not say, "It will be *difficult* to inherit heaven if you are not born again." But His earnest assurance was that it is *impossible* for anyone to enter the kingdom of God without this complete change in the life through a spiritual rebirth.

We may be socially charming, enviably educated, notably accomplished, morally unblamable, and even theologically well informed, all desirable attainments. But these advantages are not enough. The credentials of nominal Christianity will not do—church membership, liberal support of church programs, lavish charity, missionary activity, and a stout defense of the faith. All these desirable things could mark our reputation and yet we could be lost.

"The most careful cultivation of the outward proprieties of life is not sufficient."—*The Ministry of Healing*, p. 490.

When the repentant soul understands this, "his former life appears disgusting and hateful. He hates sin, and, breaking his heart before God, he embraces Christ as the life and joy of the soul. He renounces his former pleasures. He has a new mind, new affections, new interest, new will; his sorrows, and desires, and love are all new."—*The Faith I Live By*, p. 139.

INASMUCH

And the king will reply, "I assure you that whatever you did for the humblest of my brothers you did for me." Matt. 25:40, Phillips.

In November, 1966, I attended meetings in Denmark. During this time Brother H. Westerlund, at that time administrator of the Skodsborg Sanitarium, and I were together many times as we drove from place to place. Brother Westerlund is a good storyteller, and regaled me with reports of God's providences during the war and other thrilling reports of the hand of God at work in Europe.

One of these delightful experiences I want to share with you. On July 26, 1963, violent earth tremors destroyed large portions of Skoplje, Yugoslavia. In Skoplje at the time were some two hundred members of God's last-day family. About eighty-five members suffered severe losses in the quake.

When our leaders in Scandinavia heard of losses their Yugoslavian brethren sustained, they determined to help them. In these northern countries a special offering was received in the churches. From these funds twelve prefabricated homes were purchased. Each unit was to be equipped with beds, wardrobes, dining table and chairs, an electric heater, and basic kitchen equipment. Houses and equipment were loaded on railway cars and shipped to Skoplje.

Intent on being of personal help to their unfortunate Yugoslavian brethren, six men from Denmark drove by car to Skoplje to assist in the erection of the new homes.

The project completed, the day of turning over the keys to the happy families arrived. I doubt that many of the Yugoslavian members understood much of the Danish language, but they understood the language of love that made their new homes possible! They knew they belonged to a great spiritual family who cared!

Although Ellen White was speaking of children's relationship with their parents, her words in *The Adventist Home* (page 296) are also applicable to our relationship with brethren in the faith: "In doing this you are working for Jesus. He considers all these care-taking, thoughtful deeds as done to Himself."

CELL EIGHTEEN

But he was wounded for our transgressions, he was bruised for our iniquities: the chastisement of our peace was upon him; and with his stripes we are healed. Isa. 53:5.

A few years ago I visited Cell Number 18 in "the Block of Death" part of the Auschwitz concentration camp in the southern part of Poland. The Block of Death stands in some isolation from other buildings of the camp and is surrounded by a high wall, against which multiplied thousands of prisoners were executed.

Inside this dreaded building countless thousands met an unmerciful fate during those years of terror that characterized World War II in that part of Europe. But I shall not go into those repulsive details. My story centers in Cell Number 18.

Cell 18 is empty today—as are all the others in this house of infamy. Only a large wreath with appropriate wording in the Polish language marks the place where a Catholic priest died on September 14, 1941. He died of torture and starvation.

Father Kalbe was a young priest who, hearing of the plight of one of his parishioners in the camp, went to the commandant and offered to take the place of the young husband and father of three children in the death cell. The officer agreed. The young man was released to his family. Father Kalbe took his place, suffered and died in the other man's stead. Recently, our guide told us as we stood by the iron door of Cell 18, the man who had been saved by his priest visited Auschwitz and stood where we were standing.

As I stood looking into the dark, forbidding prison cell, my mind went back two thousand years to another place of death, not in Poland but outside old Jerusalem. Not inside but outside the wall. Not a cell but a cross. Here the Son of God was your substitute and mine.

"Upon Christ as our substitute and surety was laid the iniquity of us all. He was counted a transgressor, that He might redeem us from the condemnation of the law. The guilt of every descendant of Adam was pressing upon His heart."— *The Desire of Ages,* p. 753. The innocent died that the guilty might be set free. Christ took your place, my place.

THE AUTHOR SPEAKS TO YOU

This is why we thank God continually, because when we handed on God's message, you received it, not as the word of men, but as what it truly is, the very word of God at work in you who hold the faith. 1 Thess. 2:13, N.E.B.

In March, 1960, Mrs. Pierson and I were spending a few days with a fellow worker in Rhodesia. For morning worship the man of the house read from my 1960 morning devotional book *Give Us This Day.*

"We are happy to have the author of our book with us this morning for worship," Elder Baird began. "It is not often that we have the privilege of having the author of a book with us when we are reading it."

My friend paused thoughtfully, then continued, "I was just thinking about another book," he reflected, "—our Bible— we may have the Author of this wonderful Book with us every day as we read it!"

True! The Author of the world's best seller speaks to us every time we open its sacred pages. He speaks to us through the Written Word and He speaks to us through His Holy Spirit. The Bible is indeed the Inspired Word of God! It not only contains God's word; it *is* God's Word.

The believers in Thessalonica understood this and it brought joy to the apostle Paul's heart. Joyfully he wrote, "This is why we thank God continually, because when we handed on God's message, you received it, not as the word of men, but as what it truly is, the very word of God at work in you who hold the faith."

In the metropolitan museum a visitor gazed long at Rembrandt's picture of "An Old Woman." Moved by the life the great painter had infused into his work, the man murmured half aloud, "That is not a picture; it is the old woman herself."

"The Scriptures are to be received as God's word to us, not written merely, but spoken. . . . So with all the promises of God's Word. In them He is speaking to us individually, speaking as directly as if we could listen to His voice."—*The Faith I Live By,* p. 9.

"Hang in memory's hall the precious words of Christ. They are to be valued far above silver or gold."—*Ibid.*

THAT WHICH WE HAVE SEEN AND HEARD

That which we have seen and heard declare we unto you. 1 John 1:3.

The Lord's messenger knew well that before the return of our Lord, God's people would pass through a time of testing. The truth that God had given, Satan would seek to take away, to destroy either by direct attack or by subtle undermining. Today, in most lands, the overt attacks are not as frequent or as violent as once they were. Seventh-day Adventists have earned a degree of acceptability in most Christian circles. Our effective medical institutions have broken down prejudice. Our programs of welfare and disaster relief have warmed hearts that might otherwise be hardened toward us.

We are now entering the more dangerous period of the evil one's warfare—the subtle undermining of confidence in the message and the movement. We should not be surprised. Both the Word of God and the Spirit of Prophecy have warned us to expect a falling away, an erosion of faith just prior to the Second Advent.

In such a time of testing, God's true people will be strengthened in their faith by personal experiences they have had with the Lord and His saving truth. With doubt and deception hard pressing, they will not be moved. Speaking from a firsthand knowledge of Jesus and His last-day message, they will declare what they have both seen and heard of His goodness and the power of His truth.

"In the proclamation of the messages, every specification of prophecy has been fulfilled. Those who were privileged to act a part in proclaiming these messages have gained an experience which is of the highest value to them; and now when we are amid the perils of these last days, when voices will be heard on every side saying, 'here is Christ,' 'here is truth,' while the burden of many is to unsettle the foundation of our faith which has led us from the churches and from the world to stand as a peculiar people in the world, like John our testimony will be borne."—*Selected Messages*, book 2, pp. 387, 388.

"That which we have seen and heard declare we unto you."

What a blessed fellowship with well-established believers in a precious faith that neither threats nor subversion can take from us!

162

IS VIOLENCE THE ANSWER?

There is no fear in love; perfect love drives out all fear. 1 John 4:18, T.E.V.

"Death on the highways, a pack a day, cheating from top to bottom in our society, get rich quick, break up of the family, faltering in foreign policy, reckless debt—these have destroyed nations before us," one correspondent writes of the United States in our day. "Unless there is a change, deep down in the American people," she continues, "a genuine crusade against self-indulgence, immorality—public and private—then we are witnesses to the decline and fall of the American Republic. . . . First, every one of us has to clean out weakness and selfishness and immorality of all types."—Sunday *Telegram* [Portland, Maine], Feb. 9, 1963.

In recent years there have been young and old alike endeavoring to change the old order of things through resorting to violence and burning. From Watts to Washington, from Minneapolis to Miami, inner cities shuddered in paroxysms of rock throwing, fire bombing, shooting, and looting.

On American campuses violence and anarchy swept from campus to campus until, as one writer declared, the destruction threatened "disruption of the process of higher education in the United States" *(U.S. News and World Report,* May 6, 1968).

When "the establishment" has been burned down, with what is it going to be replaced? When physical flames are extinguished the fires of hatred and frustration still burn in human hearts. The looters are angry. The looted are angry. The police are angry. The taxpayers are angry. Violence is not the answer. There must be some power that can eliminate bitterness, hatred, frustration, and fear from the human soul.

There is such a power, and that power is *love*—the love of Christ! "There is no fear in love; perfect love drives out all fear." Only Christ in the heart—only *Christ's love* in the heart—will drive out selfishness, self-indulgence, and immorality. Christ alone is the sure and lasting remedy for a world racked with violence and anarchy. Only Christ can quench the flames of fear and hatred. "Perfect love drives out all fear."

163

THERE IS SOMETHING NEW UNDER THE SUN

All things are wearisome; no man can speak of them all. Is not the eye surfeited with seeing, and the ear sated with hearing? What has happened will happen again, and what has been done will be done again, and there is nothing new under the sun. Eccl. 1:8, 9, N.E.B.

Solomon was tired, jaded, and a bit cynical. The years had slipped by quickly and the years certainly had taken their toll on the monarch turned rich playboy-scholar. Love, learning, and laughter—he had tried them all. But he was not happy. Even the cycle of nature seemed endless and purposeless to him. Solomon learned what every disciple of the devil learns sooner or later—none of this sophisticated excitement satisfies the hunger of the human heart!

There is nothing new about sin. Lot's friends lived it up in the roaring cities of Sodom and Gomorrah. Love-ins are no phenomenon of the 1970's. Moses had one of these orgies on his hands fifteen hundred years before Christ.

Every new generation believes it is tripping a pioneer trail into both the problems and solutions of its day. They are only partially right. Sin in its varied forms merely changes cloaks and daggers. "The cycle of human life is repeated over and over again with each new generation."—*The SDA Bible Commentary,* Ellen G. White Comments, on Eccl. 1:3, p. 1063.

John the beloved disciple laid the ax at the root of the tree when he wrote, "Everything the world affords, all that panders to the appetites or entices the eyes, all the glamour of its life, . . . is passing away" (1 John 2:16, 17, N.E.B.). Whether it is Lot, Moses, Solomon, or Ben Smith in Sodom, Gomorrah, Jerusalem, Chicago, or Harlem, sin is still sin and there isn't anything very new or glistening about it! It still robs and kills. It robs us of our senses now and kills our hope of eternal life beyond the years.

Nothing new? Yes, there *is* something new under the sun for the child of God who seeks. God has a new heart, a new life, a new joy, a new assurance in the here and now. He also has a new heaven, a new earth, a new mansion, and a new eternity for all who decide to accept them. There is hope and help and happiness for all who choose the high road of God's love.

UP FROM THE MIRE

Create a pure heart in me, O God, and give me a new and steadfast spirit.
Ps. 51:10, N.E.B.

It was a sad scene. Handsome King David, popular leader of Israel, had fallen. His fall was not a political defeat, nor had enemy armies put to route the armed forces of Israel. David had fallen victim to the archenemy of mankind. Satan plumbed his weakness and the man of God found himself not only an adulterer but a murderer. Self-condemnation and remorse wrung his soul. Reaching out to God for peace and pardon, the fallen monarch cried out, "Purge me with hyssop, and I shall be clean: wash me, and I shall be whiter than snow. . . . Create in me a clean heart, O God" (Ps. 51:7-10).

The appeal of Israel's king is still the heart cry of every truly penitent soul today. A clean heart is still our greatest need. When the Holy Spirit has revealed to us our true condition before God, we are made aware of our shortcomings and uncleanness. We cry out for help. Thank God He hears and is ready to respond.

Our minds usually hold the key to victory to our struggle against evil. The battle of life is won or lost in the mind. "The thoughts will be of the same character as the food we provide for the mind."—*Testimonies,* vol. 5, p. 544. God will help clean up our thinking, but He must have our cooperation. We must select reading material that is uplifting, and keep our eyes on only that which is pure. We must make a covenant with our eyes. There are the television programs that draw us away from our Saviour. Trashy reading that panders to the lower nature must be replaced with literature that lifts our souls Godward. The Word of Life will play an important role in our quest for clear thinking and clean living.

Job asks a penetrating question: "Who can bring a clean thing out of an unclean?" (Job 14:4). The answer is obvious. We cannot of our own effort cleanse ourselves. But there is help. "God be praised, he gives us the victory through our Lord Jesus Christ" (1 Cor. 15:57, N.E.B.).

With our will on the right side, and with the help of our Saviour, our prayer for cleansing will be answered.

PULLING THE WORLD TOGETHER

Grow up into him in all things, which is the head, even Christ: from whom the whole body [is] fitly joined together. **Eph. 4:15, 16.**

"New York is a city without glue," one writer states in analyzing some of the divisive elements in that great metropolitan area. Then he widens the scope of disintegration, "The whole world is coming apart, the global village is about to disintegrate. The whole human race seems to be ripping open at the seams."

One who thoughtfully reads the daily paper or receives the news on television or over the radio might easily agree that elements from every point of the compass seem to be pulling the peoples of earth in all directions at once.

Multitudes in many lands are looking anxiously for some power, some emerging strong man—someone, just anyone, who can pick up the pieces and bring us together again.

Tracy Hilton found the solution to the world's enigma. The nine-year-old was sprawled on the rug putting together a jigsaw puzzle. As the picture began to take shape he exclaimed, "Oh, it's Jesus!"

Tracy continued perseveringly until the last crooked piece was in place. There before him was the full face of the Master.

"The instructions say to turn the picture over carefully," his mother said. Slowly he turned the puzzle over and there was a map of the world.

"Oh, Mother," Tracy shouted with delight, "when I got Jesus together the world is together all right, too!"

Tracy didn't know it, but he was paraphrasing Paul's words in our text today. In Christ "the whole body [is] fitly joined together." When Christ finds His proper place in the hearts of men, divergent elements can be drawn together. Unfortunately the time will never come in this sin-cursed world when enough of the world's leaders and followers will open their hearts and let Jesus come in and fitly join us all together.

But, praise God, the time is not far distant when Christ will personally step in and do the pulling together Himself. Signs on every side insistently remind us that in "a little while, . . . he that shall come will come, and will not tarry" (Heb. 10:37).

WHEN THEY FINALLY REALIZED

When they finally realized who he was, they rushed back to Jerusalem to tell the others. **Mark 16:13, T.L.B.**

"When they finally realized who he was"—the words burned their way into my thinking. I read them over and over again. Is it possible that some of us who have been Seventh-day Adventist Christians for many years may someday wake up and realize just who Jesus really is?

In recent months several young people have spoken to me of their new discovery—all of a sudden they realized who Jesus really is and what He wishes to be to them!

Take Bill, for instance. His father and mother spent years in the mission field. They rendered faithful service to the cause of God. Bill himself was reared a Seventh-day Adventist. In his early teens he was baptized. When I spent an hour visiting with him on the campus of one of our schools in a distant land, he described his new discovery.

"It's wonderful," he assured me and his face reflected the inner feeling of joy he had discovered in Christ. "For the past year now I've been praying and working for the other members of my family. Our home is different now. We have finally realized who Jesus really is!"

Fred's dad is a leader in our educational work. "I've been an Adventist all my life," he told me as we chatted in a Sabbath school room of one of our large new church buildings. "I've been a good moral kid, I guess, but somehow Jesus was just Someone in a storybook. He wasn't real to me. But not now! I know Him and I love Him. I'm trying to serve Him!"

How do we finally realize who He is and what He wants to do for us? When we begin really talking to Him in prayer; when we begin hearing Him speak to us through His Word, through sweet communion, through nature, through His many providences; when our prayers are answered, when help comes, when peace replaces care, when, though our problems are not taken away, we find solutions in Him, we will realize who He truly is. What a glorious discovery! When this beautiful realization finally dawns, we, like the disciples, will rush "to tell the others" the blessed news.

"HOW SHALL HE NOT WITH HIM"

He that spared not his own Son, but delivered him up for us all, how shall he not with him also freely give us all things? Rom. 8:32.

Did you ever stop to think about which is the more difficult for us to accept, justification or sanctification? Justification, of course, is an act of God that restores a sinner to a place with God that he would occupy if he had never fallen. Justification is preceded by conviction, repentance, and confession on the part of the sinner. Only God, through Christ, can effect the act of justification.

Sanctification, as we frequently affirm, is the work of a lifetime. Briefly it may be defined as the process of the justified sinner becoming more and more like his Lord, more Christlike.

Which is "easier"? We might reply, "Justification, for it is an act of God; all I must do is believe. Sanctification is that daily struggle with sin facing the challenge of old habits and human tendencies—this is much more difficult."

From a human viewpoint this reaction is natural. Paul has encouraging news for us in our text for the day! But first a sobering thought—the act of justification demanded a solution to man's sin problem even before Adam transgressed God's law in the Garden. How could God justify man and yet Himself be just? This was the sorest problem of eternity. God solved it. Jesus Himself would pay the awful debt. He would leave heaven, His place by the Father's side, the fellowship of the angelic host, come down to a world in rebellion, face the fiercest tests with which Satan ever confronted mankind, overcome, and then die upon a cross. Thus, through faith in that act of atonement man might be justified.

Justification then posed the more difficult problem. God solved it through Jesus. And if God in His love and mercy could overcome the tremendous problem He faced in saving a lost sinner, surely He is able to provide hope and help for him after he begins his walk in the Christian way! And, thank God, He does. Paul reminds us: "He that spared not his own Son, but delivered him up for us all, how shall he not with him also freely give us all things?"

"WHO LOVETH TO HAVE THE PREEMINENCE"

I wrote unto the church: but Diotrephes, who loveth to have the pre-eminence among them, receiveth us not. 3 John 9.

We find men like Diotrephes in our churches and schools today more frequently than one could wish. Diotrephes was an ambitious man and a troublemaker. It is not uncommon that these two traits of character go together.

We are not told just what office or position Diotrephes was ambitious to attain. Perhaps he coveted the church eldership or at least to be elected a deacon in his local congregation. Or it may be he was secretly hopeful that he would be elected the president of his conference (if there was a conference in John's day).

At any rate his aspirations were born of an unholy ambition. Evidently the burden of Christian service did not constrain him. Rather he sought position for prestige or glory.

It is likely that Diotrephes had read the words of Christ when the mother of James and John came to Him with her petition, "Grant that these my two sons may sit, the one on thy right hand, and the other on the left, in thy kingdom." The Saviour replied, "Whosoever will be great among you, let him be your minister, and whosoever will be chief among you, let him be your servant" (Matt. 20:21, 26, 27).

Diotrephes is not the only man who goes down in sacred history as one "who loveth to have the preeminence." Absalom was a man of unholy ambition, and he resorted to sneaky tactics to achieve his goal. He sought to ingratiate himself in the hearts of his father's subjects by being overly friendly and too solicitous of their welfare. Then he would spring the trap: "Oh, that I were made judge in the land . . ." he would subtly purr, "I would do him justice!" (2 Sam. 15:4).

There are still Diotrepheses in the church today. There are still those who, like Absalom, stoop to subtle undermining approaches to gain their ends. There are still those who, like the disciples, clamor "which of them should be accounted the greatest" (Luke 22:24).

Of such, Jesus says, "How can ye believe, which receive honour one of another, and seek not the honour that cometh from God only?" (John 5:44).

169

KITES RISE AGAINST THE WIND

When he was in Rome, he sought me out very diligently, and found me.
2 Tim. 1:17.

Onesiphorus was the kind of man who never gave up. He persevered. The assignment may have been baffling, frustrating, and time consuming, but when he set out to do a job he stayed at it until he could announce "mission accomplished." Evidently Paul's friend had difficulty in locating the apostle, for he wrote, "He sought me out very diligently and found me." Dr. Taylor paraphrases this simply, he "searched everywhere." Onesiphorus was not daunted by difficulty, futility, or adversity.

Perseverance is a great characteristic for a Christian. He needs much of it in his everyday victorious walk with the Lord. Without perseverance, Jesus said, we will never make it to the kingdom. "He that shall endure unto the end, the same shall be saved" (Matt. 24:13).

In fact, perseverance is a coveted quality in any person's experience. One cannot hope to make a success in any worthwhile project in life unless he has some "stick-to-itiveness." It is much easier when the task proves formidable, and the going tough, to just throw down tools and let someone else face the music for a while. Anyone can give up, but anyone can't succeed if his "giver-upper" functions prominently in his efforts.

Someone said, "Persistent people begin their success where others end in failure." The British statesman Burke once counseled, "Never despair, but if you do, work on in despair." Both these statements contain a great deal of wisdom; we need it in our Christian experience and in our Christian service.

Thomas A. Edison, like Onesiphorus, was a man of great perseverance. He never seemed to give up. After 187 failures in a certain experiment he exclaimed, "We are making progress. Now we know 187 things that won't work." And he went on to succeed—because he persevered!

Of course your lot in life is a difficult one. Of course the task you are expected to do is formidable. It can't be done? Stay by it! You will win with God's help. You may have to rest a bit, but don't quit. God is counting on you. Your church is counting on you. Persevere—be an Onesiphorus!

A BLIND MAN SEES

And he, casting away his garment, rose, and came to Jesus. Mark 10:50.

Our text today depicts the glorious climax of a sinner's quest for salvation. Jesus was on His way to Jerusalem. As He passed through Jericho, Bartimaeus, a blind beggar, "sat by the highway side begging." When he heard Jesus of Nazareth passing by, he cried out, "Have mercy on me" (Mark 10:46, 47). His appeal was heard. Healing came.

Several beautiful thoughts emerge from our story today.

Bartimaeus was persistent. Jesus was his one hope of healing. Although bystanders sought to quiet him, "he shouted even more loudly" (verse 48, T.E.V.). No one was going to keep him from Christ and His healing power. Bartimaeus possessed a persistent faith and it was rewarded.

The blind man responded immediately to the Saviour's call. There was no hesitancy, no questioning. When Jesus called, Bartimaeus "threw off his cloak" and "jumped up and came to Jesus" (verse 50, T.E.V.). Many hesitate when the Saviour extends His invitation of mercy. They question. They argue. They delay. Not Bartimaeus. He responded like a shot! He was determined not to miss his moment of opportunity.

There was no question in Bartimaeus' mind what he wanted. "I want to see again" (verse 51, T.E.V.). He had lived long enough in darkness. He wanted sight! When we go to a doctor or dentist, we go seeking relief from some particular pain or discomfort. We know what we want.

Coming to Jesus demands self-examination. It requires riddance from definite sins and shortcomings. "He shall confess that he hath sinned in that thing" (Lev. 5:5).

Bartimaeus' theology may not have been perfect, but his quest for salvation was sincere. He addressed Jesus as the "Son of David." This title may also have carried with it the thought of a conquering descendant of David leading Israel to national prominence. Though his doctrine may not have been fully mature, his faith was strong. Here was the one Person who could meet his need. He came to Him in simple faith. His need was met. Our initial step in applied theology is a personal reaction of love to Jesus and His proffered salvation.

Bartimaeus' experience may—yes, *must*—be ours.

IT'S NO FUN WHILE IT'S HAPPENING

Now no chastening for the present seemeth to be joyous, but grievous: nevertheless afterward it yieldeth the peaceable fruit of righteousness unto them which are exercised thereby. **Heb. 12:11.**

The famous artist Norman Rockwell was once asked how he was able to breathe such vibrant life into his paintings of everyday people.

"Because," he replied, "I never look for doll prettiness in my models. I look for people who have suffered—who have known hardships and heartaches, failure and poverty and shattered hopes, but through it all have never cast aside their faith."—DOROTHY CLYCE SMITH, "How to Look Beautiful," *The Signs of the Times,* Nov., 1962, p. 15.

David became a man after God's own heart. His was a life of suffering. Some of that suffering he brought upon himself. Some God permitted to befall him to purge his life from sin and to make him what God wanted him to be.

"Doll prettiness"—a superficial beauty—has no depth. It reveals no strength of true character. It has no message of hope or challenge for those who behold it. The affliction of the morrow may well turn it to darkest despair—or, on the other hand, it may be molded and matured by the pangs of suffering!

This molding, maturing process is not normally a pleasant experience. It may leave its wounds and the hurt may linger for years. But the end may well make it all worth while. It may well yield "the peaceable fruit of righteousness," making us more Christlike, kinder, more loving, more understanding, more thoughtful of those whom our lives touch.

Dr. Taylor paraphrases Paul's words to the Hebrews thus: "Being punished isn't enjoyable while it is happening—it hurts! But afterward we can see the result, a quiet growth in grace and character."

How is it with you, my friend; do you react and rebel, do you withdraw into a shell of bitterness and resentment when the oppressive hand of affliction rests upon you? Or do you joyously accept the leadings of the Lord in your life, and permit even the clouds of suffering He allows to enter your life experience to make for you a more glorious sunset?

172

REINS OF POWER IN HIS HANDS

Jesus came and spake unto them, saying, All power is given unto me in heaven and in earth. Matt. 28:18.

The context of our scripture for today is interesting. Let us read verses 16 and 17:

"Then the eleven disciples went away into Galilee, into a mountain where Jesus had appointed them. And when they saw him, they worshipped him: but some doubted."

Only a few hours before, the disciples' hopes were dashed as they beheld their beloved Master upon the cross. Surely He would not permit these evil men to take His life! He would exert His power; He would come down. He would deliver Himself. But He didn't! Gnawing doubts tore relentlessly at wavering faith. Where was the power that cast out devils, healed the sick, raised the dead?

After all these blows, all these bitter disappointments, little wonder the inspired writer added those three words, "but some doubted." Their world seemed to have utterly collapsed. Now what did they have to live for?

But the Saviour did not leave them in their discouragement and depression.

Now once more He stood before them—this time in resurrection splendor. Even now His disciples were divided. Some worshiped, some doubted. At such a moment Jesus spoke words of assurance. Neither the cross nor the grave had robbed Him of His power.

The God-man of Galilee still holds in His hands the reins of power in both heaven and earth. Jean Paul Richter, a serious historian, describes the impact the risen Lord has made upon ensuing history: "That crucified Jew with His pierced hands has lifted the gates of empires off their hinges, has turned the streams of the centuries into new channels, and still governs the years."—Quoted by G. T. Anderson, in the *Review and Herald,* April 4, 1968.

We have nothing to fear today if we are in His care. Days of bitter disappointment and discouragement may be our lot. Problems that beggar solution may be ours. When such times are upon us, let us remember that all power is still in His hands. Do not doubt. Tomorrow will be a brighter, fairer day!

A QUESTION ANSWERED

And God said unto Moses, I AM THAT I AM: and he said, Thus shalt thou say unto the children of Israel, I AM hath sent me unto you. Ex. 3:14.

A startled shepherd, actually a prince in exile, asked the question. God answered it, but not completely. Centuries passed before it was finally answered—or perhaps it has not been fully answered even today. Only in eternity will we understand all that is involved in the question and its fullest answer.

The prince in exile was Moses. The place was the backside of a Midian desert among a flock of sheep belonging to his father-in-law. The time was approximately a millennium and a half before the birth of Christ. Now for the question.

God had just revealed to Moses the role he was to play in the deliverance of Israel from Egyptian bondage. The startled shepherd was overcome with the implications of the assignment. "And Moses said unto God, Who am I, that I should go unto Pharaoh, and that I should bring forth the children of Israel out of Egypt? And he said, Certainly I will be with thee. . . . And Moses said unto God, Behold, when I come unto the children of Israel, and shall say unto them, The God of your fathers hath sent me unto you; and they shall say to me, What is his name? what shall I say unto them?" (Ex. 3:11. 12).

In other words, who is this God that will bring deliverance? God's reply? "I AM THAT I AM." But "I AM"—who?

For centuries the question remained. The amplified answer came in a beautiful revelation of our "many-sided," all-sufficient Saviour, Jesus Christ. In the fullness of time He appeared to fill the gap so long empty. "Jesus said unto them [the Jews], Verily, verily, I say unto you, Before Abraham was, I am" (John 8:58).

How gloriously Jesus provided the long-delayed answer to Moses' question. "I am the bread of life" (chap. 6:35). "I am the way, the truth, and the life" (chap. 14:6). "I am the light of the world" (chap. 8:12). "I am the good shepherd" (chap. 10:11). "I am the door" (verse 7). "I am the resurrection, and the life" (chap. 11:25).

Someday, if faithful, we may understand better what His answer to a startled shepherd in Midian truly means.

OUR LIVES MIGHT BE DIFFERENT TOO!

Believe his prophets, so shall ye prosper. 2 Chron. 20:20.

While meeting appointments in Johannesburg, South Africa, I had lunch with Mr. and Mrs. Michael Coetzee. Mrs. Coetzee's mother, Sister Pretorious, is a daughter of Henry Wessels. Ellen White sent a number of testimonies to Henry; she had told him his most valuable possessions would turn to ashes unless he responded to God's plea to follow Him.

Henry bought a necklace of diamonds costing about 25,000 dollars. The necklace was placed in a bank vault for safekeeping. Later, while he and his wife were in Australia, a financial crash wiped out their cash position. When they returned to Johannesburg they went to the bank to get the necklace. They planned to sell the diamonds to have some cash to live on. When they opened the box, to their astonishment, they found nothing but a chain of ashes, in the shape of the necklace, lying on the velvet pad in the box.

In their remorse they remembered Ellen White's plea and warning. Never again did they doubt the Spirit of Prophecy.

At one period in his experience Philip Wessels, Henry's older brother, was growing cold in his relationship with God. A straight testimony came from the Lord's messenger warning him against the course he was following. In her letter, Ellen White described how in vision she had seen Philip with his arm in a sling. When he read the letter he scoffed.

Later Brother Wessels caught his arm in a threshing machine. He had to carry his badly mangled arm in a sling for the rest of his life.

Elder A. W. Staples told this story to me one day:

"I happened to be in the same church in which Philip Wessels was worshiping the day Sister White's death was announced. When the announcement was read Philip arose, weeping, and holding up his withered arm in a sling, bore testimony to the work of the Lord's messenger. 'The Wessels family would have had a much different history,' he said sorrowfully, 'if they had only followed the admonition of God's servant.' "

The history of many lives would be different if we only followed more faithfully the admonition of His messenger.

BEAUTIFUL MEMORY OR POWERFUL PRESENCE?

And they talked together of all these things which had happened.
Luke 24:14.

As the two disciples walked together on the way to the village of Emmaus, they were reliving many thrilling experiences of the past few years and of the past few hours. "They talked together of all these things which had happened." Their minds and conversation were veritable battlegrounds of conflicting emotions. Memory had taken over!

He *was* who He declared Himself to be—the divine Son of God. Their memories were flooded with scenes of miracles. They spoke again of the water turned to wine, of the nobleman's son who, at the point of death, had been healed by the Master's word.

Not all of the memories were pleasant ones! Their beloved Leader had been criticized, accused, maligned: "He hath spoken blasphemy"; "Behold a man gluttonous, and a winebibber"; "Thou hast a devil" (Matt. 26:65; Matt. 11:19; John 7:20). They beheld Him denied, betrayed, forsaken, abused, crucified.

Later, memories turned again to glad reality—"Then . . . came Jesus and stood in the midst. . . . Then were the disciples glad, when they saw the Lord" (John 20:19, 20). Here they beheld for themselves the confirmation of the angel's words, "He is not here, but is risen" (Luke 24:6).

Years afterward the apostle Paul wrote, "Remember . . . Jesus Christ . . . raised from the dead" (2 Tim. 2:8).

The tense of the Greek verb in Paul's words indicates not a single act but a continuing state to last forever. Remember Jesus forever risen, forever present, is the apostle's thought. A beautiful memory can be a treasure to cherish. A powerful Presence means even more.

"Never feel that Christ is far away. He is always near. His loving presence surrounds you. Seek Him as One who desires to be found of you. He desires you not only to touch His garments, but to walk with Him in constant communion."—*The Ministry of Healing,* p. 85.

Jesus may be to us not just a beautiful memory but a powerful Presence.

176

GIVE THYSELF WHOLLY

Meditate upon these things; give thyself wholly to them; that thy profiting may appear to all. **1 Tim. 4:15.**

Darrell Peterson became interested in the Advent message. As he studied each week with Pastor Donaldson from the local Adventist church, Darrell drank in the truth.

When Henry Kline heard of Darrell's interest in the message Henry was disturbed.

"Darrell, don't you know those Seventh-day Adventists will take 10 per cent of your income if you join them?" Henry asked.

"Ten per cent of my income?" Darrell queried. "What do you mean?"

"I mean just that," Kline replied. "As soon as they get you into their church they will demand that you pay 10 per cent of your income to them. They call it tithe."

Darrell was disturbed. Pastor Donaldson had never mentioned anything like this to him. In fact, the question of church support had not come up. "I'll find out about it when the pastor comes to my house for our Bible study Tuesday evening," Darrell said to himself.

After the Bible study was finished Tuesday night and Pastor Donaldson was preparing to leave Peterson's home, his young friend spoke, "Pastor," he began hesitantly, "I hear that if I become a member of your church I will have to pay 10 per cent of my income to the church. Is this true?"

Pastor Donaldson was a wise young worker. Laying his hand on Darrell's shoulder and looking him straight in the eye, he began, "Yes, this is true," he said soberly. "God does ask for 10 per cent of our increase. I will study this with you shortly. But that is not all. In addition to our tithe, which belongs to Him, He asks us to give freewill offerings to support His work around the world. But God doesn't stop there. He will ask you to give your sons, your daughters, perhaps, to send them to India, to Africa, or some other far-off place. In fact, the God who gave His Son for you, in return asks you to give everything to Him. It is so little we can give; He has given us so much!"

"Meditate upon these things; give thyself wholly to them."

GOD DOES THE IMPOSSIBLE

And Jesus looking upon them saith, With men it is impossible, but not with God: for with God all things are possible. Mark 10:27.

In 1951 Mr. and Mrs. Clyde Harris of Pendleton, Oregon, handed over to the General Conference of Seventh-day Adventists the Harris Pine Mills organization worth several millions of dollars. Some people even inside the church were very skeptical about a church operating in such a competitive field of business.

Like the bumblebee that according to all the laws of aerodynamics can't fly, so the Harris Pine Mills just can't operate successfully as a Seventh-day Adventist Christian institution in such a climate as it is obliged to operate.

In the first place, preachers can't operate a huge empire of unfinished-furniture plants, sawmills, ranches, tree farms, fleets of trucks, and what not. But with God's help and with top-flight managers in the plants, Harris has operated successfully and grown under church supervision for more than twenty years. Today it is the largest unfinished-pine-furniture producer in the United States.

Businesses like Harris Pine just can't operate and keep the Sabbath. But Harris Pine does just that. Before sundown Friday evening all plants are shut down.

Even the boilers and the lumber-drying kilns keep the Sabbath at Harris Pine Mills. Boiler inspectors and timber experts said it would be technologically ruinous to shut down boilers and drying kilns every week. The boilers would be ruined. The lumber would be spoiled. But the boilers and the kilns are shut down every Friday evening before sunset and started up again shortly after sundown Saturday night. There has been no damage to boilers or lumber.

A businessman would know the problems faced in using student labor—classes, socials, extracurricular activities, immaturity, high wages. A business organization would find it difficult to operate successfully with such handicaps. Harris Pine employs more than two thousand students in its branch plants. Such a fine army of young men and women are helped through school each year. It can't work, but it does work when God is at the helm.

YOU MAKE THE DECISION

But of the fruit of the tree which is in the midst of the garden, God hath said, Ye shall not eat of it, neither shall ye touch it, lest ye die. Gen. 3:3.

"I don't see why God killed Adam and Eve for eating the fruit in the Garden of Eden." Bill's brow furrowed belligerently as he threw the challenge to his pastor.

"Did God really *kill* Adam and Eve?" Pastor Wilkins asked. "Suppose I were to tell you that if you jumped over the Niagara Falls you would die. If you went ahead and jumped into that foaming fury, could you or anyone else charge me with killing you?"

Bill thought a moment. "No, I guess no one could say that," he replied slowly. "You only told me what would happen if I jumped."

"That's right!" the pastor continued. "And that's just the way it was with God and Adam and Eve in the beginning. He placed the options before them. He explained the blessings that would be theirs if they were obedient. He also warned of the consequences of disobedience. Of their own free will they chose to disobey. They suffered the results. God did not force them!"

Suffering the results of my own choice is a lesson I learned some years ago—the hard way. I was driving through South Carolina. I had appointments to meet and I was in a hurry. The signs along the road indicated the speed limit was 55 miles an hour. I was not unaware of the penalty for exceeding the speed. But I was in a hurry. I chose to drive faster than fifty-five. It cost me 15 dollars for my choice.

Now the State of South Carolina did not make me drive that fast. I exceeded the speed limit of my own choice and I paid the penalty.

God doesn't kill people for sinning. Sinners die as the result of making wrong decisions. They but reap the results of their own choice. From the beginning God has made the options clear. "I have set before you life and death," He declares (Deut. 30:19). Through the apostle Paul He makes clear the result of our choice. "The wages of sin is death; but the gift of God is eternal life through Jesus Christ our Lord" (Rom. 6:23).

179

CAN'T GET THE STREAKS OFF

Wash you, make you clean; put away the evil of your doings from before mine eyes; cease to do evil. Isa. 1:16.

Some years ago Elder J. L. Dittberner was making a pastoral call. He noticed that the windows of the home he was in were streaked with dirt—they needed a good washing. The lady of the house was embarrassed.

"Elder, I am so embarrassed," she exclaimed. "I know my windows are dirty and they need washing. In fact, my little neighbor girl comes in to see me frequently and she always says, 'Auntie, why don't you wash your dirty windows?' "

"You see, Pastor," the sister continued, "there is a double glass. Smoke and dirt somehow have gotten down between the glass panes and I can't get inside to wash the dirt!"

There's "dirt inside" in the experience of too many of us— and sometimes it is "hard to get at." Those with whom we come in contact—like the little girl visitor—will detect the dirt. We can't hide it. And we won't be happy as long as it is there!

"He that covereth his sins shall not prosper" (Prov. 28:13).

"Many are unhappy because they are unholy. Purity of heart, innocence of mind, only can be blessed of God. When sin is cherished, it can in the end produce nothing but unhappiness; and the sin which leads to the most unhappy results is pride of heart, the lack of Christlike sympathy and love."—*Testimonies*, vol. 6, p. 53.

Our only hope for peace, for happiness, is to let God get down "between the panes" by His Holy Spirit and wash away the dirt of sin. "Wash you, make you clean," the Lord implores us; "put away the evil of your doings from before mine eyes; cease to do evil."

David felt his need for cleansing. He also knew his source of help and the channel through which that help was available —wholehearted confession of guilt and earnest prayer. "Wash me throughly from mine iniquity," he pleaded with God, "and cleanse me from my sin. . . . Purge me with hyssop, and I shall be clean: wash me, and I shall be whiter than snow" (Ps. 51:2-7).

You and I may be individuals after God's own heart, when we get the dirt inside cleansed away!

THE "CAT" WAS UNTOUCHED

Thou shalt not be afraid for the terror by night; nor for the arrow that flieth by day; nor for the pestilence that walketh in darkness; nor for the destruction that wasteth at noonday. Ps. 91:5, 6.

My message today is based upon the story of a cat—not a house cat or a tomcat or a wildcat. The "cat" I am talking about was a huge earth-moving machine owned by Harris Pine Mills and valued at $72,000.

The Harris "cat" had been loaned to a neighboring timber company to help fight fires caused by lightning. Just where the "cat" was operating on this fateful day, a sudden gust of wind caught the flames and they exploded in a firestorm that drove all the workmen away from the area. All the fire-fighting equipment including the "cat" had to be abandoned. The men had to escape for their lives.

In that raging inferno the fire fighters were sure their expensive machinery was destroyed. Nothing could escape the fury of the flames as they swept through the forest.

When the fire had passed, the men made their way back across the blackened earth, through the ghosts of scarred, smoking tree remnants. When they reached the spot where they had abandoned their equipment they found it just as they had expected—charred, twisted, melted by the intense heat of the fire—that is, all but the Harris Pine Mills "cat"! The huge earthmover stood defiantly in the midst of the black disaster—in a circle of greenery—its motor still running. It was untouched by the inferno that had destroyed most everything around it. The foliage in the tops of the trees above the "cat" was black and lifeless. But the "cat" purred on—a miracle of God's protecting hand that is unshortened today!

Sometimes the terror by night, the arrow by day, the pestilence in darkness, and the destruction at noonday is rebuked in behalf of God's property as well as on behalf of God's sons and daughters. If the Lord can spare an iron cat in the midst of a blazing inferno, He can surely care for you and for me in our everyday lives when we may be threatened.

We need to be sure that we are, indeed, dwelling "in the secret place of the most High!" Then we "shall abide under the shadow of the Almighty" (Ps. 91:1).

HAPPINESS DOESN'T COME WITH CONFETTI

Many waters cannot quench love, neither can the floods drown it: if a man would give all the substance of his house for love, it would utterly be contemned. S. of Sol. 8:7.

"I'm thirsty!" It was Linda at three o'clock in the morning. Husband, Fred, feigned sleep.

"Honey, I'm thirsty," again the plaintive call.

Fred stirred slightly. It was three o'clock on a dark, wintry morning. The water was downstairs in the cold kitchen. The only slightly conscious husband thought of the cold, creaky trip down the stairs. At three o'clock in the morning it was a grim prospect.

Fred threw back the cover, stumbled into his bathrobe and slippers, negotiated the creaky stairs, weathered the cold blast of the open refrigerator, poured the glass full of water, and labored back upstairs.

"Thank you, dear!" Linda murmured appreciatively. "You are a good husband."

Linda hadn't said, "Please, dear, go downstairs and get me a glass of water." She hadn't threatened, badgered, or whined. All she had said was, "I'm thirsty." Fred responded.

When I heard Fred tell the story later he explained, "There was only one thing in the world that made me get up at three o'clock in the morning and go down into a cold kitchen to get my wife a drink of water—it was love. I may be short on many other qualities, but when it comes to that girl I have plenty of love."

It takes plenty of love to make a happy home! Love transforms a man or a woman. It makes one thoughtful, kind, unselfish, and understanding. It takes a lot of thoughtfulness, kindness, unselfishness, and understanding to turn even a well-furnished house into a little heaven. That kind of love comes from above. It is closely akin to Christ's love.

Happiness—true happiness at home—does not begin with confetti. It begins when two hearts are overflowing with the love of God—a love that makes them thoughtful even in little things.

PROTEST? YES!

He brought me to the banqueting house, and his banner over me was love. S. of Sol. 2:4.

Protest demonstrations are no phenomenon peculiar to the current decade. They had them in Paul's day! Luke describes a scene not uncommon to the 1970's. There was a riot in Ephesus created by one Demetrius, a silversmith. The spread of a gospel denouncing idol worship, he felt, threatened his rights and security as a craftsman. He took to the streets.

Appealing to personal interest and superstition, Demetrius whipped up the emotions of the mob with techniques of inflammatory propaganda, familiar in our day. The inspired account in Acts nineteen reads much like a current news report of what might be happening in our own community. It reeks of hostility and hate.

"At this their anger boiled and they began shouting. . . . A crowd began to gather and soon the city was filled with confusion. Everyone rushed to the amphitheater, dragging along Gaius and Aistarchus. . . . Inside, the people were all shouting, some one thing and some another—everything was in confusion. In fact, most of them didn't even know why they were there. . . . They started shouting again and kept it up for two hours" (Acts 19:28-34, T.L.B.).

Many who protest today would tear down the very government that assured them the right to protest. Yet they have no better plan to replace the establishment they seek to burn and destroy. Banners, slogans, aroused tempers, shouting, are not enough. We need to find some answers and some solutions, as well as raise questions and protest.

Of course our society is sick. Inequities do exist. Agreed, some changes need to be made in certain areas.

Christ's weapons of protest? A dynamic love. A self-denying love—love that cared, love in action! During the days of the apostolic church His love protest swept Palestine, spanned the continent, leaped the seas. Today His message of compassionate salvation reaches out to every kindred, tongue, and people.

With His banner of love over us we can move the world!

JESUS WAS A MAN

Remember that Jesus Christ of the seed of David was raised from the dead according to my gospel. 2 Tim. 2:8.

"Jesus Christ of the seed of David"—several passages in the Word of God remind us that Jesus was of the seed of David—therefore He was a man, as well as the Son of God.

I like the way Dr. Taylor paraphrases the first portion of our text: "Don't ever forget the wonderful fact that Jesus Christ was a Man, born into King David's family" (T.L.B.).

"Don't ever forget"—a calculated emphasis of the authorized version's "remember." Here is a fact that we must ever keep in mind. There is a reason! This reason is a "wonderful fact." Here was nothing commonplace, nothing ordinary. Here was a fact never paralleled in the history of heaven or earth—God born into a human family! Heaven reached low to place divinity in the arms of humanity—Jesus Christ held close to Mary's heart!

The Son of God partook of the experiences common to humanity. Like other children about Him Jesus "grew, and waxed strong" (Luke 2:40). He was hungry (see chap. 4:2). He was weary after a day of toil (see John 4:6). He was "acquainted with grief" (Isa. 53:3). He experienced sorrow (see Matt. 26:37). He knew the gnawing claims of poverty (see Luke 9:58). Like all men He resorted to sleep, to rest a heavily taxed body (see chap. 8:23).

Christ's humanity links Him very closely with the needs of mankind—with your needs and mine! "This High Priest of ours understands our weaknesses, since He had the same temptations we do, though He never once gave way to them and sinned."

He "understands our weaknesses"—His humanity enables Him to enter into our feelings. He understands our hopes, our joys, our disappointments, our frustrations, and our failures! And, Paul says, He "has gone to heaven itself to help us" (Heb. 4:15, 14). "He who was one with God has linked Himself with the children of men by ties that are never to be broken."—*Steps to Christ,* p. 14.

Blessed thought—the Son of God became the Son of man that He might better serve us both now and forever!

TWO WAYS—YOU CHOOSE!

See, I have set before thee this day life and good, and death and evil.
Deut. 30:15.

When prisoners arrived at the Auschwitz concentration camp in south Poland during World War II, their bolted freight cars were opened in the Birkman section of the camp and they crowded out onto the railway ramp. In August, 1971, I stood on this ramp and sought to reconstruct this scene of horror that hundreds of thousands of human beings, young and old, experienced.

The prisoners were not given any food during the journey from their homes to the camp. They were crowded into the freight cars far beyond capacity. No sanitary facilities were provided. They were going they knew not where. Many were told they were being resettled in lands from which their fore-fathers had migrated.

In long lines these hapless wretches filed past camp doctors. These doctors, by the wave of the hand, sent some of the prisoners to the camp to live and to work, and by the same token sent others to nearby crematoriums where they were to die in gas chambers. Those considered physically capable of productive labor lived. Those whom the camp doctor at a glance decided were unfit for work died within a few hours' time.

The flick of a man's hand determined their wretched fate —life or death. The human being concerned had no choice, no voice in the decision.

For every person born into this world there are two ways. One is God's way. The other is Satan's way. One is the good way that leads to life. The other way leads to death.

God's Word makes this clear: "See, I have set before thee this day life and good, and death and evil."

Which way we take is not determined by the flick of a man's hand. It is not dependent upon our physical condition. It is determined by our own choice—"See, I have set before thee." In other words, make your decision. Good or evil, life or death—it is up to you, to me. If we are saved it will be because we have *chosen* to be saved. If we are lost it will be because we have *chosen* the way that ends in eternal death.

185

HIS SHIRT FOR GOD

For all these have of their abundance cast in unto the offerings of God: but she of her penury hath cast in all the living that she had. Luke 21:4.

During the Week of Prayer, Petro, an African evangelist, came to his mission treasurer with a request that he be given an advance of a month's salary.

"Why do you need this advance?" the treasurer asked.

"Oh, sir, you see, we will be receiving the Week of Sacrifice offering in our church on Sabbath and I wish to give a month's salary for the offering," Petro explained simply.

The treasurer was surprised. "But Petro," he asked, "how can you afford to give so much? You have a wife and six children to support."

Petro beamed. "My wife and I have talked this over," he replied happily, "and we have everything all planned. You see we have a garden and this will provide food for us during the month. I have two shirts and I have already sold one so we will have money to buy salt and a little oil for our relish. We will get along just fine."

The treasurer paused thoughtfully. Then Petro continued with a large smile creasing his black face, "It is wonderful how the Lord blesses us when we go to Him. We do so want to return to Him a good Week of Sacrifice offering."

A month's salary! Half of his shirts sold for food in order to bring a good Week of Sacrifice offering! What commitment!

This African worker's salary was not a large amount when compared with gifts that are made by God's people in more affluent countries, but perhaps in the books of heaven it was reckoned much greater than some of us give for the Week of Sacrifice. How many of us give a *month's* salary? How many of us sell a sizable share of our wardrobe in order to give liberally to the cause of God? In fact, how real is our love for God and how truly eager are we to see His work finished?

We do well to remember Petro, his shirt, and his liberal offering. We do well to remember the one Petro emulated when he gave so liberally: "For they have given a little of what they didn't need, but she, poor as she is, has given everything she has" (Luke 21:4, T.L.B.).

DIAMONDS TODAY—DUST TOMORROW

And Lot lifted up his eyes, and beheld all the plain of Jordan, that it was well watered every where, before the Lord destroyed Sodom and Gomorrah, even as the garden of the Lord, like the land of Egypt, as thou comest unto Zoar. Then Lot chose him all the plain of Jordan; and Lot journeyed east: and they separated themselves the one from the other. Gen. 13:10, 11.

There was trouble between Abram's herdsmen and those of his nephew, Lot. Grazing grounds were poor—not enough for the herds of both men. Water was scarce and the whole situation spawned ill feeling between Abram's men and Lot's men. There could have been tension between the two men themselves. Abram made sure that that did not happen.

One day Abram spoke to his nephew: "Let us go our separate ways: if you go to the left, I will go to the right; or if you take the right I will go to the left." The choice was Lot's!

"And Lot, lifting up his eyes and looking on the valley of Jordan, saw that it was well watered everywhere; . . . it was like the garden of the Lord, like the land of Egypt. . . . Lot took for himself all the valley of Jordan, and went to the east, and they were parted from one another" (Gen. 13:9-11, Basic English).

As Lot gazed out over the well-watered plains and the cities that lay before him, he thought only of the prosperity that would come to him if all that he saw belonged to him. What wealth! He would be the head of a large and prosperous family! He made a decision that was to affect not only his own future but the eternal future of some members of his household. "Then Lot chose him all the plain of Jordan; . . . and Lot dwelled in the cities of the plain" (verses 11, 12).

What a tragic decision! Soon Lot and his family were not only *in* Sodom, most of them were soon *of* Sodom. They were not only in Sodom, Sodom was in them. What appeared diamonds to Lot as he looked over the land became dust on the morrow. You know well the sad ending of the story—all the result of a wrong choice.

"Short and decisive are the steps that lead men down from high and holy ground to a low level. In a moment decisions may be made that fix one's condition forever."— *The Ministry of Healing,* p. 510. Solemn thought!

187

MARY'S SECRET

There is really only one thing worth being concerned about. Mary has discovered it—and I won't take it away from her! Luke 10:42, T.L.B.

Martha was busily engaged in caring for the creature comforts of Jesus during one of His visits to Bethany. While Martha took thought for the many little chores of the home pressing for attention, Mary, her sister, sat at the Master's feet drinking in every word He spoke.

Martha needed help in straightening the house and in preparing the meal.

" 'Sir, doesn't it seem unfair to you that my sister just sits here while I do all the work? Tell her to come and help me.'

"But the Lord said to her, 'Martha, dear friend, you are so upset over all these details! There is really only one thing worth being concerned about. Mary has discovered it—and I won't take it away from her!' " (Luke 10:40-42, T.L.B.).

"There is really only one thing worth being concerned about." Mary of Bethany understood a secret of successful Christian living you and I must know today. She had learned to place first things first.

"Personal contact with Christ, to sit down in companionship with Him—this is our need."—*Education*, p. 261. Mary's experience must become ours. In the midst of life's endless round of pressing cares and activity we, too, must learn to sit at Jesus' feet.

To sit down in companionship with Jesus is not just a beautiful phrase; it is a real experience. It becomes ours when we take time to speak with our Lord in prayer and when we listen to Him speak to us through His Word. It is a two-way conversation. It makes the Master a very real part of our life.

"As Mary once devoutly sought the eternal truth, the
  better part,
  And sat, enwrapt in holy thought at Jesus' feet with
  burning heart,
Even so, is all my heart's desire fixed, dearest Lord, on
  Thee alone.
  Oh make me true and draw me higher, and make Thyself, O Christ, my own."—*Unknown.*

A COMPLETE REFORMATION

Well, whatever you do, whether you eat or drink, do it all for God's glory. Live in such a way as to cause no trouble either to Jews, or Gentiles, or to the church of God. 1 Cor. 10:31, T.E.V.

"Reformation signifies a reorganization, a change in ideas and theories, habits and practices" *(Selected Messages,* book 1, p. 128), inspiration reminds us. Both our thinking and our living will be affected by true reformation. Some of us need our thinking changed. Many of us need our life-styles altered. We all need help—and need it desperately. "The time has come for a thorough reformation to take place."—*Testimonies,* vol. 8, p. 251.

Webster defines *reform* "to amend or improve by change of form or removal of faults or abuses; to put an end to [an evil] by introducing a better method or course of action."

It is evident that we, as God's people, are not what we should be. We need amending and improving. An end must be made to evil, and some better courses of action are to be followed. We need changing. We need renewing—we need a reformation. "Unless there is a decided reformation among the people of God, He will turn His face from them."—*Ibid.,* p. 146. "God's people will not endure the test unless there is a revival and a reformation."—*Ibid.,* vol. 7, p. 285.

This amending and improving must reach into every phase of our lives—even into some of those areas often labeled externals—what we eat, what we drink, what we wear, where we go. It is the whole man—his body as well as his heart and mind—that needs a change, a reformation. There must be *"a most decided reformation in eating, drinking, and dressing" (ibid.,* vol. 6, p. 377; italics supplied).

"God calls upon every church member to dedicate his life unreservedly to the Lord's service. He calls for decided reformation. All creation is groaning under the curse. God's people should place themselves where they will grow in grace, being sanctified, body, soul, and spirit, by the truth. When they break away from all health-destroying indulgences, they will have a clearer perception of what constitutes true godliness. A wonderful change will be seen in the religious experience."—*Counsels on Health,* p. 579.

IT COSTS, BUT IT PAYS

Rachel is weeping for her children and she cannot be comforted, for they are gone. Jer. 31:15, T.L.B.

"Don't stop now! Don't stop now!" It was the voice of a concerned father during a camp meeting appeal in South Africa.

"Don't stop, pastor, please don't stop," he pleaded. "My boy is out there in the congregation and he has never given his heart to the Lord. Make one more appeal. Perhaps he will respond."

At the close of my Sabbath morning sermon and as the Holy Spirit came in among us, I was appealing for those in the large congregation who had never given their hearts to the Lord to do so. Many responded. I was just ready to close when the agonized whisper behind me reached my ears. How could I stop when one father's son had not yet surrendered? To this father nothing was more important than for that son of his love to be saved. He would give possessions, money, even life itself, to assure his son's salvation.

Jeremiah's words in our text do not refer to a parallel experience in the life of Rachel, but they surely convey the anguish of a parent who realized, perhaps too late, that his child is not saved.

How much are these boys and girls of ours really worth? What price would we pay to assure them a place in the kingdom?

Perhaps even now you are deciding where your children will attend high school or college this fall. Will it be the conference academy or the union college? Will it be the local high school? This may not be an easy decision. It costs to send young people to Seventh-day Adventist academies and colleges these days.

One can attend a local school with little financial outlay. Why not just keep John and Helen at home and let them attend school locally? You could save a lot of money, *but* if you send them to a school where Christ occupies no place in the curriculum or in the experience of the teachers—*will you save John and Helen?* This is the important question!

SPIRIT OF THE PIONEERS

Righteousness exalteth a nation: but sin is a reproach to any people. **Prov. 14:34.**

The following words depict graphically the spirit of the intrepid pioneers who hewed a nation of the wild, fertile ground of the United States.

"They were people who knew that life is always a struggle, and accepted it on those terms. Men drowned crossing rivers, died in blizzards, in the waterless heat of summer, by falls from horses, by Indian arrow, by white man's bullet. What would be a simple scratch today, killed then. Many died at birth or in childhood of diseases which are of little risk today. . . . That sudden face at the window could be your salvation, bringing food or powder—or it could be death by arrow, hatchet or club. Nature, which gave life, could also take it. Their reality was super-harsh, but they set their faces into it, as into the killing north wind. . . . Their problem was not surplus; it was survival. The pioneers didn't brood about life— they lived it."—PAUL ENGLE, "Are We Losing Our Pioneer Spirit?" Copyright 1971 by the National Wildlife Federation. Reprinted from the December/January issue of *National Wildlife* Magazine.

What of America in 1975? Have we lost our pioneer spirit, our will to win through any obstacles? Some of our friends in other lands fear we have lost that spark that made America great!

President John F. Kennedy once wrote, "Too many Americans have lost their way, their will, and their sense of historic purpose." Then he challenged America to get moving.

Perhaps Seventh-day Adventists can learn some lessons from the spirit of *our* pioneers. The men and women who, under God, founded this movement were workers of courage.

Could it be that too many Adventists "have lost their way, . . . their sense of historic purpose"? Have we forgotten where we came from and where we are going?

Perhaps we need to recapture the spirit of the pioneers, to learn again to make the Advent message and its early triumph our cause—one for which we are willing to give everything, even to life itself. It's something to think about!

A POST OFFICE WITHOUT A LETTER DROP?

And he said unto them, Go ye into all the world, and preach the gospel to every creature. He that believeth and is baptized shall be saved; but he that believeth not shall be damned. **Mark 16:15, 16.**

Can you imagine a post office without a letter drop? I read that in the city of Pittsburgh, Pennsylvania, some years ago a million-dollar post office building was erected. A big official opening was carried out. Well-known speakers spoke at length. The band played, and all the other trimmings deemed essential on such an occasion were part of the program. Everything was fine—with one exception—there was no place to post letters!

God has entrusted to His last-day church the great assignment of preaching His gospel of the kingdom to everybody everywhere. Fully to preach this message that will save men and women is the very reason for our existence as a church. How will we give an account of our stewardship in the day of judgment if we have done many other good things and failed in that which is most important?

If you should read in the morning paper, "Theodore Roosevelt is dead!" that would not be news. You would lay aside your paper and observe it was history, not news. But when you read, "Jesus Christ died for me!" this is good news today and every day. In fact, it is the best news mankind has ever received.

News isn't released to be kept secret. It is meant to be published, and the good news of the gospel is to be published everywhere—in Tokyo and in Tanganyika, in Bombay and in Buenos Aires, in London and in Los Angeles. This worldwide, world-shaking commission is the first work of the Seventh-day Adventist Church.

You have a part to play in this challenging assignment. I have a part. The scope of our task involves not only our own country but every country on earth. Every member of the church has a role to play. We can all pray. We can all give. We all have a part. If *your* church is not a strong supporter of world missions it is like the post office with no place to mail a letter—it has forgotten the very reason for its existence! You may need to change some things!

192

SOMETIMES THE PRICE IS HIGH

Again, the kingdom of heaven is like unto a merchant man, seeking goodly pearls: who, when he had found one pearl of great price, went and sold all that he had, and bought it. Matt. 13:45, 46.

Helena loved the Lord Jesus. She determined to make Him first in her experience through a life of complete obedience to His commandments. Her father threatened to kill her if she were baptized. The "pearl" bore a high price tag. But Helena's quest was not to be diverted.

The day of the baptism came. Helena went down into the racing waters of the river with her pastor. Two shots rang out. Both the pastor and Helena disappeared beneath the water. Both were quickly recovered by loving friends. Only the pastor survived. The "pearl" cost Helena all she had—her life.

"In the parable the merchantman is represented as selling all that he had to gain possession of one pearl of great price. This is a beautiful representation of those who appreciate the truth so highly that they *give up all they have to come into possession of it.*"—*Selected Messages,* book 1, p. 399. (Italics supplied.)

Not many of us may be called upon to experience martyrdom. Sometimes, however, it is easier to die for Christ than to live for Him! Nagging, cutting opposition in the home, searing blasts of temptation, the ridicule of those whom we love because we stand for truth, renunciation of a world we have grown to love—any of these may obstruct our quest for the Pearl of Great Price.

The man in the parable sold *all that he had* in order to obtain the pearl. The Pearl of Great Price cannot be had today for a lesser price. "He is a gift, but only to those who give themselves, soul, body, and spirit, to Him without reserve."—*Christ's Object Lessons,* p. 116.

"All that he had"—the price is still the same today. It will cost us our pride, our selfishness, our idols; it may demand our pleasure, our friends, our job, even our life—but Christ and His righteousness, His salvation, is worth any price we pay!

AFFLUENCE OR POWER?

Then Peter said, Silver and gold have I none; but such as I have give I thee: In the name of Jesus Christ of Nazareth rise up and walk. Acts 3:6.

Two churchmen stood gazing admiringly at a beautiful new church school complex.

"Well, John," one of the pastors said, half chiding, half boasting, "we can't say what the apostle said, 'Silver and gold have we none!' "

"True," replied his friend a bit ruefully, "and neither can we say, 'Rise up and walk.' "

The two churchmen were not Seventh-day Adventists, but they could have been. With our capital investments in church buildings, schools, medical institutions, and publishing houses running well into the hundreds of millions, we can no longer say, "Silver and gold have I none." With an annual world budget of approximately $60 million, we give evidence of wealth and prestige.

But can we say, "Rise up and walk"? Has affluence made us spiritually strong? Are the gleaming institutions that we have built, the bank accounts we have amassed, true barometers of spiritual power in the church?

Perhaps God's answer to this question is found in His message to the Laodiceans, "Thou sayest, I am rich, and increased with goods, and have need of nothing; and knowest not that thou art wretched, and miserable, and poor, and blind, and naked" (Rev. 3:17).

"Not only does the Laodicean church claim to be rich, but she also makes the fatal mistake of considering that these riches are the result of her own labors."—*The SDA Bible Commentary,* on Rev. 3:17.

We thank God for His blessing upon this church—for the fine schools, hospitals, publishing houses, and church buildings He has given us. We need every one of these important structures and many, many more just like them.

Fine, *but*—wealth without power can never finish the work. Nothing can take the place of Spirit-filled men and women, young and old, who have committed all to their Master. Spirit-filled members who can say "Rise up and walk" are the great need of the hour—God's hour!

WHEN DO YOU GIVE YOUR FLOWERS?

And Joanna the wife of Chuza Herod's steward, and Susanna, and many others, which ministered unto him of their substance. Luke 8:3.

Inspiration doesn't tell us much about Joanna—only that she was the wife of Chuza, King Herod's business manager. As such she may well have been a person of some influence. Dr. Luke identifies her as one of the women "which had been healed of evil spirits and infirmities" (Luke 8:2). As one who had personally experienced the power of Christ in her life, she felt a debt of gratitude toward the One who had brought help and healing.

We read that Mary Magdalene, Susanna, and Joanna provided for Him out of their own resources. Of this labor of love the *Seventh-day Adventist Bible Commentary* says, "It may well be said that this group of devout women constituted the first women's missionary society of the Christian church."—On Luke 8:3.

"At every opportunity Joanna revealed her love for the Master. And Jesus understood this practical manifestation of gratitude. The spices and ointments with which she would have helped to anoint the Saviour's body in death (Luke 23:55, 56; 24:10) were but a continuing love gift begun during His lifetime."—*The Ministry,* February, 1969, p. 43.

To be able to speak a few words of sincere *appreciation* at the proper time is a gracious trait.

"There are many to whom life is a painful struggle; they feel their deficiencies and are miserable and unbelieving; they think they have nothing for which to be grateful. Kind words, looks of sympathy, *expressions of appreciation, would be to many a struggling and lonely one as the cup of cold water to a thirsty soul.* A word of sympathy, an act of kindness, would lift burdens that rest heavily upon weary shoulders. And every word or deed of unselfish kindness is an expression of the love of Christ for lost humanity."—*Thoughts From the Mount of Blessing,* p. 23. (Italics supplied.)

Many struggling ones in the world about us are thirsty for the cup of cold water—a few flowers of appreciation before the tomb. In other words, we could do with more Joannas.

BUILDING UP THE REDEEMER'S KINGDOM

Love each other with brotherly affection and take delight in honoring each other. **Rom. 12:10, T.L.B.**

Are you eager to see the gospel preached to all the world, the work finished, and Jesus come soon, very soon? Listen: "Nothing will so successfully defeat the devices of Satan and his emissaries, nothing will so build up the Redeemer's kingdom, as will the love of Christ manifested by the members of the church."—*Testimonies,* vol. 5, pp. 167, 168.

This is an amazing statement. It speaks of building up the Redeemer's kingdom, and it doesn't say a word about money, institutions, planning, or programs. It does, however, single out the most potent force in all the world—love. This is the love *of* Christ—here it is not speaking of love *for* Christ! This experience teaches us not only to love Christ but to love as Christ loved. When you and I love those around us as Christ loves them, men and women will be asking the way Zionward and the Redeemer's kingdom will be built quickly.

Jesus emphasized this precious way of personal involvement in a finished work: "This is my commandment: that you love one another as I have loved you" (John 15:12, Phillips).

When we love those with whom we come in contact as Christ loves them, they will surely become aware of it. We will let them know by our attitudes, our words and most of all by our deeds. "Love cannot long exist without expression."—*The Ministry of Healing,* p. 360. We express love by a thousand little acts of kindness, thoughtfulness, and helpfulness.

In a greedy, covetous, and indifferent world these warm demonstrations of love will set us apart as the "peculiar people" God intends we should be (1 Peter 2:9). People will seek to learn what makes us different.

This does not please the evil one, Satan. "He is not pleased to see the Redeemer's kingdom on earth built up."—*The Acts of the Apostles,* p. 74. So he continually seeks to keep brotherly love—the love of Christ—out of the church. He sows seeds of suspicion and evil surmising in our midst.

We can be part of Satan's defeat and the triumph of God's kingdom. And we can do it by cherishing the love of Christ in our hearts!

STAY BY IT—YOU WILL SUCCEED!

So let us not become tired of doing good; for if we do not give up, the time will come when we will reap the harvest. Gal. 6:9, T.E.V.

Henrik Landeng, a graduate from our college in Norway, had one all-consuming ambition—to go to Spitzbergen and sell books. At the time, there were only some two thousand Norwegians in Spitzbergen and it was very difficult to secure a government permit to visit the large frozen island.

Henrik was not deterred. Persistently he visited the government office seeking to secure a permit to visit the field of his choice. Officers assured him there were enough books in Spitzbergen and they did not need the ones he proposed to sell.

Undaunted Henrik returned a year later. The answer was still No. In the meantime, the determined youth sold many books in his homeland. The third year he still made no progress in securing a permit to visit Spitzbergen. Undeterred in his decision the youth decided upon another plan.

With two large suitcases filled with books young Landeng made his way to a Norwegian port and slipped aboard a boat Spitzbergen bound. He stowed away in a lifeboat until he was half a day out to sea, then went to the purser and offered to pay his fare. The officer refused to take his money. He also declared Henrik could not land when the ship docked.

After several unsuccessful attempts, Henrik finally slipped past the guards on the dock with his books. It was two o'clock in the morning and broad daylight in that part of the world. Young Landeng got busy selling books without delay. Just before the gangplank was drawn up for the return journey that afternoon, Henrik dashed aboard with two almost empty suitcases. He had sold all but two books. One of these he sold to the captain of the ship. Persistence paid off.

Sometimes we have been tempted to give up when the goal was almost attained. When a job was tough we gave up rather than battling through to victory. Of course there are problems. Of course there are disappointments. Of course there is opposition. But if we stay by the job the Lord will see us through!

IS GOD A KILLJOY?

I have come in order that they might have life, life in all its fulness. John
10:10, T.E.V.

"Old Jack must be a good Christian, Daddy," little Bert
announced as he came in from the mule barn.

"Old Jack a Christian?" the surprised father replied. "Why
do you think that?"

"Because, Daddy," Bert responded brightly, "he has such a
long face!"

Unfortunately too many people are under the impression
that everything worthwhile, everything that is exhilarating and
challenging, everything that is fun, becomes suspect when
God appears on the scene.

Others find just living—growing up, enjoying good, wholesome recreation, laughing, loving, working, succeeding in
life—a very stimulating and rewarding experience. It is challenging to excel at something one enjoys—flying, swimming,
painting, farming, computer-programming. When life moves
along evenly and successfully one finds many rewards in just
living. Many feel no need of anything more. God just does not
enter their picture. If He were to do so He would be a jarring
note, a detractor from the good life—or so they suppose.

Such a concept of God must be repudiated. The living God
personifies the full life. He does not decry it. Jesus Christ became man that He might reveal the character of His Father
to a world in rebellion. What a God Christ revealed! Jesus was
no supine, lackluster killjoy. He lived life to the full. He advocated the abundant life! "I have come," He declared, "in order
that they might have life, life in all its fulness."

The Master was not content to live in a corner. He moved
in the center of life. He was where the action was. He lived.
He loved. He conquered. There was never a dull moment in
the unfolding drama of Christ's life. True there were heartaches, disappointments, apparent defeats, but there were also
rewards, successes, and joys abounding.

Jesus is on the side of living—joyous living. He exclaimed,
"I have come in order that they might have life, life in all its
fulness."

This life may be yours in Christ Jesus!

READ IT AND WEEP

Therefore be ye also ready: for in such an hour as ye think not the Son of man cometh. **Matt. 24:44.**

Two statements from the Spirit of Prophecy should make a lasting impression upon the heart of every Seventh-day Adventist who reads them. One graphically describes the condition of the world immediately prior to the return of our Lord. The other depicts the condition inside the remnant church during the same period. Read them with me. First, the one dealing with the world about us:

"At the same time anarchy is seeking to sweep away all law, not only divine, but human. The centralizing of wealth and power; the vast combinations for the enriching of the few at the expense of the many; the combinations of the poorer classes for the defense of their interests and claims; the spirit of unrest, of riot and bloodshed; the worldwide dissemination of the same teachings that led to the French Revolution—all are tending to involve the whole world in a struggle similar to that which convulsed France."—*Education,* p. 228.

Now read the statement describing conditions obtaining among the professed people of God during the ominous times just described.

"When the professed people of God are uniting with the world, living as they live, and joining them in forbidden pleasures; when the luxury of the world becomes the luxury of the church; when the marriage bells are chiming, and all are looking forward to many years of worldly prosperity—then, suddenly as the lightning flashes from the heavens, will come the end of their bright visions and elusive hopes."—*The Great Controversy,* pp. 338, 339.

"Anarchy" challenging both human and divine law—familiar? Great financial combines growing richer; the poor joining in defense of their rights, even their very existence; the spirit of unrest—sound familiar? "Riot and bloodshed"—heard about any of this lately? Godless subversion, spiritual and political—familiar, too, isn't it?

Read these inspired statements over and over again prayerfully—won't you? Here are vital messages for every child of God today!

199

THE MINISTRY OF ENCOURAGEMENT

To Timothy, my dearly beloved son: Grace, mercy, and peace, from God the Father and Christ Jesus our Lord. I thank God, whom I serve from my forefathers with pure conscience, that without ceasing I have remembrance of thee in my prayers night and day; greatly desiring to see thee, being mindful of thy tears, that I may be filled with joy; when I call to remembrance the unfeigned faith that is in thee, which dwelt first in thy grandmother Lois, and thy mother Eunice; and I am persuaded that in thee also. 2 Tim. 1:2-5.

The apostle Paul practiced the ministry of encouragement. He knew how to make those with whom he served feel loved and needed. Read those words he wrote to Timothy in more modern language:

"To: Timothy, my dear son. May God the Father and Christ Jesus our Lord shower you with his kindness, mercy and peace. How I thank God for you, Timothy. I pray for you every day, and many times during the long nights I beg my God to bless you richly. He is my fathers' God, and mine, and my only purpose in life is to please him. How I long to see you again. How happy I would be, for I remember your tears as we left each other. I know how much you trust the Lord, just as your mother Eunice and your grandmother Lois do; and I feel sure you are still trusting him as much as ever" (2 Tim. 1:2-5, T.L.B.).

Would a letter like this one bring courage to *your* heart? To know that someone we love, and in whom we have great confidence, is praying for us is a great source of encouragement. We are not meeting the problems of the day alone. We are not fighting the battles of life without help from outside! Someone is thinking of us! Someone is praying for us—in the daytime while we are at work, in the hours of the night watch while we are asleep! We know because he has told us so, as Paul told Timothy. Likewise we need to encourage others.

"We are too indifferent in regard to one another. Too often we forget that our fellow laborers are in need of strength and cheer. Take care to assure them of your interest and sympathy. Help them by your prayers, and let them know that you do it."—*The Ministry of Healing*, pp. 492, 493.

HE IS FOR YOU!

All we like sheep have gone astray; we have turned every one to his own way; and the Lord hath laid on him the iniquity of us all. Isa. 53:6.

No two of us are exactly alike. Some of us are introverts. Some are extroverts. Most of us are ambiverts. Yet we all use the same twenty-six letters of the alphabet to communicate. We use them to express joy, to denote sorrow. We comfort the bereaved. We counsel the erring. We praise. We condemn. We sing. We pray. In all our moods we employ the same adaptable vehicle—the alphabet. The spiritual man, the worldly man, the saint, the sinner, the law-abiding and the criminal, the learned and the unlearned, all alike employ these twenty-six letters to express themselves.

The alphabet is one of the most adaptable, most accommodating devices known to man!

When Jesus tells us He is the "Alpha and Omega" (Rev. 1:11)—the whole alphabet—He wishes to impress upon us the great fact that He can and will adapt Himself with divine exactitude to our every need.

"We have turned every one to his own way," the gospel prophet has rightly said. These different ways create varied needs. Isaiah's needs were not the same as those of the apostle Paul. Jesus could help them both. Your needs may not be the same as mine. Jesus meets them all!

Other needs—physical and temporal—press in upon the child of God. The Sermon on the Mount is dry reading when the cruse of oil has failed and the barrel of meal is dry. Sometimes the fruits of the Spirit appear irrelevant when one's disease-racked body writhes with pain. The Ten Commandments are always present truth, but they read less convincingly by the bedside of a dying loved one when hearts are burdened with grief.

"Lo, I am with you alway" (Matt. 28:20), He assures. "Seek ye first the kingdom of God, and his righteousness; and all these things shall be added unto you" (chap. 6:33), is the promise when we bring to Him our temporal, physical, and spiritual needs. His help is adaptable to every human requirement—to *your* need.

LEAVE IT THERE

Unto us a child is born, unto us a son is given: and the government shall be upon his shoulder. **Isa. 9:6.**

"Come to me, all of you who are tired from carrying your heavy loads, and I will give you rest. Take my yoke and put it on you, and learn from me, for I am gentle and humble in spirit; and you will find rest. The yoke I will give you is easy, and the load I will put on you is light" (Matt. 11:28-30, T.E.V.).

Too many of us attempt to carry our burdens alone. Too often in so doing we find ourselves crushed beneath the load. We become discouraged. Our faith is severely tried. Doubt creeps in. Some give up. We need to be reminded frequently that *"the government shall be on his shoulder"*—not on ours.

The Basic English translation of our text reads: "The government has been placed in his hands." Here is the best and only truly safe place to leave it—in His hands. He is willing and able to carry the load!

Have a closer look at the One who extends to you this gracious invitation. The inspired writer describes Him as the "El Shaddai" (Gen. 17:1, margin)—"the God who is able," "the God who is enough." When the burden presses heavily upon you today, remember "El Shaddai"—He is able to lift the load, to give you opportunity to catch your second breath. He will renew your courage and send you forth with increased strength and faith. He is the God who is able—able to meet your need, able to solve your problems.

You can't see any way to solve your problem—no visible source of help for lifting your burden? Bless your heart, God doesn't expect you to *see* your way out. He isn't dependent upon *visible* resources to ease the strain. Look at it this way. A God who can create an earth, a sun, a moon, a host of stars out of nothing and keep them hanging on nothing can surely solve our little problems, can't He? And He won't need anything visible to begin with, either.

"In the darkest days, when appearances seem most forbidding, fear not. Have faith in God. He knows your need. He has all power. . . . Fear not that He will fail of fulfilling His promises."—*Prophets and Kings*, p. 164.

Leave the government in *His* hands!

THE MIRACLE MAN

For to us a child is born, to us a son is given; . . . and his name will be called "Wonderful Counselor." Isa. 9:6, R.S.V.

One can scarcely exhaust the beautiful thoughts in our text for today. I wish to select but one for our consideration. "His name will be called *'Wonderful Counselor.'* " This, of course, was speaking of the Messiah to come—your Saviour and mine.

The prophet's word "wonderful" is derived from a Hebrew root *pehleh*—meaning literally "miracle." The life of Jesus *was* one succession of miracles. His virgin birth was a miracle. His sinless life was a miracle. His ministry on behalf of sin-sick, disease-ridden, lost humanity was a miracle. His touch opened blind eyes and loosed tongues dumb from birth.

Deaf ears were unstopped. Diseased bodies were made whole. Sick minds were restored. Sinners were snatched from the pit of degradation. After He had successfully met every challenge with which evil men and demons confronted Him, He was nailed to the cross. The grave received Him but could not hold Him. His resurrection upon the third day was a miracle assuring freedom to countless men and women of all ages.

Forty days after His resurrection He ascended to His Father—another miracle—a crowning act of divine power providing an earnest that a host which no man can number will follow Him when He finally leads captivity captive on the first resurrection morning.

The apostle Paul sums up the miracle that was Christ and is Christ when he wrote to Timothy: "Without controversy great is the mystery of godliness: God was manifest in the flesh, justified in the Spirit, seen of angels, preached unto the Gentiles, believed on in the world, received up into glory" (1 Tim. 3:16).

He is still wonderful! He performs miracles today! To illustrate His wonder-working power, He heals the sick in America. He casts out demons in the Orient. He saves from sin in Africa. He raises the dead in the South Seas. He steadies the halting saint in Europe. He rescues the backslider in Australia. The passing of time has not diminished that wonderful miracle-working power of the Son of God. And what is more important to you, He *can* and *will* meet your need today—and every day if you will only let Him!

WHERE I FIND GOD

Then said they unto him, What shall we do, that we might work the works of God? John 6:28.

Where is God? I will tell you where *I* find God. I find Him where the Gospel writers place His Son, Jesus Christ—where the action is. I find Him in His last-day church at work, in those who have committed their lives and talents to Him in loving, meaningful service.

I find Him in the lives of student missionaries I have met in many lands. Dedicated, eager, venturesome, these young people have left family and friends. Some have delayed a year of formal education to find fulfillment in service for their Master in distant, needy lands.

I find Him in the inner cities of North America where scores, perhaps hundreds, of committed Seventh-day Adventist young men and women seek to reveal Him to those who are spiritually and materially destitute.

I find Him in the experience of a widow who sacrificed to see the work of God advance. She heard an appeal for funds to send our church papers and books to believers in lands where it is difficult to obtain these treasures. She brought two fifty-dollar notes and placed them in the hands of her pastor who made the appeal.

I find Him in the work of a consecrated layman in Nashville, Tennessee, who for many years has been visiting the inmates of a large nearby penitentiary. Faithfully each weekend he ministers to the spiritual needs of the prisoners. I have accompanied him. I know the good work he has done.

I found Him in the patient, suffering service of a pain-racked sister I met years ago in the West Indies. Although confined to her bed and gnarled with arthritis, she cheerfully served her Master. Every year souls were baptized as the result of her labor. She reached her Ingathering goal and in other ways uncomplainingly worked the works of God.

Throughout the mainstream membership of God's remnant church I see Him at work in the lives of thousands of His chosen ones. Some are active, some are confined by circumstances, but these committed ones lift Him up in life and service. They, too, work the works of their Master.

I FIND GOD IN CHRIST

God . . . hath reconciled us to himself by Jesus Christ, and hath given to us the ministry of reconciliation; to wit, that God was in Christ, reconciling the world unto himself. 2 Cor. 5:18, 19.

I find God in Jesus Christ—in His life, in His love, in His service, in His teachings. "God was in Christ," the apostle Paul tells us. The Lord's messenger adds: "By coming to dwell with us, Jesus was to reveal God both to men and to angels."— *The Desire of Ages,* p. 19. When you and I find and know Christ we will have found and we will know God, for "God was in Christ."

"Jesus called his disciples to him and said: 'I feel sorry for these people, because they have been with me for three days and now have nothing to eat. I don't want to send them away without feeding them, because they might faint on their way home.' . . .

"Then he took the seven loaves and the fish, gave thanks to God, broke them and gave them to the disciples, and the disciples gave them to the people. They all ate and had enough" (Matt. 15:32-37, T.E.V.).

When men saw Christ, moved with compassion, feed hungry men and women they were given a glimpse into the compassionate heart of the Father, for "God was in Christ."

"They came to Bethsaida, where some people brought a blind man to Jesus and begged him to touch him. . . . Jesus again placed his hands on the man's eyes. This time the man looked hard, his eyesight came back, and he saw everything clearly" (Mark 8:22-25, T.E.V.).

When men saw Christ heal the sick, the maimed, and the halt, they beheld the power of God at work, for "God was in Christ." When they beheld the Master comforting the brokenhearted, encouraging little children, caring for the poor, they were witnessing the love of God in action.

When Christ spoke of the law, the Sabbath, the signs of the times, His death, His resurrection, His second advent, He was passing on to His listeners the truth about God. Each doctrine reveals something of the nature and the character of the Father. Through these great truths, through His life, His love, and through His service, Christ introduces men to the Father!

YOU MUST ROLL AWAY THE STONE!

Then they took away the stone from the place where the dead was laid.
John 11:41.

You are well acquainted with the story of how Lazarus was raised from the dead. The Gospel writer records that the tomb "was a cave, and a stone lay upon it." Jesus could easily have commanded the stone to be removed by the word of His power. A voice that can raise the dead can surely move a stone. But the Master had a part for His disciples to play in raising Lazarus. "They took away the stone from the place where the dead was laid."

Humanity has a part to play in raising the spiritually dead. Christ is able to save souls today without our help, but He doesn't—He wonderfully includes the human factor!

"As His representatives among men, God does not choose angels who have never fallen, but human beings, men of like passions with those they seek to save. Christ took humanity that He might reach humanity. A divine-human Saviour was needed to bring salvation to the world. And to men and women has been committed the sacred trust of making known 'the unsearchable riches of Christ.' Ephesians 3:8."— *The Acts of the Apostles,* p. 134.

The human role in raising the spiritually dead is twofold— *living* and *working.* They are important in this same order. Before we can serve acceptably we must live acceptably. Before we can share our faith we must have a faith to share. Before we can make Christ real to others He must be real to us.

"If you would draw sinners out of the swift-running current, your own feet must not stand on slippery places."— *Gospel Workers,* p. 274.

"Those who have experienced the love of Christ cannot be idlers in the Master's vineyard. They will see opportunities for helping others in their steps to Christ. Partaking of Christ's love, they will labor for the souls of others. Let every soul copy the Pattern, and become missionaries in the highest sense, winning souls to Jesus."—ELLEN G. WHITE, in *The Youth's Instructor,* Oct. 20, 1892, p. 328.

What are you doing to roll away stones in your neighborhood?

HE INHERITED IT FROM HIS MOTHER

I know how much you trust the Lord, just as your mother Eunice and your grandmother Lois do; and I feel sure you are still trusting him as much as ever. 2 Tim. 1:5, T.L.B.

" 'Come, ye blessed of my Father, inherit the kingdom that is prepared for you from the foundation of the world.' Here He tells you to be a partaker of His joy, and what is that? It is the joy of seeing of the travail of your soul, fathers. It is the joy of seeing that your efforts, mothers, are rewarded. Here are your children; the crown of life is upon their heads, and the angels of God immortalize the names of the mothers whose efforts have won their children to Jesus Christ."— *Child Guidance,* pp. 567, 568.

On the glorious day when these words of promise shall become glad reality Mother Eunice will surely be among the jubilant throng of mothers who will see the reward of their labors.

Eunice was a woman of faith and trust. She inherited a legacy of faith from her mother, Lois, and passed it on to her son, Timothy. This family tradition of faith stood young Timothy in good stead during his ministry for Christ. A mother fitted with faith is one of the greatest gifts a man can receive. It equips him for fruitful service in this world and helps prepare him for a sphere of wider service in the world to come.

The Word of God in the hand and life of a committed mother is a source of power! Add to this the ingredient of a rich faith—an abiding trust. The result is a Timothy—a man of God rich in the heritage of his mother. Such a mother's "influence will reach on through time into eternity" *(The Adventist Home,* p. 240).

When the victors' crowns are dispensed on that glad day "many will raise their crowns in sight of the assembled universe and, pointing to their mother, say, 'She made me all I am through the grace of God.' "—*Messages to Young People,* p. 330.

Mrs. Pierson, in a marginal note on this statement wrote, "I think fathers are going to be included in this, too!" I hope so!

NO PARTY CRIES!

And a certain Jew named Apollos, born at Alexandria, an eloquent man, and mighty in the scriptures, came to Ephesus. **Acts 18:24.**

From our text today at least four points are clear about Apollos. He was a Jew. He was born in Alexandria. He was an outstanding speaker. He was a giant in the Word of God.

As we read on we learn other interesting things about this talented man. He was converted under the preaching of John the Baptist. He became a traveling evangelist and during his stay in Ephesus he met two other committed Christian workers—Priscilla and Aquila, also converted Jews. These two soldiers of the cross, who evidently had been longer in the way, took a special interest in Apollos and "expounded unto him the way of God more perfectly" (Acts 18:26).

It is evident from Luke's account of Apollos' experience that he earned the confidence of the church members in Ephesus during his ministry there, for when he prepared to leave for Achaia "the brethren wrote, exhorting the disciples to receive him" (verse 27). While preaching in Corinth, Apollos, his eloquence blessed of God, became very popular among certain believers, who began to exalt him above some of his brethren. Others were strong supporters of Paul, Peter, or Christ (see 1 Cor. 1:12).

Apollos, however, was not a man to encourage cliques in the church. Later, when Paul requested him to return to Corinth, Apollos declined. It may well have been his repugnance of anything that savored of self-exaltation, and he decided it would be best to stay away from Corinth.

Cliques may be the downfall of any church. When men and women, whether in Apollos' time or in our time, begin to band together in little parties, espousing their own little causes, separating from the main body, there is bound to be trouble.

Paul likewise abhorred cliques: "Brothers, for the sake of our Lord Jesus Christ I beg of you all to drop these party-cries. There must be no cliques among you; you must regain your common temper and attitude" (1 Cor. 1:10, Moffatt).

More Apolloses and Pauls in some churches today would be a great blessing!

DO WE ASK AMISS?

Ye ask, and receive not, because ye ask amiss. James 4:3.

You pray—your prayers are not answered. Is this *your* experience? For too many it is! The Lord's promises are conditional. If we fulfill the conditions, He will hear us. We will have answers to our prayers. If the heavens appear closed against us, perhaps we should search out the cause for our failure. There are causes of failure in our prayer life. The failure is on our part, not on God's.

Disregard of God's Word, disobedience, and presumption will close the doors of heaven to us. Israel on their way to Canaan discovered this. "I spake unto you; and ye would not hear, but rebelled against the commandment of the Lord, and went presumptuously up into the hill" (Deut. 1:43).

When hardened Israel disregarded and disobeyed God and presumed upon His goodness, "the Lord would not hearken to your voice, nor give ear unto you" (verse 45). They asked amiss.

Secret sin interrupts our connection with heaven. "If I regard iniquity in my heart, the Lord will not hear me" (Ps. 66:18).

Those about us may never be aware of our transgression. It may be hidden from husband, wife, brother, sister, son, or daughter. But we cannot hide our sins from God. Nothing is more certain of severing our connection with God than sin that we felt no one knew about. Perhaps no one but God does know, but He will not hear us if we persist in iniquity. We "ask amiss."

Self-indulgence closes God's ear to our petitions. Our text for today declares it. "Ye ask, and receive not, because ye ask amiss, that ye may consume it upon your lusts."

When we display selfishness, when we ask God for things merely to satisfy our own "lusts"—to get what *we* want for our own selfish desires, we "ask amiss." Self-indulgence silences our voice in God's ear.

If you pray and nothing happens, better undertake some earnest self-examination. There is reason for prayer failure. It is not with God. It is with the individual. It is because, knowingly or unknowingly, we "ask amiss." With God's help we can change this picture!

HUNGERING AND THIRSTING

Blessed are they which do hunger and thirst after righteousness: for they shall be filled. Matt. 5:6.

Thousands around the world—in many lands—are hungering and thirsting. They are not satisfied. They have an innate yearning for something better. From Vietnam a Buddhist priest reflects this longing in a letter.

"When I was a baby, my mother thought I would die. She became so fearful that she took me to the temple and dedicated me to Buddha. As my life was preserved, she gave credit to the gods and prepared me to become a Buddhist priest. I accepted her guidance. I was sent to the monastery for training. I donned the yellow robe. I took vows of celibacy to mortify the flesh and live an ascetic life. I lived with the other monks, and Buddhism became for me a way of life; but it did not bring peace. I yearned for something that would quench the thirst of my soul. One day when I was in this frame of mind, a young man from your mission office introduced me to a Bible course. The lessons made such an impact upon my mind that I set about enlisting my fellow monks in the same course. At least three of them are now studying the lessons. I am now attending your Sabbath morning service."

"No human agent can supply that which will satisfy the hunger and thirst of the soul. But Jesus says, 'Behold, I stand at the door, and knock: if any man hear my voice, and open the door, I will come in to him, and will sup with him, and he with me.' 'I am the bread of life: he that cometh to me shall never hunger; and he that believeth on me shall never thirst.' Rev. 3:20; John 6:35."—*Thoughts From the Mount of Blessing,* p. 18.

It is the Spirit of God who stimulates the hunger, creates the thirst. He reveals to us our inner selves. We understand our need for help. At the foot of the cross we discover the better way. The precious Word of God becomes at once our guide and our daily diet. The spiritual hunger is satisfied.

"The Lord shall guide thee continually, and satisfy thy soul in drought, and make fat thy bones: and thou shalt be like a watered garden, and like a spring of water, whose waters fail not" (Isa. 58:11).

DO YOU TRULY WANT THE LORD TO COME?

As soon as the crop is ready, he sends his reapers in without delay, for the harvest-time has come. **Mark 4:29, Phillips.**

You truly want the Lord to come soon! You say so! You mean it! How long you've worked and prayed and lived for that glorious day of glad fruition. Of course you want Jesus to come! But really now, how *much* do you mean it? If you mean it enough to actually do something about it, you can help speed that day.

Ellen White declares: "It is the privilege of every Christian not only to look for but to hasten the coming of our Lord Jesus Christ."—*Christ's Object Lessons,* p. 69. Ever stop to think of it this way? We can actually help hasten the day of our Lord's return.

How? That's a good question. Revelation has the answer:

"Were all who profess His name bearing fruit to His glory," the Lord's servant says, "how quickly the whole world would be sown with the seed of the gospel. Quickly the last great harvest would be ripened, and Christ would come to gather the precious grain."—*Ibid.*

If all of us were truly living the life of Christ we would be hastening the second coming of Christ! If our lives were a constant testimony to the grace and saving power of our *risen Lord,* more people around us would be looking forward with anticipation to our *returning Lord!* If the fruits of the Spirit of Christ were more of a reality in our lives, the advent of Christ would be more of a reality in the lives of those with whom we associate—in our homes and in our communities.

Jesus, in our text for the day, said practically the same thing: "When the fruit is brought forth, immediately he putteth in the sickle, because the harvest is come" (Mark 4:29).

Notice when the fruit is produced, *immediately* comes the harvest. When with God's help we have part in bearing the fruit we also have part in hastening the harvest!

When we love as Christ loved, when we are longsuffering, gentle, good, meek, as was our great Exemplar, we are bearing fruit to His glory. We are also hastening His return.

It is worth *thinking* about! It is worth *praying* about! It is worth *doing* something about!

"THY FAITH HATH MADE THEE WHOLE"

And Jesus said unto him, Go thy way; thy faith hath made thee whole. And immediately he received his sight, and followed Jesus in the way. Mark 10:52.

A blind beggar sits by the dusty roadside on the outskirts of Jericho. Bartimaeus had heard of Jesus. It was his supreme desire to contact this Man of Galilee of whom he had heard so much. Perhaps the great Teacher would remove his affliction and make him see.

As he sits Bartimaeus hears the tread of many feet. A crowd is approaching. Who can it be? "When he heard that it was Jesus of Nazareth, he began to cry out, and say, Jesus, thou son of David, have mercy on me" (Mark 10:47).

Others by the wayside seek to silence the importunate beggar. But there is no quieting him. Here is his one chance to escape from a world of darkness, and no one is going to deny him. He cries out with such insistence that Jesus and His entourage pause.

The Saviour calls for Bartimaeus. The blind man "rose, and came to Jesus" (verse 50). He comes with such haste he sheds his ragged coat. Nothing will impede his response. He must be healed!

"Thy faith hath made thee whole," Jesus declared. "And immediately he received his sight, and followed Jesus in the way."

Here is the gospel in action. Here is the good news acted out before our very eyes. Here is a soul who feels his need: "Have mercy upon me." Here is a Saviour with the help needed: "Jesus stood still, and commanded him to be called" (verse 49). Here is a demonstration of saving faith: "Thy faith hath made thee whole." Here is gratitude for the help received, here is loyalty to the One who effected the healing: "He received his sight, and followed Jesus in the way." What a moving vignette of saving grace! What a graphic depiction of the stages of discipleship!

Jesus' grace and Bartimaeus' faith combined to bring restoration to his needy soul.

Salvation comes when a sense of need and a persevering faith find a searching Saviour!

THE HANDS OF JESUS

And Jesus put forth his hand, and touched him. **Matt. 8:3.**

"I've always wanted beautiful hands," Sylvia sighed. "Mine are anything but beautiful—protruding veins, long, plain fingers, not much to look at!"

"But you have useful hands," her friend comforted. "They were just made for spanning the octaves on the piano or covering the keyboard of a typewriter! And after all, it's what these hands of ours *do* that counts more than how they look."

Hands! Hands! I got to thinking about hands—Jesus' hands. No doubt they were strong, calloused hands, for they were working hands. They must have been browned from exposure to the warm sun. They must have been rough, for He spent so much time in the great outdoors.

But the Saviour's hands were tender hands. See them laid upon the heads of little children. How gently He caressed their tousled hair. That loving touch warmed their hearts and drew them to Him. "Suffer little children," he said, "and forbid them not, to come unto me: for of such is the kingdom of heaven" (Matt. 19:14).

Our text for today identifies the hands of Christ as power-filled, cleansing hands. When His hand touched the leper "immediately his leprosy was cleansed" (chap. 8:3). The man with this living death became clean when the hand of Jesus was laid upon him.

Christ's hands delighted little children, cleansed lepers, opened blind eyes, soothed fevered brows, cast out devils, raised the dead—what hands!

There is more to the story. Those brown calloused hands were pierced for you, for me! "I have graven thee upon the palms of my hands" (Isa. 49:16), He declares. Even upon the cross those hands were stretched out in a worldwide embrace to draw to Himself every repentant sinner.

When He comes in the clouds of heaven, bright beams of light will shine forth from those nail-pierced hands, "and there was the hiding of his power" (Hab. 3:4).

Those hands of love healed and helped two thousand years ago. They are still outstretched to heal, to help, to save, today!

WHERE ARE THE WATCHMEN?

But if the watchman see the sword come, and blow not the trumpet, and the people be not warned; if the sword come, and take any person from among them, he is taken away in his iniquity; but his blood will I require at the watchman's hand.

So thou, O son of man, I have set thee a watchman unto the house of Israel; therefore thou shalt hear the word at my mouth, and warn them from me. Eze. 33:6, 7.

Something is happening to American churches and American pulpits. " 'The church is dying. . . . Religious institutions have come to the end of the line. I doubt if there will be any left by the end of the 1970's.' "—Speaker at Associated Church Press and Religious Communications Congress in Chicago, quoted by A. S. Maxwell, in *Signs of the Times,* August, 1970.

Something is happening to American educational institutions. "Faster than the pulpits of the land can attract young people to Christ the colleges turn them out as skeptics and agnostics."—Editorial, *Christianity Today,* Sept. 11, 1961.

Something could happen to the Seventh-day Adventist Church and its institutions! "And the dragon was wroth with the woman, and went to make war with the remnant of her seed, which keep the commandments of God, and have the testimony of Jesus Christ" (Rev. 12:17).

Satan will not leave our church unscathed, especially its schools. Something to consider carefully and prayerfully is the possibility that the same apostasy into which other churches have been betrayed may come knocking at *our* door.

So God has a ringing word of warning to His watchmen today. Who are His watchmen that He challenges to be on the alert in our text? Our ministers and teachers first, but also every worker in the church is a watchman. Every church officer and Sabbath school teacher is included. In fact, every church member must be on guard in this age of apostasy.

When the pillars of the gospel have been so widely abandoned, God's watchmen must be alert. When uniformitarianism and evolution are replacing the Flood and the blood; when secularism, humanism, and syncretism are eclipsing the cross and the Ten Commandments, God is depending upon watchmen—watchmen who will stand up and speak up!

THOU ART MY GOD!

O God, thou art my God; early will I seek thee: my soul thirsteth for thee, my flesh longeth for thee in a dry and thirsty land, where no water is. Ps. 63:1.

David's words in the sixty-third psalm reveal God in a very personal relationship with His earthbound children. To the psalmist God was no distant, unreachable, impersonal deity. David lived and moved in an atmosphere charged with the presence of his heavenly Father. "O God, thou art *my* God!" the sweet singer of Israel exults.

Read the whole psalm and note the many personal claims David makes in these verses: "Early will *I* seek thee." "*My* soul thirsteth for thee." "*My* flesh longeth for thee." "*I* have seen thee." "*My* lips shall praise thee." "*My* soul shall be satisfied." "Thou hast been *my* help." "Thy right hand upholdeth *me.*" It is as though the psalmist had said, "Yes, Lord, You belonged to Abraham, to Isaac, and to Jacob. You were the God of those leaders of the past, but most of all, O God, You are *my* God, You belong to me. You are mine, and I am Yours in a very personal experience!"

What God was to David the same heavenly Father desires to be to every one of us. He desires you and me to enjoy this same personal relationship. With the psalmist we may cry out with assurance, "O God, thou art *my* God!" If there is on our part the same heartfelt longing and seeking that characterized David's approach to his Father above, we, too, may know Him as personally as David knew Him. When you and I can truthfully declare, "My soul thirsteth for thee," we will also be able to say, *"I* have seen thee" and *"My* soul shall be satisfied."

"Jesus knows us individually, and is touched with the feeling of our infirmities. He knows us all by name. He knows the very house in which we live, the name of each occupant. He has at times given directions to His servants to go to a certain street in a certain city, to such a house, to find one of His sheep.

"Every soul is as fully known to Jesus as if he were the only one for whom the Saviour died."—*The Desire of Ages,* pp. 479, 480.

Blessed thought—He is ours and we are His!

WHEN DEATH THREATENS—THEN WHAT?

He that dwelleth in the secret place of the most High shall abide under the shadow of the Almighty. Ps. 91:1.

Soldiers of an enemy army invade the privacy of your home. They threaten the life or the purity of members of your family. You have the potential fire power to kill the invaders and protect your loved ones. What would the child of God do under such circumstances? Would you shoot, and break the commandment that says, "Thou shalt not kill," or would you meekly submit and let your family suffer death— or worse?

The situation ethicist counsels that every situation must be evaluated as an isolated experience. One must not be bound by the age-old tenets of a long-dead code demanding that under no circumstance is one free to take the life of a fellow human being. Some murders, we are told, are not only positively justifiable, they are a blessing to humanity.

What would I do if I were confronted with a traumatic situation such as the one I mentioned in the beginning? Quite frankly I do not know *what I* would do, but I know *what God* would do! He would have a solution to the situation all planned, and He would handle the situation in such a way as to bring honor and glory to His name.

"Whoever will rely wholly upon divine grace," Ellen White reminds us, "may make his life a constant testimony for the truth. No one is so situated that he cannot be a true and faithful Christian. However great the obstacles, all who are determined to obey God will find the way opening as they go forward."—*Testimonies*, vol. 5, p. 182.

As I told an uneasy passenger in an airport departure lounge recently, "God has not promised always to spare our lives under every circumstance. But as long as He has a work for me to do I will 'abide under the shadow of the Almighty' and leave the threatened perilous moments of my life in His hands and let Him handle such a situation as He sees best." If I have made Him first during the days of tranquillity He will not forget me in the hour of adversity. I will not need to take things into my own hands and decide what is best!

TOUCHING THE LORD'S ANOINTED

The Lord forbid that I should do this thing unto my master, the Lord's anointed, to stretch forth mine hand against him, seeing he is the anointed of the Lord. 1 Sam. 24:6.

Murder was in Saul's heart. As he searched the caves and crevices for David he was intent on putting a final end to the young rebel. No one could dispute *his* throne and live. Saul was God's anointed leader of Israel. But because the king had turned his back upon the Lord, the kingdom was soon to be taken from him. Already David had been selected as his successor.

Now, in his search for David, Saul came unattended into the very cave where David and his men were in hiding.

"Now is your chance!" some men whispered to David in the darkness. "Surely this is the hour the Lord Himself has appointed you. Has He not declared He would deliver your enemy into your hand?"

"The Lord forbid that I should do this thing unto my master, the Lord's anointed," David replied, "to stretch forth mine hand against him, seeing he is the anointed of the Lord."

You know well the rest of the story. Saul's life was spared. David refused to raise his hand against one whom the Lord had placed in the position of leadership.

"The conduct of David toward Saul has a lesson." That lesson is, "We should be careful not to take into our hands the work of judging that belongs to God."—*The Ministry of Healing,* p. 484.

It is easy to sit back and judge those who have been placed in leadership positions. You know the pattern. The Sabbath school superintendent had prepared an uninteresting program. Perhaps the critic did not know that one or two key participants in the Sabbath school had let the superintendent down, or something else went wrong over which the leader had no control.

Next time you are tempted to judge the Sabbath school leader, the pastor, the local elder, the conference president, or any other leader, remember God's warning: "Touch not the Lord's anointed!"

A FIRM HAND—FULL OF FLOWERS!

Wives, adapt yourselves to your husbands, that your marriage may be a Christian unity. Husbands, be sure you give your wives much love and sympathy; don't let bitterness or resentment spoil your marriage. Col. 3:18, 19, Phillips.

One wise man describing a happy, successful marriage, declared: "It is where the husband meets a marital crisis with a firm hand—full of candy or flowers!"

It takes a lot of tender love and care to make a happy home. Tenderness puts the flowers in the firm hand, it puts love in the firm voice. Tenderness places others first, self last. Tenderness adapts wives and husbands to one another in a beautiful Christian unity that the apostle Paul was speaking of.

Love and sympathy create tenderness. Tenderness is care in its most attractive dress. Tenderness makes the husband or wife considerate, ever solicitous of others' needs and wishes. Tenderness is the expression of the softer emotions. When tenderness reigns, the despot's bitterness and resentment are forced to flee.

Tenderness must be expressed. "In many families there is a great lack in expressing affection one for another. While there is no need of sentimentalism, there is need of expressing love and tenderness in a chaste, pure, dignified way. Many absolutely cultivate hardness of heart and in word and action reveal the satanic side of the character."—*The Adventist Home,* p. 198.

Tenderness should be manifest not only between husband and wife, but among all members of the family. "Tender affection should ever be cherished between husband and wife, parents and children, brothers and sisters. Every hasty word should be checked, and there should not be even the appearance of the lack of love one for another. It is the duty of everyone in the family to be pleasant, to speak kindly.

"Cultivate tenderness, affection, and love that have expression in little courtesies, in speech, in thoughtful attention."— *Ibid.*

Do *you* reveal tenderness and love in *your* home "in little courtesies, in speech, in thoughtful attentions"? If not, why not begin today?

TEST IT!

If there be a prophet among you, I the Lord will make myself known unto him in a vision, and will speak unto him in a dream. **Num. 12:6.**

In the April 27, 1972, issue of the *Review and Herald,* Rene Noorbergen asks two pertinent questions: "Is the Spirit of Prophecy real? Do you really believe that Ellen White was a prophet of God?"

Author Noorbergen then proceeds to answer his own questions: "I am no longer afraid of questions such as these. I have answered them not through blind emotion but through personal discovery. Don't take my word for it. Study the prophetic gift. . . . Test it. Approached with a prayerful attitude, it will give your faith an entirely new turn and will turn your belief into conviction, a conviction that through His prophets God will keep guiding His work."

What Rene Noorbergen has found many of us discovered years ago. God speaks to our hearts through the appealing pages of *The Desire of Ages, Steps to Christ,* and *Thoughts From the Mount of Blessing.* We love our Saviour more when we spend a "thoughtful hour" contemplating the final scenes of His life. Heaven and our heavenly Father are just a little nearer, a little dearer after we have read from these volumes that exalt our Saviour.

We even discover our minds are clearer, our health more vibrant when we follow faithfully the inspired counsel the Lord has left for us in the writings of such books as *The Ministry of Healing* and *Counsels on Diet and Foods.* The messenger of the Lord deals with the whole man—our physical and mental needs as well as our spiritual enlightenment.

We have seen the work prosper and expand when counsel given by the Spirit of Prophecy was followed. Schools have been opened, medical institutions established, publishing houses have come into being and prospered, new work has been started and developed under the direction of the Lord's messenger. Countless times the Lord has made known His will and way through visions, dreams, and other avenues of direct communication with Ellen White.

I also can add with confidence, Don't take my word for it. Study the prophetic gift. Test it for yourself.

IT WILL BE ALL RIGHT

Believe in the Lord your God, and you shall have success! Believe his prophets, and everything will be all right! 2 Chron. 20:20, T.L.B.

In the permissive days in which we live, Seventh-day Adventist schools must be kept different from those in the world about us. From kindergarten through graduate school they must be distinctively Seventh-day Adventist, following the inspired instruction the Lord has given His last-day church.

So many churches have lost their schools. Educational institutions once founded upon the Lord Jesus Christ and Christian principles are today adrift upon a sea of doubt. Once they lost their foundational faith, they lost contact with the church.

In the same way many churches have also lost their mission. They have little left except a watered-down gospel of social action.

God still calls His people to be a separate people. We should operate schools that are different. "Be ye not unequally yoked together with unbelievers: for what fellowship hath righteousness with unrighteousness? and what communion hath light with darkness? And what concord hath Christ with Belial? or what part hath he that believeth with an infidel? And what agreement hath the temple of God with idols? for ye are the temple of the living God; as God hath said, I will dwell in them, and walk in them; and I will be their God, and they shall be my people" (2 Cor. 6:14-16).

If our schools are not different from those about us, what incentive is there for parents to pay tuition and other expenses to send their children to Seventh-day Adventist schools? "There has been an effort to mold our school after other colleges. When this is done, we can give no encouragement to parents to send their children" *(Testimonies,* vol. 5, p. 21) to a Christian institution.

If we are to keep our schools different, if they are to accomplish what God desires them to accomplish, if everything is to be "all right" among God's remnant people, our text for today lays down the only safe formula: "Believe in the Lord your God, and you shall have success! Believe his prophets, and everything will be all right!"

THOSE DON'TS!

And if it seem evil unto you to serve the Lord, choose you this day whom ye will serve. Joshua 24:15.

"Why is it always like this?" stormed Linda. "Don't do this! Don't do that! You can't go here! You can't go there! All religion is, is do's and don'ts, can's and can'ts. I am fed up with it all!"

"Now, Linda," an older friend soothed, "is it really all that bad? I don't read in the Bible that anyone *has* to do anything. The way I read it a person can do anything he wants to do. In fact, God made provision for everyone to do exactly as he wishes!"

Linda softened slightly at the unexpected reply.

"You must have heard something I haven't," she continued, the fire fading from her eyes. "All I ever hear of religion is *don't, don't, don't,* and I am getting to hate it."

Linda was not the first teen-ager rapidly turning rebel over the don'ts and can'ts she felt composed religion as she knew it. Actually, her older friend was correct. The true religion of the Word doesn't *make* anyone do what he does not want to. In fact, God gives everyone the privilege of doing exactly as he chooses!

When a beneficent Creator made man in the Garden of Eden, He made Adam a creature with the power of choice. He was not created a mere automaton—a toy in God's hand forced to do what God required. *He could do as he pleased!*

This truth of man's free choice is as old as the human race. In his day Joshua reminded the people of God that the course they followed was a matter of their own desire and decision. "Choose you this day whom ye will serve!" The Israelites themselves decided who would be their master.

Daily you and I face similar choices. Daily we hear the voice of God, "Choose *you* this day." God places the options before us. The decisions are ours. Whether or not we serve the Lord is up to us. We decide. The Omnipotent One will never force us. We may take the path of our own choosing.

And—it is a solemn thought as well—whether or not we are eternally saved is our choice.

HOW ABOUT THE BOARD IN YOUR OWN EYE?

And why beholdest thou the mote that is in thy brother's eye, but considerest not the beam that is in thine own eye? Or how wilt thou say to thy brother, Let me pull out the mote out of thine eye; and, behold, a beam is in thine own eye? Matt. 7:3, 4.

"Poor man," I mused pityingly, "he really doesn't have much hair left!" He was a good man, this colleague of mine, a very capable man, but he was surely losing his hair—fast! So I felt sorry for him.

Then one day I was viewing some color moving pictures a friend of mine had taken. There *I* was in one of the scenes, and I saw myself at an angle I couldn't see when I looked into the mirror each morning.

No, it couldn't be—surely I had more hair than that! But the awful truth was out! If anything, I had less "covering" than my friend whom I had been feeling sorry for!

Sometime later I told my friend the story. We both had a good laugh. "I could have told you that a long time ago," he chided.

How human it is for all of us—to see something undesirable in someone else before we discover the same lack in our own self!

I can hear Jesus speaking to me in the modern paraphrase of Dr. Taylor:

"Why worry about a speck in the eye of a brother when you have a board in your own? Should you say, 'Friend, let me help you get that speck out of your eye,' when you can't even see because of the board in your own?" (Matt. 7:3, 4, T.L.B.).

How quick most of us are to criticize—to see the faults in others. How slow we are to see our own shortcomings. How faint our praise; how loudly ring our accusations and condemnations.

There is a work that needs to be done in the life of each of us—the work of self-examination. "Check up on yourselves. Are you really Christians? Do you pass the test? Do you feel Christ's presence and power more and more within you? Or are you just pretending to be Christians when actually you aren't at all?" (2 Cor. 13:5, T.L.B.).

How is it with *you,* my friend?

WOMEN'S RIGHTS?

"Is it right that, because he had no son, our father's name should disappear from his family? Give us our property on the same footing as our father's brothers." **Num. 27:4, N.E.B.**

Perhaps they were the forerunners of the modern women's lib movement. Perhaps this is too ambitious a claim to lay for the five daughters of Zelophehad, a direct descendant of Joseph. At least they believed in women's rights, and they took their "grievances" to "Moses, to Eleazar the priest, the chiefs, and all the community." We read about it in the twenty-seventh chapter of the book of Numbers.

"A claim was presented by the daughters of Zelophehad son of Hepher, son of Gilead, son of Machir, son of Manasseh, son of Joseph. Their names were Mahlah, Noah, Hoglah, Milcah and Tirzah. They appeared at the entrance of the Tent of the Presence before Moses, Eleazar the priest, the chiefs, and all the community, and spoke as follows: 'Our father died in the wilderness. He was not among the company of Korah which combined together against the Lord; he died for his own sin and left no sons. Is it right that, because he had no son, our father's name should disappear from his family? Give us our property on the same footing as our father's brothers' " (verses 1-4, N.E.B.).

The appeal of the five sisters was not dismissed lightly by either Moses or the Lord. Note the sequel to their entreaty.

"So Moses brought their case before the Lord, and the Lord spoke to Moses and said, 'The claim of the daughters of Zelophehad is good. You must allow them to inherit on the same footing as their father's brothers' " (verses 5-7).

In recent years there has been much agitation over the role women are to play in present-day society. Most professions are open to either male or female applicants today. Federal law forbids discrimination on the basis of sex in practically all areas of employment. A President of the United States, when asked whether America would ever have a woman President, replied: "When she is the best candidate available we will have a woman president, but not just because she is a woman."

"But remember that in God's plan men and women need each other" (1 Cor. 11:11, T.L.B.).

ALONE WITH GOD

And when he had sent them away, he departed into a mountain to pray.
Mark 6:46.

The crowds that thronged the Saviour's preaching were too great for any synagogue or meeting place of His day. So Jesus led them to the gentle slopes of nearby hills, to the glistening seashore, or to the grassy fields, and there He opened to them the Word of life. The Master loved these spots close to nature. Somehow the words the Creator spoke had new meaning in the midst of His own creation. He spoke of the lilies of the field, the olive trees, the birds of the air, the shining stars above, and each conveyed to His hearers some special line of truth that gripped their hearts.

Through the centuries God has spoken to His people through His special book of nature. Not only in His public ministry but in His personal devotions, the Saviour sought the sylvan sanctuaries of the mountainside to commune with His Father. "He departed into a mountain to pray" (Mark 6:46). "To Him each quiet retreat was a sacred temple."—*The Desire of Ages,* p. 290.

"By communion with God in nature," Ellen White says, "the mind is uplifted, and the heart finds rest."—*Ibid.,* p. 291.

As a new Adventist still in her teens and the only one of her faith in the family, it was not always easy for Dollis to find a place and time for prayer. So she followed her Saviour out under His starry heavens. There beneath the glorious Florida full moon she could pour out her heart to God. With the sweet odor of summer flowers perfuming the air and with the low whispering of the pine trees in her ears, the young schoolteacher felt very near to her Maker as she knelt in the soft warm sand and talked with Him.

How many of those earnest prayers out in nature were answered! Within five months of her own baptism Dollis' mother joined her in church fellowship. Later her father and her older sister took the same step. A friend entered a Christian college to prepare for service in the Lord's vineyard.

Following the Master out onto the mountainside, or by the seashore, or just onto the white Florida sand under the starry heavens may become for any child of God a route of victory.

A NAME WORTH A REGIMENT

Therefore God raised him to the heights and bestowed on him the name above all names, that at the name of Jesus every knee should bow—in heaven, on earth, and in the depths. **Phil. 2:9-11, N.E.B.**

In *Decision* magazine Robert C. Vaughan tells the story of Samuel Benfield Steele, inspector of the Canadian Northwest Mounted Police. Steele, with nerves to match his name, played an important role in the development of the police force, especially in the policing of the construction of the Canadian Pacific Railway in British Columbia. In the Canadian *Who Was Who* the profile of Samuel Steele, according to Vaughan, contains this sentence, "His coming meant order, his presence meant justice; his name was worth a regiment."—*Decision* magazine, October, 1972, p. 3.

There is another of whom this might be said—One whose banner over us is not the Maple Leaf but the banner of love—the Lord Jesus Christ: "His coming meant order, his presence meant justice; his name is worth a regiment."

Into an untold number of lives Jesus Christ has brought order. Men and women, boys and girls with problem-plagued, frustration-filled lives have found meaning and order through the loving name, the perfect life, the vicarious death of the Man of Calvary.

The precious name of Jesus has brought justice not only to individuals but to whole communities. Whole islands, like Mussau in the South Pacific, where heathenism and ignorance had spawned degradation and filth and fear, have been transformed into healthy, happy, law-abiding communities when the all-prevailing name of Jesus became the law of love.

The name of Jesus Christ is indeed "worth a regiment" and far more! No army that ever marched has had such far-reaching power for good as the transforming name of Jesus.

Marshal all the great names of all lands and all time; include Alexander and Aristotle, Cicero and the Caesars; include Napoleon Bonaparte and the French men of letters; add all of your present-day heroes and favorites in any field, still there is that name above all names—that Man before whom all others will someday bow!

His name is indeed worth a regiment many times over!

JESUS THE GREAT RESTORER

The Spirit of the Lord God is upon me; because the Lord hath anointed me to preach good tidings unto the meek; he hath sent me to bind up the brokenhearted, to proclaim liberty to the captives, and the opening of the prison to them that are bound. Isa. 61:1.

Jesus was a restorer. He was more than a restorer of truth that had been obscured beneath ceremonialism, truth that had been forgotten and ignored. As our text today reveals— the Lord was "anointed" to "preach good tidings," "bind the broken-hearted," "proclaim liberty to the captives" of sin. He also was "to proclaim the acceptable year of the Lord, and . . . to comfort all that mourn" (Isa. 61:2).

The Master fulfilled all that the gospel prophet foretold. See Jesus on the Sabbath day confronted with a needy man and an accusing band of Pharisees. Jesus spoke to the unfortunate man, "Stretch forth thine hand. And he stretched it forth; and it was restored whole" (Matt. 12:13).

How the "oil of joy" must have flowed in the man's being, how the act must have clothed him with "the garment of praise"! His poor, lame hand was restored full of strength because he had come in contact with the Great Restorer.

Pause by the Master's side as a crowd brings to Jesus the blind man in Bethsaida. The sightless one's friends "besought him to touch him" (Mark 8:22). Jesus "put his hands . . . upon his eyes, and made him look up: and he was restored, and saw every man clearly" (verse 25).

"He was *restored*." Who could know the joy this act of love kindled in the healed man's heart? How he must have loved the Saviour—the first face he had ever seen was that of his great Benefactor. So it was—everywhere the Saviour went He restored peace to troubled hearts. He restored hope to lost souls. He restored confidence to the discouraged.

Jesus is our example. We are to follow in His steps. How much repairing and restoring is needed in the world today!

Our sin-sick planet is filled with broken minds, broken homes, broken hearts. How much restoring these lonely, bitter, faithless lives need! How much love and understanding they cry out for. Like our Saviour before us, you and I may become restorers in our homes, in our country, in our day!

HOW SHALL I BRING THE ARK OF GOD HOME?

And David was afraid of God that day, saying, How shall I bring the ark of God home to me? 1 Chron. 13:12.

A new pastor in southern France began visiting his parishioners to get acquainted. One couple—community leaders and anxious to make a good impression—anticipated his visit. One day when the man returned from work his wife said the pastor had been there.

"What did he say?" the husband asked.

"He asked, 'Does Christ live here?' and I didn't know what to say," the wife answered.

The man's face flushed. "Why didn't you tell him that we were respectable people?"

"He didn't ask that."

"Why didn't you say that we read our Bible and offer our prayers?"

"He didn't ask that either."

More vexed, the man asked, "Why didn't you say that we are always at church?"

"He didn't ask that either," sobbed the wife. "He only asked, 'Does Christ live here?'"

The pastor's question struck the couple with new force. Slowly, their lives changed. Gradually they grew to expect Christ, not dead, but gloriously alive in their home.

This question is for you, for me! Does Jesus live in *my* home?

In our text today David did not have Christ in the home in mind when he asked the question, "How shall I bring the ark of God home?" He was speaking of bringing the actual ark of the covenant back to its rightful place in the Temple. Nevertheless, can we not rephrase the words of Israel's king and re-emphasize a continuing challenge of the Word with which every child of God is confronted—How shall I bring Christ into *my* home? How can I make Him an abiding guest in *my* family?

God wishes to make our homes little heavens on earth—where Jesus dwells. The home should be the father's kingdom. Mother should be the queen, and it should be the children's paradise. Ellen White declares: "The sweetest type of heaven is a home where the Spirit of the Lord presides."—*The Adventist Home*, p. 15.

FAULTFINDING IS OUT

Why beholdest thou the mote that is in thy brother's eye? Matt. 7:3.

Judy was plump. Not nearly so slim as the day Jack married her. And Jack never let her forget it. He never lost an opportunity to poke fun at her obesity. Something soon happened to that home—and then to the church membership of that young couple. If Jack had been more thoughtful, the story might have been different.

Faultfinding can be very subtle. "Never should either . . . [husband or wife] indulge in a joke at the expense of the other's feelings. Never should either the husband or wife in sport or in any other manner complain of each other to others, for frequently indulging in this foolish and what may seem perfectly harmless joking will end in trial with each other and perhaps estrangement."—*The Adventist Home,* p. 177.

We often guard our tongue better in public than at home. But if we want the presence of Christ, we will cherish kindness and love, the spirit of tenderness and forbearance. "By the grace of God you can succeed in making each other happy, as in your marriage vow you promised to do."—*The Faith I Live By,* p. 259.

Faultfinding can be a sore spot. Benjamin Franklin had good advice on that subject: "Keep your eyes wide open before marriage, and half shut afterwards." When we bury the hatchet, it should remain buried. "The heart of his wife should be the grave for the faults of the husband, and the heart of the husband the grave for his wife's faults."—*The Adventist Home,* p. 177.

A young friend of mine was planning to marry. It seemed to me a terrible mistake, and I labored with him half the night trying to talk him out of it. But love is not only blind, it is also deaf. They were married. What a tragedy!

The young man started out well in the ministry. Very shortly he was pastoring large churches. But he soon dropped by the wayside because of his wife's cutting criticism. She failed to remember that her heart should be the grave of the faults of the one she had promised to love, honor, and cherish till death parted them. Love will dig deep graves for faults—and seal them in forever!

MAKE IT WARM AND CHEERFUL!

Use hospitality one to another without grudging. **1 Peter 4:9.**

In the Third Epistle of John two persons are mentioned. One, "the wellbeloved Gaius," and Diotrephes "who loveth to have the preeminence." These two church members to whom John is writing were men of different dispositions.

It is evident from John's short Epistle that Diotrephes was a troublemaker. He also manifested a degree of indifference, if not hostility, toward the needs of visiting saints. He "receiveth us not." But Diotrephes' lack of hospitality did not stop there. He was "not content therewith, neither doth he himself receive the brethren, and forbiddeth them that would, casteth them out of the church." Dr. Taylor translates John's words: "He not only refuses to welcome the missionary travelers himself, but tells others not to, and when they do he tries to put them out of the church" (3 John 10, T.L.B.).

On the other hand Gaius was a man renowned for his Christian hospitality. "Dear friend, you are doing a good work for God in taking care of the traveling teachers and missionaries who are passing through. They have told the church here of your friendship and your loving deeds. I am glad when you send them on their way with a generous gift. For they are traveling for the Lord, and take neither food, clothing, shelter, nor money from those who are not Christians, even though they have preached to them. So we ourselves should take care of them in order that we may become partners with them in the Lord's work" (verses 5-8, T.L.B.).

"Wellbeloved Gaius" merited a place in sacred history as a man of great hospitality. His deeds were in keeping with the instruction of the inspired Peter to "use hospitality one to another without grudging," "cheerfully share your home with those who need a meal or a place to stay for the night" (T.L.B.).

We have all known men and women like Gaius—warm, thoughtful hosts and hostesses who are always ready to share their home with those passing through. It may be a serviceman, an unexpected visitor at church, or a minister from the conference office. Their homes are always open, there is always an extra place at the table.

Warm Christian hospitality is a gift from God!

ON BONNETS AND POTATOES

If ye have faith, and doubt not, . . . ye shall say unto this mountain, Be thou removed, and . . . it shall be done. Matt. 21:21.

Years ago in the Southland a young lady asked her brother to give her money for a college education.

"I'd like to, sis," he replied, "but I can't help you. Unless," as an afterthought he added, "you can use this." In an offhand manner he flipped the girl a fifty-cent piece.

Jean accepted the challenge. In those days fifty cents would buy something. That half-dollar bought Jean some cloth. From the cloth she made a bonnet—you can see this happened quite a few years ago. The bonnet sold for several times the amount of her original investment.

After earning several dollars making bonnets, Jean decided to raise potatoes. She was able to do all of the work herself except the plowing. She contracted a neighbor boy to do this. Her crop was good. She reinvested. Potatoes and bonnets put Jean through college. It started with fifty cents.

Of course, it costs money to get an education. Most likely you can't make it on bonnets these days—but with potatoes or some other practical investment you may get through. If your parents can't help you much, don't give up! Where there's still a will there is still a way. Actually, you will appreciate your academy or college education more if a lot of your own sweat and tears have made it possible.

"Let the youth who need an education set to work with a determination to obtain it," Ellen White says. "Do not wait for an opening; make one for yourselves. Take hold in any small way that presents itself."—*Christ's Object Lessons,* p. 334.

I heard an educator friend of mine say one time: "It is true that there are parents who cannot afford to send their children to our schools, but I have never yet heard of a case where the parents had a strong desire for their boy or girl to be in a Christian school, and where the child had an equally strong desire, that it was not possible to work something out some way for that child to receive a Christian education."

Whether it takes bonnets, potatoes, or something else, when September comes, be in a Christian school where God wants you to be. Move a mountain!

THE UNSUNG HERO

The Lord grant unto him that he may find mercy of the Lord in that day: and in how many things he ministered unto me at Ephesus, thou knowest very well. 2 Tim. 1:18.

Onesiphorus was a man who helped others. Paul writes of "how much he helped me at Ephesus" (2 Tim. 1:18, T.L.B.). Perhaps he had the gift of "helps" that Paul speaks of in his letter to the Corinthians (1 Cor. 12:28). Nothing more is mentioned in Holy Writ about the help Onesiphorus rendered to the apostle in Ephesus, but evidently this assistance was well known to Timothy, and we may imagine what some of the "helps" may have been.

At Ephesus Paul encountered problems and some opposition. In the synagogue for three months he worked tirelessly in an effort to persuade men for Christ.

Perhaps during this intensive evangelistic crusade Onesiphorus was by Paul's side encouraging and supporting his elder as well as working personally with those who gathered in the place of worship. Evidently Paul's effort was not as fruitful as hoped, for "some rejected his message and publicly spoke against Christ" (Acts 19:9, T.L.B.). During those difficult days of opposition Onesiphorus stood right by Paul.

For two years longer the evangelistic team of Paul and Onesiphorus continued their work in Ephesus. Because of the opposition in the synagogue they moved their meeting place to the "school of one Tyrannus." There are always problems inherent in moving a series of meetings from one hall to another. Interested people must be given careful instructions regarding the new address and encouraged to attend. Details concerning arrangements in the new location must be cared for. These may not have been as complex in Paul's day, but no doubt Onesiphorus was there assisting and encouraging.

The gift of "helps" today is still a blessed one. To serve as an elder, a deacon, or a deaconess, to help in the Sabbath school, the Community Services, with the juniors, or in the Pathfinders, is a worthwhile contribution to the work in any church. There may not always be words of appreciation and acclaim, but it is still a blessed work to be an Onesiphorus today—to be a helper in God's work!

THE GOOD OLD DAYS

Say not thou, What is the cause that the former days were better than these? for thou dost not inquire wisely concerning this. Eccl. 7:10.

On January 31, 1902, Mrs. L. Flora Plummer, at the time corresponding secretary for the General Conference Sabbath School Department, wrote a letter to Elder A. G. Daniells, president of the General Conference. It reflects some of the sincere, selfless philosophy of our earlier workers. It is not a bad thing that we should refresh our minds with the healthy attitudes of some of the "good old days" we too easily forget.

"DEAR BROTHER DANIELLS: I wish so much that I could have your kindly help and advice, just as I used to have it fifteen years ago. I am discouraged. I really am. This department is costing too much in dollars and cents. From May 20, 1901, to February 1, 1902, it has cost $591.50. This includes my wages up to January 1, 1902 and everything I had paid from this office. It is too awful much. And I have been estimating the average monthly cost, now that we are in full running order, and it will run about as follows: Rent, $10.00; Stenographer, $20.00; Postage, $15.00; Printing $10.00; Miscellaneous, $4.00; Mrs. Plummer, $36.00; Total, $95.00.

"Now, Brother Daniells, my dear good friend, I can say to you what I would not say to others. My efforts are not worth to the cause any such sum as that. I cannot make them worth it. It seems wicked to spend such an amount for all I can do, now when money is of so much value to the cause. Truly, I am distressed over this. I love the work, and am doing all I can, but the work I am doing is not worth that much money and I can never make it worth it. I can see no way of cutting down expenses either. I watch them all the time. Everything is high-priced in this 'prosperous' city, and I am greatly depressed by the situation. Sabbath is drawing on, and I have not time for more, but I could not go home tonight without writing you."

The Preacher reminds us that usually it is not helpful to dwell too long on "the good old days." We agree. Sometimes, however, the sincere selflessness of those who served in yester-year is a challenge to us today!

NO SUBSTITUTE ROCK

For their rock is not as our Rock. **Deut. 32:31.**

When Moses spoke these words the people before him were comparatively young people. The old guard had passed off the stage of action. A new generation was to shape the destiny of Israel. God's man was passing on to them some timely counsel in language they understood, for the land in which they had dwelt for forty years was indeed a land of rocks.

Moses wished to impress upon his young hearers that "there is none holy as the Lord: for there is none beside thee: neither is there any rock like our God" (1 Sam. 2:2). The false gods of the world about them could never suffice. Fulfillment would come only through *their Rock,* spelled with a capital *R.* "For their rock is not as our Rock." There is no substitute for the living God!

People in our day—young and old—are still trying "other rocks"—the kinds spelled with the lower-case *r,* and they are still finding that "their rock is not as our Rock."

Some seek fulfillment in the rock of *humanism.* A humanist, one writer explains, "is one 'whose belief consists of faith in man and devotion to human well-being.' Faith in man is substituted for faith in God."—HAROLD LINDSELL, in *Christianity Today,* Sept. 11, 1970, p. 5. We should cultivate faith in our fellow men, we should be concerned with their well-being, but the rock of humanism "is not . . . our Rock."

Some seek fulfillment in the rock of *materialism.* We live in a grasping, greedy era. People, young and old, want more and more and more of this world's goods—more *things.* Through the acquisition of *things* they hope to find peace and happiness. But they find as Jesus once said, "Real life and real living are not related to how rich we are" (Luke 12:15, T.L.B.).

Today millions seek solutions to the mysteries of the universe and of life in the rock of *evolution.* In so doing they do away with the Rock of Ages, His Word, His creative and redemptive power, His second advent. But evolution poses as many problems as it solves. The rock of evolution "is not . . . our Rock."

No rock Like Our "Rock"

There is none holy as the Lord: for their is none beside thee: neither is there any rock like our God. 1 Sam. 2:2.

If you have ever traveled in the Holy Land you will understand well why Bible writers have so much to say about rocks and stones. There are mounds and mountains of rock. Pastures and roadside wastes are strewn with stones of all sizes.

In the Word of God the Lord is referred to as the Rock—emphasizing the everlasting stability and reliability of the Most High. The inspired author of the first book of Samuel declared God's ultimate supremacy when he wrote "neither is there any rock like our God." Yet millions today seek satisfaction and fulfillment in other rocks—other gods. As we noted in our reading yesterday, humanism, materialism, and evolution are some of the spurious rocks. There are others.

There is a theological liberalism abroad in the Western world today that is a close relative of humanism. It denies the supernatural. Miracles are "out." This liberal interpretation of the Word does not accept the deity of Christ, the virgin birth, His vicarious atonement, or bodily resurrection.

A gospel with no Saviour from sin, no returning Lord, no forever heaven, "is not as our Rock." Here is no satisfying substitute for the Rock of our salvation.

To replace the broken cisterns of theological liberalism, we have offered to us the equally shattered cisterns of a new morality. No more restrictions. No more being fenced in. According to the new morality, there are no absolutes, no ultimates. Everything is determined by the situation. The Ten Commandments according to the new morality would place the qualifying word "ordinarily" before each of the ten precepts. "Ordinarily thou shall not steal," et cetera.

With no standard of right or wrong but the loving thing of the moment, where are we? This is not truth from the Christ who said, "It is easier for heaven and earth to pass, than one tittle of the law to fail" (Luke 16:17). "If ye love me, keep my commandments" (John 14:15). Liberalism is man's philosophy, not God's saving message. This "is not as our Rock."

Substitute rocks will not satisfy. "Neither is there any rock like our God."

THE OCCULT IS NO SUBSTITUTE

Let no one be found among you who makes his son or daughter pass through fire, no augur or soothsayer or diviner or sorcerer, no one who casts spells or traffics with ghosts and spirits, and no necromancer. Those who do these things are abominable to the Lord, and it is because of these abominable practices that the Lord your God is driving them out before you. Deut. 18:10-12, N.E.B.

I was flying from Madras to Bangalore, South India. The big jet was filled with young yogis from the United States. I was the only person on the aircraft not in this party touring the holy places of Mother India.

Next to me was sitting a young American from California. We were soon in conversation. I was curious to know what had led this youth with a Christian background to give up his faith in Christ and embrace the occult.

"Friend, what have you found in yoga that you did not have in Jesus Christ?" I asked after we had become acquainted.

The young man paused thoughtfully, then replied honestly, "Nothing."

For a few minutes I continued tactfully to press the claims of Christ upon him, but he changed the subject.

Many, especially among the youth today, are seeking fulfillment in the occult. Some universities and even high schools have offered courses in witchcraft, and there has been no shortage of enrollees. More than a thousand daily newspapers in the United States carry well-read astrology columns. Some radio stations include horoscopes in their daily programs. Stores offer personalized horoscopes from computers. England has thousands of admitted witches.

Those who turn to the occult for fulfillment do so largely as an escape from their problems or from the problems of the world about them. To such seekers David Wilkerson, Teen Challenge leader, has this wise counsel: "Don't play around with devil games. Avoid Ouija boards, séances, and tarot cards. Don't believe in horoscopes. Trust your guidance and future completely to Jesus."—*Maturity Manual,* p. 60.

Jesus is the solution to our problems. The rock of occultism "is not as our Rock" (Deut. 32:31).

THE PRICE OF POWER

I intreated thy favour with my whole heart. Ps. 119:58.

God has promised the gift of His Holy Spirit to provide requisite power to proclaim His last-day message to every kindred, tongue, and people. There are yet great lands of earth outwardly closed to the heralds of the three angels' messages. The peoples in these lands, too, must hear this truth from the personal messenger, through the printed page, over the ether waves of radio or TV, or through some medium of divine provision we may know nothing about at present.

We know the message will do its work, but we know also that power beyond our own human planning will be required to accomplish the task. The power is promised but there are conditions laid down. There is a price to pay. God demands it. *The price of power is everything—everything we have or are!*

"I intreated thy favour with my whole heart," the psalmist declared. He knew the price of power. He sought God with his whole heart. Again he speaks on the subject: "Blessed are they that . . . seek him with the whole heart" (Ps. 119:2). God wants our heart, our *whole* heart. Only then can He trust us with His power, the power of the Holy Spirit—the only power adequate for the challenge before us.

"Surrender your will and way to Him. Make not a single reserve, not a single compromise with self. Know what it is to be free in Christ."—*The Ministry of Healing,* p. 514. Our hearts, our wills, our ways—all His. Here is the formula for power.

"Nothing," the Lord's messenger declares, "is apparently more helpless, yet really more invincible, than the soul that feels its nothingness and relies wholly on God."—*Prophets and Kings,* p. 175. *Surrender* and *nothingness* are not strong words in man's vocabulary, but they hold the secret to God's power in the language of heaven.

"There is no limit to the usefulness of one who, by putting self aside, makes room for the working of the Holy Spirit upon his heart, and lives a life wholly consecrated to God."—*The Desire of Ages,* pp. 250, 251.

The price of needed power is everything. When God's church—you and I—is willing to pay the price, *the power will come.* The work will be finished. Why do we keep God waiting?

"RAISE THE DEAD"

And as ye go, preach, saying, The kingdom of heaven is at hand. Heal the sick, cleanse the lepers, raise the dead, cast out devils: freely ye have received, freely give. Matt. 10:7, 8.

I checked and double checked the following story with Elder L. C. Naden, then president of the Australasian Division. He affirmed, after careful investigation, that the story is true.

From his hillside home a pastor heard the loud sound of wailing in the distance. In his native land of New Guinea this meant a death had occurred in a village in the valley. For several hours the sad lament continued. The pastor felt a strong impression that he should go to the heathen village to help.

After walking for some time the pastor reached the village and pushed his way through a crowd of mourners gathered in the home of the deceased. There on the mud floor lay the dead woman—a young mother. By her side were two small children and her husband, all weeping bitterly.

Already arrangements had been made to dispose of the body according to the custom of this primitive area. The woman, who had been ill for several days, was not only "dead" (which in local language could mean that she was in a coma), she was, according to the report, "dead finished," which in pidgin English meant certainly, truly dead.

The pastor's heart was touched by the scene before him. For these poor mourners there was no blessed hope of a resurrection morning, no life beyond the grave. Perhaps God would perform a miracle in their midst.

"Would you like me to pray?" he asked.

"But she is dead!" they responded. "It is too late!"

"It is never too late for my God," he assured them. They agreed he should pray.

Simply and earnestly this child of God pleaded with his heavenly Father for a miracle that would bring faith and deliverance to these primitive villagers.

As the prayer ended the woman on the floor drew a long breath, opened her eyes and sat up! God restored her to her family. He also brought faith to the village. In fact, in 1967 I flew over several villages in the area that are today Seventh-day Adventist villages because God still raises the dead!

HIS FACE TOWARD US

Blessed are they that hear the word of God, and keep it. **Luke 11:28.**

"Are you there, Father?" asked the 8-year-old boy of his father in the small hours of the night.

"Yes, my boy, I am here." ·

"Is your face turned toward me, Daddy?"

"Yes, son, my face is toward you. But why do you ask that question?"

"Everything is all right, then, Daddy, if your face is turned toward me. Good night."

So it is with your life and mine in the dark hours. The outlook today, in this world of sin and suffering, is far from encouraging, but the uplook was never brighter! In such a time as this, our only source of faith and confidence is a heavenly Father—not far distant, but One who is near—His face turned toward us.

Our new-fashioned society needs the old-fashioned faith in God and His Word. Something to hold us steady in the storm. A faith that will help us see through and beyond these present distresses to a better, brighter day ahead. That faith is more than a vague something. It rests in Someone; that Someone is God.

We find God in God's book—the Bible. Can any more timely admonition come to us today than these words of the Master: "Search the scriptures" (John 5:39). The time has come for us to brush away the dust of neglect from our Bible, and study it diligently every day. Jeremiah rejoiced in the sweet messages of God that came to him through inspiration. "Thy words were found, and I did eat them; and thy word was unto me the joy and rejoicing of mine heart" (Jer. 15:16). Job's evaluation of the Scriptures may be found in his words, "I have esteemed the words of his mouth more than my necessary food" (Job 23:12).

His face is toward us waiting to commune with us—waiting to give us wisdom, instruction, and help through the pages of His Word. There are promises waiting for us to claim, words of comfort for the sorrowing, words of challenge for the strong, messages of hope and cheer for the fainthearted.

Where is *your* Bible just now, my friend?

DELIVERED UNTO SATAN

Cling tightly to your faith in Christ and always keep your conscience clear, doing what you know is right. For some people have disobeyed their consciences and have deliberately done what they knew was wrong. It isn't surprising that soon they lost their faith in Christ after defying God like that. Hymenaeus and Alexander are two examples of this. 1 Tim. 1:19, 20, T.L.B.

Hymenaeus and his friend became confused regarding an important point of doctrine, declaring that the resurrection of the saints "is past already" (2 Tim. 2:18). Evidently the apostasy of Hymenaeus not only led to total shipwreck of his own faith but he was active in destroying the confidence of others.

Because of this blasphemy and disrupting influence among the saints, it seems likely he was disfellowshiped or otherwise disciplined—"delivered unto Satan," the apostle writes. Evidently church action had no salutary effect upon Hymenaeus, for when Paul wrote his second letter to Timothy, Hymenaeus was still in apostasy.

It is a sad experience when modern Hymenaeuses wander off into the tempting fields of false doctrine. It is more regrettable when they feel the imperative resting upon them to disturb other church members with their apostate teachings.

It is one thing for members to differ on peripheral interpretations of Scripture. The church is broad enough to embrace such divergent views on minor issues. Through the years many have taken different views of the 144,000 and certain other prophecies of Daniel and the Revelation. They were not points essential to salvation. Private interpretations, not blatantly advocated, caused no rupture in the church. There was no problem.

To actively advocate divergent views against the counsel of brethren of experience is quite another matter. Activity that creates confusion and erodes faith inevitably invites spiritual disaster. Paul's resort to discipline was the only course left for him to pursue.

"Whosoever transgresseth, and abideth not in the doctrine of Christ, hath not God. . . . If there come any unto you, and bring not this doctrine, receive him not into your house, neither bid him God speed: for he that biddeth him God speed is partaker of his evil deeds" (2 John 9-11).

GETTING THROUGH TO GOD

Behold, the Lord's hand is not shortened, that it cannot save; neither his ear heavy, that it cannot hear. Isa. 59:1.

"I just don't seem to be able to get through to God." The young man seated by my side in the college lounge was distressed. He wanted to live the Christian life. He wanted victory. But heaven seemed closed to him. He just couldn't seem to "get through to God."

This frustrated youth was not the first one who has found difficulty in getting through to God. Many a halting saint has suffered the same trauma. Many have been swept over the brink of discouragement because of their failure to get through.

If we can't get through—if we pray and nothing happens—there is a reason. When God declares His "hand is not shortened" and His ear is not heavy, He means what He says. He is accessible. He is willing, He is able, to answer our petitions.

Read on in Isaiah's counsel in chapter fifty-nine. Verse two unveils one cause of prayer failure. "Your iniquities have separated between you and your God, and your sins have hid his face from you, that he will not hear."

"Your *iniquities* . . . your *sins*" "have separated," "have hid." Here is the reason our prayer voice is too frequently muted—*sin in our life!* If we persist in wrongdoing, God "will not hear" us! It is either break with sin or break with God. It is just that simple.

Indifference also is an impediment to answered prayer. The Bible makes this clear. "I have called, and ye refused," God declares. "I have stretched out my hand, and no man regarded; but ye have set at nought all my counsel, and would none of my reproof" (Prov. 1:24, 25).

Despite our knowledge of God's will we go our own heedless way. He calls, we refuse to hear. He stretches out His hand, we disregard. While the door of mercy stands ajar we have opportunity to enter. One day that door will close. "Then shall they call upon me, but I will not answer; they shall seek me early, but they shall not find me" (verse 28).

"Now is the accepted time" (2 Cor. 6:2), God says. We need to get through to God *today*—before probation closes.

MOMENTARY ADVANTAGE OR ETERNAL INHERITANCE?

Alexander the coppersmith did me much evil: the Lord reward him according to his works. . . . Notwithstanding the Lord stood with me, and strengthened me; that by me the preaching might be fully known, and that all the Gentiles might hear: and I was delivered out of the mouth of the lion. 2 Tim. 4:14-17.

It is likely that Alexander the coppersmith was a Roman Jew. When Paul was arrested and tried before the Roman court it would appear that Alexander testified against the old apostle. The coppersmith had had occasion to become acquainted with Paul in Ephesus, but he testified against Paul when he was on trial for his life in Rome.

Paul was never a man to hide his faith in Christ, and as he stood bravely before the court there is little doubt that he would speak most eloquently of his Saviour and the salvation His death extends to all. Here was an assembly of Gentile hearers and Paul would surely make Christ known to them.

For some reason, not mentioned in the Inspired Word, Alexander found it expedient to accuse the apostle during his trial. This testimony evidently contributed to the adverse decision of the court. He "did me much harm," Paul later wrote to Timothy. The Centenary Translation by Montgomery gives Paul's words an even more damaging intent: "Alexander, the coppersmith, manifested bitter hostility toward me."

Alexander the coppersmith is the timeless type who places momentary advantage above an eternal inheritance. Frequently those who follow such a course reach for two worlds and in the end lose both. While it served his purpose Alexander perhaps feigned friendship with the man of God. When he gained his end he turned against Paul.

Paul warns succeeding generations of men of such perfidy. "Beware of him," he warns (2 Tim. 4:15, Moffatt). He also declares that such unscrupulous individuals will someday receive their just rewards. "The Lord will punish him" (verse 14, T.L.B.).

Perhaps Paul had in mind such men as Alexander the coppersmith when he wrote to the Galatians: "Whatsoever a man soweth, that shall he also reap" (Gal. 6:7).

WATCH THOSE CAVES UNDER YOUR HOUSE!

If the foundations be destroyed, what can the righteous do? **Ps. 11:3.**

In January, 1959, Zichen Zusen Bolder, a small Belgian village on the Dutch border, experienced a tragic happening. For centuries their homes had been undermined by the villagers themselves quarrying out sandstone from which they built their houses. Beginning in Roman times, the caves now extended some thirty miles, honeycombing the earth beneath their homes.

When the crash came, houses, churches, people, disappeared as a thin crust of earth gave way. Some people were killed, others injured. Many were missing. Tragedy left the villagers stunned—their loved ones and homes gone.

Similarly, there is some undermining of the Christian faith today that has resulted in cracks in the foundation of some ecclesiastical structures. Mechanistic evolution as a theory of origins has worked its insidious way into many churches and schools of so-called Christian lands. The Bible is ridiculed. Everything supernatural is repudiated. What cannot be explained by the scientific method is considered suspect. The Creation story is scorned. The divinity of Christ is denied. The law of God is flaunted. The idea of a Second Advent is ignored. The existence of God is rejected.

God's remnant church will not escape the subtle undermining influences of modern, Christless, faithless theology. Satan is even now at work to weaken the pillars that gird this message. He does his work subtly, sometimes under the guise of making the truth "relevant."

The messenger of the Lord warns us, "There will be a removing of the landmarks, and an attempt to tear down the pillars of our faith."—*The SDA Bible Commentary,* Ellen G. White Comments, on Rev. 18:1-5, p. 985. The evil one will leave no stone unturned in his effort to undermine faith in the pillars of truth. He will ridicule. He will create doubts. He will introduce unproved data. He will make black appear white, and by plausible arguments error will be presented as truth.

In these days we need to guard well our homes and our churches, for "if the foundations be destroyed, what can the righteous do?"

WHERE OUR HEARTS ARE

Wherever your treasure is, there your heart and thoughts will also be. **Luke 12:34, T.L.B.**

"Dear Brother Reinhard," the letter began. "When we were young God called my wife and me to Africa. We served Him gladly for many years until our health broke and we had to return to our homeland.

"Now I am 85 years old. My dear companion has gone to rest, and I soon will follow her. My thoughts still go out to Africa, where there is so much to be done. The need is still so great, and time to finish the work is so much shorter than it was when we went to Africa for the first time many years ago.

"Yesterday I went to the funeral home to find out what a very simple funeral would cost. They told me the cheapest is $200. I have left this sum in my savings account in the bank and have given them the necessary instructions.

"The rest of our life's savings—it is not much—I have sent to the General Conference for the work in needy Africa. Use it for the spreading of the third angel's message. It is very late.

"I can live on the small income I receive each month, as I do not need much of this life's goods anymore. May God bless the work in Africa and may Jesus come very soon!"

Since writing these words and making this liberal offering to a finished work, this saint of God has fallen asleep in Jesus. His works do truly follow him!

In Abraham's day the old patriarch was called upon to offer up his own son as a sacrifice to God. He did not hesitate. His most precious possession was on the altar. His treasure was where his heart was—with God. No sacrifice was too great.

From Abraham's experience in giving, the Lord has a lesson for his children in 1975: "The lesson was given to shine down through the ages, that we may learn that there is nothing too precious to be given to God."—*Our High Calling,* p. 191.

"There is nothing too precious to be given to God"—what a lesson! What a challenge! If these words strike a responsive chord in our hearts, all that we have—nothing withholding—will be on the altar for Him! "Wherever your treasure is, there your heart and thoughts will also be."

243

THE *SINE QUA NON* OF THE GOSPEL

Jesus answered and said unto him, Verily, verily, I say unto thee, Except a man be born again, he cannot see the kingdom of God. John 3:3.

Here is one of the most vital truths in the Word of God. It is the very core of the Christ-centered Advent message. It is the *sine qua non*. We must not fail to grasp the import of John's words!

"Jesus answered and said unto him, Verily, verily, I say unto thee, Except a man be born again, he cannot see the kingdom of God."

Jesus makes it clear. The new-birth experience is an absolute necessity. There is no choice in the matter. We simply can never enter the gates of Paradise and spend eternity in the Master's kingdom unless an encounter with Jesus has changed entirely these sin-prone lives of ours. He alone can do it! Thank God, He will if we will but permit Him to do it.

The Word makes it clear the agency Heaven uses in bringing about this marvelous transformation—it is the Holy Spirit. "And when he [the Comforter] is come, he will convince the world of sin" (John 16:8, margin).

Then to the smitten heart the Holy Spirit whispers softly, "Behold the Lamb of God, which taketh away the sin of the world" (chap. 1:29). "Little by little, perhaps unconsciously to the receiver, impressions are made that tend to draw the soul to Christ. . . .

"No one sees the hand that lifts the burden, or beholds the light descend from the courts above. . . . Then that power which no human eye can see creates a new being in the image of God."—*The Desire of Ages,* pp. 172, 173.

The new birth is not some halfway, incomplete experience. It goes to the very root of our trouble—the sinful heart. "A new heart also will I give you, and a new spirit will I put within you: and I will take away the stony heart out of your flesh, and I will give you an heart of flesh" (Eze. 36:26). Our heart, our "desperately wicked" heart, must be completely changed! In one of the languages of southern Mexico the word for *conversion* means literally "his heart returned to God's presence."

Have you experienced the new birth?

REMEMBER!

Remember that Jesus Christ of the seed of David was raised from the dead according to my gospel. **2 Tim. 2:8.**

Three blessed and encouraging thoughts emerge from the reading of our text for today. The apostle Paul admonishes us to *remember* three great truths:

1. *"Remember . . . Jesus Christ . . . raised from the dead."* Multitudes in non-Christian lands follow the teaching of men who today are dead and buried. I have visited the Shwe Dagon Pagoda in Rangoon, Burma, and the Temple of the Tooth in Kandy, Ceylon. In these two places, according to Buddhist tradition, repose the relics of the Buddha. In old Arabia is the tomb of the prophet Mohammed. China claims the remains of Confucius. These men are dead and buried. But, Paul reminds us, "Remember . . . Jesus Christ . . . raised from the dead"!

As the songwriter proclaims:

"I serve a risen Saviour, He's in the world today;
I know that He is living, whatever men may say!"

Copyright 1933 by Homer A. Rodeheaver. © Renewed 1961. The Rodeheaver Co., Owner. All rights reserved. Used by permission.

The risen Lord is by our side. When we face the vicissitudes of life we do not face them alone! When frustrations threaten, when doubts assail, when the way is almost unbearable—"Remember . . . Jesus Christ . . . raised from the dead."

2. *"Remember . . . Jesus Christ of the seed of David."* Not only the risen Christ but the Son of man who lived life, faced problems as we meet them, is to be an encouragement to each follower of the Saviour. Not only the glorified Christ but the tempted Christ is our source of strength. He has been over the road before you. He can enter into your experience. He has help for you!

3. *"Remember . . . Jesus Christ."* Remember the good news. It is still "the power of God unto salvation" (Rom. 1:16) in 1975 as it was in the first century after Christ. When the present or the future looks dark or hopeless—"Remember . . . Jesus Christ." When you try and fail and you think there isn't any use of trying again, "Remember . . . Jesus Christ."

NOT JUST A NEW COAT OF PAINT

Therefore if any man be in Christ, he is a new creature: old things are passed away; behold, all things are become new. 2 Cor. 5:17.

The new birth is not a patched-up life with a few reformations wrought. It is not a question of conveniently covering up some secret sins or gaining outward victory over some of the evil tendencies that plague us. Paul declares the child of God must become a "new creature." The change is not like repairing an old building and putting on a new coat of paint. The old structure must be demolished. A new edifice rises in its place. The Balinese in the Orient call it "putting on a new way of life."

"When the Spirit of God takes possession of the heart, it transforms the life. Sinful thoughts are put away, evil deeds are renounced; love, humility, and peace take the place of anger, envy, and strife. Joy takes the place of sadness, and the countenance reflects the light of heaven."—*The Desire of Ages,* p. 173.

To some the new birth comes in a dramatic way, as it did to Saul on the road to Damascus. Under the influence of a Spirit-filled sermon, during the heartbreak of tragedy, in the presence of death, the Holy Spirit speaks in such clear tones that there is no chance for the sinner to mistake Heaven's will. Amid a light from heaven a voice is heard declaring, "I am Jesus whom thou persecutest." The Saviour is revealed in all of His beauty and loveliness. The heart is broken, the whole course of an evil lifetime is changed in a moment.

The new birth does not come to all in such a glorious way. Not to everyone comes a cataclysmic Damascus Road experience. Many grow up in Christian homes. At mother's knee they hear and accept the stories of God's love and redemption. As they grow, so their understanding of spiritual concepts develops apace. Have they not been truly born again? The servant of the Lord answers this question.

"A person may not be able to tell the exact time or place, or to trace all the circumstances in the process of conversion; but this does not prove him to be unconverted. . . . Little by little, perhaps unconsciously to the receiver, impressions are made that tend to draw the soul to Christ."—*Ibid.,* p. 172.

"I WAS IN PRISON"

The Lord give mercy unto the house of Onesiphorus; for he oft refreshed me, and was not ashamed of my chain. **2 Tim. 1:16.**

Paul's friend Onesiphorus was a prison worker. He visited the old apostle while he was in chains. "He was never ashamed of my being in jail," Dr. Taylor paraphrases the last part of our text in *The Living Bible.* Onesiphorous brought encouragement and help to God's man suffering imprisonment. It was a great work he did!

Years ago when I visited the beautiful island of Guadeloupe in the French West Indies, I met Sister O'Neil, one of our church members. Sister O'Neil's husband was a tailor by trade. One night a man broke into her husband's shop and made off with quite a supply of merchandise. Later the man was apprehended, tried, and sentenced to a prison term.

Like Onesiphorus, Sister O'Neil became a prison worker. She visited the man in jail, gave him literature and Bible studies. He became a Sabbath school member. His life was so changed that before the end of his term he was released. When I visited Guadeloupe, I went to the prison to visit Sister O'Neil's Sabbath school and Bible class. There I met thirty to forty men who were studying the truth. Already twelve had been baptized in the prison.

Sister O'Neil "was never ashamed of . . . [their] being in jail." She is a twentieth-century Onesiphorus.

In Nashville, Tennessee, for many years Leonard Haswell has led out in an effective program of prison visitation and of holding church services in the prison. I have visited the prisoners in the State penitentiary with him. I heard one of the inmates, serving as the Sabbath school superintendent, make a moving appeal to others present to give their hearts to Christ. Through the years more than 140 have been baptized as a result of his visiting and holding meetings in the prison.

Brother Haswell "was never ashamed of . . . [their] being in jail." He is a twentieth-century Onesiphorus.

Referring to those who visit prisoners, the Master said, "Verily I say unto you, Inasmuch as ye have done it unto one of the least of these my brethren, ye have done it unto me" (Matt. 25:40).

ARBEIT MACHT FREI

There is a way which seemeth right unto a man, but the end thereof are the ways of death. **Prov. 14:12.**

As I walked into the Auschwitz Concentration Camp near Oswiecim, Poland, I read the words in large metal letters over the entrance. They are in the German language. *ARBEIT MACHT FREI*—"work makes free."

Those hapless thousands who passed beneath these words of irony discovered that all that was freed from the camp was the smoke from the crematoriums where the bodies of those who perished were consumed.

The words promised much. They were a snare and a delusion. The promised freedom proved to be a tragic death.

So it is with the sinner or the halting saint who chooses what appears to be the easy way. The way of ease, the way of pleasure, the way of escape, the way of transgression promises much. It leads to death, from which there is no resurrection.

Pilate discovered that the easy way out—the way of compromise—leads only to distress and ruin in the end. He yielded to the demands of the crazed crowd that Jesus should be condemned and released.

"Rather than risk losing his position, he delivered Jesus up to be crucified. But in spite of his precautions, the very thing he dreaded afterward came upon him. His honors were stripped from him, he was cast down from his high office, and, stung by remorse and wounded pride, not long after the crucifixion he ended his own life. So all who compromise with sin will gain only sorrow and ruin. 'There is a way which seemeth right unto a man, but the end thereof are the ways of death.' "— *The Desire of Ages,* p. 738.

Sometimes in our indifference we say by our lives, if not by our words: "It doesn't matter." "I'll do as I please." "I'll go where I wish." "God isn't interested in these little things—these externals!"

Isn't He? "God has placed in His Word no command which men may obey or disobey at will and not suffer the consequences. If men choose any other path than that of strict obedience, they will find that 'the end thereof are the ways of death.' "— *Patriarchs and Prophets,* pp. 360, 361.

WHOSE SLAVE ARE YOU ANYWAY?

I speak this way, using the illustration of slaves and masters, because it is easy to understand: just as you used to be slaves to all kinds of sin, so now you must let yourselves be slaves to all that is right and holy. **Rom. 6:19, T.L.B.**

"I'm not any man's slave! I'm a free individual!" I can just hear your strong denial of bondage—*you* are no man's slave! You are your own boss! No one is going to tell *you* what to do!

Wait a minute! Don't be too hasty or too sure! Sometimes even Seventh-day Adventist Christians have trouble with the master-slave relationship. You see, a person may be a slave to an obnoxious habit.

The dictionary defines a habit as "a way of acting that has become fixed through repetition." Judging, criticizing, gossiping, lying, stealing, lustful thinking, impure actions, swearing, smoking, drinking, gambling, are only a few of the evil habits that plague even the professed Christian's pathway.

"One evil habit, if not firmly resisted, will strengthen into chains of steel, binding the whole man," the Lord's messenger declares *(The Ministry of Healing,* p. 510). These bonds must be broken. We must be free! We must become slaves of a new Master! "Just as you used to be slaves to all kinds of sin, so now you must let yourselves be slaves to all that is right and holy."

For forty years George Ora Smith was a slave to tobacco. His body was saturated with the poison. Taking the name of the Lord in vain was also a way of life with George—that is, until Christ and His truth fully possessed George's heart. Then things were different—vastly different. Through imparted strength from his new-found Saviour, George found deliverance—freedom from the old habits. No longer was he a slave. The Word of God replaced love for the world. The house of God replaced the theater in George's experience. He found a new Master. He became a slave to "all that is right and holy."

There is help for every one of us! "Through the power of Christ, men and women have broken the chains of sinful habit."—*The Acts of the Apostles,* p. 476.

Every one of us may become "slaves to all that is right and holy" through Jesus Christ our Lord!

PETER'S GOD STILL LIVES!

He [Peter] . . . declared unto them how the Lord had brought him out of prison. **Acts 12:17.**

There was a loud, insistent knock at the door. Elder and Mrs. Conference President cringed. They were sure they had heard that same knock before when Brother President had been taken away by the secret police and after a brief "trial" was thrown into prison for fifteen long years.

The second banging on the door was even more insistent. But how could it be—Brother President had been released from prison only four days before. What could they want this time?

"You go to the bedroom," Mrs. President said softly. "I'll answer the door."

It *was* the secret police. This time they hustled Mrs. President off to the station without giving her time even to pack the basic needs for a stay away from home. Her husband followed. Both pleaded with the police to disclose the cause of her detention. Their appeals were fruitless.

The distraught woman was taken to an inner room of the prison and ordered to change into prison garb. For the next three mornings she was forced to join a work detail.

Friday came. Sister President explained she could not work on the Sabbath.

"You do what you are told here!" her tormentors said.

The next morning our sister was awakened.

"Come with me, quickly and quietly," a guard ordered.

Mrs. President rose hurriedly. The guard led her to the dressing room. Her own clothes were returned to her.

"Dress quickly!" she was told.

The guard took her to the gate of the prison.

"Go quickly," he said. "You are free!" There was no further explanation.

It was almost Sabbath school time. Sister President hurried straight to the church. Here she found all the church members had spent the entire night praying for her.

What a praise and prayer service followed! Sister President never learned the cause of her brief imprisonment.

Peter's God still lives!

A WORD FOR OUR EDUCATORS

My brothers, not many of you should become teachers, for you may be certain that we who teach shall ourselves be judged with greater strictness. James 3:1, N.E.B.

A Christian father had just left his son in the college men's dormitory for the first time. As he drove home a flood of mixed emotions surged through him. In his study a few hours later he penned these thought-provoking words to the dean of men:

"As I drove away from your school and from your dormitory, I felt as though I had left part of my life behind. We drove home to a broken circle. Our boy was gone. He is missing because of our deliberate choice to take him out of his home and place him in your home. This choice was based on confidence in you and the faculty of your school, and in the specific contribution dormitory life can make to his character.

"Most of all, dean, I want my son to learn to know and love God, for this is life eternal. I want him to find happiness and the greatest security on earth in a very personal acquaintance with the God of heaven. This can be if the very atmosphere of the dormitory invites the sweet Spirit of God as a constantly honored guest. . . .

" First of all, dean, we want you to be the kind of man we want our boy to become. . . . You will leave an imprint on his soul, and we want it to be after the pattern of God."

Administrators in our educational institutions, teachers in our classrooms, have a wonderful privilege; likewise, they have a tremendous responsibility! Whether yours is the delicate work of molding the minds of kindergarten tots, or whether you have the demanding assignment of dealing with graduate students, yours is an awesome opportunity!

Fathers and mothers throughout the mainstream of Adventism are much concerned about the uniqueness of our church and our schools. They want their children to be nurtured in the Bible-based, Christ-centered Advent message. They are willing to sacrifice in order to send their children to Seventh-day Adventist institutions because they expect them to be different—to maintain their distinctive Adventist atmosphere.

IT MUST BE THE REAL THING!

We speak that we do know, and testify that we have seen. John 3:11.

The story of Jacob and Esau is familiar. Jacob knew the birthright would someday be his and his greatest desire was to receive it, together with all the blessings and privileges that would accompany it. As a spiritual child of God, Jacob regarded this birthright as "the object of his longing."

But Jacob's experience was too much like many professed Christians today. "While he thus esteemed eternal above temporal blessings, Jacob had not an experimental knowledge of the God whom he revered. His heart had not been renewed by divine grace."—*Conflict and Courage,* p. 60.

We would say today that Jacob was a church member but that he was not converted. He made a profession without a corresponding practice being present in his life. Jacob understood little of God's great plan of salvation until he was on his way from Beersheba to Haran and the Lord swung the gates of God ajar in a dream. The deceiver beheld "a ladder set up on the earth, and the top of it reached to heaven: and behold the angels of God ascending and descending on it" (Gen. 28:12).

Later at the brook Jabbok in an hour of crisis Jacob truly met his Lord in a genuine conversion experience. Here his heart was renewed by divine grace. Here he began a new experiential walk with God.

The deeply spiritual class in soul-winning techniques was finished. Ellen, the daughter of a prominent church member, lingered a moment to speak with her instructor.

"Elder," she began hesitantly, "I have been a Seventh-day Adventist all my life. I believe this message, but——" and Ellen faltered a moment. "Somehow tonight through the Holy Spirit you have given me a new understanding of all that He desires to be to me. I understand for the first time my great need and His boundless saving power. I am certain that a new walk with Jesus is just ahead for me, and I am so happy."

There are still modern-day Jacobs who have "known the truth," but who through the leading of the Spirit are finding the joy of knowing the Christ of the truth as well. They speak "what they know" from personal experience.

IT BEGINS AT HOME!

First . . . show . . . piety at home. 1 Tim. 5:4, Weymouth, 4th ed.

If Jesus Christ is truly in our home, all who come in contact with us will know about it, for our religion is most clearly revealed in our home. We talk about revival and reformation. There is no better place for this revival and reformation to begin than in our homes.

It has been said that men will wrangle for religion, write for it, fight for it, die for it. Anything but live for it.

How sad.

Religion is the best armor in the world, but the worst cloak.

"First . . . show . . . piety at home," Paul told Timothy, for religion, like charity, must begin within our own four walls.

We usually associate sanctification with the church. But God says it begins at home. Our biggest test is not in public or the church. It is in the home—how we relate to our husband, wife, father, mother, son, daughter, brother, or sister. This is the acid test of our religion.

It is a sad paradox that those we should love the most are often loved the least. Those who should have a barrelful of our tenderness, compassion, courtesy, and a forgiving spirit often get only a thimbleful.

Have you ever heard a husband, perhaps a Seventh-day Adventist husband, curtly interrupt his wife or children in a manner he would never use in speaking to his boss or someone else he wished to impress? Have you ever been such a husband?

Have you ever heard a wife, perhaps a Seventh-day Adventist wife, whine or nag at her husband or children in a manner she should never think of using in dealing with friends outside the family circle? Have you ever been such a wife?

Sons and daughters also need to remember that piety begins at home.

"How many dishonor Christ and misrepresent His character in the home circle! How many do not manifest patience, forbearance, forgiveness, and true love! . . . If parents will strive for unity in the home by inculcating the principles that governed the life of Christ, dissension will be driven out, and unity and love will abide there."—*The Adventist Home,* p. 178.

HEARTS OF THE CHILDREN TO THEIR PARENTS

Behold, I will send you Elijah the prophet before the coming of the great and dreadful day of the Lord: and he shall turn the heart of the fathers to the children, and the heart of the children to their fathers. Mal. 4:5, 6.

In a church headquarters office far from Washington a father was discussing mission problems with several leaders. During the conversations the telephone rang. Elder Strand (not his real name) answered.

Learning the call was long distance, the church leader raised his hand requesting silence. As the telephone conversation continued most of the talking was done by the person on the other end of the line. Tears began to trickle down Elder Strand's cheeks.

"Bad news," one of the men whispered softly. "Perhaps a loved one has passed away."

The telephone conversation ended. Elder Strand replaced the receiver on the telephone, turned, buried his face in his hands and wept.

"My boy! my boy!" he sobbed. Then in a voice charged with emotion, he told the story.

"It was my boy, Ted, in America. We left him there to complete the school year in college. The past four years Ted has been caught up with the fads and the frustrations of other teen-agers in America. He had no time or inclination for spiritual things. There were hours of anxiety and heartache. My wife and I have prayed earnestly for him, but he was too busy."

Elder Strand paused, eyes glistening, then continued with feeling, "That was Ted! He's changed! He was telling me what Jesus had done for him during a recent revival at the college. He didn't talk like my boy. He told me he was sorry for the heartaches he had caused his mother and me. He spoke of the change that has come into his life. He assured me this is for real. Thank God!"

Describing the work of revival just before Jesus returns, the Lord's messenger writes: "The Spirit of God rested upon them. . . . The hearts of parents were turned to their children, and the hearts of children were turned to their parents." —*The Story of Redemption*, p. 359.

Blessed assurance!

A BATTLE FOR ALL OF US

I spake unto thee in thy prosperity; but thou saidst, I will not hear. This hath been thy manner from thy youth, that thou obeyedst not my voice. Jer. 22:21.

"This hath been thy manner from thy youth." Jeremiah's appeal to Jehoiakim, king of Judah, was to break the fetters of evil habit that bound him.

How many of us are Jehoiakims today—we need freedom from the thongs of evil habit. "There are some who are seeking, always seeking, for the goodly pearl," the Lord's messenger writes. "But they do not make an entire surrender of their wrong habits. They do not die to self that Christ may live in them. Therefore they do not find the precious pearl."—*Selected Messages,* book 1, pp. 399, 400.

The righteousness of Christ will never cover these "wrong habits" of ours, these practices that may have been our manner from our youth, or some we developed later in life. Whichever it may be or whatever they may be, if the robe of Christ's righteousness is to cover us, these wrong habits must go. "Every worldly habit and idea that is not in harmony with the mind of God should be renounced."—*Fundamentals of Christian Education,* p. 517.

Only the Holy Spirit is able to supply strength for certain victory over these evil tendencies. "If the heart is not kept under the control of God, if the Holy Spirit does not work unceasingly to refine and ennoble the character, the old habits will reveal themselves in the life."—*Christ's Object Lessons,* p. 50.

This battle confronts most of us much of the time! "Every man has corrupt and sinful habits that must be overcome by vigorous warfare. Every soul is required to fight the fight of faith. If one is a follower of Christ, he cannot be sharp in deal, he cannot be hardhearted, devoid of sympathy. He cannot be coarse in his speech. He cannot be full of pomposity and self-esteem. He cannot be overbearing, nor can he use harsh words, and censure and condemn."—*The SDA Bible Commentary,* Ellen G. White Comments, on Gal. 5:6, p. 1111.

Thank God there is help! "For I can do everything God asks me to with the help of Christ who gives me the strength and power" (Phil. 4:13, T.L.B.).

"TOO MUCH TO ASK?"

And so, dear brothers, I plead with you to give your bodies to God. Let them be a living sacrifice, holy—the kind he can accept. When you think of what he has done for you, is this too much to ask? Rom. 12:1, T.L.B.

"I have been to God today," Jonathan Edwards is quoted as saying, "and given myself, all that I am and have, to God so that I am not in any respect my own; I can challenge no right to this understanding, this will, these affections that are in me; neither have I any right to this body or any of its members; no right to this tongue, these eyes, these ears, this smell or taste. I have given myself clear away and have not retained anything as my own. I have been to God this morning and told Him that I gave myself wholly to Him, so that for the future I will challenge no right to myself in any respect."

Jonathan Edwards understood what it means for a person to present all he is and has to Christ. This is exactly what Christ asks of each of us today—*everything.*

In the first eleven chapters of his Epistle to the Romans, Paul deals largely with that which a Christian believes and why he believes it. He explains what it truly means to become acquainted with Christ and His salvation from sin. Beginning with chapter twelve, the apostle turns to another phase of the Christian's experience—service. He wants us not only to know how to *love* Christ, he also wants us to know how to *serve* Him in love.

Before we can serve Him, Christ must have all there is of us! Jonathan Edwards placed everything upon the altar of sacrifice and service! We must do the same. It must be a complete offering, "the kind he can accept."

"In giving ourselves to God, we must necessarily give up all that would separate us from Him. Hence the Saviour says, 'Whosoever he be of you that forsaketh not all that he hath, he cannot be my disciple.' Whatever shall draw away the heart from God must be given up. . . . We cannot be half the Lord's and half the world's. We are not God's children unless we are such entirely."—*Steps to Christ,* p. 44.

256

ARE YOU TRULY LIVING?

For me to live is Christ, and to die is gain. Phil. 1:21.

Some forty years ago, John and Betty Stamm were missionaries of another church in China. They were murdered by a gang of bandits ranging through the province. Upon arrival at the mission station some days later, friends found only heaps of debris and ashes—all that was left of the buildings.

Searching through remains of what had once been the Stamms' home, a fellow missionary found the flyleaf of Betty's Bible. In an entry dated December 8, 1934, the young missionary wife had penned these words: "Lord, I give up my purposes and plans, all my desires, hopes, and ambitions, and accept Thy will for my life. I give my life, my all utterly to Thee to be Thine forever.

"I hand over to Thy keeping all my friendships, my love; all the people whom I love are to take second place in my heart. Fill me and seal me with Thy Holy Spirit. Work out Thy whole life in my life at any cost now and forever. 'For me to live is Christ, and to die is gain.' "

"To live is Christ, and to die is gain." Betty Stamm knew the meaning of Paul's words. Her plans, her purposes, her desires, her hopes and ambitions, her will—all had been yielded to the will and the guiding hand of God.

Such a complete surrender to Christ is described by the pen of inspiration: "Consecrate yourself to God in the morning; make this your very first work. Let your prayer be, 'Take me, O Lord, as wholly Thine. I lay all my plans at Thy feet. Use me today in Thy service. Abide with me, and let all my work be wrought in Thee.' This is a daily matter. Each morning consecrate yourself to God for that day. Surrender all your plans to Him, to be carried out or given up as His providence shall indicate. Thus day by day you may be giving your life into the hands of God, and thus your life will be molded more and more after the life of Christ."—*Steps to Christ,* p. 70.

We begin to truly live only when we fully surrender all that we have or are to Christ. Only then can we say with Paul, "For me to live is Christ, and to die is gain."

WHAT SORT OF PATTERN DO YOU PROJECT?

In all things shewing thyself a pattern of good works. Titus 2:7.

Recently in a Western city motel room I found a copy of that incomparable book *The Desire of Ages.* Opening it, my eyes fell on these thought-provoking words (on pages 280 and 281 of that special edition):

"True character is not shaped from without, and put on; it radiates from within. If we wish to direct others in the path of righteousness, the principles of righteousness must be enshrined in our own hearts. Our profession of faith may proclaim the theory of religion, but it is our practical piety that holds forth the word of truth. The consistent life, the holy conversation, the unswerving integrity, the active, benevolent spirit, the godly example—these are the mediums through which light is conveyed to the world."

From these inspired words several great truths shine forth:

1. Character is not something we *put on.* It is an inward experience that *shines through.* Reputation and true character are not necessarily synonymous. Reputation is what people think us to be. Character is what we are. Our reputations may be developed by an outward show. Character is developed by what we truly are deep inside.

2. We can't give to others what we ourselves do not possess. We cannot share a Christ with those around us who is not enshrined in our own hearts. We must know Him personally before we can make Him known to others.

3. A theory of religion is not enough. Unless our doctrines are translated into everyday, practical piety, we have little to offer those with whom we come in contact. The test of any man's theology is the sort of practicing Christians it produces. We can best preach the law by having Christ, in whose heart the law is hidden, enshrined in our hearts. We can best preach the Sabbath when we are truly acquainted with Christ the Lord of the Sabbath!

4. The most effective catalyst for our creed is a truly consistent Christian life.

It is not enough to say, "Do as I say, not as I do." Our living must square with our preaching—seven days of every week.

258

HE COULDN'T BACK DOWN

The king was grieved, but because of his oath, and because he didn't want to back down in front of his guests, he issued the necessary orders. Matt. 14:9, T.L.B.

An alley cat fleeing from a mangy dog found himself atop a telephone pole. Long after the frustrated canine had abandoned the chase, the cat, stranded on the dark, lofty perch, yowled loud and plaintively. A few feet away an irate citizen appeared in his second-story window and endeavored to induce or frighten the distraught feline to quiet down. Failing in his peace-keeping mission, the interrupted sleeper called the fire department to help the cat down the pole. After considerable coaxing, the firemen were successful in restoring quiet to the neighborhood. All this commotion simply because the alley cat had never learned to back down.

Alley cats are not the only creatures who have not learned to back down. Human beings sometimes find themselves in awkward situations created by their own wrong course of action but they are unwilling to admit their mistake.

Herod is a tragic example of such an individual. At a birthday party Herodias' daughter had pleased the king and his party with her dancing. In a reckless moment "he vowed to give her anything she wanted" (Matt. 14:7, T.L.B.).

This was an opportunity for Herodias to even an old score with John the Baptist. At her "urging, the girl asked for John the Baptist's head on a tray. The king was grieved, but because of his oath, and because *he didn't want to back down* in front of his guests, he issued the necessary orders" (verses 8, 9, T.L.B.; italics supplied).

Backing down is simply being willing to admit mistake and to renege on a rash commitment. Backing down requires humility. Many of us are not overly blessed with this Christian trait of character.

To save a situation that involves being true to God or dealing fairly with a brother sometimes requires a Christian to humble himself and "back down." To react with gracious humility in such circumstances is a blessed characteristic. It is not easy but it is right! Why not try it next time you foolishly maneuver yourself into such a plight? Learn to back down.

A MAN OF THE CROSS

Then said Jesus unto his disciples, If any man will come after me, let him deny himself, and take up his cross, and follow me. Matt. 16:24.

Stephano was a new convert to the Advent message in the Congo. He was a working man and the Sabbath problem soon confronted him. Stephano explained carefully to his superior just why he could not work on the seventh day of each week.

Stephano's employer was sympathetic but one little problem required attention. A list was kept of all employees and their attendance or absence from work. It was noted daily. If a worker was absent because of illness a certain sign was noted on the worksheet. If he was absent with permission to care ior some personal matters a different kind of sign appeared by the man's name.

Stephano's absence because of his religious convictions perplexed the head man for a few moments. What sign could he put after this conscientious man's name? He pondered a moment. Then his face lighted up.

"I'll put a cross by Stephano's name," he announced, "for Stephano is a man of the cross!"

"A man of the cross"—what a high tribute! Certainly here is a title every child of God should covet!

"If any man will come after me, let him deny himself, and take up his cross, and follow me."

In these words Jesus makes it clear that there is a close relationship between denying self and following Christ and bearing His cross. We cannot become men of the cross until self has been successfully dealt with.

"The warfare against self is the greatest battle that was ever fought. The yielding of self, surrendering all to the will of God, requires a struggle; but the soul must submit to God before it can be renewed in holiness."—*Steps to Christ,* p. 43.

"The greatest battle that was ever fought"—not the battle to remain faithful when tempted to work on God's Sabbath, but *self* is our greatest struggle! As long as Christ occupies second place in our devotions we cannot successfully face the tests of obedience. Stephano had no problem about Sabbath observance. He had made Jesus first in his life. He was a man of the cross.

HE WILL NOT FAIL US

Asa called upon the Lord his God and said, "There is none like thee, O Lord, to help men, whether strong or weak; help us, O Lord our God, for on thee we rely and in thy name we have come out against this horde. O Lord, thou art our God, how can man vie with thee?" 2 Chron. 14:11, N.E.B.

Good King Asa had faithfully served the Lord during days of peace and prosperity. He had done all within his power to crush the agencies of apostasy that had infiltrated Judah. God's blessing rested richly upon him.

When an overwhelming enemy force threatened to destroy him and his people, naturally and confidently Asa turned to the Lord for help. He poured out his heart to God when destruction was at the door. "There is none like thee, O Lord, to help men, whether strong or weak; help us, O Lord our God, for on thee we rely and in thy name we have come out against this horde. O Lord, thou art our God, how can man vie with thee?"

God heard Asa's earnest petition. The Ethiopian hordes were put to flight. The faith of the king of Judah in his God was vindicated.

The God of Asa is still strong on behalf of His trusting, threatened children in 1975. We may turn to Him in adversity just as confidently as we speak to Him in prosperity. Asa's petition may be our petition.

"The prayer of Asa is one that every Christian believer may fittingly offer. We fight in a warfare, not against flesh and blood, but against principalities and powers, and against spiritual wickedness in high places. See Ephesians 6:12. In life's conflict we must meet evil agencies that have arrayed themselves against the right. Our hope is not in man, but in the living God. With full assurance of faith we may expect that He will unite His omnipotence with the efforts of human instrumentalities, for the glory of His name. Clad with the armor of His righteousness, we may gain the victory over every foe." —*Prophets and Kings*, p. 111.

You and I need not fear whatever lot may be ours this day. We are in the hands of the God of Asa. In the hour of crisis, decision, or need, we may pray Asa's prayer. Asa's God will not fail us!

PLANE CRASH IN ALASKA

For he shall give his angels charge over thee, to keep thee in all thy ways.
Ps. 91:11.

While flying through the treacherous Aniak Pass in Alaska in June, 1971, Pastors Ronald Breingan and Joseph Chythlook were involved in a plane crash. En route through the pass their plane, a Cessna 180, encountered severe turbulence. Pastor Chythlook, the Eskimo pilot, attempted to alter course and return to Aniak. During the maneuver the plane was caught in a down draft and thrown to the ground.

The crash shattered the windshield, blew the doors off, and sheared the right wing from the fuselage of the plane. Fortunately the two men were only badly shaken up.

Clawing his way out of the wrecked plane, Pastor Breingan stood up to assess the damage. Before he could reach back into the cockpit to help his pilot, a severe gust of wind picked the plane up and turned it over with Pastor Chythlook still strapped inside. One-hundred-miles-an-hour winds slid the wrecked craft down a hillside.

Staggering after the battered wreckage, Ron pulled Joe to safety—still miraculously preserved without serious injury. The only injuries the men suffered were a wound on the Eskimo pastor's forehead and a torn triceps muscle in Ron's right arm.

For two days the battered missionaries fought for survival against the elements. The howling wind swept their plane about so that the men were forced to move a short distance away for safety. Thus they were without shelter.

On Friday rescue planes located the hapless pastors. Because of fierce winds a helicopter at first was unable to land, but two paramedics were dropped to render assistance. Two hours later the helicopter landed and picked them up.

That week the Breingan family happened to be on the General Conference office family's fellowship of prayer list. In writing to me of the experience, Mrs. Breingan said: "I am so thankful for a God who watches over His people in the hour of peril and for friends in the world headquarters office who care enough to pray for those of us who serve in faraway places."

FROM DISCIPLE TO DESERTER

Demas has deserted me. 2 Tim. 4:10, T.L.B.

How much we learn about Demas and his relationship with Paul the apostle and the gospel of the Lord Jesus Christ in these four words—"Demas has deserted me"! Paul's second letter to Timothy in which these words appear was written from Rome during the days of his second imprisonment. He realized that his days on earth were numbered.

On a number of occasions I have visited the Mamertine dungeon in Rome where, some commentators believe, Paul was imprisoned when he wrote the words of our text. It is a dark, forbidding hole made completely secure in later years with only an opening in the top through which food and other bare necessities were lowered to inmates below.

The city of Rome had been burned. Nero, that callous tyrant, desired to divert the suspicions of his people from himself by a planned persecution of the Christians. It is possible this climate contributed to Paul's arrest. "After a time the unbelieving Jews" fastened "upon Paul the crime of instigating the burning of Rome. . . . Paul was placed in a gloomy dungeon. . . . Accused of instigating one of the basest and most terrible of crimes against the city and the nation, he was the object of universal execration."—*The Acts of the Apostles,* pp. 489, 490.

Languishing in a dungeon, accused of a crime in which he had no part, with only a small inaccessible hole in the roof of his cell, Paul needed friends. The warm assurance of God's love and care burned brightly in the old apostle's heart, but under such circumstances he no doubt yearned for words of encouragement that those who shared his blessed hope might speak.

At such an hour, Paul wrote, "Demas has deserted me." The apostle tasted the bitter dregs his Lord had drunk when "all the disciples forsook him, and fled" (Matt. 26:56). With Job he could lament, "They whom I loved are turned against me" (Job 19:19).

Demas is the timeless type of the fair-weather friend. While life flows along evenly and smoothly the Demases stay by. They are much in evidence when friendship costs little or nothing. But when the going is rough and friendship makes demands on time, or cash, or even life itself, they become deserters.

"POLARIZED" AND "POLARIZERS"

You must not think that I have come to bring peace to the earth; I have not come to bring peace, but a sword. Matt. 10:34, N.E.B.

Polarization is an ugly word in any language. It smacks of enmity, tension, and accentuated separation. It is dividing people into opposing camps. Can such a mission of division be part of the ministry of our Lord? Yet He says, "I have not come to bring peace, but a sword."

The Bible is a book about polarization. The Old Testament leaves no doubt as to man's sinfulness at one end of the spectrum and God's holiness at the other. Thank God His Word also makes clear how sinful man may be reconciled to a sinless God, how the gulf may be bridged.

Many of God's mighty ones in Old Testament times were polarized or polarizers. Abraham, Joseph, and Daniel would not compromise with the worldly elements about them. They were fully committed to the will, the way, and the word of the Lord. To this extent they were polarized.

Joshua and Elijah were polarizers. In the face of great odds and certain personal loss they called God's people to decision: "Choose you this day whom ye will serve" (Joshua 24:15); "How long halt ye between two opinions?" (1 Kings 18:21). In their day God's people were challenged to be separate—to be different—poles apart from the world around them. There must be no compromise!

The New Testament is just as fracturing in its pronouncements. Right is right. Evil is evil. There is no no man's land in the great controversy between Christ and Satan. Every man is either in one camp or the other. This is what the gospel is all about—polarization—life or death, salvation or damnation.

It is not that Christ deliberately desires to spawn division. He makes this clear over and over in His Gospels. What His desire for His people is, "That they may be one, as we are" (John 17:11). But no one knows better than Christ that frequently the claims of the gospel, once spurned, turn the rejector against the believer.

Don't be surprised if polarization comes even inside God's last church today. It is no more popular to follow Jesus fully now than it was in His day!

LOYALTY CEMENTS THE TIES

[Our] first duty [is] to show loyalty to the family. 1 Tim. 5:4, N.E.B.

A fine worker in this cause labored alone without the help of a wife who had stood faithfully with him for many years. In many respects she was both his right and left hand. They worked together "in tandem." Then something happened. A too close relationship developed with another couple in the church.

In due course these new friends were brought into the inner circle of the family. A friendship that began perhaps innocently enough between two of the spouses grew into too intimate a relationship. After some months the home was broken. For years the aggrieved husband labored alone. Someone who had no right had entered that sacred circle.

Loyalty is the *sine qua non* of a truly happy home.

Our "first duty" is "to show loyalty to the family." Another inspired writer counsels: "There is a sacred circle around every family which should be preserved. No other one has any right in that sacred circle. . . . The wife should have no secrets to keep from her husband and let others know, and the husband should have no secrets to keep from his wife to relate to others."—*The Adventist Home,* p. 177. Friends and acquaintances may be many and dear, but they are not to meddle in the home life. This circle is sacred.

In fact, every member of the family has a part to play in maintaining love and loyalty in the home. "Each of you must love his wife as his very self; and the woman must see to it that she pays her husband all respect" (Eph. 5:33, N.E.B.). It is a two-way street—for both husband and wife.

There is a part for the children too! They must be loyal to the family circle. There must be no betrayal here. "Children, obey your parents in the Lord: for this is right" (chap. 6:1). "Honour thy father and thy mother" is the first commandment with a promise, "that thy days may be long upon the land which the Lord thy God giveth thee" (Ex. 20:12). A happy Christian home depends upon the love and loyalty of the whole family—the husband, the wife, and the children. "Self-control on the part of all the members of the family will make home almost a paradise."—*My Life Today,* p. 84.

HOW MAY WE KNOW FOR CERTAIN?

You ought not to be astonished, then, when I tell you that you must be born over again. John 3:7, N.E.B.

If we are not born again we shall never gain heaven. Jesus says: "Verily, verily, I say unto thee, Except a man be born again, he cannot see the kingdom of God" (John 3:3). Therefore we must be certain we have entered into this experience. The grave consequences of failure here admit of no guesswork, no speculation. How may we know when we have experienced the new birth? Jesus gives us a practical test by which to try our experience: "Wherefore by their fruits ye shall know them" (Matt. 7:20), He said. The Spirit works invisibly, but the results are visible. There will be an outward demonstration of the inward transformation.

The new birth is evident by *life* service, not *lip* service. Some folks seem to feel they must tell everyone they are born-again Christians. When the Spirit has completely changed our life others will *know* without our telling them. Those who work with us on the job will know. Our secretaries and fellow office workers will know. Those who ride with us on the bus or train will know.

Most of all, those in our own homes will know a change has been wrought. Our husbands and wives will know. The sharp words, the unkind criticism, the growling, the nagging, will go. In their place will be kindness, thoughtfulness, love, encouragement, and helpfulness. Someone has said even our dogs and cats will know when a raging sinner becomes a practicing saint—no more temper tantrums or door slamming.

Paul further describes the transformation wrought when we "put on the new man" (Eph. 4:24). The person who has been born from above has put away lying. He speaks truth with his neighbor. He does not let the sun go down upon his wrath. If he has stolen, he steals no more. No corrupt communication proceeds from his mouth. "Bitterness, and wrath, and anger, and clamour, and evil speaking" have been put away. He is tenderhearted, forgiving, even as God for Christ's sake forgives the sinner (see Eph. 4:24-32). In short, one who has been born again is a completely changed person.

YOU AND I MAKE THE CHOICE

Finally, brethren, whatsoever things are true, whatsoever things are honest, whatsoever things are just, whatsoever things are pure, whatsoever things are lovely, whatsoever things are of good report; if there be any virtue, and if there be any praise, think on these things. Phil. 4:8.

Browsing through my files recently I came across this striking poem:

The Viewpoint

I read a book last week.
The author dipped his facile pen in fire
And seared raw facts into my brain.
Up from the mire he dragged dark truth
And flaunted it.
And, as I read, I knew his soul was warped;
His mind must know despair, thinking all truth
Was ugliness laid bare.

And then I read another book.
The author sat upon the very throne of truth
And used a pen far mightier than a sword.
He wrote of youth triumphant, clean and fine.
He wrote of sin, compassion in each line.
He wrote of love—it blossomed like a rose
Sprung from good soil. He wrote of One,
Giver of that great trinity of gifts,
Life, love, and beauty; and when he was done
I knew somehow my stumbling feet had trod
The trail he'd blazed for me to his Friend, and God!

—*Author Unknown*

Francis Bacon wrote, "Reading maketh a full man." What we read determines not only how we spend our time, but, to a large extent, what we *are*. If we fill our minds with rich ennobling thoughts from godly writers our own lives will be enriched—we will be drawn closer to our Creator. If we choose to sate our minds with that which is sensuous and degrading our characters will be molded by these carnal authors.

You and I make the choice!

267

STRENGTH, NOT LENGTH, COUNTS

But when he saw the wind boisterous, he was afraid; and beginning to sink, he cried, saying, Lord, save me. Matt. 14:30.

While visiting in Rotterdam, Holland, Elder M. E. Lind heard much about a certain family. All of the sons were in the church and living exemplary Christian lives despite many difficult experiences. Elder Lind decided to visit the home.

He found the wife and mother in bed recovering from a long illness. After a brief pastoral conversation, Elder Lind spoke of her boys. The mother's eyes brightened.

"I understand your sons are now with you in the church," the pastor observed.

"Yes," the mother replied, "but it was not always so. For many years they wandered away from the Lord and the church." She then explained some of the circumstances that brought discouragement and apostasy but finally conviction and return.

"It was prayer that brought them back," she said certainly.

"What did you say to the Lord?" the pastor asked, interested in what petitions had so moved the arm of Omnipotence.

The woman on the bed thought for a moment, then, rather embarrassed, she explained, "Pastor, I only prayed a very short simple prayer, 'Lord, save my boys,' but I spoke those words to my heavenly Father countless times every day during those seventeen years!"

A four-word prayer repeated earnestly and endlessly brought results. It is the *strength, not the length,* of our prayers that counts with God.

When the rolling sea threatened to envelop him, Peter uttered but three words. The Saviour heard that anguished cry, "Lord, save me" (Matt. 14:30)—and answered. Peter's life was preserved. When a flurry of rocks was about to end his life, Stephen's prayer was short—eight words. (See Acts 7:60.)

Many of our prayers will be much more comprehensive than these we have noted, but Ellen White reminds us, "Long prayers are not essential."—*The SDA Bible Commentary,* Ellen G. White Comments, on James 5:16, p. 939.

Our God is only a prayer away! It is the *strength,* and not the length, of that prayer that determines its effectiveness.

IT MAKES A DIFFERENCE

Jesus answered and said unto him, Verily, verily, I say unto thee, Except a man be born again, he cannot see the kingdom of God. John 3:3.

A Frenchman living permanently in England sought and secured British citizenship. Meeting a friend of his on the street a day later, he was greeted by him.

"I see you are British now," the friend began, "but I don't suppose it makes a great deal of difference, does it?"

"Indeed it does," the former Frenchman replied, experiencing a surge of excitement in his newly acquired status. "Yesterday Waterloo was a tragic defeat. Today it is a glorious victory!"

It is so in the new-birth experience. When the Lord Jesus comes into our life things are gloriously changed. Through His grace and by His strength the old life of sin and defeat becomes a radiant life of victory.

Man's natural, sinful state is made clear in the Scriptures. "All have sinned, and come short of the glory of God" (Rom. 3:23), Paul declares.

"The natural man receiveth not the things of the Spirit of God" (1 Cor. 2:14), he says.

How then can man ever hope to enter into the new-birth experience? How can a lost sinner find that exciting life of victory? Alone he cannot—it is impossible, but help is at hand!

"The Son of man is come to seek and to save that which was lost" (Luke 19:10). Today the Saviour works through His Holy Spirit. "I will pray the Father, and he will give you another Comforter" (John 14:16). "He will reprove the world of sin" (chap. 16:8). "He," Jesus declares, "shall teach you all things, and bring all things to your remembrance, whatsoever things I have said" (chap. 14:26).

Sometimes the heart is powerfully moved by a Spirit-filled sermon and the seeds of revival are sown. Sometimes the reading of a scriptural portion or receiving a message through a Spirit-filled song stirs the soul and prompts to something better. A word kindly spoken by a friend inquiring into one's spiritual condition can light the fire of desire for a new life.

The Holy Spirit is ready to work for everyone who will permit Him—right now!

269

THE CHOSEN PEOPLE

Is there any advantage then in being one of the chosen people? . . . Yes, of course, a great deal in every way. Rom. 3:1, 2, Phillips.

Elder R. S. Watts and I were flying from Salisbury to Nairobi in August, 1961. Soon after take-off a young woman approached us.

"Aren't you men Seventh-day Adventist ministers?"

A bit surprised, we affirmed that we were.

"I thought I recognized you," she continued, and then went on to explain that she had met each of us at different places in the past.

Later, after our new friend had returned to her seat in the fore section of the plane, the stewardess brought from her a handwritten note:

"I am so glad you men are on this plane. You see, this is my first flight and I was a bit uneasy. But with those of like faith it is almost like relatives. It gives one who is weaker a comfortable feeling to know there are other members of God's family on board the plane."

It is a precious experience belonging to God's worldwide family—"one of the chosen people." "God can bestow no higher honor upon mortals than to adopt them into His family, giving them the privilege of calling Him Father."—*Fundamentals of Christian Education,* p. 481.

I have heard more than one person say they felt nearer to brothers and sisters in Christ than they did to some of their own flesh and blood relatives who were not Seventh-day Adventists. This is understandable. When we are "one of the chosen people" we have the same common bond of love for Christ and His last-day message. We have similar interests. We have the same motivating love. "The love of Christ constraineth us" (2 Cor. 5:14). Our understandings of the Word of God are parallel. We have the same goals. We share the same blessed hope. We are striving to reach the same heaven. Indeed we are all one in Christ Jesus.

What a glorious day it will be when the family of God on earth becomes the family of God in heaven!

You and I must be there—as members of "the chosen people" throughout eternity.

"IF HE IS ANYTHING LIKE YOUR DOCTOR"

You yourselves are the letter we have, written on our hearts, for everyone to know and read. It is clear that Christ himself wrote this letter and sent it by us. It is written not with ink on stone tablets, but on human hearts with the Spirit of the living God. 2 Cor. 3:2, 3, T.E.V.

Some years ago D. W. Hunter was Ingathering in the Telugu country of South India. When the Hindu rajah learned Elder Hunter was connected with our Narsapur Hospital he was interested immediately.

"Several years ago my little daughter was seriously burned when a pot of boiling rice overturned on her," the rajah explained. "A native practitioner gave her what care he could, but when he removed the bandages he found the left arm had grown fast to her side in the scar tissue. It appeared my little daughter would be deformed the rest of her life.

"Finally we heard of Narsapur Hospital and the wonderful things the doctors there could do. So we took our child to Narsapur. Dr. Clark took her in, did many skin grafts, gave her tender, loving care for nearly a year."

The rajah paused, called his little 7-year-old daughter into their room. "Look at her now," he exclaimed appreciatively. "She can use her arm just as freely as you or I."

There was a hint of emotion in the Hindu man's voice as he continued. "But that isn't what I want to tell you—as wonderful as it is. You see, Dr. and Mrs. Clark loved my little girl. They had no children and the doctor would carry my daughter through the hospital and call her his little girl." Tears welled up in the rajah's eyes as he concluded, "Mr. Hunter, I don't know your Jesus. But if He is anything like Dr. and Mrs. Clark, I want to know more about Him."

"In every one of His children, Jesus sends a letter to the world. If you are Christ's follower, He sends in you a letter to the family, the village, the street, where you live. Jesus, dwelling in you, desires to speak to the hearts of those who are not acquainted with Him. Perhaps they do not read the Bible. . . . But if you are a true representative of Jesus, it may be that through you they will be led to understand something of His goodness, and be won to love and serve Him."—*Steps to Christ,* p. 115.

SEPTEMBER 23

"SO I KNELT DOWN AND PRAYED AGAIN"

Three times I prayed to the Lord about this, and asked him to take it away.
2 Cor. 12:8, T.E.V.

"I find myself using a lot of formal expressions in my prayers to my heavenly Father," a friend once wrote to me. "This morning, I caught myself repeating a set of stereotyped phrases in prayer when there was something more vital that I should have been praying about—my low number of baptisms and many other urgent matters. Of course, I have recently moved, and that is an explanation we like to give, but it is far from a satisfactory excuse for not having accomplished more. So I knelt down and prayed again, and did a little better, I think."

"So I knelt down and prayed again." This pointed, piercing phrase fairly leaped out at me! It challenged my own praying. No doubt, frequently I also could profitably kneel down and "pray again" after having had a somewhat stilted conversation with the Lord.

As members of God's great family we all desire to be more successful in our labor for Him. Did you ever stop to think about it?—our success has a very close relationship with our prayer life. The servant of the Lord says:

"A worker [church employed or otherwise, I believe] cannot gain success while he hurries through his prayers and rushes away to look after something that he fears may be neglected or forgotten. He gives only a few hurried thoughts to God; he does not take time to think, to pray, to wait upon the Lord for a renewal of physical and spiritual strength. He soon becomes weary. He does not feel the uplifting, inspiring influence of God's Spirit. He is not quickened by fresh life. His jaded frame and tired brain are not soothed by personal contact with Christ."—*Testimonies,* vol. 7, p. 243.

Hurried prayers, petitions filled with too-worn clichés, vain repetitions, are not the prayers of power.

Perhaps it would be well sometimes for many of us to kneel down and pray again. It just might be that we would be more successful in the Lord's work.

I LOST THE BATTLE TODAY

Even though the desire to do good is in me, I am not able to do it. **Rom. 7:18, T.E.V.**

"Today I'm going to live for Christ! His will is my will. Today is going to be a day of victory. I know it will be!"

Ever begin the day with this glowing resolution filling your mind and warming your heart? Of course you have! Your waking thoughts were of your Saviour and of His goodness to you. With His love flooding your soul you literally rolled out of bed onto your knees. God was real to you. You talked with Him. You heard His voice speaking to you. You were on the mountaintop. What a sweet communion with your Master.

Then something happened. You met Bill or Linda or someone else who was not your favorite friend. Of course, you don't *dislike* this particular person, but your personalities clash. Linda talks too much about too many things and about too many people. What Bill says or does rather rubs your fur the wrong way. You know what I am talking about.

On such a day this less-favored friend is running true to form. What he says irks you. It stirs old resentments. The fine fire that was burning in your heart when you left the trysting place with Jesus suffers from a few drops of cold water.

Then before you have prayed your way through this encounter, you find yourself in the midst of another situation you cannot handle. More problems. More tests. More cold water on that sacred flame.

Despite your best efforts things continued to go wrong. What happened? Perhaps Ellen White had the answer:

"Man is to make earnest efforts to overcome that which hinders him from attaining to perfection. But he is wholly dependent upon God for success. Human effort of itself is not sufficient. Without the aid of divine power it avails nothing. God works and man works. Resistance of temptation must come from man, who must draw his power from God. On the one side there is infinite wisdom, compassion, and power; on the other, weakness, sinfulness, absolute helplessness."—*The Acts of the Apostles*, p. 482.

Perhaps we were depending too much upon our own strength and too little upon what God must do for us.

THE FOUNDATION OF ALL VICTORIES

The Spirit of the Lord God is upon me; because the Lord hath anointed me to preach good tidings unto the meek; he hath sent me to bind up the brokenhearted, to proclaim liberty to the captives, and the opening of the prison to them that are bound. Isa. 61:1.

The Temperance Department's fine Five-Day Plan to Stop Smoking has brought freedom from the noxious weed to some 11 million people around the world, according to E. H. J. Steed, secretary of the department. One of these men, says Pastor Steed, is Bill Blaine, a man living in Sydney, Australia. Doctors had given him two or three months to live. Each morning he coughed until he cried. One day he was coughing and crying and blaspheming. "God," he said, "You don't exist. If You do, why don't You help me?" That day he saw in the press a small notice about Seventh-day Adventists offering a community service—the Five-Day Plan to Stop Smoking.

Bill attended and faithfully followed the plan. After five days he was no longer smoking fifty cigarettes a day. He rose and testified on the last day that even though he had cursed God, now he was free through God's saving grace. He lived two more years, during which time he constantly told his story in churches, halls, and on street corners.

For thirty-two years his wife had suffered his drinking bouts, his smoking and cursing. Her prayers were answered. He died trusting in Jesus.

The world is a prison house of intemperance. To help bring deliverance from this enslavement is a challenge to every Seventh-day Adventist, for "temperance alone is the foundation of all the graces that come from God, the foundation of all victories to be gained" *(Temperance,* p. 201).

Bad habit, false desire, and corrupt practices have bound men to appetite and lustful living which dethrone reason, blind social relations, and stifle spiritual experience in the illusive search for the good life. *"Never* will men practice temperance in all things until their hearts are renewed by divine grace. . . . Our work for the fallen will achieve *real success* only as the grace of Christ reshapes the character and the soul is brought into living connection with God."—*The Ministry of Healing,* pp. 179, 180. (Italics supplied.)

THEOLOGY OF THE EMPTY PEW

But though we, or an angel from heaven, preach any other gospel unto you than that which we have preached unto you, let him be accursed. Gal. 1:8.

During a recent twelve-month period more than three hundred thousand members left one of the large Christian denominations in a European country. In a neighboring land hundreds of Christian church buildings stood empty, many of them for sale. Seventh-day Adventists have bought a number of these buildings for ridiculously low prices. In other countries church attendance has fallen off sharply; churches have been consolidated or closed.

I traveled through two great lands recently. Large churches with thousands of names on their church rolls stood practically empty—even on Christian high days such as Easter, less than fifty people worshiped in buildings with seating accommodations for two thousand. The fires in the hearts of the people had gone out. Their interest was gone. Their faith was gone. There was nothing left!

Such a lack of interest in the Christian gospel and the church is not surprising. When seekers after God come to the place of worship they expect to be fed spiritually. Too many have found politics instead of righteousness, the social gospel in place of the saving gospel. They are psychoanalyzed instead of transformed. They go away unfed. As one unknown writer has said, "If men receive stones when they ask for bread they will probably stop coming to the bakery." This is just what is happening in too many Christian churches around us. Too many stones, too little bread!

Is this what we want in the Seventh-day Adventist Church? Do we want our churches empty, the faith of our members gone? You and I both reply to those questions with a resounding No! Then we must assure that those basic Christian truths that made us Seventh-day Adventists keep us Seventh-day Adventists! Christ our Creator as well as our Redeemer. Christ our Advocate as well as our Friend. Christ our Example in commandment keeping as well as in social action. Christ the author and the finisher of our faith—the whole Christ—is still the central theme of the Advent message.

275

IS THIS REALLY WHAT YOU WANT?

They hated knowledge, and did not choose the fear of the Lord. **Prov. 1:29.**

I have just been listening to George Putnam, one of America's outstanding radio news commentators for nearly forty years. He caught my attention when he said, "I want to talk to you today about our schools and our teachers." Mr. Putnam went on to pay tribute to the multiplied thousands of loyal, capable men and women who help make up the teaching staff of American schools.

Abruptly Mr. Putnam changed the course of his talk. He turned his attention to those occupying teaching posts who are not so loyal in their schools. He scored those activist pedagogues who spend too much time attacking the Government or espousing offbeat causes. The speaker singled out radical educators who advocate the use of marijuana and call for violent revolution on their campuses.

Mr. Putnam pointed out that a teacher has a captive audience and for several hours a week he is in a position to pour hate and doubt instead of math and literature into youthful ears.

In the classroom too many of the youth of our generation have been fed a diet of infidelity and doubt, disobedience and lawlessness. Too many have been forced to drink from the wells of paganism, sitting under teachers who not only are not Christians but avowed anti-Christian activists. Under the guise of "acquiring a broader culture," boys and girls have been filled with the refuse of yellow-sheet fiction. Subtly and not so subtly they have been exposed to a godless hypothesis.

"Philosophical speculation and scientific research in which God is not acknowledged are making skeptics of thousands. In the schools of today the conclusions that learned men have reached as the result of their scientific investigations are carefully taught and fully explained; while the impression is distinctly given that if these learned men are correct, the Bible cannot be."—*The Ministry of Healing*, p. 439.

Is this the kind of educational institution you wish to attend? Is this the kind of pagan philosophy you want your son or daughter to be subjected to hour after hour in a captive audience?

TIME TO WAKE UP!

And that, knowing the time, that now it is high time to awake out of sleep: for now is our salvation nearer than when we believed. **Rom. 13:11.**

Lights are going out in many parts of the world. Yesterday it was China, North Korea, North Vietnam. Tomorrow it may be in Burma, Burundi, or Bangkok that doors to the gospel may be closed. There are many troubled lands. America faces grave problems that perplex her leaders. All these things add up to one fact—Bible prophecy is fast fulfilling before our very eyes. "When ye see these things come to pass," Jesus said, "know ye that the kingdom of God is nigh at hand" (Luke 21:31).

The hour is late—very late. Our time is short—very short. We can no longer say that we live in the eleventh hour of this world's history. We can scarcely say we live at five minutes till midnight. Rather we live in the final fleeting moments of time. Jesus' coming is near, very near. "Verily I say unto you," the Saviour warns, "This generation shall not pass, till all these things be fulfilled" (Matt. 24:34).

In such an awesome hour one would expect every youth, every adult member, of God's remnant church to be atingle with expectancy, straining every nerve to help in warning a world of impending doom—and the coming of our great Deliverer.

Instead, the messenger of the Lord declares, "The stupor of death is upon many who profess Christ."—*Testimonies,* vol. 5, p. 387. She makes an appeal to every young man, every young woman, who has been mesmerized by the gaudy, giddy world in which we live, "Awake, I beseech you, from the sleep of death."—*Ibid.,* p. 466.

How sad, how utterly tragic—God's church, God's youth, asleep at their posts in an hour of peril.

We do not have an eternity, or a millennium, or a century in which to accomplish our God-given task. Perhaps some Advent youth of our day may not have even a normal lifetime to meet this challenge, to fill this need.

"It is high time to awake out of sleep," the apostle Paul commands. If this message was timely for the members in Rome during Paul's day, it is much more urgent in ours.

277

"WHAT LIES BEFORE ME IN THE DARKNESS?"

He brought them out of darkness and the shadow of death, and brake their bands in sunder. **Ps. 107:14.**

"Father," said a dying heathen girl, "Father, where am I going? What lies before me in the darkness? Oh, Father, I am afraid. Help me! Help me!"

"My little girl," groaned the stricken man, "I cannot tell. There are other lives beyond, though the body decays in the grave, but . . . "

"Oh, Father, are they happy lives? Or will I suffer there? Can you give me hope? What do your books say? Tell me! Help me!"

But the father knew nothing more. Not even his love for his dying child could pierce the impenetrable pall shrouding so much mystery and terror. In the darkness the slender fingers tightened upon the father's hand, then faltered, loosened, and grew cold in death.

In the Americas, in Africa, in Australia, in Europe, in Asia, in the islands of the sea, men and women, boys and girls, ask the same questions. "What lies before me in the darkness? Can you give me hope? What do your books say?" Some of these questioners may be *your* neighbors. What are *you* doing to answer them? What message of hope do *you* have for those around you?

> One hundred thousand souls a day
> Are passing one by one away
> In Christless guilt and gloom.
> Without one ray of hope or light,
> With future dark as endless night,
> They're passing to their doom.
> —S. J. STONE

"Two hundred millions of people lie down every night hungry in body," John R. Mott writes, "but one thousand million lie down without God, and without Jesus Christ." What an awesome picture! What a staggering realization!

What a challenge to the youth of the Advent Movement. What a challenge to the young people in *your* church. What a challenge to *you*.

RISE AND SHINE!

Arise, shine; for thy light is come, and the glory of the Lord is risen upon thee. Isa. 60:1.

"Arise, shine." These two insistent words constitute a clarion call to every young man and woman in God's church in 1975. They are "the words of Christ through the gospel prophet" *(Thoughts From the Mount of Blessing, p. 43).* They come as a burning challenge to every child of God in these thrilling closing hours of earth's history. In the great drama so rapidly unfolding about us, you and I are challenged to play an active part.

"For thy light is come, and the glory of the Lord is risen upon thee." The sixtieth chapter of Isaiah deals with the glorious finishing of the work of God and with the new earth state. The prophet vividly describes an unusual awakening, both within the ranks of God's professed people and among those who will respond to their message of truth. A great ingathering of souls is pictured before Jesus returns and the new earth becomes a reality.

In the preceding chapter the prophet depicts the people as waiting in vain for light (Isa. 59:9). They were in "darkness." They were like the dead (verse 10). Now, what a contrast! The darkness is dispelled. As the fiery fingers of the dawn push back the shades of night, so the glory of the Lord shall arise and the "gross darkness" covering the people shall be dispelled.

What a glorious panorama of the triumph of God's work in the world. "This message will close with power and strength." —*Early Writings,* p. 278. We are a part of a divine movement destined to triumph in a blaze of glory—the glory of the eternal God and of His Son, Jesus Christ. But before that triumph there is a work to do.

God says first, "Arise." The word used here is a call of the Lifegiver. The spiritually dead of Isaiah 59 must live. They must arise as from the dead. A dead light bulb cannot dispel darkness. Neither can a dead Christian shine for God. We must first arise from our spiritual apathy and shake off the graveclothes of indifference. The times demand a fresh, vibrant, living experience in the things of God. If you are spiritually dead or dying, God calls you—"Arise."

279

YOUTH ABLAZE FOR GOD

Let no man despise thy youth. 1 Tim. 4:12.

"Total evangelism is the supreme goal of Missionary Volunteering," Theodore Lucas, former world youth leader, once said. "Brilliant and unprecedented are the manifestations of divine power even now through youthful lives devoted to the cause of truth and righteousness. Thousands are being baptized because of their endeavors."

Advent youth around the world confirm Elder Lucas' words.

The young people of South America responded to God's call to action. In São Paulo, Brazil, fifty Voice of Youth efforts were held during two years. The results? Four hundred and thirty-four were baptized. In the state of Paraná five new churches were raised up by Missionary Volunteer evangelists.

In Tanzania, Africa, Samuel Roi accepted the Advent message while attending a government school in Mwanza district. Samuel was so on fire with his new-found faith that the headmistress of the girls' section of the school invited him to come and tell her girls why he had become a Seventh-day Adventist.

Three and one-half hours after he began, Samuel completed his one-sitting evangelistic effort, and when he made an appeal for any of the young women who wished to join him in the Seventh-day Adventist Church to stand, thirteen stood.

Youthful Hernan of southern Mexico learned the truth from lay preacher Francisco Roblero. When Hernan read *The Great Controversy,* which Francisco had lent him, the young man was thrilled with the message he found in its pages. He wanted the book but he did not have the money to buy one. This did not deter Hernan. He simply set out to copy the whole book by hand! He took many long days to accomplish the task, but he stayed at the job until it was completed.

Not only that—Hernan shared his faith with many others in his community. Of course, there was opposition, and some persecution, but within two years' time El Porvenir had a Sabbath school with 120 members. Thirty have been baptized and more are studying.

God has a faith-sharing assignment for *you,* too!

"IN NORTH AMERICA TOO!"

They shall be mine, saith the Lord of hosts, in that day when I make up my jewels. Mal. 3:17.

When Velma, a young housewife in Emmett, Idaho, accepted the Advent message, her husband threatened divorce and considered having her committed to an institution. Through a providentially directed series of events, she soon won her married sister, Loretta. Then the two young women went to work for God in an earnest soul-winning endeavor. Relatives, friends, neighbors—all received literature or were approached personally with the claims of the message.

One by one there were baptisms in the struggling little Emmett church. The interest created by these two young women, whom their pastor called firebrands for God, grew until Elder Martin decided a public effort must be held to reap the harvest. The meetings were greatly blessed of God. Among those making their decision for present truth were the husbands of Velma and Loretta, and other members of the families.

In a little more than one year sixteen persons were influenced to accept God's truth by this young wife and mother. During the first eighteen months after Velma was baptized, church attendance in Emmett jumped from between fifteen and twenty to between sixty-five and seventy-five.

A group of our black youth in Philadelphia decided to hold a public evangelistic crusade in a difficult area of their city. Night after night these young people preached in their tent. Day after day they visited in the homes of the interested people. Soon they were holding more than two hundred Bible studies with candidates for the kingdom of God. The last I heard, a goodly number, young and old, had been baptized.

These are not mission stories from the West Indies, from Africa, or South America. This is what happened when young people whose hearts were full of the love of God went to work for Him right here in North America! There are thousands more like Velma and Loretta and our black youth in Philadelphia whom the Lord can and will use if He is only given the opportunity.

ON THE MARCH FOR GOD

O God, when thou wentest forth before thy people, when thou didst march through the wilderness; Selah: the earth shook, the heavens also dropped at the presence of God: even Sinai itself was moved at the presence of God, the God of Israel. Ps. 68:7, 8.

When God marched "through the wilderness" in the days of ancient Israel, things happened. Miracles were performed— "the earth shook," "the heavens . . . dropped," "Sinai itself was moved." because the presence of God was in that place.

"A work similar to that which the Lord did through His delegated messengers after the Day of Pentecost He is waiting to do today. At this time, when the end of all things is at hand, should not the zeal of the church exceed even that of the early church?" —*Testimonies,* vol. 7, p. 33.

It has been said that after Cicero, the great Roman orator, finished an oration, spellbound people crowded around and cried, "How well you spoke!" But when Demosthenes, the Grecian leader, spoke, the aroused crowds shouted, "Let us march!"

Young people, I pray that God will strike fire in your heart today—a fire that will compel you to cry out, "Let us march!" Let us march first to the foot of the cross, and there in sincere repentance yield ourselves anew to the Man of Calvary. Then let us march to the upper room, where in quiet confidence we may be filled with Pentecostal power.

Then let us march to the dark counties and districts, to the unentered cities in North America and Europe. Let us march to the ends of the earth, our hearts aglow with the love of Christ and with a passion for souls that will not burn out this side of the kingdom.

Let us march and *march* and MARCH until the last stronghold of heathenism or unbelief has fallen. Let us march until the banner of our coming King has been planted victoriously in every land and on every tiny atoll—on earth's most distant outpost. Let us march and keep on marching until the gates of Paradise swing open before us, and with the vast host of the redeemed we enter the City of God to spend eternity with our Saviour!

Wake up and march!

WITH ALL YOUR HEART

With all your heart do what God wants, as slaves of Christ. Eph. 6:6, T.E.V.

Years ago Dr. and Mrs. Philip Nelson left a lucrative practice in the United States, responding to a call to India as medical missionaries. When furlough time came in 1964 there was a shortage of doctors in the field. Dr. Nelson remained nearly a year to fill a need at our mission hospital in Ranchi, northeastern India.

Finally the day of departure arrived. They were heading home on their first furlough! The first leg of their journey was by car across north central India to Delhi. In the nation's capital they would board the plane to Africa, where they planned to visit Mrs. Nelson's father and sister in Malawi before proceeding to the U.S.A., their homeland. Near Allahabad—"God's Own City"—two punctures brought their trip to an unplanned interruption. There was no second spare tire, so the doctor left Mrs. Nelson in the car close to an Indian village while he caught a ride to Allahabad to purchase another tire. When he returned a few hours later he found his dear companion cruelly murdered. It was a heartbreaking experience!

Some time later Dr. Nelson wrote to a friend, unburdening his heart after the tragedy. This beautiful heartsearching letter reveals that this missionary doctor knew what Paul was talking about in our text for today—"with all your heart do what God wants, as slaves of Christ." With Dr. Nelson's permission, I share with you one paragraph of this challenging letter:

"Sister White said that when God gave His Son to redeem man He poured out all heaven in one gift. It seemed to me that when I lost Ruby, I poured out all I had in one gift to India. It has inspired me to give what is left of me in a deeper, more meaningful consecration than ever before. I will go anywhere He leads me. I will bear any burden He lays upon me. I will make any sacrifice He calls upon me to make. I will live a life fully dedicated to Him, every moment of every day."

What a surrender! What consecration! What yielding to the will of God under every circumstance!

"With all your heart do what God wants"—nothing less is acceptable to Him whose slave you have chosen to be!

THERE WAS A GREAT RAIN

And it came to pass in the mean while, that the heaven was black with clouds and wind, and there was a great rain. **1 Kings 18:45.**

For nearly five years parts of Northern Transvaal, South Africa, had experienced a cruel drought. The ground was parched and cracked; once-lush grazing lands were burned up. Thousands of head of cattle perished. Families living in the area were rationed to a few gallons of water a week for all household purposes. It was a crisis hour.

Pastor J. J. B. Combrinck invited pastors of other churches in the area to join him in a season of fasting and prayer for rain, but had hardly any response. After six weeks of waiting Brother Combrinck decided that Seventh-day Adventists would have to pray alone before total disaster visited his district.

The local newspaper splashed the news on the front page: "Seventh-day Adventists to Pray for Rain!" The local radio station likewise heralded the news several times on Friday. Reaction in the community ranged from restrained to open scoffing.

The Sabbath dedicated to prayer and fasting dawned as hot and forbidding as hundreds of other days before it. Humanly speaking, the prospects for rain were most unfavorable.

In the Seventh-day Adventist church that day Pastor Combrinck studied with his people the conditions of answered prayer. Most of the afternoon was spent in earnest entreaties to God that the drought might be broken.

Describing what happened later, Pastor Combrinck in a letter to me wrote: "When our people reached their homes late Sabbath afternoon the sky had suddenly become overcast, and within half an hour a soft rain began to descend. The showers lasted for more than two days. In fact, the rains continued regularly for some weeks. Many have testified that God heard the prayers of Seventh-day Adventists. Far and wide the rain has continued to fall, only a few places are still dry."

The God of Elijah is not dead in our day. He is still the master of the elements. He still remembers the needs of His people. You may need rain. You may need some other blessing urgently. When we pray as Elijah prayed we may expect to be heard and helped as Elijah was heard and helped.

GOD'S ANSWERS

Now unto him that is able to do exceeding abundantly above all that we ask or think, according to the power that worketh in us, unto him be glory in the church by Christ Jesus throughout all ages, world without end. Amen. **Eph. 3:20, 21.**

Do you ask for—

SALVATION?
"Sirs, what must I do to be saved? And they said, Believe on the Lord Jesus Christ, and thou shalt be saved" (Acts 16:30, 31).

PARDON?
"I alone am he who blots away your sins for my own sake and will never think of them again" (Isa. 43:25, T.L.B.).

VICTORY?
"Thanks be to God, which giveth us the victory through our Lord Jesus Christ" (1 Cor. 15:57).

POWER?
"You will be filled with power when the Holy Spirit comes on you" (Acts 1:8, T.E.V.).

PEACE?
"God's *peace, which is far beyond human understanding,* will keep your hearts and minds safe, in Christ Jesus" (Phil. 4:7, T.E.V.).

JOY?
"You *love* him, although you have not seen him; you *believe* in him, although you do not now see him; and so you *rejoice* with a great and glorious joy" (1 Peter 1:8, T.E.V.).

WISDOM?
"If any of you lacks wisdom, he should *pray to God,* who will give it to him; for God gives generously and graciously to all" (James 1:5, T.E.V.).

HEALTH?
"Beloved, I wish above all things that thou mayest prosper and be in health, even as thy soul prospereth" (3 John 2).

There is a blessed fullness about God's dealing with His children. He "is able to do exceeding abundantly above all that we ask or think."

A VIPER IN THE VOLUME?

A road may seem straightforward to a man, yet may end as the way to death. Prov. 14:12, N.E.B.

An Indian gentleman was in his library searching for a book. After a few minutes he located the desired volume and, standing on a stool, he reached to retrieve it from a high shelf. As he pulled the book from its musty corner he felt a sharp pain in his finger like the prick of a pin.

The man paid no attention to the discomfort at the time. "I thought someone had left a pin or a sharp paper clip in the book," he told his wife later.

Soon the injured finger began to swell. Then his whole arm was affected. Too late he discovered that what he thought was a common pin was in reality a small and poisonous viper that had found its way into his library.

Vipers hide in many volumes today. As people read, they are enamored by charming word pictures and bewitched by subtle suggestions of the evil one, many times unaware that their minds are being poisoned. But in the judgment the record will reveal that the serpents among the books caused the downfall of countless souls.

"God has given to His people the choicest reading matter. . . . Keep choice, elevating literature ever before the members of the family. Read our books and papers. Study them. Become familiar with the truths they contain. As you do this, you will feel the influence of the Holy Spirit. Every moment of life is precious, and should be spent in preparing for the future immortal life. Let the mind be stored with the elevating, ennobling themes of the Word of God, that you may be ready to speak a word in season to those who come within the sphere of your influence. The reading of our publications will not make us mental dyspeptics. None of us will receive the bread of life to our injury, but as these books are read, the mind will be furnished with that which will establish the heart in the truth." —*My Life Today,* p. 89.

Do we sometimes select vipers when we might just as easily choose victory?

CHOOSE CAREFULLY WHAT YOU READ

For the Lord giveth wisdom: out of his mouth cometh knowledge and understanding. **Prov. 2:6.**

An educator friend of mine was conducting the Week of Prayer in one of our overseas colleges. During counseling periods he discovered a number of students had been adversely influenced as the result of reading a book written by an agnostic author. The volume was a subtle work of rationalizing. Sin is not sin, the author declared, it is merely anything you *think* is bad. If you *think* a certain course of action is right and acceptable, it is.

A faculty member, without reading the book himself, unwittingly placed it in the hands of a student who was "looking for something to read." The volume passed through many hands and considerable damage was done before the results came to light.

The Lord's servant underscores the need of our exercising great care in the books we read: "Books from the pens of infidels should have no place in the libraries of those who would serve God. They will make better kindling material for your stove than food for the mind. Infidel books have been a cause of ruin to many souls. Men have studied these books of Satan's inspiration, and they have become confused in regard to what was truth. Satan stands at the side of him who opens an infidel book, and he will educate the mind that peruses such literature, and so bewitch the soul that it will be almost impossible to break the infatuation."—*Our High Calling*, p. 276.

"Those who value their soul's salvation should shun infidel writings as they would shun the leprosy."—*Ibid.*

Little wonder Ellen White added this bit of wise counsel: "To the youth I would say, Be careful what you read. So long as the mind is directed into wrong channels by an improper course of reading, it is impossible for you to make the truth of God the constant subject of meditation. If there was ever a time when a knowledge of the Scriptures was more important than any other, that time is the present. I appeal to old and young, Make the Bible your textbook. Here you will find the true standard of character."—*Ibid.*

287

AFTER THE PEACE SYMBOLS?

When they shall say, Peace and safety; then sudden destruction cometh upon them. 1 Thess. 5:3.

As I write these words in August, 1972, the world stage is monopolized by peace movements. Despite government leaders' best efforts to de-escalate combat in several trouble spots of earth, multiplied thousands of voices are demanding *peace* NOW. These demands fill the newspapers, clog the airwaves, deface our signs and fences. "We want peace, *now!*" is the loud clamor of thousands of marchers demanding the end of war.

Many of these peace movements are spearheaded by youth wearing peace symbols around their necks, on rings or bracelets. Peace signs are everywhere—on bumper stickers, in windows, on fences, and even on well-patched levis. This is, indeed, a generation avowedly seeking peace.

The Word of God has something to say about peace—or the absence of it—in our day. Instead of peace, the Saviour declared that our generation would be rather a time of war and rumors of war: "And ye shall hear of wars and rumours of wars: see that ye be not troubled: for all these things must come to pass, but the end is not yet. For nation shall rise against nation, and kingdom against kingdom" (Matt. 24:6, 7).

Commenting on this scripture, Teen Challenge leader David Wilkerson says, "I think that this Scripture must help a Jesus Person to realize that as this age draws to a close there will be no peace and the issue of world peace for the follower of Christ cannot be a dominating one.

"The whole cry for peace," Mr. Wilkerson, in his *Maturity Manual,* page 30, declares, "is a sign of the nearness of Christ's coming." And, he may well have added, rather than spending time battling the establishment with peace slogans, the youth of our day might better spend time preparing for the appearance of the Prince of Peace whose early appearing such movements foretell.

While a world fights for peace around us, God's people should be seeking the Prince of Peace and "the peace of God, which passeth all understanding" (Phil. 4:7), to prepare us for the sudden destruction just ahead. This is God's true peace movement!

"OPs" AND "NOPs"

So you are no longer outsiders or aliens, but fellow citizens with every other Christian—you belong now to the household of God. Eph. 2:19, Phillips.

Dr. Alonzo Baker was presenting a paper to a group of church leaders gathered for a conference on management. The speaker was emphasizing the blessing of serving in a Christian institution with a Christian atmosphere. He opened his remarks with a story that warmed my heart.

"There is a difference in working with Christian colleagues and with those not of our faith," Dr. Baker declared. "Let me illustrate what I mean. Recently my wife and I were invited to a social occasion in Santa Monica. Most of the people attending were doctors and their wives. Some were Adventists; some were not—about half and half. We were sitting with Dr. Joan Coggin and her mother. As people came into the room and were introduced, I would ask, 'Are they Adventists?'

"Dr. Coggin answered very cryptically, 'OP,' or 'NOP.'

"At first, I did not understand so sought an explanation. 'I know what WPA is, what FTC is, what SEC is, but what is this OP and NOP you keep talking about?'

"She replied, 'OP is Our People; NOP is Not Our People.'

"I want to tell you, brethren, there is a difference between OP and NOP!"

All of us who have experienced the warmth of fellowship with those of like precious faith at home or in some distant land will agree with Dr. Baker. I have traveled in many different lands, but I never feel I am "away from home" when I am with Seventh-day Adventists. It matters not what their cultural background, their nationality, or race may be, if they are OP I am right at home. My fellow workers tell me they feel the same way.

OPs all speak the same language. It is not English, not French, not Pidgin, not Chinese, not Spanish, not German. It is the Advent language. It is a cordial handclasp, a contagious smile, and a warm demeanor. This says "I love you" in OP language. It makes one feel good "to belong"!

I agree with Dr. Baker. "There is a difference between OP and NOP." May the Lord ever keep it so!

SPEAKING THE SAME LANGUAGE

How sweet are thy words unto my taste! yea, sweeter than honey to my mouth! Ps. 119:103.

Henry Rocher, a French citizen, was traveling through Poland by train. Early one morning as he sat in his compartment he picked up his Bible and began to seek strength for the day. Sitting on the seat beside him was an old Russian woman. She recognized God's Word by the black cover and the gold-edged pages.

Her face lighted up. Reaching down beside her, she pulled out a big book of her own from between a loaf of hard, black bread and a piece of cheese.

Quickly she thumbed through her precious book until she found Luke 2:11. Though she spoke a different language, she was able to pierce the Babel barrier by pointing to the text in her Bible and asking with her eyes if he believed in the Saviour. The Frenchman rustled the leaves of his Bible, located Luke 2:11 and with a smile nodded.

There was another murmur of pages. This time the text was a short one in which the word *disciple* was prominent. Again a questioning look in the bright eyes brought an affirmative reply.

Mr. Rocher reached and took the other Bible. Locating 1 Corinthians 1:3 in both books, he returned the Russian woman's Bible. She read the apostle's words: "Grace be unto you, and peace, from God our Father, and from the Lord Jesus Christ."

Both faces lighted up with a joy that comes only to those who know the Lord Jesus Christ. No words had been spoken, but both experienced the reality of the communion of the saints—through the medium of the Word.

"How sweet are thy words unto my taste!" the psalmist exclaimed, "yea, sweeter than honey to my mouth!" To the Hebrew of David's day honey was "a symbol of all that was pleasant to the palate" *(The SDA Bible Commentary,* on Ps. 19:10).

How precious should be the Word of God to His people today! Are His words sweeter to you than honey? How frequently do you partake of its precious nectar?

HOLY SPIRIT LOVE

The fruit of the Spirit is love. Gal. 5:22.

"The fruit of the Spirit is love." Read it again—and again! Ponder it well. Pray about it! It is a fact you and I must not lose sight of. As members of God's remnant church we pray for the outpouring of the Holy Spirit. We plead with Him to come into our midst in Pentecostal power. We feel our need of Him as we face the challenge of taking the Advent message across our breakfast table, across our street, across our nation, across the oceans, across the world!

The Holy Spirit is *power*. It is power to *serve*. It is also power to live! Sometimes the living is more difficult than the serving. The evidence of the Spirit's power in our living will be seen in the measure of *love* that shines through our daily life. *"The fruit of the Spirit is love."* If the Spirit truly abides within, love—the love of Christ—will be evident in all our contacts with those about us.

Of course we will love our friends. It is not difficult, usually, to love those who love us. We naturally respond to affection that flows "usward" in loving words and thoughtful deeds. There is no problem in returning such affection. But the fruit of the Spirit is more than love toward those who love us!

"Love your enemies" (Luke 6:27), Jesus says.

The love that flows from the Holy Spirit dwelling in our hearts and lives is an affection that includes loving those who are against us. When the love of Christ is in our hearts we will love those who make life difficult for us, those who oppose our plans in school, on the job, in the Sabbath school, or in the church program. It helps us love those whose personalities do not mesh easily with ours, who "rub us the wrong way," who seem frequently to say things to wound or disappoint us. This love will provide grace to return a soft answer when the natural response would be a curt or cutting reply.

This is "Jesus love," for such a love is not a natural reaction. It comes from above! This love of which Paul speaks is a love that draws a circle around both friend and "irritater" alike, and takes them both in.

GOD'S WORD BRINGS JOY

Your words are what sustain me; they are food to my hungry soul. They bring joy to my sorrowing heart and delight me. Jer. 15:16, T.L.B.

Jeremiah was discouraged. Judging by human norms, the prophet during his lifetime experienced sufficient suffering and adversity to discourage any man. His neighbors plotted against him. " 'Let's destroy this man and all his messages,' they said. 'Let's kill him so that his name will be forever forgotten' " (Jer. 11:19, T.L.B.).

His friends rejected him. " 'We will report you,' they say. Even those who were my friends are watching me, waiting for a fatal slip. 'He will trap himself,' they say, 'and then we will get our revenge on him' " (chap. 20:10, T.L.B.).

Pashur the priest, in charge of the Temple, encouraged the prophet's harassment. "He arrested Jeremiah and had him whipped and put in the stocks at Benjamin Gate near the Temple. He left him there all night" (verses 2, 3, T.L.B.).

The prophet's own family rejected him. "Even your own brothers, your own family, have turned against you. They have plotted to call for a mob to lynch you. Don't trust them, no matter how pleasantly they speak. Don't believe them" (chap. 12:6, T.L.B.).

King Zedekiah was going to make certain the voice of God's man was muted forever. "They took Jeremiah from his cell and lowered him by ropes into an empty cistern in the prison yard. (It belonged to Malchiah, a member of the royal family.) There was no water in it, but there was a thick layer of mire at the bottom, and Jeremiah sank down into it" (chap. 38:6, T.L.B.).

In prison, in stocks, in the "thick layer of mire," with everyone apparently against him, the prophet experienced hours of extreme mental anguish and periods of bitter discouragement.

But through the darkness there came the voice of hope, the assurance of strength, the expectation of deliverance. It was the word of God to His suffering saint. " 'They will try, but they will fail. For I am with you,' says the Lord. 'I will deliver you' " (chap. 1:19, T.L.B.).

God's words will bring joy to your heart also if you will "eat" them as the prophet did.

APOSTLE OF POLARIZATION

And unto this people thou shalt say, Thus saith the Lord; Behold, I set before you the way of life, and the way of death. Jer. 21:8.

For forty years Jeremiah the prophet stood before Judah as a witness of truth and righteousness. It was a period of unparalleled apostasy, but God's man exemplified in life and character the worship of the true and living God.

During the cruel sieges of Jerusalem, Jeremiah was the mouthpiece of Jehovah. It took courage to predict the downfall of the house of David and the destruction of Solomon's glorious temple. Even while in prison for his ministry of repentance, Jeremiah's fearless voice spoke out insistently against sin.

As a result, Jeremiah was a man feared and disliked by many. "I am hated everywhere I go," he lamented. "I am neither a creditor soon to foreclose nor a debtor refusing to pay—yet they all curse me" (Jer. 15:10, T.L.B.).

"Woe is me!" the prophet cries out in the same verse (K.J.V.). It is as though the harassed man of God suddenly realized "that his mission, like that of Christ, is 'not to send peace, but a sword' (Matt. 10:34)."—*The SDA Bible Commentary,* on Jer. 15:10.

In a sense Jeremiah was an apostle of polarization. He preached God's message. The straight testimony was not pleasing to the majority of those who came under his ministry. But the prophet was not seeking popularity. He was endeavoring to do God's will, to preach God's Word. His preaching polarized those who heard him. There were few halfway hearers. Men spurned God's call to repent and turned against His messenger.

Jeremiah came to set sinners at peace with God, but in so doing he inevitably placed them in tension with those who spurned this proffered blessing. With the prophet there must be no "peace at any price"—God's people must "never seek, or be content with, the peace that comes through compromise with evil" (*ibid.,* on Matt. 10:34).

The Lord still sets before His people "the way of life, and the way of death." Even among the remnant there will no doubt emerge another polarization as some make their decision for life while others choose death. It will take the courage of Jeremiah to make a stand for God on the issues involved.

DRINKING AT THE LIVING FOUNTAIN

Ho, every one that thirsteth, come ye to the waters, and he that hath no money; come ye, buy, and eat; yea, come, buy wine and milk without money and without price. Isa. 55:1.

Intensity of physical activity may often hide a real thirst of the soul. Norma Lee, a young and attractive Australian girl, found this in her experience. For her it was parties, dancing, drinking, and a continual round of pleasure. But back home her godly mother, having accepted the Advent message, prayed that Norma would find the genuine and recognize the illusion before it was too late.

One night while dancing Norma was stricken with paralysis in one leg. For days she cried while her mother pointed out God's way, and His power to heal and offer a new life. Norma's willingness to believe and to accept God's plan brought a miracle, an instant rejoicing as health and strength were restored. For some months a new radiance was hers, but temptation and worldly companions turned her back to former pursuits.

One morning while on a train journey Norma fell from the carriage onto the opposite rails. A speeding, passing train severed her legs. She hovered between life and death, but the suffering re-emphasized to her the only way to happiness "without money and without price"—a price already paid by Jesus on her behalf.

From a wheel chair, Norma's testimony to other youth was of God's power to save even to the uttermost through warnings and afflictions.

The prophet Isaiah asks us, "Wherefore do ye spend money for that which is not bread? and your labour for that which satisfieth not?" (Isa. 55:2). In one year, Americans spend on liquor an amount equivalent to the total expenses of all governments and private citizens in Africa for that same period. Billions of dollars more are spent on tobacco, drugs, and pornographic literature, apart from gambling and other follies. "With our first parents, intemperate desire resulted in the loss of Eden. Temperance in all things has more to do with our restoration to Eden than men realize."—*The Ministry of Healing*, p. 129.

Isn't it time we lifted up our voices to a needy world with the prophet's appeal to drink at the living fountain?

"MY LIFE IS MY MESSAGE"

You are all the letter we need, a letter written on our heart; any man can see it for what it is and read it for himself. **2 Cor. 3:2, N.E.B.**

During a visit to Bombay in 1969 I saw huge posters commemorating the centennial anniversary of the birth of Mohandas Gandhi—the father of the Indian nation. On this poster were these significant words: " 'My life is my message.'— M. GANDHI."

Though he was not a Christian, Mahatma Gandhi was a dedicated leader. The gospel of Christ, especially the Sermon on the Mount, had been a definite influence upon his life. Many of these principles were exemplified in his life.

"My life is my message"—it would be a wonderful testimony if this could be said sincerely and truthfully of every Seventh-day Adventist Christian. The world today is in need of more "legible Christians."

The apostle Paul had this in mind when he wrote to the believers in Corinth. He referred to his converts as his "epistles." He needed no letters of introduction himself, for the believers who had found Christ through his labors were sufficient proof of his apostleship. The lives of Paul's converts were Paul's message.

"Ye are our epistle," Paul wrote, "written in our hearts, known and read of all men."

"Each believer and each church should be a letter from Christ to the world. The author of the letter is Christ. The material on which the writing is done is the heart of each believer, and that which is written is the law of God, a transcript of His character."—*The SDA Bible Commentary,* on 2 Cor. 3:3.

"What you are speaks so loudly I can't hear what you say." This is another way of saying that for weal or for woe our life is really our message. Those with whom we come in contact judge us, our Saviour, our message, and our church by what we are, what we do, rather than what we say.

WE *SHALL* SEE HIM

When he shall appear . . . we shall see him. 1 John 3:2.

We all like to see people who are famous—people about whom we have heard a great deal. Back in 1927 after Charles Lindbergh made the first solo transatlantic flight from New York to Paris, crowds flocked to the cities he visited just to catch a glimpse of the "lone eagle." I was one of them! Today when the astronauts visit a city, people mob them. They want to *see* them.

In Jesus' day it was the same. When "certain Greeks . . . came up to worship at the feast: the same came therefore to Philip . . . and desired him, saying, Sir, we would see Jesus" (John 12:20, 21). The people of Jesus' day thronged Him. They heard of His mighty miracles, how the lame walked, the deaf heard, the blind saw, the dead lived. They heard of His teaching and preaching, how peace came to troubled breasts, how lives were transformed at His word or touch. The people thronged to *see* Him.

Did you ever long to share the privilege of Jesus' contemporaries—to actually *see* the Saviour? You will, if you are faithful. John assures us it will be so: "When he shall appear . . . we *shall* see him." This is a promise of God. It will not fail.

"We shall see *him.*" Job declares we shall "behold" Him, "and not another" (Job 19:27). It will be "this same Jesus" (Acts 1:11). The Jesus who walked the dusty roads of old Galilee, the Jesus who healed the sick and raised the dead, the Jesus who comforted the sorrowing and dying, the Jesus who spake as never man spake, the Jesus who lived as never man lived, the Jesus who loved as never man loved, the Jesus who died as never man died—"This same Jesus"—we shall "behold" Him "and not another"!

"We shall see him"—what a precious privilege—what an awesome responsibility! "May God help His people to arouse and walk and work as men and women on the borders of the eternal world. Soon an awful surprise is coming upon the inhabitants of the world. Suddenly, with power and great glory, Christ will come. Then there will be no time to prepare to meet Him. Now is the time for us to give the warning message."—*Testimonies,* vol. 8, p. 37.

BITTER OR BETTER?

If thou faint in the day of adversity, thy strength is small. **Prov. 24:10.**

Do you permit adversity to make you bitter or better? No matter how filled with sunshine our pathway may be, dark clouds of disappointment or adversity are bound to appear sometime. How do you react? Do such experiences make you bitter or better?

Talk about adversity, disappointment, discouragement—Joseph knew all about such experiences. For years such was the way of life for him. But through the dark clouds he always saw the sun shining. Adversity did not discourage nor destroy him. It did not make him bitter; it made him better.

At times Joseph might well have reasoned God had both forsaken and forgotten him. Every mile of the journey down to servitude into Egypt, after he had been betrayed by his brothers, the young man must have wondered why, *why*, WHY did this have to happen to me?

The experience of the years that followed could easily have made Joseph bitter. He could have been bitter toward his brothers for mistreating him, bitter toward Potiphar's wife for "framing" him—or even toward God, who apparently had forsaken him. Joseph could well have become bitter toward life for dealing him such cruel blows. No doubt there were times of discouragement when the young man's mind was assailed with dark thoughts. But if there were, such are not recorded. Joseph's mind provided no permanent resting place for them. The man of God refused to permit adversity to make him a soured, disappointed person. He always looked for the blessings in his adversity.

How does disappointment and adversity affect *you?* Does your relationship with the Lord and your familiarity with the promises of His Word hold you firm and keep you sweet? Do such experiences make you bitter, or, like Joseph, do they make you better? "If thou faint in the day of adversity, thy strength is small."

OCTOBER 19

UMBRELLAS AND JUDGING

Judge not, that ye be not judged. For with what judgment ye judge, ye shall be judged: and with what measure ye mete, it shall be measured to you again. Matt. 7:1, 2.

Jack Solsman had five umbrellas that needed repairing before his family would be prepared for the forthcoming rainy season. Gathering them all together one morning, he took the umbrellas to a repair shop for mending. They would be ready by five in the afternoon, and he was to pick them up on the way home after work.

For lunch Jack stepped into a restaurant. After eating he went to the clothes rack, took his hat, and absentmindedly picked up an umbrella that did not belong to him.

The owner of the umbrella appeared on the scene just as Jack was walking out.

"Say, mister," the aggrieved man called out, "that's my umbrella you've taken."

Jack was terribly embarrassed. "Oh, I am so sorry," he replied as he handed the umbrella back to its rightful owner. "I guess I must have umbrellas on my mind today."

The afternoon passed quickly, and Jack forgot the incident. Shortly after work he stopped by the repair shop, picked up his five umbrellas, and made his way to the bus stop on his way home.

When the bus arrived, Jack climbed aboard with his bundle of umbrellas and found a seat. Nicely settled, he glanced around at his fellow passengers. In the seat just across from him sat the man whose umbrella he had taken by mistake at lunchtime.

Eying the five umbrellas Jack had in his hands, the man across the aisle smiled knowingly and added with a faint accusation, "Had a good day today, didn't you?"

It is easy to judge; sometimes the evidence appears to be airtight. We see the man with the umbrellas in his hands; he must have stolen them. But we could be wrong. It is, therefore, better for us to read again the words of Christ in His sermon on the mount and hold our judgment.

"Judge not, that ye be not judged. For with what judgment ye judge, ye shall be judged: and with what measure ye mete, it shall be measured to you again."

CHRIST CARES FOR OUR PEOPLE PROBLEMS

And that he might reconcile both unto God in one body by the cross, having slain the enmity thereby. **Eph. 2:16.**

They hadn't spoken for many years, yet they were members of the same Seventh-day Adventist church. When I went to their church for a revival I knew no refreshing could come unless the high wall of partition that separated these two brethren was broken down. I prayed, I visited, I appealed. The Spirit worked. I saw the emotional dam break and those two strong men embrace and with tears streaming down their leathery cheeks sob out requests for forgiveness.

What broke the dike of hatred? Christ in the heart of each one. Christ is not divided against Himself, and when He is admitted into two hearts He breaks down any partitions and draws those two hearts together. Estrangement cannot exist when Christ comes into a heart or a home!

Though Paul in his letter to the Ephesians was speaking of demolishing the wall between Jew and Gentile, he might well have applied his words to two persons with people problems when he spoke of Christ as the One who "might reconcile both unto God in one body by the cross, having slain the enmity thereby."

The Christian ethic decrees that men and women should live at peace with those around them. Sometimes this is not easy, for all people are not easy to live with. As one saint once prayed, "Dear Lord, please make all the bad people good and the good people easy to live with."

Personalities, dispositions, sometimes clash. Tensions and bad feelings follow. With no Christ at the door of the heart to mellow the life and keep the temper in check, trouble is bound to follow.

But Christ can make a difference. Little Jean once explained, "When Satan knocks at my heart's door I just send Jesus to answer the door. When Satan sees Jesus he gets away in a hurry!"

Christ doesn't take away our people problems, but He gives us special grace to get along with some of the saints who aren't so easy to live with. Who knows, someone probably thinks you and I are among those who aren't easy to live with, so we all need Christ in our hearts.

CHRIST CARES FOR OUR SIN PROBLEM

When they were come unto a place called Golgotha, that is to say, a place of a skull, they gave him vinegar to drink mingled with gall: and when he had tasted thereof, he would not drink. And they crucified him. Matt. 27:33-35.

One of the most gripping pictures to come from the pen of God's inspired servant depicts the crucifixion scene. Let us read it reverently again:

"The spotless Son of God hung upon the cross, His flesh lacerated with stripes; those hands so often reached out in blessing, nailed to the wooden bars; those feet so tireless on ministries of love, spiked to the tree; that royal head pierced by the crown of thorns; those quivering lips shaped to the cry of woe. And all that He endured—the blood drops that flowed from His head, His hands, His feet, the agony that racked His frame, and the unutterable anguish that filled His soul at the hiding of His Father's face—speaks to each child of humanity, declaring, It is for thee that the Son of God consents to bear this burden of guilt; for thee He spoils the domain of death, and opens the gates of Paradise. He who stilled the angry waves and walked the foam-capped billows, who made devils tremble and disease flee, who opened blind eyes and called forth the dead to life,—offers Himself upon the cross as a sacrifice, and this from love to thee. He, the Sin Bearer, endures the wrath of divine justice, and for thy sake becomes sin itself." — *The Desire of Ages*, pp. 755, 756.

Sin demanded death. "Sins are forgiven only if blood is poured out" (Heb. 9:22, T.E.V.).

On Calvary blood was indeed poured out. A solution to man's sin problem was found in the death of God's sinless Son. The gulf that separated man from his Maker has been bridged. The separating partition has been removed. Because there was a Calvary the alien becomes a citizen of the kingdom. The stranger becomes a member of the family—a son, a daughter, of God. The vile sinner becomes the redeemed saint. Man is brought back to God. Man's Creator becomes man's Redeemer.

It is hard to believe, but it is blessedly true. As one who had experienced the joy of salvation exclaimed, "When I look at my sinful self I can't see how I can be saved. When I look at Jesus I can't see how I can possibly be lost."

MAKE IT PUBLIC IF NECESSARY

Euodias and Syntyche, I beg of you by name to make up your differences as Christians should! **Phil. 4:2, Phillips.**

It was many years ago. I was still very young. I was very foolish. In the early days of my mission experience I had written a series of articles on India for my hometown paper back in America. I had played up the sensational and some things that were not too complimentary to the people of the country. The facts were true, but I was very unwise in writing as I did.

Somehow these articles fell into the hands of some young Indian college students where I was invited to conduct the Week of Prayer. Upon my arrival and during the first day or so of meetings I was aware of a very cold atmosphere. Something was wrong. So I called together several of the young men whom I knew especially well, explained my apprehension, and asked them frankly what the trouble was. They told me. My articles had been read by the students; my foolishness was unmasked. The sensitive feelings of the young people had been wounded.

There was only one thing to do. I had made a bad mistake, the influence of which had spread through the whole student body. Righting such a wrong could be done only one way—a public confession. The Lord gave me grace. The mistake was acknowledged publicly. The whole atmosphere of the student body changed. I experienced the full forgiveness of the young people, and we enjoyed a fine, warm, blessed Week of Prayer.

"For open sin, open confession is required" *(The Desire of Ages,* p. 811), Ellen White writes. "Every open sin should be as openly confessed."—*Gospel Workers,* p. 216.

Private personal sins we do not proclaim from the housetops. But when our misdeeds are common knowledge in the church or in the community our confession should be as far reaching as our mischief has been.

If making wrongs right privately is difficult, it takes much more grace to get up and publicly proclaim we have erred. But it is the only way to have full peace with God. The Lord will not forsake us in such an hour. "My grace is sufficient for thee" (2 Cor. 12:9), He promises.

THE LAW OF ACTION AND REACTION

Blessed is he that considereth the poor: the Lord will deliver him in time of trouble. **Ps. 41:1.**

God's Word enjoins a loving care and attention for those who are less fortunate than ourselves—those who are in need. "We should remember the poor" (Gal. 2:10), Paul reminds us. "Give to the poor" (Matt. 19:21), Jesus instructed the rich young ruler in His day. "Blessed is he that considereth the poor," the psalmist says in our text today. "He that hath pity upon the poor lendeth unto the Lord" (Prov. 19:17), the wise man adds.

Moses summed it up nicely when he wrote: "If there be among you a poor man of one of thy brethren within any of thy gates in thy land which the Lord thy God giveth thee, thou shalt not harden thine heart, nor shut thine hand from thy poor brother" (Deut. 15:7).

God's last-day messenger echoes the appeal of Bible writers: "All around us we see want and suffering. Families are in need of food; little ones are crying for bread. The houses of the poor lack proper furniture and bedding. Many live in mere hovels which are almost destitute of conveniences. The cry of the poor reaches to heaven. God sees; God hears."—*Testimonies,* vol. 6, p. 385.

"If Christ is abiding in us, our hearts will be full of divine sympathy. The sealed fountains of earnest, Christlike love will be unsealed."—*Prophets and Kings,* p. 719.

When we follow God's invitation to extend sympathetic help to those in need He promises rich blessings that will return to gladden our own lives. "Cast thy bread upon the waters: for thou shalt find it after many days" (Eccl. 11:1), the preacher lays it down. "The Lord will deliver him in time of trouble," the psalmist promises. "That which he hath given will he pay again" (Prov. 19:17), the wise man declares. "Thou shalt have treasure in heaven" (Matt. 19:21), Jesus assures.

"It is as we give ourselves to God for the service of humanity that He gives Himself to us. No one can give place in his own heart and life for the stream of God's blessing to flow to others, without receiving in himself a rich reward."—*Thoughts From the Mount of Blessing,* p. 81.

GETTING ON SPEAKING TERMS WITH GOD

Take with you words, and turn to the Lord: say unto him, Take away all iniquity, and receive us graciously: so will we render the calves of our lips. **Hosea 14:2.**

I was in a large and ornate basilica in Europe. Near the entry were a number of small kiosks resembling telephone booths. I saw men and women approach the kiosks and kneel quietly. By their moving lips I knew they were speaking softly to someone inside. Presently a black-sleeved arm reached out and a hand touched the penitent. He or she arose and walked away. They had come for confession.

The prophet Hosea reminds the seeker after peace that as he approaches the Most High he must "take with you words" and Ezra urges him to "make confession unto the Lord God" (Ezra 10:11).

Sin silences the voice of God to us. Communications are cut. We must then get back on speaking terms with our heavenly Father. The wall of partition that separates us from God must be broken down. There is only one way to deal with this situation. The long silence must be ended. Communications must be restored. We re-establish our relationship by "taking words," confessing our sins to God.

Charlotte Elliott's beautiful hymn, "Just as I Am," expresses it well.

We come to Christ just as we are—

> Just as I am without one plea
> But that Thy blood was shed for me . . .

And Augustus Toplady's classic hymn, "Rock of Ages," makes it clear that we have no righteousness of our own to recommend us.

> Nothing in my hand I bring,
> Simply to Thy cross I cling.

Only through the blood and merits of Jesus can we approach God for forgiveness.

God's Word declares we need confess our sins only to Him. "For there is one God, and one mediator between God and men, the man Christ Jesus" (1 Tim. 2:5). "Secret sins are to be confessed in secret to God."— *The Desire of Ages*, p. 811.

DON'T READ THIS IF YOU HAVE NEVER MADE A MISTAKE

Confess your faults one to another, and pray one for another, that ye may be healed. The effectual fervent prayer of a righteous man availeth much. James 5:16.

"Will you please go with me to my pastor? I need to make some things right with him." The young lady speaking to me was attending a camp meeting. "You see, I have said some very unkind things about him because he won't sponsor the kind of socials I want. Some of the things I've said are not true, and I want to make things right so that I can truly live for Christ."

Many young people—and many older people as well—need to make some things right if they are ever to experience revival and be prepared for the soon coming of Jesus. The influence of many a prayer meeting has been neutralized because participating members had things in their lives that needed to be confessed before they could be right with God.

True revival will come only when we are right with our fellow men as well as with God! If you and I are on better terms with the angels than we are with our brethren, there is something wrong with our religion.

Peace with God may be only a confession away for some troubled saints. "Confess your faults," the apostle admonishes. Notice whose faults we are to confess. *Your* faults, not someone else's. It is much easier, and much more in keeping with the old sinful nature, to confess or talk about the faults of others. It is a blow to our ego to admit that we have been wrong. But the way to peace with God is through peace with those about us.

If we would be reconciled to God we must first be reconciled to our fellow man. "Therefore if thou bring thy gift to the altar, and there rememberest that thy brother hath aught against thee; leave there thy gift before the altar, and go thy way; first be reconciled to thy brother, and then come and offer thy gift" (Matt. 5:23, 24).

It is not easy to say, "I am sorry. I was wrong. Please forgive me." It is not easy to confess our faults, but it is God's way, and it is the right way. It is the only way we will find forgiveness, peace, and restoration with God. Don't delay if you need to make some things right with others! "Confess your faults."

MAKE IT SPECIFIC

And it shall be, when he shall be guilty in one of these things, that he shall confess that he hath sinned in that thing. Lev. 5:5.

"Many are zealous in religious services, while between them and their brethren are unhappy differences. . . . God requires them to do all in their power to restore harmony. Until they do this, He cannot accept their services. The Christian's duty in this matter is clearly pointed out."—*The Desire of Ages*, p. 311.

We may be able to explain the 2300 days perfectly. We may be faithful in our tithe paying and the support of our church financially. We may be in Sabbath school promptly every Sabbath morning. We may be an officer in our church, a teacher in the Sabbath school, a leader of the youth, *but* if we can't get along with those around us, if there is unresolved trouble between us and other church members or other persons, we must straighten those things out before revival can come.

If you have spoken that which was untrue or un-Christian about someone, you must go to that person and confess your fault. *You must be specific in your confession.* You must "confess" that you have "sinned in that thing," the Word of God declares.

"True confession is always of a specific character, and acknowledges particular sins. They may be of such a nature as to be brought before God only; they may be wrongs that should be confessed to individuals who have suffered injury through them; or they may be of a public character, and should then be as publicly confessed. But all confession should be definite and to the point, acknowledging the very sins of which you are guilty."—*Steps to Christ*, p. 38.

Then to make our experience even more difficult, inspiration says we must go as the chief offender: "If you have committed one wrong and they twenty, confess that one as though you were the chief offender. Take them by the hand, let your heart soften under the influence of the Spirit of God, and say, 'Will you forgive me? . . . I want to make right every wrong, that naught may stand registered against me in the books of heaven. I must have a clean record.' "—*Our High Calling*, p. 370.

In the spirit of Christ we are to go to those whom we have wronged, confess specifically our mistakes, go as the chief offender and humbly ask the one we have wronged to forgive us.

CHRIST CARES FOR PROBLEMS OF NATIONALITY

Nation shall rise against nation, and kingdom against kingdom. **Matt. 24:7.**

One of the signs that Jesus will soon return is the national enmity in our world today. Sometimes nation may be against nation in overt warfare. In other instances it is a battle of pressures, a battle of words, a battle of influences. One needs but to read today's paper, to listen to the daily news on the radio, or view it on TV, to be thoroughly briefed on national tensions and hatreds which exist in many parts of our modern world.

Christ in the heart changes all this.

A friend of mine visited the city of Jerusalem in 1972. There in that country so torn by national and cultural hatreds a group of Seventh-day Adventist Christians gathered to celebrate the Lord's Supper. Both Jews and Arabs were numbered among the participating saints.

My friend described with emotion the scene of an Arab washing the feet of his Jewish brother and then the Jew girding himself and serving his Arab brother. It was indeed a moving experience. While all around hatred and violence flared, in the house of God members of two differing cultures, in whose hearts Jesus had set up His throne, could kneel and serve each other in the ordinance of humility and then partake of Communion together. *Christ made the difference.*

In one land in Eastern Europe a Seventh-day Adventist traveler was visiting in the home of Seventh-day Adventist workers. At four o'clock in the afternoon one of the national leaders raised his hand to silence the conversation.

"It is eight o'clock in Washington now, and the brethren in the General Conference are leading out in the world fellowship of prayer. We always join them, for we also belong to the great world family of God's remnant church."

Though the political ideology espoused in this land frequently leads to outbursts of differences with American policy, when Jesus is in the hearts of members in one land and also in the hearts of members in another land, the nationality gap is closed. In such hearts nations cease to rise up against nations. Jesus Christ cares for problems of nationality differences.

THE SLAVE WHO IS KING

Paul and Timothy, slaves of Jesus Christ. Phil. 1:1, T.L.B.

In Paul's day a slave could receive his freedom by selling himself to one of the heathen gods. In this Greek practice the owner and the slave went to the temple where the owner received the purchase price (money that the slave had saved) and the slave supposedly was sold to the god. Thus he became the property of the god and was to all intent and purpose free.

Perhaps it was this custom that Paul had in mind when he referred to Timothy and himself as "slaves of Jesus Christ." The King James Version of our text uses the word "servants" rather than "slaves." The original Greek *doulos* meant literally "one bound," hence "a bondservant" or "a slave."

Paul uses this term *doulos* several times in his Epistle to describe the Christian's relationship to Christ. In so doing he reminds every Christian that he is the absolute possession of Jesus. Herein lies the difference between a servant and a slave. A servant is more or less free to do as he pleases. A slave is the purchased possession of his master. He is not at liberty to do as he chooses.

We have been purchased as Christ's love slaves. We belong to Him. He paid the price with His own life's blood upon the cross of Calvary. "You have been bought and paid for by Christ, so you belong to him" (1 Cor. 7:23, T.L.B.). "God paid a ransom to save you . . . , and the ransom he paid was not mere gold or silver. . . . He paid for you with the precious lifeblood of Christ, the sinless, spotless Lamb of God" (1 Peter 1:18, 19, T.L.B.). We thus become Christ's absolute possession. We can never belong to anyone but Christ.

Because of this new relationship with Jesus we owe Him our absolute obedience. A slave does not go and come as he pleases. His life is under the complete control of his master. His master's will becomes his will. His life is controlled by the decisions and the planning of his master. With the purchased possession of Christ it must be ever thus. We belong to Him. His will becomes our will. His planning directs our lives.

This is no relationship of which we are to be ashamed. For as an old saying goes, "To be His slave is to be a king."

MAKE CHRIST THE HEAD!

Husbands, love your wives, as Christ loved the church and gave himself up for her. **Eph. 5:25, R.S.V.**

The home of a young couple had been broken. The husband bitterly blamed religion for the trouble. I reminded him it was not Christ and Adventist teachings that triggered the dissension. It was the *absence of Christian practice.* Christ in the heart of the husband and Christ in the heart of the wife will draw them together in union and love. He never divides.

Reverence for Christ makes husbands and wives unselfish, kind, and loving. Love for Christ draws the family together. Make Christ "first and last and best in everything" is the counsel given a newly married young couple. "Constantly behold Him and your love for Him will daily become deeper and stronger as it is submitted to the tests and trials. . . . As your love for Him increases, your love for each other will grow deeper and stronger."

Christian love is much like a wheel, whose spokes come nearer to one another the closer they come to the center. The closer we are to Christ, the closer we come to each other.

Paul told husbands, "Love your wives, even as Christ also loved the church, and gave himself for it." "So ought men to love their wives as their own bodies. He that loveth his wife loveth himself" (Eph. 5:25, 28).

What greater challenge is there for husbands when we think of the supreme sacrifice our Saviour made in leaving heaven—the association of the angelic host and the fellowship with the Father—to come to this world and give Himself upon Calvary that you and I might live. As husbands such a love should be in our hearts toward our wives—a love that will inspire us to give even our lives for those whom we love, if necessary.

Ellen White sums it up this way: "If Christ indeed is formed within, the hope of glory, there will be union and love in the home. Christ abiding in the heart of the wife will be at agreement with Christ abiding in the heart of the husband. They will be striving together for the mansions Christ has gone to prepare for those who love Him."—*My Life Today,* p. 84.

WITH WORDS *AND* ACTIONS

Let every one of you who is a husband love his wife as he loves himself, and let the wife reverence her husband. **Eph. 5:33, Phillips.**

A dear old couple went as missionaries to Africa from Switzerland more than sixty years ago. Every time I saw Brother and Sister Matter, after I became acquainted with them in their later years, the love light was glowing brightly in their eyes when they looked at and talked to each other. *Love will find expression in looks.*

One woman from a divorce-marred home told me that in all the years she had lived with her husband he had never told her he loved her. Many homes could be saved if there were just a little more expression of love and appreciation.

A laconic, hard-working man lost his wife of fifty years. He was riding back from the funeral with the pastor.

"John," the pastor said, "Mary was a good wife, wasn't she?"

"Yes," John answered.

"You loved your wife, didn't you, John?"

"Yes, Pastor. Mary was a wonderful wife. I did love her. And once I almost told her so."

Sometimes we freely give expressions of appreciation to those we wish to impress. But we forget those considerate words at home where they are most needed and treasured. *Love will find expression in words.*

But it is not enough to look at our wives tenderly or whisper loving phrases in their ears. Actions speak louder than words. Sometimes it's a good idea to show our love by drying the dishes, vacuuming the rugs, and emptying the trash.

The wife of one of our workers in Africa told a group of women that although she had been married for thirty-three years, it always did something for her when her husband gave her violets—for she loved violets. That thoughtful husband expressed his appreciation in a tangible, practical manner. *Love will find expression in actions.*

"Make the home a Bethel, a holy, consecrated place," we are counseled. "Keep the soil of the heart mellow by the manifestation of love and affection."—*Counsels to Parents and Teachers,* p. 114. A home where love dwells and finds expression is a home where angels delight to dwell.

309

LETTERS OF RECOMMENDATION

Ye are our epistle written in our hearts, known and read of all men. 2 Cor. 3:2.

Recently I went into a large cafeteria in a Southern city for lunch. I selected the food that appealed to me and made my way to an empty table near the cashier's counter.

About halfway through my meal the cashier came to my table.

"Pardon me, sir, but aren't you a minister?" she asked.

"Yes, I am," I replied, thinking perhaps she had noticed that I paused to ask the blessing before eating.

"By any chance, are you a *Seventh-day Adventist* minister?" she persisted.

I was surprised.

"Yes, I am a Seventh-day Adventist minister," I confirmed, "but what makes you think so?"

"Well," she continued, "I thought I had seen you before. I asked one of the waitresses to go by your table and see whether you had coffee with your meal. She returned and said, 'No.' 'Go and look again,' I told her, 'and see if he is eating meat.' She returned the second time with a negative reply, so I felt quite sure you were a Seventh-day Adventist minister."

I visited further with her, discovered her husband was the owner of the cafeteria and she was a member of the Seventh-day Adventist Church. I had met her some years before when I was serving in that conference. How glad I was that I had not disappointed her in the diet I had selected.

In our text for today the apostle Paul declares: "You are all the letter we need, a letter written on our heart; any man can see it for what it is and read it for himself" (2 Cor. 3:2, N.E.B.).

Each one of us is a "letter" from our church. We are "known and read" by those with whom we come in contact. Many know what Adventists believe and teach. May God grant that our letter-lives may always ring true!

DON'T FORGET THAT SWORD!

Take your stand then with truth as your belt, righteousness your breast-plate, the gospel of peace firmly on your feet, salvation as your helmet and in your hand the sword of the Spirit, the Word of God. Above all be sure you take faith as your shield, for it can quench every burning missile the enemy hurls at you. **Eph. 6:14-17, Phillips.**

A seventeenth-century Covenanter in Edinburgh, Scotland, was taken to the gallows to pay for his religious convictions.

"Have you one last request?" he was asked.

"Yes," the condemned man replied. "I would like to pray one last prayer and sing one last psalm before I die."

"Your request is granted."

The man of God prayed long and earnestly. He then broke out in song. He had chosen as his last praise to God the long Psalm 119—all 176 verses. As he sang, the clatter of hoofs was heard. A horseman galloped up with a last-minute pardon. The Covenanter's life was spared.

Elder G. S. Stevenson, a descendant of this Covenanter, told me this story at Otjiwarongo, Southwest Africa, in May, 1960. Had the condemned man not committed this psalm to memory he might well have died that day. His knowledge of the Word of God actually saved his physical life!

A thorough knowledge of the Word of God will be our greatest support and encouragement in the times of test and trouble ahead for God's people. We "should be preparing for what is soon to break upon the world as an overwhelming surprise, and this preparation . . . [we] should make by diligently studying the word of God."—*Prophets and Kings*, p. 626.

This is the day as never before when God's people need to turn to the Bible and make its precious promises our very own.

"Flee to the neglected Bible; the words of inspiration are spoken to you; pass them not lightly by. You will meet every word again, to render an account whether you have been a doer of the word, shaping your life according to the holy teachings of God's word."—*Testimonies*, vol. 1, p. 508.

IT THROWS A LOT OF LIGHT

Study to shew thyself approved unto God, a workman that needeth not to be ashamed, rightly dividing the word of truth. 2 Tim. 2:15.

An elderly black saint loved her Bible dearly. A friend, desiring to assist her in the study of the Word, presented her with a commentary on the Scriptures.

A few days later the friend dropped by to see how she was enjoying the commentary.

"Auntie, how do you like the book I gave you?"

A pearly white smile creased the black face.

"That sure is a good book," the saint of God replied, "but the Bible sure does throw a lot of light on that book!"

The Word of God throws much light on the here and now as well as upon the eternal world. Nothing must take its place in the daily program of God's remnant people in these closing hours of earth's history. The Scriptures must ever remain pre-eminent among us!

"Many think that they must consult commentaries on the Scriptures in order to understand the meaning of the word of God, and we would not take the position that commentaries should not be studied; but it will take much discernment to discover the truth of God under the mass of the words of men." — *Fundamentals of Christian Education,* pp. 187, 188.

"Let them destroy my works," Martin Luther once cried out. "I desire nothing better; for all my wish has been to lead souls to the Bible, so that they might afterwards neglect my writings."—D'AUBIGNÉ'S *History of the Reformation,* p. 205.

Melanchthon, Luther's contemporary in the Reformation, declared that "we ought not to interpret Scripture by the Fathers, but the Fathers by Scripture. 'How often has not Jerome been mistaken!' said he; 'how frequently Augustine! how frequently Ambrose! how often their opinions are different! and how often they retract their errors! There is but one Scripture, inspired by the Holy Ghost, and pure and true in all things.' "—*Ibid.,* p. 178.

The Word of God throws lots of light on lots of different subjects and many varied situations. "Study to shew thyself approved unto God."

NEVER TWENTY-TWO

See, I have set before thee this day life and good, and death and evil.
Deut. 30:15.

Nickie was 21; he'll never be 22. On a recent Wednesday, at twelve minutes after 9:00 A.M., he climbed to the fifteenth floor of a downtown office building in San Francisco, broke into a vacant office, and jumped to his death. He was hung up on drugs.

At 21, Nicholas Paolini seemed to have his future assured. He was good-looking, intelligent, a gifted musician. He was a junior at the university, studying business administration; he had begun on a baseball scholarship. In high school he was an all-city catcher and captain of his team. In studies he was straight B.

His older brother, Fred, looking back on the tragedy, traces Nickie's decline into the drug world. It started, he said, with pot in his senior year in high school, and went on to other drugs as he found "new friends" at the university.

Nickie's family tried in quiet, often desperate, ways to help him. He loved his family and didn't want to hurt anybody. When his father tried to help, Nickie turned away to avoid the pain he would cause his father. He gave up his song-writing contract with music agents because his associates in the music world were leading him to drugs.

However, all the future for Nickie and all the hopes of his family were shattered that Wednesday. He went with some of his new drug-world friends. An hour or so later he was dead.

In high school Nickie probably would have felt insulted if it were suggested he would die a suicide because of his pot habit. But one wrong choice led to another.

The choice between life and death is as verily set before us today as it was before ancient Israel. God's way is different—instead of 3-D in danger, damage, death, it comes in 3-L—light, love, life. The choice is before each of us, and God invites us to make the right choice.

DON'T BE TEAMED WITH THE WRONG PERSON

Don't be teamed with those who do not love the Lord, for what do the people of God have in common with the people of sin? How can light live with darkness? And what harmony can there be between Christ and the devil? How can a Christian be a partner with one who doesn't believe? 2 Cor. 6:14, 15, T.L.B.

The young woman sitting before us had almost made up her mind—almost but not fully and irrevocably, we hoped.

"Fred's a good, clean, upright Christian," she was saying only half convincingly. "It is true, he is not a Seventh-day Adventist, but we have talked it over and he has agreed to study our message."

I had heard that argument before. I knew how such a venture usually turns out—after the fish is caught there is no more need to put bait on the hook.

"I just can't live alone," Jeanie continued. "I need someone to love me—to encourage me, to help me. Fred is so kind and tender with me now; I'm sure he will be considerate of my religious convictions." Jeanie looked wistfully out the window hoping, I suspected, that either her pastor or I would understand and at least not make it hard for her. She and Fred were terribly in love. That love was sure to make things turn out all right!

There is little help or encouragement for one who goes through spiritual life alone—alone to church, alone in prayer, alone in the study of the Word, alone to church gatherings. It is a desolate experience. Yes, Jeanie understood. She had thought of all this carefully and prayerfully, she assured us.

I do not know what decision Jeanie made. The right one, I hope. For I know the unhappy experience of Katie and Henry, of Marilyn and Orville, of Bill and Carol. Their stories are all the same. Young faith, high hopes, brief happiness, unplanned conflicts, frequent misunderstandings, distant coolness, open resentment, bitter disillusionment, love dies—and a marker is placed upon the grave of another unequal marriage.

"Can you afford to have such terrible odds against you in fighting the battle for everlasting life?"—*Messages to Young People,* p. 441.

LIP OR LIFE?

This people draw near with their mouth and honor me with their lips, while their hearts are far from me, and their fear of me is a commandment of men learned by rote. Isa. 29:13, R.S.V.

The last meeting of the retreat had come. Young people from the nearby Adventist colleges were gathered together for the farewell service. For some time all was quiet. Then one by one young voices praised God and renewed their consecration to His cause.

One young woman, not a Seventh-day Adventist, listened intently, her heart evidently warmed by what she had witnessed at this unusual gathering of young Christians. But her brow was knit with evident concern. At last she spoke.

"Several months ago I was introduced to the writings of Ellen White," she began, "and I have learned to treasure these precious books. I've read *Steps to Christ, The Great Controversy, Messages to Young People,* some of the *Testimonies,* and others."

The other young people, noting the voice of a newcomer, listened intently to her positive testimony. Linda spoke on.

"I recognize in Ellen White's writings the same voice I hear when I read the Bible," she explained. She paused a moment, then continued, "There is one thing that perplexes me, however. Why is it that you Adventist young people profess so much love for Christ and still you do not live in harmony with the counsel He has given you through His chosen messenger?"

The silence was eloquent. Some of the surprised youth looked at one another questioningly. Many just looked down— as Linda mentioned, kindly but frankly, life-styles she found among young Seventh-day Adventists that somehow to her didn't square with the "red books."

Finally some braver souls responded hesitantly. Yes, there were things that should be different, and with God's help they would be different in the days ahead! The meeting closed on a serious, challenging note.

Linda's question is still a good one for all of us, regardless of our age group. Why is it that we profess to love Christ so much, and still we do not live in harmony with the counsel He has given us through His chosen messenger?

Do we love the Lord by our *lips* or by our *lives?*

MOLECULES OR A CREATOR?

By the word of the Lord were the heavens made; and all the host of them by the breath of his mouth. Ps. 33:6.

"A soup of amino acid-like molecules, formed in pools some 3 billion years ago, interacted with oxygen and other elemental constituents of the Earth, probably giving rise to the first organization of matter which possessed the properties of life.

"Evidence indicates that nearly two million living species and millions of extinct species are descendants of this early form of life." So read an excerpt from a 205-page volume, *Science Framework for California Public Schools,* quoted in *These Times,* June, 1970.

Is this explanation of the beginning of life more easily accepted than the words of the psalmist?

The mechanistic evolutionary hypothesis honeycombs the school systems of the world today. In biology, geology, astronomy, in practically every area of learning, the seeds of unbelief in God's Word are being sown. In referring to the subject areas just mentioned, a one-time president of the Science League of America said, "All are dependent on evolution for their proper understanding." The tragic thing about it all is that such theories are being foisted upon our children and youth as proved fact!

Scientists who believe in the Word of God vigorously dispute such statements. Garrett Vanderkooi, a research professor in the University of Wisconsin, declares evolution to be "a theory with such a vast scope, and which by its very prehistoric nature cannot be proved" *(Christianity Today,* May 7, 1971, p. 13).

"There is no theory in existence today that even begins to explain the origin of life by natural means," Professor Vanderkooi continues. "The pat answers given in high school and beginning college textbooks on the origin of life simply do not hold up when submitted to biochemical analysis."—*Ibid.*

Which will we accept, "a soup of amino acid-like molecules formed in pools some 3 billion years ago" or "by the word of the Lord were the heavens made"? I choose God. I believe "he spake, and it was done; he commanded, and it stood fast."

"BROTHER SAUL"

And Ananias went his way, and entered into the house; and putting his hands on him said, Brother Saul, the Lord, even Jesus, that appeared unto thee in the way as thou camest, hath sent me, that thou mightest receive thy sight, and be filled with the Holy Ghost. Acts 9:17.

Ananias of Damascus is not one of the loudly proclaimed heroes of the New Testament, but his attitude toward Paul, soon after the apostle's conversion, reveals a beautiful example of Christian love and forgiveness. Let us have a look at the story recorded in Acts 9:10-18.

"Now in Damascus there was a disciple by the name of Ananias. The Lord spoke to this man in a dream, calling him by his name. 'I am here, Lord,' he replied" (Acts 9:10, Phillips).

Saul had been an implacable enemy of the infant Christian church. His avowed mission to Damascus was to search out those in "the Way," as the early Christians were called. He was committed to stamping out the hated sect—probably Ananias included.

When the Lord spoke to Ananias first about his role in rehabilitating the great persecutor, Ananias understandably demurred. He pleaded, reminding the Lord of this man Saul's record—how he had come from Jerusalem to imprison or kill all who called upon God's name.

The Lord told Ananias not to fear, that Saul was one whom He had chosen to do a great work for Him. With this assurance Ananias hesitated no longer. He followed his Lord's instructions, proceeding immediately to Judas' home on the street called Straight. There he met the dread persecutor. Now note how Ananias addressed the man he had feared.

"Brother Paul, the Lord Jesus, who appeared to you on the road, has sent me so that you may be filled with the Holy Spirit and get your sight back" (Acts 9:17, T.L.B.).

Ananias' greeting, *"Brother* Saul," is a sublime example of Christian love, forgiveness, and brotherliness! You and I need to cultivate this spirit of love, forgiveness, and brotherliness more, too!

"GO TELL THAT FOX!"

At that same time some Pharisees came to Jesus and said to him, "You must get out of here and go somewhere else, for Herod wants to kill you." Jesus answered them: "Go tell that fox: 'I am driving out demons and performing cures today and tomorrow, and on the third day I shall finish my work.' " Luke 13:31, 32, T.E.V.

Jesus was no coward. It required courage to throw out such a challenge to the unscrupulous ruler of Galilee. It required courage to remain within Herod's reach and carry on His work in the face of such threats.

The God-man who came as your Saviour and mine was no cringing coward. On occasions His form was bowed with anguish, but never with fear or cowardice. Though He was meek, humble, kind, and compassionate, the Man of Galilee was no weakling. Jesus Christ provides the world in all ages with the greatest display of raw courage ever witnessed.

Jesus began His ministry in Nazareth, which was, in some respects, His hometown. It is not always easy to witness in our hometown where everyone may know us too well. But Jesus courageously called sin by its right name in His hometown. He staked His claim to divinity, to the Messiahship, right here before His fellow townspeople. He rebuked the rulers of the synagogue. The results?

"All the people in the synagogue were filled with anger when they heard this. They rose up, dragged Jesus out of town, and took him to the top of the hill on which their town was built, to throw him over the cliff" (Luke 4:28, 29, T.E.V.).

It required courage for Jesus to preach His despised evangel.

It required courage for Christ to defy the viceroy of mighty Rome, to confront an angry mob of His own townspeople, and to stand, as He did, before the rulers of the Jews. On many occasions He stood practically alone—but He stood! He stood for right under all circumstances, in all places, before all peoples! One of His disciples denied Him. Another betrayed Him. They all forsook Him. But He stood firm until death—the shameful death of the cross. It required real courage!

AND STILL THERE IS MORE

I am Alpha and Omega, the first and the last: and, What thou seest, write in a book, and send it unto the seven churches. Rev. 1:11.

I have stood in the Library of Congress in Washington, D.C., and looked upon the thousands of volumes packing the shelves in that great institution. There are books and manuscripts dealing with almost every subject under the sun—history, religion, politics, science, geography, fiction, poetry, prose. The list is endless.

But what do all these volumes contain? Those in the English language are simply the twenty-six letters of the alphabet arranged in varied styles. We speak of the works of the great English and American authors. Actually they wrote nothing but the twenty-six letters of the English alphabet. Each arranged and rearranged them in his own inimitable style.

Writers of English prose and verse have been doing this for centuries. Libraries, bookstores, newsstands, homes, are filled with millions of volumes written over hundreds of years. These writers have certainly given the alphabet a workout! But have they exhausted it? Are the letters less usable, less effective now than they were two centuries ago?

No! The writers of today find the alphabet as fresh and as ready to do its master's bidding as it was centuries ago. The alphabet is absolutely inexhaustible. The millions of books, brochures, papers, and magazines that will be written from now until the end of time will not in the least hamper the effectiveness of the alphabet. When the last words are written in English the twenty-six letters will be as far from exhaustion then as when they first came into being. They are totally inexhaustible!

When Jesus says, "I am Alpha and Omega"—the whole alphabet—He wishes to impress upon us that in His ability to save spiritually and to help physically and temporally, He is absolutely inexhaustible!

"He who reveals to the soul its necessity is waiting to satisfy its hunger and thirst. Every human resource and dependence will fail. The cisterns will be emptied, the pools become dry; but our Redeemer is an inexhaustible fountain. We may drink, and drink again, and ever find a fresh supply.

WHERE IS GOD?

Where is God my maker, who giveth songs in the night? Job 35:10.

A Seventh-day Adventist college student was greatly perplexed.

"I've been looking for God in my community," he lamented, "but I have been having a hard time finding Him."

The young man continued to lament what he felt was a placing of doctrine before human need in a part of his Adventist community.

"We have doctrines, moral codes, and unyielding traditions, but these are not enough," he declared. "I want to see God."

"Where is God?" This is a good question. Our young college friend was not the first to ask it. Centuries ago in Job's day perplexing questions arose. As it is in our day also, people were asking many questions. They were supplying few answers.

"Where is God my maker?"

In a decade marked by violence, racism, protest, population explosion, pollution, progress, and sudden death, this is a relevant question. It is not surprising that young people are asking such a question. In an era when large segments of mankind are approaching a future, which from a human standpoint is uniquely and utterly unknown except for its dangers, many are asking, "Where is God?"

It is true that cold doctrines, stern moral codes, unyielding traditions, are not enough. Doctrine and moral codes certainly have their place, but if the God of love and life is to shine through, these must be clothed with the warmth and the conviction of love in action, motivated by a born-again life. Those with whom we come in contact daily must see the God of love shining through our lives as we work the works of God among them.

It is not enough that unbelieving friends hear the seventh-day Sabbath truth. This is important. They must hear. But what is more basic—they must become acquainted with Jesus Christ, the Lord of the Sabbath. They must learn of Him not alone through our logic; they must meet Him daily in our lives as they behold us doing the work He did.

IT SETTLES A LOT OF QUESTIONS!

For as many as are led by the Spirit of God, they are the sons of God.
Rom. 8:14.

We are not angels in the rough who need polishing. We are not merely errant children who need reproving. We are not merely sick patients who need healing. We are sinners who need saving. We need help!

We have our part to play in the plan of redemption. We must exercise our power of choice and *choose* to respond to the call of the Saviour. We must indeed *will* to follow Him. But this is not enough, and we need help on the day of our justification when the sins of the past are cared for, and we need help every day of our lives as we seek to walk the Christian way. This help must come from outside ourselves!

"Education, culture, the exercise of the will, human effort, all have their proper sphere, but here [transforming the evil heart] they are powerless. They may produce an outward correctness of behavior, but they cannot change the heart; they cannot purify the springs of life. There must be a power working from within, a new life from above, before men can be changed from sin to holiness. That power is Christ."— *Steps to Christ*, p. 18.

Christ, by His Spirit, leads us day by day. When we are led by the Spirit we are the sons of God and this settles a lot of questions for the Christian.

The Spirit-led life settles many questions. "For as many as are led by the Spirit of God, they are the sons of God." Often we hear questions such as these: Is it wrong to go to shows, to smoke, to drink, to wear jewelry? Is it wrong to eat this or that? Is this wrong? Is that wrong? When a person is truly led by the Spirit; when Jesus is first, last, and best in everything, it is wonderful how these questions answer themselves. The question is no longer, Is this right? or, Is that wrong? The question rather becomes, Will it please Jesus?

Read Galatians 5:22-25. If we will make these words our guide in the use of our television and radios, in our choice of reading matter, the purpose of the Spirit-led experience will be more quickly realized in us.

The Spirit-led life settles a lot of questions!

DRY AND BRITTLE CHRISTIANS

And no man putteth new wine into old bottles; else the new wine will burst the bottles, and be spilled, and the bottles shall perish. Luke 5:37.

Even today in some parts of the Orient the inexorable advance of plastics and metals has been ignored and the skins of animals are still used for water bags and bottles. Through the years I saw them frequently in rural India. Fastened to the backs of knock-kneed donkeys or sleek, black buffalo, the supple bags cling to the contour of the animal's body bearing the precious liquid for drinking purposes, for washing, or for irrigating parched garden plots.

In Jesus' day genial hosts kept their wines in bottles made from skins. With each new crop new bottles were provided for the sweet nectar of the grape, for after a time the skins became dry and brittle. In such condition the bottles were unfit for use as containers. Christ used this illustration to portray the sad spiritual condition of some of the religious leaders of His day. These traditionalists had become so enmeshed in ceremony and so bogged in their own traditions that "their hearts had become contracted, like the dried-up wine skins to which He had compared them.

"While they remained satisfied with a legal religion, it was impossible for them to become the depositaries of the living truth of heaven. They thought their own righteousness all-sufficient, and did not desire that a new element should be brought into their religion. The good will of God to men they did not accept as something apart from themselves. They connected it with their own merit because of their good works. The faith that works by love and purifies the soul could find no place for union with the religion of the Pharisees, made up of ceremonies and the injunctions of men. The effort to unite the teachings of Jesus with the established religion would be vain. The vital truth of God, like fermenting wine, would burst the old, decaying bottles of the Pharisaical tradition."— *The Desire of Ages,* p. 279.

Our only safety is in knowing God and the power of His love as revealed through Christ by an experimental knowledge. Then we may become God's new skins filled with the wine of His life-giving gospel.

THE WOMAN WHO FORGOT TO DIE!

Wherefore he saith, Awake thou that sleepest, and arise from the dead, and Christ shall give thee light." Eph. 5:14.

The news was not good. According to the doctor, Elsie Brandon had just six months to live. Her heart ailment was incurable. Her legs and feet were giving trouble. It was most difficult for her to walk.

Six months to live! After careful and prayerful reflection, Sister Brandon determined that by God's grace those last six months were going to be fruitful ones. They would be spent to His glory. She was not going to just lie down and die. Every day was going to be given in service for her Saviour.

Sister Brandon set aside any thought of her ailing heart. She "forgot" her aching limbs—and what is more important, she literally "forgot to die" during the next six months. In fact, she lived for nine years after she was told that her days were numbered. During this time the little church of which Sister Brandon was a member both woke up and fired up. Inspired by the committed example of their weaker sister, they went to work with her. The church was revived spiritually and increased numerically when one sister forgot self and went to work for God!

This challenging experience set me to thinking. It reminded me of the title of a sermon I heard one time—"If I Should Wake Before I Die." Some of us are nearly dead spiritually and we need to wake up. "That is why God says in the Scriptures, 'Awake, O sleeper, and rise up from the dead; and Christ shall give you light' " (Eph. 5:14, T.L.B.).

The apostle Paul explains why we need to awaken from our spiritual stupor. "In all this, remember how critical the moment is. It is time for you to wake out of sleep, for deliverance is nearer to us now than it was when first we believed" (Rom. 13:11, N.E.B.).

We are not only near spiritual death but we are very near the end of all things. This is a critical moment, he declares. The day of our deliverance is at hand.

Many of us, like Elsie Brandon, are living on borrowed time either spiritually or physically. Her experience challenges us to wake up and live—wake up and serve to His glory!

GETTING ALONG WITH OTHERS

He did not need anyone to tell him what people were like: he understood human nature. John 2:25, Phillips.

Long before modern psychologists flooded the world markets with books on human behavior, Jesus Christ, by precept and example, left His followers a rich legacy in the field of personal relations. True Christian human relations do not require one to practice a system of clever psychology devoid of sincerity. There will be no fawning nor flattering. A winsome personality is but the outworking of an inward experience in Christ Jesus.

"We cannot gain and possess the influence that He had; but why should we not educate ourselves to come just as near to the Pattern as it is possible for us to do, that we may have the greatest possible influence upon the people?"— *Testimonies,* vol. 2, p. 618.

Let us note some principles for getting along with others that the Saviour left us by His precept and example.

Jesus felt for people in their physical frailty. He expressed His feelings in sympathy. He provided for their needs. The servant of the Lord writes: "At all times and in all places He manifested a loving interest in men."— *The Desire of Ages,* p. 86.

Jesus drew men to Him because He took a personal interest in them. He associated Himself with the hopes and the joys and problems of their everyday life. They longed for His company, for He made it evident that He found pleasure in being with them.

The apostle Paul likewise taught this concept of human relations. "Take a real interest in ordinary people" (Rom. 12:16, Phillips), he counseled the church in Rome.

What a blessed experience it is for the Christian to follow in our Lord's steps. It enables us to live peaceably and profitably with those about us. There is something wrong with a person's religion when he gets along better with the minister on Sabbath than he does with his neighbors the rest of the week.

Following in the steps of Jesus in our relations with our neighbors prepares us for the here and now—as well as the there and then!

"HE HATH TRIED ME"

But he knoweth the way that I take: when he hath tried me, I shall come forth as gold. Job 23:10.

Talk about trials and hardships—Jeremiah really experienced them! From beginning to end the prophet's life was beset with experiences that would have utterly demolished many men's faith. Pressures, persecution, isolation, misrepresentation, derision, incarceration, banishment—Jeremiah was well acquainted with them all.

The pressures of his prophetic ministry weighed inexorably upon him. God's word to the prophet was as a burning fire in his bones. "I was weary with forbearing," he lamented, "and I could not stay" (Jer. 20:9).

Persecution was predicted: "The kings of Judah, . . . the princes, . . . the priests, . . . the people of the land. . . . They shall fight against thee" (chap. 1:18, 19).

Pashur, the son of Immer, helped fulfill these words. He "smote Jeremiah the prophet, and put him in the stocks" (chap. 20:2). The man of God was flogged, then made a gazingstock to all who passed by.

Because Jeremiah was accused of treason (falsely), Zedekiah had him placed in a murky, miry dungeon. "Then took they Jeremiah, and cast him into the dungeon of Malchiah the son of Hammelech, that was in the court of the prison: and they let down Jeremiah with cords. And in the dungeon there was no water, but mire: so Jeremiah sunk in the mire" (chap. 38:6).

Along with others, including Baruch, his friend and helper, Jeremiah was later banished to Egypt in an effort to still the prophet's tongue and pen. (See chap. 43:3-7.)

Yes, Jeremiah had trials—perhaps much greater than most of us as Christians are called upon to experience. Yet through it all, the God whom Jeremiah served stood by the man who remained steadfast through test and trial.

Most of us experience misrepresentation, opposition, and perhaps even a bit of derision sometime in our lives. To some, persecution and isolation come. Few of us know the pressures of duty Jeremiah felt. But we all have tests and trials. The same God who sustained and encouraged the prophet of God two and one-half millenniums ago will stand by His people today.

"I WANT MY MONEY BACK!"

I am weary of my crying: my throat is dried: mine eyes fail while I wait for my God. **Ps. 69:3.**

Five-year-old E. W. was all ears. The minister was speaking on the nearness of Jesus' second coming and the need to sacrifice to "finish the work" and hasten the Advent.

E. W. was deeply impressed.

"After the service," E. W. told me years later, "I hurried home, got my little piggy bank, emptied out the contents and took the money to my mother."

"Mamma," E. W. said earnestly, "I want Jesus to come and I want to help in His work. Take this money and use it for Jesus."

Each evening E. W. would pray seriously for Jesus to *come quickly.* Each morning he would run to the window and look toward the eastern sky.

"I believe He is coming today—*today,* Mamma," he would say longingly.

A week or so passed. Jesus did not appear. Little E. W.'s faith was severely tried. One morning after looking disappointedly out the window he ran determinedly to his mother.

"Mamma! Mamma!" he cried. "Jesus isn't coming. Jesus isn't coming. I want my money back! I want my money back!"

Some of us today are like little E. W. We have waited long for our Saviour's return. Our problems multiply. Our faith is tested. Discouragement threatens. We feel God has forgotten us. We cry out with the psalmist: "How long wilt thou forget me, O Lord? for ever? how long wilt thou hide thy face from me?" (Ps. 13:1). "I am weary of my crying: my throat is dried: mine eyes fail while I wait for my God." And sometimes we almost say as did little E. W., "I want my money back."

Then our God in His love and mercy speaks to us. "For yet a little while, and he that shall come will come, and will not tarry" (Heb. 10:37).

"Cast not away therefore your confidence, which hath great recompence of reward," He says reassuringly (verse 35).

The delaying time is a testing time. He has not forgotten us. His promises are certain. "If I go and prepare a place for you, *I will come again"* (John 14:3).

BREAKING DOWN THE PARTITIONS

For he is our peace, who hath made both one, and hath broken down the middle wall of partition between us. Eph. 2:14.

Six soldiers in battle dress appeared at the cemetery carrying the body of a fallen comrade. The priest stopped them at the entrance.

"Was he baptized?" the man of the cloth asked.

The battle-weary veterans looked at one another helplessly.

"We don't know," they responded. "All we know is that he was our buddy. He has been killed in action. We want to bury him in your cemetery!"

The priest thought for a moment.

"I am sorry," he continued slowly, "I would like to accommodate, but if you are not certain that he was baptized I cannot permit you to bury him in this consecrated soil."

Shocked, the servicemen turned sadly away. Retracing their steps a few feet from the entrance they proceeded to dig a grave just outside the cemetery fence. As tenderly as strong, rough hands could, they laid their comrade to rest.

The next morning the six servicemen returned to the cemetery to place some flowers on the grave. They began walking around the fence in search of the spot where they had laid their buddy. How could this possibly be? There was no trace of a grave any place along the outside of the fence.

As they stood perplexed the priest appeared.

"You are searching for the grave," he began. "I could not sleep last night. I thought of my heartless act yesterday in denying you a burial place. Very early this morning I came and moved the fence out a bit to take in the grave of your fallen comrade."

A partition moved, a buddy brought in! This makes us think of what Jesus has done for each of us who desires to be taken in. "With his own body," Paul declares, "he broke down the wall that separated them and kept them enemies" (Eph. 2:14, T.E.V.).

Satan erected the barricade when he brought sin into the Garden of Eden. But we "who sometimes were far off are made nigh by the blood of Christ" (verse 13). He has taken in every one who will permit Him. Thank God the wall is gone!

WHAT IS RIGHT IN OUR OWN EYES?

In those days there was no king in Israel, but every man did that which was right in his own eyes. Judges 17:6.

"There are times when a man has to push his principles aside and do the right thing," a St. Louis cabby once declared. Perhaps unwittingly, this driver had become an exponent of a currently popular philosophy—situation ethics.

"The situationist enters into every decision-making situation fully armed with the ethical maxims of his community and its heritage, and he treats them with respect as illuminators of his problems. Just the same he is prepared in any situation *to compromise them or set them aside* in the situation if *love* seems better served by doing so," writes Dr. Joseph Fletcher. (From *Situation Ethics,* p. 26, by Joseph Fletcher. Copyright © MC-MLXVI, by W. L. Jenkins. Used by permission of The Westminster Press.)

According to this philosophy every man or woman, when confronted with a perplexing situation, or when severely tried by temptation, does that which is "right in his own eyes." He makes his own decision, not necessarily based upon inspired morality but rather upon what he feels is the loving thing to do under the circumstances.

The Word of God declares that God, not man, is the arbiter of right and wrong. In His Ten Commandments He has given us the guidelines of moral rectitude. They are "the work of God, and the writing was the writing of God" (Ex. 32:16). He gave the commandments to be kept. "Thou shalt keep therefore his statutes, and his commandments" (Deut. 4:40). Here is God's eternal and ultimate standard of right and wrong.

Love enters into every decision-making situation for the child of God—love for his Creator and Redeemer. Jesus makes the love factor clear: "If ye love me," He says tenderly, "keep my commandments" (John 14:15). The Master further declared that this love-covenant would last as long as heaven and earth shall stand. "Verily I say unto you, Till heaven and earth pass, one jot or one tittle shall in no wise pass from the law" (Matt. 5:18).

God's law—not the situation—determines what is right or wrong!

IN THE EXTREME EMERGENCY—WHAT SHALL I DO?

If any of you lack wisdom, let him ask of God, that giveth to all men liberally, and upbraideth not; and it shall be given him. James 1:5.

Situation ethics has been presented as a method of dealing with moral dilemmas. These dilemmas include such situations as defending one's home and family from an attacker, stealing to preserve life, the surgeon's dilemma when he is forced to decide which life—or any life—to save at a crucial moment. In this complex world one is confronted by many situations—no two may be identical. What is one to do? Will he find in the musty ethic of revelation the solution to his problem? Must he search frantically for some authoritative pronouncement handed down by establishment leadership?

If one's child were starving, and stealing appeared the only means of preserving the loved one's health, it could be a terrifying temptation to secure that food even at the risk of violating the commandment that says, "Thou shalt not steal" (Ex. 20:15). To protect one's own flesh and blood in the moment of lethal attack would certainly be the natural reaction of one in such a predicament. What should the child of God do under such extreme circumstances, which are certainly possibilities but not probabilities for most of us?

I am just simple enough to believe that my omnipotent God has a provision for every situation. Has He not said, "The angel of the Lord encampeth round about them that fear him, and delivereth them" (Ps. 34:7)? God has not promised to spare our lives under all circumstances. He did not spare the life of His only-begotten Son when man's existence was at stake. As long as He has a work for His child to do He will spare his life, and the lives of his loved ones. He will provide for every extreme emergency in His own good way!

What about the temptation to steal, to lie? God has promised: "There hath no temptation taken you but such as is common to man: but God is faithful, who will not suffer you to be tempted above that ye are able; but will with the temptation also make a way to escape, that ye may be able to bear it" (1 Cor. 10:13). What a blessed promise covering every conceivable situation!

THEIR FINEST HOUR

Call to remembrance the former days. Heb. 10:32.

In the November 21, 1942, issue of the *Saturday Evening Post* a challenging advertisement appeared. Standing at his church pew an American citizen was reacting to the tragic happenings in the Pacific during the early days of World War II.

He traced briefly and forcefully the gallant victories of American arms in previous wars. He dwelt upon the sacrifices America had been willing to make through the centuries to keep the fires of freedom burning in remote areas of earth. He challenged the Government to tell America the truth about the war into which we had recently been drawn.

"If we need sugar to win this war, take it.

If we need rubber to win this war, take it.

If we need steel to win this war, take it.

If we need cash to win this war, take our money and buy War Savings Stamps and Bonds!

Take everything we've got to win this war, and welcome!

Because there's one thing no one's ever going to take from you and me, so help us God,

And that's America! . . .

I say: We'll live on bread and water, if we have to, and we'll like it . . . fine!"

What a challenge these words contain when translated into the spirit and language of the Advent people engaged in this planet's final great warfare! I believe I speak for every committed Seventh-day Adventist around the world today when I say—

If God needs our children to finish the work—take them!

If He needs our TV or radio sets to finish the work—take them.

If He needs our cars or boats to finish the work—take them.

If He needs our money—even our savings—to hasten His return—take it.

Take everything we've got to finish the work, and welcome!

Because there's one thing no one's ever going to take from you and me, as Seventh-day Adventists, so help us God,

And that's the blessed hope—the certainty of seeing our Saviour face to face in the clouds of heaven SOON.

THE DIVINE MAGNET

And I, if I be lifted up from the earth, will draw all men unto me.
John 12:32.

In the twelfth chapter of the gospel of John, Jesus gives us an insight into His multisided ministry and His mighty power. He lived as never man lived. He taught as never man taught. He permitted those whom He had helped or healed to escort Him victoriously into Jerusalem in fulfillment of prophecy. As a result the name of Jesus was on every tongue. More than the Greeks were saying, "Sir, we would see Jesus" (John 12:21).

From such a platform of popularity and power Christ uttered some of the most important words of His ministry: "And I, if I be lifted up from the earth, will draw all men unto me."

Dr. William Barclay beautifully comments on those words of the Master: "It was in the magnet of the cross that Jesus pinned His hopes. And Jesus was right because love will live long after might and power and force is dead."—*Barclay Commentary,* The Gospel of John, p. 149.

Dr. Barclay continues to illustrate the penetrating power of love as revealed in the cross by using the story of Joan of Arc as written by George Bernard Shaw: "When she knew she had been betrayed to the state by the leaders of her people, Joan declared, 'I will go out now to the common people, and let the love of their eyes comfort me of the hate in yours. You will be glad to see me burnt; but if I go through the fire I will go through to their hearts forever and ever.' "

When the Son of God went through the fires of opposition and persecution, finally to be nailed to a cruel cross, Jesus went straight into the hearts of millions of men and women from every age and from every land.

Ellen White says: "I present before you the great, grand monument of mercy and regeneration, salvation and redemption—the Son of God uplifted on the cross of Calvary. This is to be the theme of discourse. Christ declares, 'And I, if I be lifted up from the earth, will draw all men unto me.' "—*The SDA Bible Commentary,* Ellen G. White Comments, on John 12:32, p. 1137.

THEY SEARCHED THE SCRIPTURES DAILY

These were more noble than those in Thessalonica, in that they received the word with all readiness of mind, and searched the scriptures daily, whether those things were so. Acts 17:11.

The apostle Paul was a preacher who encouraged Bible study. Wherever he spoke, men and women turned to the Word. The people in Berea began to search the Scriptures daily. Paul commended them for their earnestness in probing the Word.

If the Bereans needed to study the Word of God to confirm their relationship to a Christ who had but recently been in their midst, members of God's remnant church need to search the Scriptures as they prepare for a Saviour so soon to return.

As never before Seventh-day Adventists need to turn to the Bible— and study it carefully and prayerfully! The Lord's messenger emphasizes their need over and over!

We need to study the Word alone as we plead with God to guide our minds into the channels of truth that He would have us explore. We also need to study the Bible in groups. "Let small companies assemble in the evening, at noon, or in the early morning to study the Bible. Let them have a season of prayer, that they may be strengthened, enlightened, and sanctified by the Holy Spirit. . . . What testimonies you may bear of the loving acquaintance made with your fellow workers in these precious seasons when seeking the blessing of God."
—*Testimonies,* vol. 7, p. 195.

What a blessed experience would be ours if this counsel were carried out in every Seventh-day Adventist church around the world. Instead of gathering to gossip and speak idly and foolishly we could profitably spend time in small groups diligently and prayerfully seeking to know God's will for us in these last days.

Why not begin a Bible study group in your home, in your church, this very week? Revival follows Bible study—so does Pentecostal power. We all need these blessings!

WHAT HE SAYS, DO!

His mother saith unto the servants, Whatsoever he saith unto you, do it.
John 2:5.

At the marriage feast in Galilee, Jesus' mother spoke the words of our text for today. "Whatsoever he saith unto you, do it." These seven words contain a very important message for God's people today—both as a corporate church body and as individuals. Our only safety today is in doing what God tells us to do!

More and more we need to be turning to the Lord for wisdom and guidance as we deal with the work of God in our local churches, in our local conferences, in our unions, and in the General Conference. The problems are too complex for us to seek solutions in our own strength and wisdom. We need to know what the Lord has to say through His Word and through His appointed messenger. Herein lies our only safety as we seek to finish His work soon.

I have just been reading again the inspired words found in 2 Chronicles 20:20: "Believe in the Lord your God, so shall ye be established; believe his prophets, so shall ye prosper."

All of us want success in our work and we want God's work to succeed. "Believe in the Lord your God," the inspired writer declares, "and you shall have success!" (2 Chron. 20:20, T.L.B.). Believing and obeying the *Word of God* is basic to true success in the *work of God.*

The world around us purports to offer much. There are many easy solutions. But are they God's solutions to our personal problems, or to the problems of our church? This is the most important question. Many of man's human solutions do not square with God's Word. When this is true we have only one clear course open to us—*go to the Book, go to the writings of God's servant,* discover what He says through Inspiration. Then follow the instruction of Jesus' mother, "Whatsoever *he* saith unto you, do it." Follow His instructions. "God can teach you more in one moment by His Holy Spirit than you could learn from the great men of earth."— *Testimonies to Ministers,* p. 119.

Prayerfully following *God's* clear instruction—this is our only safe course today.

MARANATHA!

If anyone does not love the Lord, let him be outcast. Maranatha—Come, O Lord! 1 Cor. 16:22, N.E.B.

The only place in the Bible the word "Maranatha" appears is in our text for today. The apostle Paul in this first letter to the believers in Corinth was making an earnest appeal for them to forsake all practices that bound them to the world. He warned them frankly of the consequences they must expect if they left his appeals unheeded. Following through with an urgent call for their full surrender to the Lord Jesus, he exclaims "Maranatha!"

What does this interesting word *Maranatha* mean? Various shades of meaning are suggested. Dr. Taylor in *The Living Bible* paraphrases it "Lord Jesus, come!" Dr. J. B. Phillips uses the translation, "May the Lord come soon!" Still other modern expositors prefer to quote Paul: "Our Lord will come," as either a statement of fact or an expression of hope. Whichever wording we prefer, *Maranatha* is a good Adventist word, for it deals with the coming of our Lord.

In the early church the word *Marana* or *Maran* was used by the disciples in speaking to, or of, Christ. "It was a respectful form of address," one commentator explains. "After the resurrection it was used as an endearing term, 'Our Lord.' Early church members used *Maranatha* as a word of encouragement to one another. It was a greeting, even a watchword or a password keeping bright the hope they cherished in their hearts. *Maranatha,* 'May the Lord come soon.' "

"Our Lord *will* come"—I like *Maranatha* because of the *certainty* of the blessed hope I find in its expression. There is no question about the fulfillment of the blessed hope. "For yet a little while, and he that shall come will come, and will not tarry" (Heb. 10:37). In a world adrift upon a vast sea of uncertainty, *Maranatha* offers something to which God's believing people may tie—"Our Lord *will* come!" The Advent hope is not built upon the weak assurances of man. These promises were inspired by the living God and they will not fail. Though we have waited long, we may know hope will become glad fruition.

TOO LATE TO TURN BACK

If any man draw back, my soul shall have no pleasure in him. But we are not of them who draw back unto perdition; but of them that believe to the saving of the soul. Heb. 10:38, 39.

Years ago L. H. Olson, longtime missionary to South America, and his son were climbing a rugged peak in Zion National Park. Father, not so conditioned for the rigorous undertaking, was becoming weary.

"Let's go back," he suggested. "We are *almost* to the top. Let's settle for this and go back down!"

His young son was dismayed!

"Oh, no, Dad," he protested vigorously. "We can't go back now. It's too late! Why, we are almost there. We must keep on going until we reach the top!"

"It is not he that putteth on the armor that can boast of the victory; for he has the battle to fight and the victory to win. It is he that endureth unto the end that shall be saved. The Lord says, 'If any man draw back, my soul shall have no pleasure in him.' "—*Selected Messages,* book 1, p. 315.

If we need help to endure, that help is available from above. Note these words of encouragement to a weary saint: "If Brother J would cling to God more firmly . . . he would receive strength from above. . . . If he stands with the single purpose to obey God at any cost he will have help and strength."—*Testimonies,* vol. 4, p. 237.

Truly we are almost there! Everything in the world about us and within the church we love cries out, "We are almost there!" A multitude of voices remind us that the kingdom is but a brief span away.

"We can't turn back now"—not when the goal is within sight. This is no time for the soldier of Christ to give up! After years of enduring the struggle with God's help, how sad if we were to turn back when now we can see, as it were, glory streaming through the gates ajar. As the apostle says, "Surely we are not going to be men who cower back and are lost" (Heb. 10:39, Phillips). It is too late now to pursue such a course. Our eyes must be heavenward toward the certain victory and reward God has promised His faithful people!

335

IT PAYS!

Thou upholdest me in mine integrity. **Ps. 41:12.**

William Harrison, a real estate man, owned property adjoining our Seventh-day Adventist church in a small Southern city. To improve his plot for sale, Mr. Harrison needed a tenfoot strip of our church land. He approached the pastor with a request to purchase the strip.

The local church board might easily have reasoned, "This is a fine opportunity to exact a good price from the owner. He has to have the land; let's make him pay well for it!"

But the members of the board did not take this greedy approach. When the neighbor met the pastor a few days later he asked the price of the land.

"You are dealing with the sale of land every day," the pastor replied. "Give us what is fair."

Mr. Harrison, deeply impressed by this unusual response, gave them a liberal amount for the land. He also decided in his mind that if ever he had an opportunity to help Seventh-day Adventists he would do it.

A few months later the conference MV secretary was looking for a new youth campsite. With the pastor he visited Mr. Harrison to see whether he knew of a suitable tract of land.

"I'll try to find what you want," he assured them.

A few days later he called the pastor. "Tell your friend I have just what he wants for his youth camp. It is a large camp that has recently been closed down by the owners."

A subsequent inspection of the proffered camp revealed it to be an ideal spot, exactly what was needed for the youth of the conference. Everything was fine except the probable price. It was worth over a quarter of a million dollars.

"Let me see what I can do," Mr. Harrison suggested, when the men explained their small conference could not afford such expensive property.

Mr. Harrison met with the board of directors of the large corporation that owned the coveted camp. He explained the work of Seventh-day Adventist youth and told them that he knew Seventh-day Adventists were good people.

The conference got the land—as a *gift.* Integrity pays—sometimes even in dollars and cents!

WHAT ARE YOU THANKFUL FOR?

And you shall eat and be full, and you shall bless the Lord your God for the good land he has given you. **Deut. 8:10, R.S.V.**

The GI was very young. He was very brave. A wide grin creased his grimy face as he held up the stub of an arm for the surgeon to care for. His hand had been blown off in battle.

Dr. Robert Dunn was surprised at the grit and the smile.

"Do you mean you have lost your hand and you can still smile?" the surgeon asked incredulously.

The youth still grinned. "Doc, you don't understand," he replied courageously. "I lost my hand, but I still have my life. I'm alive and I can go home. I might have been lying out there on the hillside where so many of my buddies are. I'm thankful to be alive!"

Today is Thanksgiving Day for those who live in the United States. In some lands another day has been set aside for Thanksgiving. Whoever we are, wherever we live, every one of us has something for which to be thankful.

Like the young soldier, we should all be thankful we are alive. Think of the millions of young men from many lands who lost their lives in World War I and World War II, in Korea, in the Middle East, in Africa, in Vietnam. They loved life. They had loved ones at home. They had much to live for.

If you and I have health and strength we have much for which to be thankful. Through the years my work has taken me frequently into hospitals and leper colonies. As I see young and old cut down by incurable disease, some with members of their bodies missing, I thank God for health and strength. We may not have all of the "things" of this world we would like, but if we have health and strength we have a great deal for which to be thankful.

During visits to Europe in recent years I have visited the former concentration camps. Six million people suffered and died in these camps in the thirties and forties of this century. You and I should be thankful for freedom!

Yes, you and I have much for which to be thankful on this Thanksgiving Day—for our Saviour and Friend, Jesus, for His Word, for the gift of eternal life, for the blessed hope of Christ's soon return, and oh, so much more!

EVER HAVE YOUR FACE SLAPPED?

Ye have heard that it hath been said, An eye for an eye, and a tooth for a tooth: but I say unto you, That ye resist not evil: but whosoever shall smite thee on thy right cheek, turn to him the other also. Matt. 5:38, 39.

Her seventy years did not deter Sister Garnesecchi from serving her Lord courageously in her native Genoa, Italy. As a literature evangelist she was ringing doorbells one day in a neighborhood near her home.

"Who is there?" a rough voice called out at one house.

"A friend," Sister Garnesecchi replied sweetly.

"I have no friend," came the terse reply from inside.

"Of course you do," our sister continued, "and I've come to call on you today."

The door opened suddenly and a tall craggy-faced woman loomed up in the doorway. Without warning, the woman of the house raised her bony hand and gave Sister Garnesecchi a resounding slap on the cheek.

Quickly the literature evangelist regained her composure.

"Why did you slap me?" she inquired calmly. "Since you do not hesitate to slap a woman of seventy years, you are welcome to slap my other cheek as well. After all, my Lord was mistreated. Should I be unwilling to suffer also?"

The tall woman of the house was embarrassed. Her angry outbursts had not often been met with the sweet spirit of Jesus.

"I'm so sorry," she apologized. "Do come in."

Sister Garnesecchi stepped into the front room and was seated. An order for literature was taken and a cash contribution to the work of her church was received. A lasting friendship was established.

"Do not retaliate," the Lord's messenger admonishes. "So far as you can do so, remove all cause for misapprehension. Avoid the appearance of evil. Do all that lies in your power, without the sacrifice of principle, to conciliate others. . . .

"If impatient words are spoken to you, never reply in the same spirit. Remember that 'a soft answer turneth away wrath.' And there is wonderful power in silence. Words spoken in reply to one who is angry sometimes serve only to exasperate. But anger met with silence, in a tender, forbearing spirit, quickly dies away."— *The Ministry of Healing,* pp. 485, 486.

GIVING TO THE CHIEF

Then the people rejoiced, for that they offered willingly, because with perfect heart they offered willingly to the Lord: and David the king also rejoiced with great joy. 1 Chron. 29:9.

One of our church members in Natal, South Africa, was watching an African workman rounding up his two cows.

"Are you selling your cattle?" Brother Torlage asked.

"No," the African replied, "our chief needs money and I am going to give him one of my cows."

"One of your cows?" Brother Torlage gasped in astonishment. "You have only two and you are going to give one of them to your chief? Why don't you give him some bananas or some garden produce? You can't afford to give one of your cows!"

"But, sir, you don't understand," the African's voice was filled with emotion. *"This is for my chief,* and I must make a gift worthy of him!"

A gift worthy of his chief! Nothing less would be thinkable!

Some non-Christians in lands afar put us to shame in giving. R. J. Borrowdale, longtime missionary to India, once gave me a little insight into the giving habits of Southern Asia's people.

"The average Hindu villager gives more than one fourth of his income for his religion," Elder Borrowdale explained. "First there are the direct offerings the Hindu worshiper brings to his temple. Then there are times and seasons when pilgrimages must be made to distant temples or faraway rivers. These journeys cost in time and money. There are also votive offerings and festivals at which certain people in the community are to be fed. Adding it all up, I believe these religious demands require at least a fourth of the Hindu's income!"

In the beautiful island of Bali the people believe their homeland is the property of the gods. The island bounties have been given to the people only in trust. To express their gratitude for this sacred trust they spare nothing in giving the best they have to their gods!

Giving—giving of our very best, above and beyond the tithe which already belongs to God—should be a joyful experience for the willing child of God.

VICTORY CERTAIN

The word of God grew and multiplied. **Acts 12:24.**

Perhaps Dr. Luke had several objectives in mind when he wrote the book of Acts. One of them, and perhaps the most important of them all, was to record accurately the marvelous advance of the early Christian church in taking the gospel into all parts of the world. The good news of the living Saviour, who died, rose, and lives spread like fire in the stubble from Jerusalem to Rome, the capital of the world, in thirty short years.

The book of Acts is punctuated with exultant reports of victory and progress. The thrilling saga of power and advancement starts with Peter preaching at Pentecost. By chapter 6, verse 7, Dr. Luke could report: "The word of God increased; and the number of the disciples multiplied in Jerusalem greatly; and a great company of the priests were obedient to the faith."

The good news reached out into all parts of Palestine and into Samaria, and Luke wrote: "Then had the churches rest throughout all Judaea and Galilee and Samaria, and were edified; and walking in the fear of the Lord, and in the comfort of the Holy Ghost, were multiplied" (Acts 9:31).

The conversion of the apostle Paul added impetus to the forward leap of the gospel, and the message entered Antioch. Cornelius was converted. The news at this juncture was: "The word of God grew and multiplied."

Two other thrilling progress reports appear in chapters 16 and 19: "And so were the churches established in the faith, and increased in number daily" (verse 5). And "So mightily grew the word of God and prevailed" (verse 20).

The paean of power reaches its peak of crescendo as the book of Acts closes with a shout of triumph concerning the ministry of Paul: "Preaching the kingdom of God, and teaching those things which concern the Lord Jesus Christ, with all confidence, no man forbidding him" (chap. 28:31).

Today God's message of Christ's imminent return is reaching out into all parts of the world with speed and mighty power. Soon another shout of victory will mark its completion! Nothing can hinder its certain triumph!

PEACE OR PIECES?

There is no peace, saith the Lord, unto the wicked. Isa. 48:22.

You have heard the expression "Christian nations." Quite likely you live in such a country. Actually, there are no truly Christian lands today. Nations and governments are made up of individuals. Unfortunately, the human "heart is deceitful above all things, and desperately wicked" (Jer. 17:9). In such hearts the principles of righteousness, the principles of Christ, cannot exist. In too many "Christian nations" righteousness has given way to selfishness, and God has been supplanted by a materialistic humanism. Political expediency prevails over moral principle. Such a milieu of materialism is fertile soil for greed and war.

Yet the "peace issue" is paramount in our day. Practically every major city in America and many in foreign lands have witnessed huge peace demonstrations demanding the end of war. "We will have peace if we have to fight for it" is the mood of our decade.

Peace, even world peace, is not a political problem to be settled solely by governments. Peace, true peace, is a spiritual experience that must first be enjoyed by individuals. Only truly born-again followers of the Lord Jesus Christ can enjoy "the peace . . . which passeth all understanding" (Phil. 4:7).

"There is no peace, saith the Lord, unto the wicked." World peace is not so much a matter of one nation getting along with another nation as it is a matter of humankind getting along with God. The wicked man—the man who is not right with the Almighty—cannot find peace until first he is reconciled with God. Real peace comes when man is in right relationship with his God. "We have peace with God through our Lord Jesus Christ" (Rom. 5:1).

Peace is the opposite of war. Peace is the cessation of war. This is true in both the spiritual and the political worlds. When the guns are quiet, when the killing stops, when politicians cease hateful accusations, war is over. When enmity toward God disappears, when forgiveness of sin is experienced, when victory over the carnal nature is achieved—all through the grace and power of Jesus Christ—then spiritual peace reigns in the life.

341

GETTING WEARY OF THE WAR

Let us not get tired of doing what is right, for after a while we will reap a harvest of blessing if we don't get discouraged and give up. Gal. 6:9, T.L.B.

For years the world clamored for the cessation of hostilities in Vietnam. Streets and campuses in many lands were choked with protesters demanding the war be brought to an end. Banners and bull horns proclaimed to the world that the fighting must stop. People were killed and wounded in the cause of peace!

Old and young, rich and poor, black and white grew weary with the protracted blood-letting and suffering. "Stop the war —at all costs" was the common cry. Victory through arms became secondary. People were tired of killing and sacrificing. "When will it all end?" were the words on millions of lips. The world was worn out waiting for the end to come. But finally the end, of a sort, did come. The cease fire was signed. An uneasy peace settled upon a war-weary land.

For nearly six thousand years another great controversy has been raging. In more recent decades the struggle has intensified. Years ago the battle should have been over, but the conflict drags on. Men and women for long anxious years have been praying and working for the end. "When will it all end?" "Will it ever end?" war-weary veterans ask, almost in despair.

Never fear, the controversy *will* be over. "Then shall the end come" (Matt. 24:14). "He that shall come will come, and will not tarry" (Heb. 10:37). These words of God will not fail.

It is so easy to give up when the way is long and difficult, when trials and temptations press in upon us. "What's the use?" "Will it ever end?" In times like these, remember the words of the Saviour and don't give up: "He that shall endure unto the end, the same shall be saved" (Matt. 24:13).

An unknown poet has words of courage for us:
"When things go wrong as they sometimes will,
When the road you're trudging seems all uphill,
When funds are low and the debts are high,
When you want to smile but you have to sigh,
When care is pressing you down a bit,
Rest if you must, but don't you quit."

342

HOW ABOUT YOU?

The name of God is blasphemed among the Gentiles through you.
Rom. 2:24.

In the last twelve verses in his Epistle to the Roman Christians, the apostle Paul delineates the sins of the Gentiles in some detail. It is indeed a lurid list, as all who have read Paul's words will agree. As Christians, members of God's remnant church, we shudder as we read the heinous transgressions of unbelievers. Secretly, perhaps unconsciously, we may thank God we are not as these terrible people.

"But wait a minute!" Dr. Taylor paraphrases Paul's words, "You are just as bad. When you say they are wicked and should be punished, you are talking about yourselves, for you do these very same things" (Rom. 2:1, T.L.B.).

It is easy to wrap about us a pious garment of innocence when we may be even more guilty than the world about us! We are God's people. We have the truth. We are preaching God's last message!

This is just about what the Jews were saying. "You know what God wants you to do, and you have learned from the Law to choose what is right; you are sure that you are a guide for the blind, a light for those who are in darkness" (verses 18, 19, T.E.V.).

Then Paul challenges God's people in his day—perhaps he has a message for you and me in our day! "You teach others— why don't you teach yourself? You preach, 'Do not steal'—but do you yourself steal? You say, 'Do not commit adultery'—but do you commit adultery? You detest idols—but do you rob temples? You boast about having God's law—but do you bring shame on God by breaking his law?" (verses 21-23, T.E.V.).

What an indictment—teaching others while they themselves were castaways, doing the very things they condemned in others.

Then God's loving-kindness and ever willingness to help is revealed: "Surely you know that God is kind because he is trying to lead you to repent!" (verse 4, T.E.V.).

343

GOD'S ADDITION

If you confess with your lips that Jesus is Lord and believe in your heart that God raised him from the dead, you will be saved. **Rom. 10:9, R.S.V.**

This is God's arithmetic problem. It's just as simple as two plus three equals five. Add it up for yourself. "Confess with your lips that Jesus is Lord" plus "believe in your heart that God raised him from the dead" equals "you will be saved."

It looks simple on paper and it *is* simple if we keep Jesus very much in our reckoning. Confession plus faith equals salvation. Now let's have a second look—especially at the first part of the problem—"If . . . Jesus is *Lord.*"

We know Jesus as our Saviour, as our Great Exemplar, as our High Priest, and as our coming King, but do we know and accept Him as *Lord* of our life? This is important. In fact, it is the *sine qua non* of salvation. If we are to be saved we must know Him not only as our risen Saviour, the One who gloriously conquered death, we must also acknowledge and accept Him as our present Lord—the One who has the right to control our lives.

When Jesus is mentioned in the New Testament by the Greek name *kurios*—Lord—the inspired writer wishes to impress us with His authority, His power, His divinity—His right to reign in our lives. In describing this Jesus to us, the apostle Paul declares, "He is the highest Ruler, with authority over every other power" (Col. 2:10, T.L.B.).

By the power of our Lord Jesus Christ, the heavens, the earth, and "all things created" exist, for "all things were created by him, and for him" (chap. 1:16). Jesus Christ, the Son of God, was not only the Creator of the world, He is also its Sustainer. The winds, the waves, the tides obey His will. Without Him nothing exists. He is indeed Lord of the universe.

What Christ is to the universe He must be to every one of His earthborn children—Lord and Master, in complete control. We must acknowledge Him as the undisputed Sovereign of our being. Our words, our thoughts, our actions, will be under His control when "Jesus is Lord" of our lives. When we believe that He is to control the living as well as raise the dead, and when this truth becomes the motivating factor in our lives then indeed we will be in the vestibule of heaven.

JESUS—THE DELIVERER

But when he saw Jesus afar off, he ran and worshipped him, and cried with a loud voice, and said, What have I to do with thee, Jesus, thou Son of the most high God? I adjure thee by God, that thou torment me not. For he said unto him, Come out of the man, thou unclean spirit. Mark 5:6-8.

What a scene—Jesus stepping from His little boat onto the shores of Gadara confronted with a raving demon-possessed creature storming out from nearby cliffs. Arms flailing wildly, his long, matted hair flying in the breeze, broken handcuffs clanking, shrieking as he ran, the wild man of the tombs bore down upon the Saviour and His disciples. The disciples fled in terror, but Jesus stood His ground.

With the same voice of authority that stilled the storm-tossed waves of Galilee, Jesus spoke to the on-rushing man. The wild man's rush slackens, wavers, and he comes to a halt a few feet from the Master.

"Come out of the man, thou unclean spirit," Jesus commands. Somehow in his confused mind, "the unfortunate . . . [man realizes] that One is near who can save . . . [him] from the tormenting demons. . . . [He falls] at the Saviour's feet to entreat His mercy; but when . . . [his] lips are opened, the demons speak through . . . [him], crying, 'What have we to do with Thee, Jesus, Thou Son of God? art Thou come hither to torment us?' "—*The Ministry of Healing*, p. 96.

You remember the rest of the story—the demons' request to enter a herd of swine rooting on the hillside, Jesus' acquiescence, and the hogs' destruction when they plunged over the cliff into the sea.

In our day Jesus Christ, the Son of God, still delivers from evil spirits—very real evil spirits—as real as those who possessed the man of Gadara. I have personally witnessed the power of my Saviour casting out evil spirits in old India, once in Palianappapuram and once in Achampati, both in Tinnevelly district of South India. The demons came out when commanded to do so in the name of the Lord Jesus Christ. It was just as real, just as challenging, as was the Gadara confrontation two millenniums ago.

Jesus is the same Deliverer today that He was then. Moreover, His delivering power can and must be felt in your life.

1975 DEVIL POSSESSION

"Jesus, Son of the Most High God! What do you want with me?" Mark 5:7, T.E.V.

Two important truths challenge us in today's text. First, Jesus was the "Son of the Most High." The words are those of the evil spirits who were in possession of the poor man living among the tombs of Gadara when Jesus commanded them to leave him. Even these evil spirits acknowledged the divinity of Jesus Christ. The fact that He was the "Son of the Most High" must ever be uppermost in your thinking and mine as we face the problems and the prospects of our day.

The Man you and I have accepted as Lord and Saviour is not bound by the bonds of humanity. Jesus Christ was not only a good man, He was and is indeed the God-man. He is still the Son of the Most High! This is important for us to remember in our struggle against the evil one.

Now an even more sobering thought—we may be devil-possessed today. "Not like the man of Gadara," you protest. Perhaps not, but devil possession in 1975 can be just as real, just as menacing, just as devastating in our sophisticated society as it was among the tombs of Gadara.

Note these words of inspiration referring to another experience of deliverance in Jesus' day:

"There are multitudes today as truly under the power of evil spirits as was the demoniac of Capernaum. All who willfully depart from God's commandments are placing themselves under the control of Satan. Many a man tampers with evil, thinking that he can break away at pleasure; but he is lured on and on, until he finds himself controlled by a will stronger than his own. He cannot escape its mysterious power. Secret sin or master passion may hold him a captive as helpless as was the demoniac of Capernaum."—*The Ministry of Healing,* pp. 92, 93.

But Jesus Christ is still the great Deliverer! Help is at hand if we request it!

"No cry from a soul in need, though it fail of utterance in words, will be unheeded. Those who consent to enter into covenant with God are not left to the power of Satan or to the infirmity of their own nature."—*Ibid.,* p. 93.

346

JESUS THE GREAT DISTURBER

Those who saw what happened were telling everyone about it, and the crowd began pleading with Jesus to go away and leave them alone! Mark 5: 16, 17, T.L.B.

When Jesus cast out the evil spirits from the man of Gadara, the reaction to the miracle on the part of the local citizenry may seem to us indefensible. It is easy to feel they should have been glad and rejoiced when one of their unfortunate countrymen was delivered from the legion of demons.

Think it through a bit more carefully. Life in these parts of Gadara had been peaceable until Jesus came. Then He arrived and unsettled and disrupted the routine of their lives. Jesus disturbed their life pattern of pigs, pay, and pleasure. Naturally, they resented His intrusion.

Many people don't like to be disturbed—neither in Jesus' day nor in ours! People want to be left alone. They don't want to be disturbed. "I'm comfortable!" "I'm satisfied." "Leave me alone." This is too frequently our reaction today—so why should we condemn the people of Gadara when they reacted thus?

When Jesus by His Holy Spirit comes to members of His remnant church in an effort to change some life patterns and prepare us for His soon coming, too many of us don't want to be bothered. When through revelation He disturbs our habits of eating, drinking, dressing, pleasure seeking, and selfish inactivity, our natural reaction is, "Go away and leave us alone." We are comfortable as we are.

When Jesus by His Holy Spirit invites us to active service—to hand out literature, visit the sick, give Bible studies, attend evangelistic meetings, too many of us respond like the Gadarenes: We want to see the work finished, but we don't like being disturbed. "We are tired. Sabbath is our only free day. We have something else we want to do. Go away and leave us alone. Don't disturb our comfort, our leisure, our money, our possessions." Jesus disturbs people!

JESUS IS LORD

He is Lord of lords, and King of kings. Rev. 17:14.

"Under New Management"—frequently we see this sign staring at us from the window or the wall of some business enterprise. This, of course, is calculated to communicate to the reader that things are different inside. There has been a change of management. Things are better now—the food is more inviting, the service is much improved, the quality of the products for sale is superior—because the business is under new management. People who know how to "run" things better are now in charge of affairs.

Management does make a difference, a big difference, whether it is in the operation of a business or in living the Christian life.

When sin or self predominated, the great consideration was, "What do *I* want?" "What are *my* rights?" "What do *I* think?" "What will make *me* happy?" When Christ takes over, when *Jesus* becomes Lord of our life, things change. "What will *Jesus* think?" "What does *Jesus* want me to do?" "What will please *Jesus?*" When we are under new management Jesus will not only be "Lord of lords" in the universe, He will be Lord of lords in our everyday lives!

When Jesus is Lord everything we have will be surrendered to Him. Our money, our property, our music, our reading, our eating, our drinking, our playing, our social activities—every decision of our life will be made with *Jesus* uppermost in our minds.

"When natural inclination draws you in the direction of fulfilling some selfish desire, set the Lord before you as your counselor, and ask, 'Will this please Jesus? Will this increase my love for my best Friend? Will this course grieve my dear Saviour? Will it separate me from His company?' "—*The Faith I Live By*, p. 237.

Jesus "gave himself *for* us" (Titus 2:14). In return He demands everything *from* us. There can be no reservation. It is not enough to sing about Him, talk about Him, use His name in our prayers. He must become a living reality in our lives. He must become the controlling factor. He must indeed be Lord of all lords to us every moment of every day.

DEATH HOLDS NO TERROR

Yea, though I walk through the valley of the shadow of death, I will fear no evil: for thou art with me; thy rod and thy staff they comfort me. Psalm 23:4.

Did you ever wonder what thoughts course through the mind of a child of God as he faces lingering but certain death from cancer? In a recent issue of *These Times* I read a moving testimony, "Testament of Faith," by Mrs. Gwen Ford, written shortly before her death from cancer.

Mrs. Ford's voice of courage preserved by the printed page breathes hope and help for every child of God. I have culled a few gems for your encouragement:

"During my hospitalization the fact that I had or had had cancer could not make me dismal for more than a moment, so close and real was the presence of Christ. . . . I left the hospital rejoicing, never doubting that cancer for me was finished. . . .

"I knew that God was not unmindful of my plight. His life, His presence, His strength brought comfort in the valley of the shadow. The prayers offered by my bedside, especially when I was too ill to pray myself, and the consciousness of the other prayers by friends and loved ones then distant, brought comfort and assurance. . . .

"The Lord's presence and the promises from His Word can buoy us up and help us through experiences, which otherwise we would not be able to endure. . . .

"Stripped of my ability to walk and work, I am constantly thrown upon the divine power. . . .

"Life can still be full of challenge and interest even for the invalid. . . . With so much apparently gone, I appreciate better and find how very much more is really left. . . .

"What then of the future? Medically speaking, the bone cancer is expected to spread until finally the liver or lungs are affected, and the end thus hastened. If this is the Lord's will for me, I can await it without dread, and say, 'Ebenezer. . . . Hitherto hath the Lord helped' me.

"When my death comes, it will not be a tragedy—a cutting off, an untimely event—but a full fruition of the Lord's plan for my life."

What a blessed hope is ours in Christ Jesus!

"WHAT STUPIDITY!"

For we dare not make ourselves of the number, or compare ourselves with some that commend themselves: but they measuring themselves by themselves, and comparing themselves among themselves, are not wise. 2 Cor. 10:12.

After reading our text for the day in the King James Version of Scripture, read Dr. Taylor's paraphrasing of Paul's words in *The Living Bible:* "Oh, don't worry, I wouldn't dare say that I am as wonderful as these other men who tell you how good they are! Their trouble is that they are only comparing themselves with each other, and measuring themselves against their own little ideas. What stupidity!"

"What stupidity!" What is the apostle talking about? To whom does he refer as being guilty of stupidity? Those "who tell you how good they are." Those who compare "themselves with each other, . . . measuring themselves against their own little ideas."

The servant of the Lord has something to say about such people: "I was shown that there was too much comparing ourselves among ourselves, taking fallible mortals for a pattern, when we have a sure, unerring pattern. We should not measure ourselves by the world, nor by the opinions of men, nor by what we were before we embraced the truth."—*Testimonies,* vol. 1, p. 406.

"Tens of thousands, full of ambition for distinction and display, have been ruined because they have lost sight of principle. They have measured themselves among themselves, and compared themselves with themselves. Their eager grasping for credit and reward has resulted in diminished spirituality. This is a lesson all should study carefully, that they may be warned against selfishness and avarice, against pride which destroys love for God and corrodes the soul."—*Selected Messages,* book 2, pp. 184, 185.

There is only One to whom we may look with perfect confidence as our true example—Jesus. "He is our true Pattern, and each should strive to excel in imitating Him."—*Testimonies,* vol. 1, p. 126.

If we truly have an experience with the Lord our eyes will be upon Him rather than upon those about us.

FACING A FIRING SQUAD

O love the Lord, all ye his saints: for the Lord preserveth the faithful, and plentifully rewardeth the proud doer. **Psalm 31:23.**

During a recent visit to Poland a story of faithfulness during the dark days of World War II came to my attention. Stanislaw, as we shall call the young Polish husband and father, was pressed into forced factory labor by the occupying power. About the middle of the first week Stanislaw spoke to his supervisor about being excused from work on God's holy Sabbath. The response was quick and decisive.

"There is a war on. There will be no exceptions to your weekly work program!" his superior snapped. Efforts to reason with the man were futile.

Sabbath morning when Stanislaw failed to appear for work, soldiers banged on the door of his apartment. Without even time to bid his wife and children good-by, he was hustled into a motor vehicle and driven to a secluded woods in one part of the city. "We know how to deal with workers who refuse to obey orders," one of his armed captors spat. "We shoot them!"

Stanislaw was blindfolded and stood by a wall. His persecutors tried to coerce him—he was offered his freedom if he would work. The young man was firm. Exasperated the soldiers jerked the blindfold from his eyes and shoved him back into the car, and he was taken to a place of custody.

The next weekend the same scenes were enacted. Blindfolded and against the wall for the second time he heard the ominous crack of rifle bolts putting cartridges into chambers for firing.

"Don't you have a wife, some children, you love?" the soldiers tantalized. "This is your last chance to save your life! This morning we are going to kill you if you do not obey."

"I have a wife and I have two small children whom I love dearly," Stanislaw replied calmly. "I want to live and I am willing to serve, but I must obey my God."

With an oath an officer jerked off the blindfold and muttering angrily he shoved Stanislaw back into the car, and they drove back to headquarters.

The result of obedience? Stanislaw was set free.

NO NEUTRALITY

Anyone who is not for me is really against me; anyone who does not help me gather is really scattering. Matt. 12:30, T.E.V.

In times of war there have always been neutral countries. These nations do not take sides. Theoretically they do not favor any of the warring countries.

The word *neutral,* according to the dictionary, means "not engaged on either side; not aligned with a political or ideological grouping." Neutrality may be possible in time of war or in the struggle of party politics. There is one warfare, however, where no one can escape being engaged on one side or the other. In the confrontation between good and evil, between Christ and Satan, neutrality is impossible. Polarization is inevitable. Jesus makes this clear in our text for the day. "Anyone who is not for me is really against me."

Today the battle lines are being drawn on the issue of revelation. *Is* the Bible the Word of God, or does it merely *contain* the Word of God? In the world around us there is a movement away from the revelation of the Word to the opinions of men. Some of these opinions are far from the clear teachings of God's Holy Scriptures.

Seventh-day Adventists believe the Bible is indeed God's Word—His message to the world and to His people throughout all ages. For us there can be no equivocation.

God has likewise spoken to His church through the writings of the Spirit of Prophecy. Seventh-day Adventists believe the writings of Ellen White were inspired of God to bring hope and help to His remnant church. "Satan will work ingeniously, in different ways and through different agencies, to unsettle the confidence of God's remnant people in the true testimony." —*Selected Messages,* book 1, p. 48.

"In the great conflict for the soul of man, there is no middle ground; neutrality is impossible (see *The Desire of Ages,* p. 324). Every man is either a patriot or a traitor. He who is not wholly on the side of Christ is wholly on the side of the enemy, that is, the weight of his influence is in that direction. To be almost, but not wholly, with Christ is to be, not almost, but wholly against Him."—*The SDA Bible Commentary,* on Matt. 12:30.

TWENTY-FIVE MINUTES TO LIVE

How do you know what is going to happen tomorrow? For the length of your lives is as uncertain as the morning fog—now you see it; soon it is gone. James 4:14, T.L.B.

Richard Cooper is scheduled to die for strangling two women in a sordid hotel. Twenty-five minutes before the death march begins the prison chaplain sits in front of his cell visiting casually with the condemned man. Richard wants no religion. He wants to die for his crime.

Attendants prepare the cyanide pellets and the acid that will mix in buckets under the chair in the gas chamber. A telephone line is kept open just in case a last-minute reprieve should be called in. Richard has requested that his body be given to a medical school for experimentation. He discussed the prospect with his chaplain.

In twenty-five minutes Richard Cooper will be dead. The chief physician and the warden pay brief visits to the cell. The warden shakes hands with the youth and says good-by. Two guards accompany Richard to the gas chamber. Seated in the chair, he glances at the grim-faced witnesses outside. Straps are placed around the youth's waist, chest, legs, and arms.

The door is closed tightly. The warden nods. A lever is pulled. The pellets drop into the acid. Eight and a half minutes later the prison physician pronounces Richard Thomas Cooper officially dead.

Another soul for whom Christ died has slipped into eternity—unprepared.

Twenty-five minutes to live!

Accident, tragedy, illness strike with lightning suddenness sometimes. We may not have even twenty-five minutes to prepare for eternity. "Hold yourselves ready, therefore, because the Son of Man will come at the time you least expect him" (Matt. 24:44, N.E.B.). We might not be anymore prepared to meet our Maker than was Richard Thomas Cooper.

Some people don't care for this kind of story. I don't like them either. Neither does God—when He has made every provision for a different ending for every soul who will turn to Him. But that turning should be NOW.

YOU MAY NEED TO PAY SOMETHING BACK

If the wicked restore the pledge, give again that he had robbed, walk in the statutes of life, without committing iniquity; he shall surely live, he shall not die. Eze. 33:15.

"Please help me," the letter appealed, "I don't know to whom else I can turn, and I believe you will help me."

I continued reading the letter.

"Many years ago I was working in an office where I had access to the safe. Over a period of years I took several hundreds of dollars that did not belong to me. I have not been happy. My conscience has troubled me continuously. I know the only way to find peace is to pay this money back. I want to be right with God, and I want you to help me arrange with my former employer for me to return the money in installments over a year's time. Won't you please help me!"

Of course I would help. I contacted the employer concerned. As expected, he was more than willing to receive the money and he was willing to forgive the mistake that had been made. Arrangements were made. A little over a year later I inquired of my employer friend how things turned out.

"Fine!" he assured me. "The money came back regularly. The account is paid in full, including interest."

Personal peace with God, revival and reformation in the church, cannot come until restitution of that taken from a fellow man has been made in full. Are *you* seeking peace when there is some outstanding account you need to settle?

Many a church member who would never dream of holding up a filling station or of reaching a hand into an employer's till, perhaps still needs to make restitution—to God.

"Will a man rob God?" the prophet asks, "Yet ye have robbed me. But ye say, Wherein have we robbed thee? In tithes and offerings" (Mal. 3:8).

We are just as guilty when we put our hand in God's pocket as when we steal from a fellow man. We may be guilty of robbing God in offerings as well as in tithe. It is easy sometimes to "tip" God a little instead of being honest with Him in both tithes and offerings. Perhaps we need to do a little giving again, either to God or to a fellow man, before we can truly be at peace with God.

THE PERIL OF RE-ENTRY

And as they came down from the mountain, Jesus charged them, saying, Tell the vision to no man, until the Son of man be risen again from the dead. Matt. 17:9.

Technologists tell us that one of the most dangerous stages of a moon flight is when the spaceship re-enters earth's atmosphere. At this point of the return journey terrific heat threatens to destroy the spaceship. If the astronauts successfully negotiate this re-entry process they will soon be safely back with their fellow human beings again.

Three disciples who had been with Jesus on the Mount of Transfiguration also had a re-entry problem when they left their trysting place with God and returned to face the workaday problems of life on the plain below. They very soon ran into a problem they could not handle—a man whose son was possessed of an evil spirit. Coming back down to earth after the ecstasy on the mount proved a traumatic experience—especially when they were confronted with this test. Only quick action on the part of Jesus saved the situation. Jesus did what the disciples could not do—He delivered the boy from the evil spirit.

Sometimes you and I have our re-entry problems too, don't we? There are experiences when the Holy Spirit seems to lift us right into the very vestibule of heaven—times when we bask in the presence of our lovely Jesus. It may be a Week of Prayer, a Bible conference, a sermon, the conversion of a long-prayed-for loved one that stirs our souls with the nearness of God. Like the three disciples in Jesus' day, we long to build some memorial to the experience and remain on the sacred ground forever.

But, like the disciples, we must go down. We must leave our mountain of blessing and return to the mundane milieu of everyday living. We must go back to school with its history, math, and English, to the irritations of the daily job of making a living, to the wife or husband who does not know the Lord. We must go back to the inner city, to our neighborhood where the needs are great and where the Lord has need of us!

As we make our re-entry, let us carry with us the atmosphere of heaven and be sure Jesus is by our side to help us.

355

ROUSE TO REALITY!

In all this, remember how critical the moment is. It is time for you to wake out of sleep, for deliverance is nearer to us now than it was when first we believed. It is far on in the night; day is near. Let us therefore throw off the deeds of darkness and put on our armour as soldiers of the light. **Rom. 13:11, 12, N.E.B.**

As we near the end of the old year it is well for us to be reminded that we are also nearing the end of the old world in which we live. Tremendous days are just ahead—days of fantastic opportunities and advance for the work of God. There are also days of frustration and problems—situations that will demand the best that is in every member of God's remnant church. It is indeed a critical hour.

"We are standing upon the threshold of great and solemn events. Prophecies are fulfilling. Strange, eventful history is being recorded in the books of heaven. Everything in our world is in agitation. There are wars and rumors of wars. The nations are angry, and the time of the dead has come, that they should be judged. Events are changing to bring about the day of God, which hasteth greatly. Only a moment of time, as it were, yet remains. But while already nation is rising against nation, and kingdom against kingdom, there is not now a general engagement. As yet the four winds are held until the servants of God shall be sealed in their foreheads. Then the powers of earth will marshal their forces for the last great battle."—*Testimonies,* vol. 6, p. 14.

"Only a moment of time, as it were, yet remains"—what challenging words these are! How filled with hope and glad anticipation they are for the prepared child of God! How ominous are these same words to the sleepy, lukewarm Laodicean who puts off the return of his Lord far into the future. To such the apostle directs his appeal, "It is high time now for you to wake up out of your sleep—rouse to reality." Think it over, friend of mine, are you asleep, do you need to "rouse to reality"?

Thank God, our "(final deliverance) is nearer to us now than when we first believed"!

DON'T BE A LINE STRADDLER!

Thou shalt make no covenant with them, nor with their gods. Ex. 23:32.

I was driving down a long hill in western Arizona. It was late in the afternoon. I had been driving for several days. I was tired. There had been few cars on that particular stretch and perhaps I was not as alert as I should have been. Out of nowhere a car suddenly appeared behind me with a red light flashing. I quickly pulled over to the side of the road and stopped.

The patrolman came to my car, greeted me, and asked for my driver's license. I wondered what I had done wrong. He quickly told me. "You were driving in the middle of the road back there; you were straddling the line in the center of the road." After a courteous little lecture on driving safely he sent me on my way.

I was reminded of what I had known for years—State highway departments spend thousands of dollars every year painting a dividing line to show motorists the middle of the road not so that they can straddle it but so that they can stay on the right side of it.

Of course, in most things it is good to avoid extremes and stay in the middle of the road, as we are told so frequently. I have no quarrel with this good counsel—normally. But there *are* times when the Seventh-day Adventist Christian cannot be a middle-of-the-roader with impunity. There are times when the man in the middle of the road is more than half wrong. This is when principle is involved.

Commenting on our text for today, Ellen White writes, "Those who had recently rededicated themselves to the Lord . . . realized that the line of demarcation between His people and the world is ever to be kept unmistakably distinct. They refused to enter into alliance with those who, though familiar with the requirements of God's law, would not yield to its claims."—*Prophets and Kings,* p. 570.

Inspiration makes it clear that when matters of principle are involved, the middle-of-the-roader, the compromiser, is wrong.

Don't be a line straddler!

SLIDE-RULE RIGHTEOUSNESS

Now we are seeing the righteousness of God declared quite apart from the Law (though amply testified to by both Law and Prophets). **Rom 3:21, Phillips.**

An engineer attending an evangelistic crusade in South Africa was used to calculating with a slide rule. One evening after listening to G. S. Stevenson speak on the righteousness of Christ, he was discussing the sermon with the preacher. Taking a slide rule from his jacket pocket and pointing to a place near the bottom of the rule, he said, "It seems to me it is like this. I only come up so far on the rule." He then pointed to the top of the rule. "I should be up here. I can't make it alone, so somehow Jesus comes along and fills up the gap."

Ellen White puts the same thought in these beautiful words: "When it is in the heart to obey God, when efforts are put forth to this end, Jesus accepts this disposition and effort as man's best service, and He makes up for the deficiency with His own divine merit."—*Selected Messages,* book 1, p. 382.

What a precious thought—Christ "makes up for the deficiency with His own divine merit." In our own strength we come far short, "all our righteousnesses are as filthy rags" (Isa. 64:6). There is nothing we can do to care for the past transgressions, but to confess and to believe. We *confess* our shortcomings and we *believe* God's promises of forgiveness, cleansing, and restoration. The righteousness of Christ becomes ours because we believe—by *faith.* It is a righteousness imparted to, and operating in, all who have faith in Jesus Christ.

"In its truest sense, righteousness by faith is not a *theory;* it is an *experience,* a vital change which takes place in the believer in Christ. It gives the sinner a new standing before God. . . .

"It involves a complete transformation of the life. He who has entered into this new life has experienced deep contrition, and has made sincere, heartfelt confession and repudiation of sin. With his divine Lord, he has come to love righteousness and hate iniquity. And being justified,—accounted righteous by faith,—he has peace with God."—A. G. DANIELLS, *Christ Our Righteousness,* pp. 74, 75.

ASK FOR THE OLD PATHS

Thus saith the Lord, Stand ye in the ways, and see, and ask for the old paths, where is the good way, and walk therein, and ye shall find rest for your souls. Jer. 6:16.

The words of F. M. Wilcox, at the time editor of the *Review and Herald,* spoken during a devotional at the 1936 General Conference session, deserve our attention here in late 1975:

"It is by subtle, insidious temptations, that Satan seeks to draw the disciples of Christ away from their allegiance to Him. If Satan can lead them to lose their first love in Christian experience, if he can induce them to form alliances with the world, if he can corrupt the simplicity of their faith, if he can influence them to adopt worldly policy and principles in the operation of God's work, if he can persuade them to substitute for the Bible truths belonging to this day and generation, subtle philosophies or a beautiful idealism, his purpose will be achieved. It is against dangers of this character that we need resolutely to steel our hearts and safeguard our souls. . . .

"The menace of false standards, of changing emphasis in Christian experience, threatens the remnant church today the same as it has the church in every period of its history. Israel of old affords a striking illustration. Joshua and the elders who outlived him had hardly passed away before there came onto the stage of action a new generation who knew not the Lord and who turned to the worship of Baal. Similarly, the early disciples of the Christian Era had scarce retired to their graves before their children, with new converts from heathenism, sought to remodel the gospel cause.

"How many times has this history been repeated through the centuries! Will it be repeated in the Seventh-day Adventist Church? The fathers of this movement have passed to their rest. Standards fallen from their hands have descended to us. Will we prove true to our holy heritage?

"Will we faithfully oppose the inroads of worldliness, of unbelief, of apostasy? Will we keep to the old paths of Christian faith and experience?"—*The Review and Herald,* June 1, 1936.

May God grant that with resolution we will reply, *By God's grace and strength we will!*

GROUNDED AND SETTLED

Continue in the faith grounded and settled, and be not moved away from the hope of the gospel, which ye have heard, and which was preached to every creature which is under heaven. Col. 1:23.

As we near the end there will be great danger in the church of individuals moving out in independent or irresponsible action. Frequently the servant of the Lord has reminded us that God is leading a people—"not one here and one there, but a people" (*Review and Herald,* Sept. 12, 1893).

Some weary of the "establishment" and seek to cast reflections upon the organization. Independent thought and action are extolled. Inspiration assures us, however, that organization will have its place in this movement until the work closes.

"Some have advanced the thought that as we near the close of time, every child of God will act independently of any religious organization. But I have been instructed by the Lord that in this work there is no such thing as every man's being independent. The stars of heaven are all under law, each influencing the other to do the will of God, yielding their common obedience to the law that controls their action. And in order that the Lord's work may advance healthfully and solidly, His people must draw together."—*Testimonies to Ministers,* p. 489.

"Let none entertain the thought, however, that we can dispense with organization. It has cost us much study, and many prayers for wisdom that we know God has answered, to erect this structure. It has been built up by His direction, through much sacrifice and conflict. Let none of our brethren be so deceived as to attempt to tear it down, for you will thus bring in a condition of things that you do not dream of. *In the name of the Lord, I declare to you that it is to stand, strengthened, established, and settled.*"—ELLEN G. WHITE, in *Review and Herald,* Oct. 12, 1905.

"We want to hold the lines evenly, that there shall be no breaking down of the system of organization and order that has been built up by wise, careful labor. License must not be given to disorderly elements that desire to control the work at this time."—*Testimonies to Ministers,* p. 489.

"Continue in the faith grounded and settled."

THERE IS NO QUESTION ABOUT IT

The Lord shall arise upon thee, and his glory shall be seen upon thee. And the Gentiles shall come to thy light, and kings to the brightness of thy rising. Lift up thine eyes round about, and see: all they gather themselves together, they come to thee. Isa. 60:2-4.

This is a great day to be a committed Christian—to be part of God's great movement that is pressing forward into all parts of the world, preparing people for the coming of Jesus.

The sixtieth chapter of Isaiah contains a message for our time. It is filled with assurance, progress, and a fulfillment of God's plans and purposes. One translator captions this chapter "The Enlargement of the Church." Notice the promises of God in this chapter underwriting the triumph of His work: "The Lord shall arise upon thee." "Gentiles shall come to thy light." "All they gather themselves together, they come to thee." "The forces of the Gentiles shall come unto thee." "The sons of strangers shall build up thy walls, and their kings shall minister unto thee." "I the Lord will hasten it in his time" (Isa. 60:2-5, 10, 22).

The Lord's messenger gives us further insight into this great period of activity and progress: "I saw angels hurrying to and fro in heaven, descending to the earth, and again ascending to heaven, preparing for the fulfillment of some important event. Then I saw another mighty angel commissioned to descend to the earth, to unite his voice with the third angel, and give power and force to his message."—*Early Writings,* p. 277.

Other inspired writers add their encouraging testimony. "Thy people shall be willing in the day of thy power" (Ps. 110:3). God's people will respond and do their share. "The wealth of the nations shall come to you" (Isa. 60:5, R.S.V.). The Lord will assure that ample funds are available for this great forward thrust to victory.

Ultimate triumph is assured in the Master's own words: "This gospel of the kingdom shall be preached in all the world" (Matt. 24:14). There is no question about it—*the message will be preached.* Then the Master promises, *"I will come again, and receive you unto myself; that where I am, there ye may be also"* (John 14:3).

NOT INVITED TO HIS OWN CELEBRATION

And they came with haste, and found Mary, and Joseph, and the babe lying in a manger. And when they had seen it, they made known abroad the saying which was told them concerning this child. And all they that heard it wondered at those things which were told them by the shepherds. **Luke 2:16-18.**

George R. Smoker tells the story of Mr. Good Deeds. In a certain community this gentleman lived and spread much happiness among the townspeople by his kindness and by his great and good deeds. For years the people praised Mr. Good Deeds for all he did for them.

Then one day the recipients of Mr. Good Deeds' loving care decided they would do something special for him on his birthday to express their great appreciation for all he had done. Plans were carefully laid. There would be songs written in honor of their benefactor. There would be speeches of praise. Gifts would be given, and to climax the occasion a lavish feast would be enjoyed after which Mr. Good Deeds himself would be called upon for a speech.

The celebration went off as planned. In fact, it was such a huge success the people of the town decided it should become an annual affair. In the years that followed there was more music, more food, more fun and laughter. Also there was less and less of Mr. Good Deeds. Finally one year the citizens were so occupied in making preparation for the gala event that they entirely forgot to invite Mr. Good Deeds to attend his birthday celebration!

Within a few days many of us will be observing Christmas. We know rather certainly that Jesus was not born on December 25, but any day would be appropriate to give special thought to the birth of our Lord.

In too many hearts and homes Christ has been taken out of Christmas. Gifts are lavished upon family, friends, and other "must people." How much will be given to forward the preaching of Christ's gospel? Stacks of Christmas cards and letters will be read and enjoyed. How much time will be devoted to the reading of Christ's Word?

Plan now to invite Jesus to attend His birthday celebration in *your* home!

"ON EARTH PEACE"

And suddenly there was with the angel a multitude of the heavenly host praising God, and saying, Glory to God in the highest, and on earth peace, good will toward men. **Luke 2:13, 14.**

It was Christmas Eve, 1914—the first Christmas of the long gruesome World War I. The Allied trenches were cold slits of mud in a shell-pocked turnip field. Only yards away German soldiers slogged about in similar forbidding circumstances. On both sides of the lines small Christmas gifts had been sent "up front" from families and friends back home. There was the usual bantering and small talk. An occasional shot split the cold night air.

Suddenly a British sentry shouted excitedly: "Shut up, you fellers! Listen!"

From the enemy trenches came the unmistakable strains of a concertina and rich German voices ringing out Christmas carols. Faint bursts of laughter occasionally wafted through the darkness. The British Tommies crowded to the point where their trenches most nearly approached the Germans. They listened, then they too burst into singing.

Then someone shouted, "Come on over!" Silence—then the invitation was repeated. Before long German and British soldiers were scrambling out of their trenches, swarming into the darkness in an incredible Christmas get-together.

Until a little past noon Christmas Day the unbelievable continued in that Flanders turnip field—British and German soldiers exchanged greetings, food, and souvenirs. For a few hours the hate, the will to kill, was gone. In that strange setting in Flanders there was "on earth peace" for a few joyous hours.

Someday there will be true lasting peace on earth. Someday the prediction of angel voices will become a glad and joyous reality. Someday hate and war will be forever banished. Someday the spirit of Christmas will mean much more than cessation of war, the giving of gifts, and the gorging of stomachs.

Someday "good will toward men" will be genuine. Love will flood human hearts and motivate all behavior. It will not be for a few unreal hours in a Flanders turnip field. The dawn of that blessed day will come when the Prince of Peace returns the second time. Thank God, that day will last forever.

NO ROOM IN THE INN

She gave birth to her first son, wrapped him in cloths and laid him in a manger—there was no room for them to stay in the inn. Luke 2:7, T.E.V.

What a poignant scene—the Lord of heaven come to earth to be born of a virgin and there is no room for Him! "In the city of their royal line, Joseph and Mary are unrecognized and unhonored. Weary and homeless, they traverse the entire length of the narrow street, from the gate of the city to the eastern extremity of the town, vainly seeking a resting place for the night. There is no room for them at the crowded inn. In a rude building where the beasts are sheltered, they at last find refuge, and here the Redeemer of the world is born."—*The Desire of Ages,* p. 44.

"*No room* . . . in the inn"—these words dramatically foreshadow the tragic lot of Him who came to be the Saviour of mankind. In later years there was no room in the hearts and lives of most with whom He came in contact for His tender love, His teachings, His sweet spirit, His death, His glorious resurrection. Men thronged Him but most of them simply had no room for Him in the inn of their hearts and lives.

How sad, we say! If only *we* had been there two thousand years ago *our* hearts and homes would have been wide-open!

But really, would they have been? Do we have room for Him today? Have we "room" in our lives for His insistent call to *repentance?* Do we let the fullness of His presence melt *our* hearts and make *us* truly sorry for sin? Is there "room" for His clarion call to *revival?* Have *we* responded to the stirrings of His Holy Spirit in *our* lives? Is there "room" for His anxious appeal for reformation—a real change in *our* habits and life patterns? To what extent have *we* truly changed the way we live since His challenge to change confronted us?

Have we "room" for the study of His Word, for time to talk unhurriedly with Him in prayer—"room" to manifest His Spirit, reveal His love? Is there "room" in our lives—time for sharing with others what He has done for us?

Truly now, is there room in the inn of our lives for Him today?

WHAT DOES CHRISTMAS MEAN TO YOU?

For unto you is born this day in the city of David a Saviour, which is Christ the Lord. **Luke 2:11.**

Today is Christmas. We may not celebrate it for the same reasons millions around us "observe" the day, but the birth of Christ should be a special event for every Seventh-day Adventist. Ellen White refers to the birth of the Saviour as "the greatest event of the ages" *(The Desire of Ages,* p. 44). The proclamation of the angel to the shepherds has a message of special import for each one of us:

"Today in the city of David a deliverer has been born to you— the Messiah, the Lord" (N.E.B.).

Here is an important message. Here is a personal message. Here is a message for the whole world today.

The message is *personal:* "Unto *you.*" The angel was speaking not only to the shepherds on the Judean hillside two thousand years ago, he was speaking to *you* today in 1975. The assurance of a Saviour is for *you.* It matters not whether you be rich or poor, learned or unlearned, male or female, the announcement of a Saviour is for *you.* This is a precious thought!

On this Christmas Day it may well be a good time for each of us to ask ourselves, What am I doing with this personal message? Have I accepted the precious Jesus as my personal Saviour? Has His blood covered *my* sins? If I am a church member, does the robe of His righteousness cover *me?* Do I unhesitatingly confess Him before those around me? Can all with whom I come in contact know that I am His and He is mine?

The angel not only announced the advent of a personal Saviour, he declared the Babe in Bethlehem's manger to be our personal Lord. If Jesus is Lord of your life and mine, He controls us entirely. The Lordship of Christ demands our full surrender and our utmost obedience. In His Sermon on the Mount, Jesus asked, "Why call ye me, Lord, Lord, and do not the things which I say?" (Luke 6:46). Here is a challenge for everyone of us as members of His church this Christmas Day.

"This day" make the Christ message one for our time. Instead of being carried away with the festivities of the occasion, let us prayerfully assess our relationship to the *personal, precious, present* message of the Christmas angel.

"EVERYTHING IN CHRIST"

You have everything when you have Christ. **Col. 2:10, T.L.B.**

A young high-caste Brahman in India accepted Christ as his personal Saviour and found great joy in serving his newly found Lord. One day while riding on the train, he was asked by an acquaintance about his new experience.

"You have given up a great deal to become a Christian," his traveling companion observed, a note of sympathy in his voice. "You have given up your home, your family, your job—everything. Is this not a great sacrifice to make for Christ?"

The young man thought for just a moment.

"Sir," he said sincerely, "I am frequently asked about what I have given up for Christ. It is strange, but no one ever asks about the blessings I have received since I have become acquainted with Jesus. Actually I have given up very little. 'My cup runneth over.' Now that I have Christ I have everything the human heart could ask for."

"Everything the human heart could ask for"—how like the words of our verse for today—*"You have everything when you have Christ."* The King James Version states it more succinctly: "Ye are complete in him."

Commenting on this scripture, one of the writers of *The Seventh-day Adventist Bible Commentary* says: "Literally, 'have been made full in him' (cf. Eph. 3:19; 5:18). In the sphere of the Christ, man not only may see his goal of perfection, but may also receive power to achieve it. As we accept His wisdom we become wise. Through daily communion with Him the likeness of the Divine becomes a reality within the human soul. There is nothing for this life or for eternity that man cannot receive through spiritual union with Christ. We may become complete in Him."—On Col. 2:10.

The mature human heart reaches out for love, for peace of mind, for light, for hope, for rest, for knowledge, for happiness, for security, for sympathy when things go wrong, for understanding when there are problems, for comfort when sorrow breaks our family circle.

All these are ours in Christ Jesus. He is the source of love, of knowledge, and of peace of mind. From Him flows light, hope, happiness, sympathy, and comfort.

THE GENERATION THAT FORGOT

All that generation were gathered unto their fathers: and there arose an-other generation after them, which knew not the Lord, nor yet the works which he had done for Israel. Judges 2:10.

Three verses in the second chapter of Judges provide subject matter for careful, prayerful thought on the part of God's people today.

"The people served the Lord all the days of Joshua, and all the days of the elders that outlived Joshua, who had seen all the great works of the Lord, that he did for Israel" (Judges 2:7).

As long as Joshua and many of his godly fellow leaders remained on the scene of action, the children of Israel "served the Lord" and prospered spiritually and materially. But with the passing of Joshua and his generation sad changes came in among the professed people of God. Our text for today notes these changes:

"All that generation were gathered unto their fathers: and there arose another generation after them, which knew not the Lord, nor yet the works which he had done for Israel."

These sad words should cause us serious concern, for the sequel to this bit of inspired history is sad indeed: "They would not hearken unto their judges, but they went a whoring after other gods, and bowed themselves unto them: they turned quickly out of the way which their fathers walked in, obeying the commandments of the Lord; but they did not so" (verse 17).

Everything went well with the Exodus Movement as long as Joshua's generation who had witnessed the many miracles of God's leadership were on the scene. They recalled frequently how the Lord had interposed on their behalf. A later generation that also should have remembered, unfortunately forgot.

Like the Exodus Movement, the Advent Movement has been replete with miracles of divine grace and power. God's leadership in the building up of this work around the world has been manifested over and over again.

Now we are a part of "another generation"—those early pioneers have passed off the stage of action. The miracles our founding fathers witnessed may grow dim in our eyes. We must not forget as the generation following Joshua forgot!

367

THERE'S A GREAT DAY JUST AHEAD!

And the earth was lightened with his glory. **Rev. 18:1.**

I thank God for this precious assurance of the Lord: "The great work of the gospel is not to close with less manifestation of the power of God than marked its opening. . . . Servants of God, with their faces lighted up and shining with holy consecration, will hasten from place to place to proclaim the message from heaven. By thousands of voices, all over the earth, the warning will be given. . . . The message will be carried not so much by argument as by the deep conviction of the Spirit of God. The arguments have been presented. The seed has been sown, and now it will spring up and bear fruit."— *The Great Controversy,* pp. 611, 612.

This power of the Holy Spirit will be felt in every phase of church endeavor. His energizing power will give fresh life to the wheels of organization. God's people will be constrained by a new and holy revelation of Christ and His righteousness to labor for Him. No longer will they be fearful of men's faces.

No longer will weary ministers or church officers be compelled to plead for funds to advance and finish God's work. Pentecostal endowment will open wallets, and funds will be given willingly. Houses and lands will be sold and the proceeds will gladly be turned over to the cause of God. One overwhelming passion will eclipse all others—to know God's will and to do it!

Novels and questionable literature will be laid aside as God's Word is restored to its rightful place in the home. Songs of praise will ring forth from meetings where both young and old find greater joy in worshiping God than in the boorish beat of some contemporary composition. The prayer meeting will find favor over the motion-picture production or the dramatic presentation. The chief joy of God's last-day people will be to live and labor for their Lord.

This is the experience into which you and I must enter! This experience will be but the prelude to the joys of the eternal kingdom. Today we are in the testing time. We will be tried in the fire. The wheat will be separated from the chaff; the gold and the dross will be revealed.

With God's help we must stand the test and have part in that great day when the earth will be "lightened with his glory."

IT'S A COLD WORLD OUT THERE!

From that time many of his disciples went back, and walked no more with him. John 6:66.

Years ago a missionary couple in Africa decided to leave the work for a short time and recoup their financial situation. A position in a large nearby diamond mining company was open and very tempting. They accepted—"for a year." The mission committee granted the year's leave of absence.

At the end of the year they hadn't "made quite enough money" and requested a further year's extension of their leave. At the end of the second year out of mission work, two mission leaders went to visit the couple to ascertain their plans for the future. Their reception was rather icy. They curtly informed the mission leaders they were not yet ready to return to their former posts and furthermore they felt they probably never would. Appeals on the part of the union leaders were ignored. The couple very shortly were "out of the truth."

Sometime later when our brethren were Ingathering in the vicinity they learned that the former worker was critically ill in the hospital. The men hurried to the hospital but arrived too late. Brother Blank had passed away a few hours before. Within a year Mrs. Blank was committed to a mental institution, and a short time later she too passed away.

In another part of Africa one of our national nurses decided to go for midwifery training. When she made the decision she was aware she would have trouble having her Sabbaths free. Shortly after entering the course she wrote her former nursing supervisor: "I am very sorry to tell you that I must be a 'Sundaykeeper' for one year. I have not been able to get my Sabbaths off. I hope the Lord does not come during this year, for I would not be ready."

In many evangelistic crusades I have conducted through the years, church members have told me that when the meetings started they were on the verge of leaving the church, that they had become cold, indifferent, or bitter.

It is a cold world out there. Leaving Christ, leaving the church, never solves the problems. "We ought, therefore, to pay the greatest attention to the truth that we have heard and not allow ourselves to drift away from it" (Heb. 2:1, Phillips).

GOING THROUGH

And he brought us out from thence, that he might bring us in, to give us the land which he sware unto our fathers. Deut. 6:23.

Through cars were always what I looked for when I traveled by train in India years ago. I recall one of my early trips in South India. I was going from Mettupalaiyam to Madras, where I had important appointments. After purchasing my ticket I gathered up all my luggage and began searching for the Madras car—one that would be kept on the main line and not shunted off at one of several stations en route.

At last I found my Madras car. I checked it carefully, then put my luggage aboard. Once or twice before the train pulled out I got out and looked at the station names on the side of the car—to be *absolutely sure!* Yes, there it was each time in unmistakable letters—MADRAS. Finally the train pulled out and I settled down hopefully for a night's sleep in the third-class compartment, satisfied that I was in the right car. During the night there were stops and bumpy shunting of cars, but I felt secure. The next morning, of course, I woke up in Madras— I had been on a *through* car!

I am thankful today to be a part of a movement that is going through. It is heaven bound! It came into existence at the time the prophetic word foretold. It is a worldwide movement, as inspired writers declared it would be. It is a message calling out men and women, boys and girls, "that he might bring us in, to give us the land which he sware unto our fathers."

It is right that we check our bearings frequently to assure that we are on the "through car"—one that is not going to be sidetracked or shunted off onto the wrong track. We need to check our guidebook, our heavenly timetable, the Word of God, often. As the song says, "Be sure, very sure" that we are on the right road to the kingdom. This, you and I have done carefully and prayerfully through the years. We have found the Advent message stands the test of time and thorough investigation. Its Bible-based, Christ-centered tenets give us confidence—the Advent Movement is a "through car," headed for heaven! And if we are faithful, so are we!

FAITHFUL UNTO DEATH

Be thou faithful unto death, and I will give thee a crown of life. **Rev. 2:10.**

Marie lived in a little town in the West Indies when I knew her years ago. Like practically all of the other people on her island, she belonged to the established church. One evening Marie's friends invited her to attend some meetings that were being held by an Adventist lay preacher. She found the Bible studies most interesting and continued to attend regularly.

When Marie's parents discovered where their daughter was going each evening they became very angry. When she continued to attend despite their warnings, one evening Marie's father burst into the meeting and dragged his daughter roughly outside.

When Marie began attending "Sunday School" on Saturday, it was too much for her mother. She organized a mob of religious zealots and laid wait for her daughter after an evening meeting. They tore Marie's dress from her and beat her unmercifully, leaving her in a ditch for dead.

But Marie did not die. The last time I visited her island she had been baptized and was faithfully witnessing for her Lord.

We have come to the end of another year. I have enjoyed visiting with you in your home each day during 1975. Within a few hours we will start a new year. How many more old years will slip into eternity and another new year begin we do not know. Surely there cannot be many before us. Jesus must come for His own soon.

My appeal to each one of you is to be true to the Lord Jesus Christ and His last-day message. "Do not be afraid of anything you are about to suffer. Listen! The Devil will put you to the test by having some of you thrown into prison; your troubles will last ten days. Be faithful until death, and I will give you the crown of life" (Rev. 2:10, T.E.V.).

Tests, trials, temptations are bound to come; but whatever is ahead never, never give up, never turn back from the path you have chosen, for if you are faithful, "even unto death," your reward is certain. Jesus says, "I will give thee a crown of life." Don't miss that crown!

God bless you all during 1976.